CONFIGURING THE NETWORKED SELF

ONE WEEK LOAN

D1375654

Configuring the Networked Self

Law, Code, and the
Play of Everyday Practice

Julie E. Cohen

Yale

UNIVERSITY PRESS

New Haven & London

Published with assistance from the foundation established in memory of
Philip Hamilton McMillan of the Class of 1894, Yale College.

Yale University Press books may be purchased in quantity for educational, business, or
promotional use. For information, please e-mail sales.press@yale.edu (U.S. office) or
sales@yaleup.co.uk (U.K. office).

Designed by James J. Johnson and set in Electra type by Integrated Publishing Solutions.
Printed in the United States of America.

Library of Congress Cataloging-in-Publication Data

Cohen, Julie E.
  Configuring the networked self : law, code, and the play of everyday practice / Julie E.
Cohen.
     p. cm.
  Includes bibliographical references and index.
  ISBN 978-0-300-12543-6 (pbk.)

  1. Information networks—Law and legislation.   2. Data protection—Law and
legislation.   3. Copyright and electronic data processing.   4. Internet—Law and
legislation—Social aspects.   I. Title.
  K564.C6C635   2012
  342.08′58—dc23   2011019631

A catalogue record for this book is available from the British Library.

This paper meets the requirements of ANSI/NISO Z39.48-1992
(Permanence of Paper).

10 9 8 7 6 5 4 3 2 1

For Andrew and Eli

Contents

Contents

Acknowledgments

Within the narrative of internal, unknowable creativity that animates contemporary copyright theory, writing a book is the paradigmatic act of individual authorship. The reality is quite different. Without the generosity of many wonderful colleagues, this project would never have been completed. Jack Balkin, Lara Ballard, Yochai Benkler, Michael Birnhack, Dan Burk, Glenn Cohen, Gabriella Coleman, Kevin Collins, John Deighton, Deven Desai, Donnie Dong, Terry Fisher, Oscar Gandy, James Grimmelmann, Natali Helberger, Joseph Liu, Michael Madison, Colin McClay, David McGowan, Charles Nesson, John Palfrey, Neil Richards, Stuart Shieber, Jessica Silbey, Rebecca Tushnet, Molly Van Houweling, Phil Weiser, and Jonathan Zittrain all read portions of the manuscript, ranging from a few chapters to the entire thing, and offered their comments and constructive criticisms, along with large doses of encouragement. I would especially like to note the extraordinary generosity of Terry Fisher, who convened a gathering of colleagues at his home to read and discuss the penultimate draft of the manuscript; Jack Balkin, who assigned the manuscript to his seminar students at Yale Law School; and Rebecca Tushnet, who read the entire manuscript at least twice and whose turnaround times are the stuff of legend.

In a less direct but equally important way, this book reflects the input of a diverse collection of colleagues and fellow travelers from whom, over the years, I have learned an enormous amount: Anita Allen, Jack Balkin, Ann Bartow, Yochai Benkler, Michael Birnhack, James Boyle, Dan Burk, Margaret Chon, Kevin Collins, Susan Crawford, Niva Elkin-Koren, Brett Frischmann, Oscar Gandy, Tarleton Gillespie, Chris Hoofnagle, Ian Kerr, Mark Lemley, Larry Lessig, Jessica Litman, Michael

Acknowledgments

Madison, Deirdre Mulligan, Helen Nissenbaum, David Phillips, Peggy Radin, Joel Reidenberg, Neil Richards, Marc Rotenberg, Pamela Samuelson, Daniel Solove, Madhavi Sunder, Rebecca Tushnet, and Fred von Lohmann. I owe special debts of gratitude to Dan Burk, with whom I have nurtured a shared interest in STS, information studies, and allied fields, and to Peggy Radin and Pamela Samuelson, whose wise and generous mentorship at the start of my academic career has been a continuing source of inspiration.

The ideas that form the basis for this book have emerged over the course of more than a decade of scholarly work. Portions of the manuscript are adapted from previously published work, as follows: Portions of Chapters 1 and 2 are adapted from "Cyberspace as/and Space," *Columbia Law Review* 107 (2007), 210–55. Portions of Chapters 1, 3, and 4 are adapted from "Creativity and Culture in Copyright Theory," *University of California Davis Law Review* 40 (2007), 1151–1205. A portion of Chapter 3 is adapted from "The Place of the User in Copyright Law," *Fordham Law Review* 74 (2005), 347–74. Portions of Chapter 4 are adapted from "Copyright, Commodification, and Culture: Locating the Public Domain," in Lucie Guibault & P. Bernt Hugenholtz, eds., *The Future of the Public Domain: Identifying the Commons in Information Law*, 121–66 (The Hague: Kluwer Law International, 2006). Portions of Chapters 5 and 6 are adapted from "Privacy, Visibility, Transparency, and Exposure," *University of Chicago Law Review* 75 (2008), 181–201. Portions of Chapters 7 and 8 are adapted from "Pervasively Distributed Copyright Enforcement," *Georgetown Law Journal* 95, (2006), 1–48.

As the book took shape, I benefitted greatly from the opportunity to present chapters at numerous workshops and conferences, including faculty workshops at Georgetown University Law Center, Harvard Law School, Boston University School of Law, Case Western Reserve University School of Law, and the School of Information at the University of California at Berkeley; presentations at the 2007 and 2009 annual meetings of the Society for Social Studies of Science; lectures at the Berkman Center for Internet and Society, the Yale Information Society Project, the Information Technology and Society Colloquium at New York University School of Law, the Indiana University Law and Society Colloquium, and Queensland University of Technology; and informal discussion sessions with participants in the American University Cyberlaw Colloquium and members of the Data Privacy Working Group at Harvard's Center for Research on Computation and Society.

This book was begun at Georgetown University Law Center and

Acknowledgments

completed during the year that I spent in residence as a visiting professor at Harvard Law School. I thank Deans Judy Areen and Alex Aleinikoff and associate deans Vicki Jackson, Larry Gostin, and Robin West at Georgetown and Dean Martha Minow at Harvard for their support and encouragement. Thanks also to Urs Gasser, the executive director of the Berkman Center for Internet and Society, for providing additional research funding during the Harvard year. Jennifer Locke Davitt and the staff of the Edward Bennett Williams Law Library at Georgetown as well as June Casey and the staff of the Langdell Law Library at Harvard provided heroic assistance, undaunted by a project that required a dizzying array of reference materials from multiple libraries. In addition, I am grateful for the talented research assistance provided by Theresa Coughlin, Robert Dowers, Brian Finkelstein, Sharona Hakimi, Ryan Houck, Andrew Jacobs, Amanda Kane, Chris Klimmek, and Jack Mellyn, and for the expert secretarial and administrative assistance of Suzan Benet, Peggie Flynn, and Kathryn Ticknor. Michael O'Malley at Yale University Press was a supportive and inordinately patient editor.

I have saved the most important thanks for last. I am profoundly thankful for the love and support of my family, Andrew and Eli, to whom this book is dedicated. They tolerated my absences, for the most part without complaint, endured my occasional grouchiness, and always made clear their unconditional love and support.

PART I

Locating the Networked Self

CHAPTER 1

Introduction: Imagining the Networked Information Society

O ver the last two decades, the rapid evolution of networked information and communication technologies has catalyzed equally rapid
change in the organization of economic and social activity. Spurred
by the perceived economic opportunities and threats that new digital
technologies create, powerful actors have endeavored to define and
channel flows of information in ways that serve their goals. Those efforts
have led to prolonged and often bitter struggles over the content of law,
the design of technology, the structure of information markets, and the
ethics of information use. In addition, they have stimulated heated scholarly and policy debates about what a good information society should
look like.

The ongoing debate among U.S. legal scholars and policy makers about the structure of the networked information society has two odd
features. First, the emerging regime of information rights and privileges
is publicly justified in terms of economic and political liberty, but as a
practical matter, it allows individuals less and less control over information flows to, from, and about themselves. In particular, the commercial,
legal, and technical infrastructures that define the individual experience
of the network are converging around relatively strong default protection
for intellectual property rights in information—most notably copyright
and trade secrecy—and relatively weak protection for individual privacy.
To an extent, the explanation for this is political. Advocates of strong
copyright and advocates of weak privacy share interests in strengthening
the commodification of information and in developing infrastructures
that render individual activity transparent to third-party observers. Those

entities wield considerable political and economic clout. But the gap between the rhetoric of liberty and the reality of diminished individual control is nonetheless striking.

Second, despite their practical convergence, legal and policy discussions about control of cultural information and control of personal information have remained largely separate. For the most part, the leading scholarly books on these topics do not acknowledge, much less attempt to explore, the interconnections. Within the wider public policy arena, copyright and privacy issues are rarely linked. To an extent, this disconnect also has a political explanation. Advocates of increased commodification and transparency have nothing to gain from highlighting the overlap. Advocates of "free culture" and "access to knowledge," meanwhile, tend to be uneasy with the limitations on access that privacy claims represent, and so have difficulty making common cause with privacy advocates across a broad range of issues. This uneasiness produces a second rhetorical gap, within which advocacy for human rights and human welfare in the networked information society proceeds as though "openness" were the only thing that mattered.

This book argues that the two phenomena are linked. The curious divergence between the rhetoric of liberty and the reality of diminished individual control and the failure to link copyright and privacy issues more systematically on both political and theoretical levels have a common origin. Together, they signal deep inadequacies in the conventional ways of thinking about information rights and architectures.

For the most part, U.S. legal and policy scholarship about the networked information society shares a set of first-order commitments—to individual autonomy, to an abstract and disembodied vision of the self, and to the possibility of rational value-neutrality—that derive from the tradition of liberal political theory within which legal academics are primarily trained. Those commitments shape both the prevailing understanding of the legal subject and the preferred form of analysis by which a just and intellectually defensible system of information rights is to be derived.

In each of three areas that the book will explore—copyright in cultural creations, privacy interests against surveillance, and the design of the architectures and artifacts that mediate access to networked information resources—a common pattern emerges: legal scholarship posits simplistic models of individual behavior derived from the first-order liberal commitments and then evaluates emerging legal and technical regimes that govern information flow according to the models. Theoretical frameworks organized around the core liberal individualist themes of expressive and market liberty predominate, regardless of their fit with the phenomena under investigation.

This approach has not served either theory or policy well. The models of individual behavior upon which it relies are too narrow both descriptively and normatively to yield useful insights into the relationships between copyright, creativity and culture; between surveillance, privacy, and subjectivity; and between network architecture and social ordering. Moving beyond the bounds of liberal political theory is essential if we are to understand the cultural work that regimes of information rights do and to appreciate the ways in which formally separate regimes of information rights intersect.

Human beings and human societies are constituted by webs of cultural and material connections. Our beliefs, goals, and capabilities are shaped by the cultural products that we encounter, the tools that we use, and the framing expectations of social institutions. Those processes play out in concrete contexts, involving real spaces and artifacts that we encounter as embodied beings. We cannot claim to judge cultural and social institutions from a vantage point of detached, value-neutral distance, as liberal theory would have us do. But we also cannot avoid the necessity of judging. The legal, technical, and institutional conditions that shape flows of information to, from, and about us are of the utmost importance not because they promote free speech or free choice in markets, but because they shape the sort of subjectivity that we can attain, the kinds of innovation that we can produce, and the opportunities for creation of political and ethical meaning that we can claim to offer.

This book seeks to remedy legal scholarship's theoretical deficit and, in the process, to develop a unified framework for conceptualizing the social and cultural effects of legal and technical regimes that govern information access and use. It will ask the sorts of questions with which law traditionally has concerned itself—what regime of information rights is just, and why—but it will foreground a set of considerations that legal thinking about those issues has tended to marginalize. It will consider how people encounter, use, and experience information, and how those practices inform the development of culture and identity. In particular, it will explore the ways in which social practices of information use are mediated by context: by cultures, bodies, places, artifacts, discourses, and social networks. From that vantage point, it will consider the ways in which the processes of cultural development and self-formation adapt to laws, practices, and technologies designed to impose commodification and transparency within the information environment.

In brief, I will argue that the production of the networked information society should proceed in ways that promote the well-being of the situated, embodied beings who inhabit it. That framework owes something to the theory of capabilities for human flourishing developed by Martha Nussbaum and Amartya Sen, and more recently applied to questions of information law and policy by a number of influential scholars. In the abstract, however, the statement that law should promote human flourishing tells us very little about the conditions of human flourishing in the networked information society.

We will see that law- and policy making for the networked information society serve the ultimate goal of human flourishing most effectively when they attend to the ordinary, everyday ways in which situated, embodied subjects experience their culture and their own evolving subjectivity, and when they consider the ways in which networked information technologies reshape everyday experience. To promote human flourishing in the emerging networked information society, information law and policy should foster institutional and technical structures that promote access to knowledge, that create operational transparency, and that preserve room for the play of everyday practice. We will see why the politics of "access to knowledge" should include a commitment to privacy, and why a commitment to human flourishing demands a more critical stance toward the market-driven evolution of network architectures.

Variations on a Common Theme: Freedom and Control in Information Policy and Theory

Discussions among legal scholars and policy makers about copyright, privacy, and the design of network architecture revolve inexorably around the central themes of freedom and control. One view of the ideal information society, which I will call "information-as-freedom," celebrates networked information technologies because they enable unimpeded, "end-to-end" communication and thereby facilitate the growth of a vibrant, broadly participatory popular culture. The other, which I will call "information-as-control," celebrates networked information technologies because they enable precise, carefully calibrated control of information flows and thereby facilitate the flourishing of vibrant information markets. Few legal scholars advocate either view in its purest form all the time. Policy and legal debate about any given topic, however, are inevitably driven by the clash between the two, and the different policy prescriptions that they appear to generate.

My goal in this book is to focus critical attention on what the freedom/control binary leaves out. Upon closer inspection, each vision of the information society has a hollow core. The self that is to exercise expressive freedom, or to benefit from market abundance, remains a mere abstraction, and the emergent character of the relation between self and surrounding culture remains largely unexplored. Relatedly (and not coincidentally), scholars in both groups have been spectacularly unsuccessful at grappling with a series of difficult questions about normative endpoints: about the sort of culture that a regime of copyright should seek to privilege, about the kind of subjectivity that a regime of privacy protection should seek to promote, and about the values that network architectures ought to serve.

Enclosure and the "Cultural Environment"

In the domain of copyright, the clash between information-as-freedom and information-as-control plays out in the form of a debate about the merits of broader rights and increased commodification of copyrighted content. Adherents of increased commodification point to the economic welfare that stronger property rights create. Critics of increased commodification have sought to rebut those arguments by drawing attention to the interdependence of cultural and informational goods and activities. They argue that commodification not only impedes specific economically and socially valuable activities that result from the free flow of information, but also impairs overall cultural health. Neither set of scholars, however, can explain why its preferred approach to fostering cultural progress is a good one.

Critics of increased commodification of cultural goods advance two major themes, one drawn from economic history and one drawn from natural history. The first theme invokes the "enclosure movement" in Britain. At various times from the fourteenth century to the early nineteenth century, common lands were enclosed, with drastic consequences for the commoners accustomed to using them. Legal scholars have called recent expansions of copyright a "second enclosure movement" that threatens to produce equally drastic consequences for information users.[1] Many scholars, including Yochai Benkler, James Boyle, Lawrence Lessig, Brett Frischmann, and Carol Rose, have sought to rehabilitate the "commons" from its association with tragedy and to celebrate the productivity of common cultural resources.

The second theme is that of environmentalism. Although today the idea of a natural environment seems unremarkable, that idea emerged within scientific and popular discourse only in the mid-twentieth century, during the debate that followed publication of Rachel Carson's *Silent Spring*. Scientists were beginning to understand the complex web of ecological cause and effect; naming that web gave it an independent existence invested with political meaning. Borrowing self-consciously from the history of the environmental movement, James Boyle has argued that policies favoring increased commodification of information harm a different kind of environment, constituted by society's cultural and informational resources.[2] By appropriating the complex web of political meaning centered on the interdependency of environmental resources, he sought to jump-start a political movement focused on an ecological understanding of culture and cultural processes. Other scholars have taken up the call, and count themselves part of a new movement organized around the cause of a diverse and self-sustaining culture.

In the public policy arena, academic critiques of commodification and enclosure intersect with a set of grassroots movements loosely organized around the banner of "free culture." Inspired by the successes of free and open source software, free-culture advocates argue that free and open access to informational goods is essential to both cultural progress and democratic self-government. Legal scholars, in turn, cite the free-culture movements as evidence of the vibrancy of the cultural commons, and regard free-culture advocates as the environmental activists of the information age.

Yet the metaphors of "commons" and "environment" also surface unanswered and deeply divisive questions about substantive cultural policy. Ecological analysis of "culture" does not lead unproblematically to the conclusions its advocates urge. Instead, attempts to do the "science" of cultural environmentalism have generated some very peculiar results. Many scholars appear to lose sight of the metaphoric quality of the references to "environment," pursuing explanations for culture in the realms of complex systems theory and evolutionary theory rather than in the literatures that study culture itself.[3] In the realm of culture, however, conflating metaphor with reality is a risky move. The health of ecological environments is constrained by scientific principles and therefore relatively amenable to objective measurement. Cultural environments have attributes and tendencies, but they are far less predictable, and their health is a matter of opinion. For precisely this reason, attempts to translate cultural "science" into cultural policy are open to contestation. Cultural change may be empirically and anecdotally demonstrated, but cultural harm is in the eye of the beholder.

Scholars who favor broader copyright rights and increased commodification, for their part, have preferred to seek explanations for culture within the "science" of markets, but this is hardly an improvement.[4] The environment within which artistic and intellectual culture emerges and evolves isn't a market, though it contains markets. It is a social entity, generated by patterns of human and institutional interaction. Social formations exhibit patterns and create path-dependencies, some of which can be described using economic laws, but we can't deploy economic laws to generate scientifically determinate prescriptions for their optimal form. Untangling the arguments about which patterns are better requires good descriptive and normative accounts of culture itself.

When it comes to articulating a normative theory of culture, though, both scholars who oppose increased commodification and scholars who favor it become oddly reticent. Adherents of cultural environmentalism know what they think a good culture would look like, but are sensitive to the irony of appearing to dictate how that culture should be achieved. Scholars who favor commodification do not share this difficulty—the vision they promote is that of the unfettered market in cultural works—but the terms of that theory mean they must show enthusiasm, at least in aggregate, for whatever the market turns out. Their task is then reduced to justifying whatever the market has generated, and sometimes they sound as though they have trouble believing themselves.

Establishing good descriptive and normative foundations for cultural policy requires confronting culture on its own terms, stripped of the veneer of scientism that the "environment" and "market" metaphors encourage. It requires, in other words, exactly what scholars on both sides of the debate have been trying to avoid: a theory that focuses on culture as culture and grapples directly with questions about why institutional arrangements for the production of culture matter. To decide whether the future of the "cultural environment" is in jeopardy, we need to understand how cultural processes work, why we should value them, and whether legal and institutional structures adequately take those values into account. Part II of this book develops an account of culture organized around the everyday creative practice of situated individuals and communities and explains why copyright law and theory require such an account to function effectively.

Openness and the Future of Privacy

The topics of surveillance and privacy have proved even more confounding for legal scholars of the networked information society. Here the clash between information-as-freedom and information-as-control plays out in a bewildering variety of contexts. Practices involving the collection and processing of personal information, the monitoring and logging of individual movement and communication, and the authentication of access to networked resources pervade both government and commercial activity. In each setting, privacy advocates have attempted to demonstrate that increased surveillance poses unacceptable threats to individual freedom, while advocates of increased surveillance argue that heightened surveillance promotes economic and social welfare. For all the heat that these battles generate, they shed very little light on what is really at stake on either side of the equation.

Advocates of increased privacy protection argue that flows of information about people are just as important for liberty and self-determination as flows of information to and from people. Individuals and communities are affected by flows of information about them, and by the knowledge that those flows are used to generate. In many cases the resulting systems of classification are deployed in ways that are antithetical to principles of self-determination and to principles of distributive justice. If we are concerned with individual freedom, they argue, we should be paying careful attention to practices relating to the collection and processing of information about persons and groups.[5]

Privacy advocates, however, have difficulty explaining exactly why the information flows to which they object are so harmful. One answer often given is that uncontrolled flows of personal information threaten individual autonomy and self-determination. Like allegations of cultural harm, allegations about harms to autonomy are difficult to prove. Absent visible coercion, demonstrating harm to selfhood requires a theory of the self and of the type of self-determination that privacy enables. Legal scholars of privacy have been reluctant to offer such a theory, preferring instead to advance relatively neutral conceptions of freedom. Another answer often given to explain why surveillance causes harm is that privacy promotes important social values, but the values described tend to be vague and nonspecific. No clear organizing theme— like "free culture" or the "cultural environment"—has emerged to serve as a focal point around which privacy advocacy and policy making might coalesce.

Arguments about the value of privacy, meanwhile, make many scholars on both sides of the freedom/control binary very nervous. First and most obviously, surveillance practices that revolve around the collection and processing of personal information play an important role within the vision of information-as-control. Information-driven profiling enables more precise tailoring of information services to customer needs and more precise fulfillment of security imperatives. Legal rules conferring ownership of collected personal information on data aggregators also reinforce norms of information ownership that apply to other kinds of intellectual property. Advocates of increased personal-information processing argue that privacy restrictions undermine efficiency, interfere with truth-discovery, jeopardize public safety, and hamper markets from responding to consumer preferences.[6] Yet these arguments too suffer from overgenerality; privacy opponents often cannot identify the precise gains that more information would produce.

Arguments for strong privacy protection do not sit well with open-access advocates for entirely different reasons. A political agenda based entirely on greater information openness cannot easily accommodate the goals that privacy advocates describe. Privacy may require greater access to some kinds of knowledge, but it also, and necessarily, dictates limits on access to other kinds of knowledge. Put differently, claims to increased privacy are claims about the positive value of enclosure. Privacy advocates argue that the quest for enclosure is a function not simply of the quest for profit, but also of the quest for personal security. Boundaryless space produces existential unease; boundaries, in turn, can serve important functions beyond the demarcation of commodified property. Open-access advocates resist such arguments, and one consequence of that resistance has been a fragmentation of the populist agenda that both open-access advocates and privacy advocates claim to represent.

The perceived irreconcilability of privacy and "openness" produces a very odd dynamic in which the themes of information-as-freedom and information-as-control begin to collapse into each other. Scholars on both sides invoke Sun Microsystems CEO Scott McNealy's famous statement—"You have zero privacy anyway. Get over it."[7]—with equal facility, and both sides understand the domain of appropriate policy actions to be narrowly constrained by a set of accepted parameters having to do with the primacy of private choice. The resulting arguments about the primacy of private choice no longer span the spectrum from right to left, but instead run in a circle.[8] The extreme libertarian version of the free-culture argument shades into an argument for unlimited personal choice, including unlimited personal choice to commodify the self. Meanwhile, important questions about the value of privacy and the truth gains from information processing go unanswered, and often unasked.

Understanding the ways in which disappearing privacy affects individual and social well-being requires confronting the problem of self-hood and the relationship between selfhood and surveillance in ways that the frames of autonomy, truth discovery, and free culture do not allow. Part III of this book takes up that task, developing an account of privacy organized around emerging subjectivity and explaining why society should care about the kinds of subjectivity that privacy enables.

Lost in "Cyberspace"

Debates about the shaping of the cultural environment and the appropriate scope of personal privacy have implications not only for permitted uses of information, but also for the ways that networked architectures and artifacts are designed. That discussion has been powerfully shaped by an initial narrative about "cyberspace" as experientially separate and thoroughly malleable—a place where the real-world constraints of space, body, and time are transcended and where the constraints that govern human interaction can be remade in the service of particular ideals. In a domain where everything seemed up for grabs, the clash between information-as-freedom and information-as-control became all-important; along the way, however, the combatants forgot to ask the most important question of all.

Advocates of information-as-freedom initially envisioned the Internet as a seamless and fundamentally democratic web of information, inherently unchecked by geographic borders or state-specific regulation. That vision is encapsulated in Stewart Brand's memorable aphorism "Information wants to be free." Brand's aphorism has several meanings, of which the literal, anthropomorphic one is by far the least important. It is significant, first and foremost, as an attempted statement of natural law. Information "wants" to be free in the same sense that objects with mass present in the earth's gravitational field "want" to fall to the ground. Scholars allied with this vision argued that the Internet was essentially unregulable and was therefore the ideal milieu for the realization of expressive and political freedom. Cyberspace would be "a civilization of the Mind"—or at least a separate jurisdiction, in which the laws of real space need not necessarily apply.[9] It would be subject to its own laws and constituted by the consent of its self-selected members. This framing positioned cyberspace as "empty" space: potentiality waiting to be filled up with settlements, structures, and norms, from which the constitutive legal texts of the community would then emerge.

For advocates of information-as-control, the Internet's truly revolutionary potential lay in its ability to reduce transaction costs that impeded the seamless exchange of goods, services, and speech. Put differently, they celebrated the Internet as the ideal environment for the manifestation of a different natural law: the natural law of the market. According to the natural law of the market, information does not "want" to be free at all. It derives its value precisely from the fact that it is an object of desire—a good for which people are willing to pay. For advocates of information-as-control, cyberspace was empty space to be filled up with more perfect versions of real-world institutions—markets and public squares unencumbered by the real world's unavoidable transaction costs.[10]

Of course, both visions of cyberspace were too simple. Early Internet architectures did not easily support the secure digital marketplaces envisioned by advocates of information-as-control. As Lawrence Lessig and Joel Reidenberg explained, however, the apparent ungovernability of cyberspace celebrated by advocates of information-as-freedom was neither a permanent nor a technologically necessary feature. In *Code and Other Laws of Cyberspace,* Lessig memorably assailed the utopian credo of the early Internet pioneers for its failure to acknowledge the technological contingency of cyberspace freedoms. He characterized utopian thinking about the Internet as a type of "is ism"—a confusing of the way things are with the way they must be.[11] Whether information flows freely across boundaries depends on the design of network protocols and interfaces. And to the extent that the design of information technologies is amenable to state regulation, it does not follow that information networks inevitably will produce legal and political destabilization. Information is an agent of creative destruction, perhaps, but its properties do not dictate a particular economic or political organization. Reidenberg argued that in light of the importance of digital technology as a regulatory modality, code could and should be harnessed in the service of state regulatory interests.

Among U.S. legal scholars, *Code* in particular has become the foundational text for theories about the architecture and governance of the networked information society. Post-*Code,* the two dominant visions of the networked information society have evolved into two different approaches to the design and regulation of networked information technologies. Building from *Code*'s apparent validation of their arguments about the Internet's essential regulability, scholars allied generally with the vision of information-as-control have urged that code should become a vehicle for imposing more perfect controls over information flow. They argue that information technologies should be redesigned to build in control via digital rights management and filtering capabilities, and that a broad range of service providers, from ISPs to software designers, can and should police flows of online content.[12] Other scholars, allied generally with the information-as-freedom vision of the Internet's potential, have seized on *Code*'s argument about architecture as a source of regulatory danger to fundamental liberties. Arguing that an unfettered Internet promotes personal and political freedom, they attempt to promote the design of technologies that facilitate open, anonymous interactions and relatively unconstrained access to information.[13]

Code did not, however, displace the presumption of geographic separateness that animated legal scholarship about cyberspace. Instead, Lessig articulated a vision of cyberspace that remained both fundamentally spatial and fundamentally exceptionalist. And in the debate about models of information law for the post-*Code* society, the narrative of cyberspace as experientially separate has persisted. The difference is that cyberspace has become a space to be designed to the specifications that we desire: a place where the hitherto unattainable ideal of information-as-freedom/control can be more narrowly pursued.

If this were simply a question of the allocation of rights and responsibilities in virtual space, it would not be very important. But what occurs in cyberspace is not separate from what occurs in real space. Cyberspace is not, and never could be, "a civilization of the Mind"; minds are attached to bodies, and bodies exist in the space of the world. And cyberspace as such does not preexist its users. Rather, it is produced by users, and not (in most cases) as a deliberate political project, but in the course of going about their lives. The technologies and "places" that constitute cyberspace have been assimilated into the lives of millions of ordinary people who embrace the Internet as a tool for pursuing their ordinary, real-world ends.

In the ongoing debate about the relative merits of freedom and control, the two visions of the information society have come to seem both strangely interdependent and strangely disconnected from the realities that confront Internet users. Policy debates have a circular, self-referential quality. Allegations of lawlessness bolster the perceived need for control, and objections to control fuel calls for increased openness. That is no accident; rigidity and license historically have maintained a curious symbiosis. In the 1920s, Prohibition fueled the rise of Al Capone; today, privately deputized copyright cops and draconian technical protection systems spur the emergence of uncontrolled "darknets." In science fiction, technocratic, rule-bound civilizations spawn "edge cities" marked by their comparative heterogeneity and near imperviousness to externally imposed authority. These cities are patterned on the favelas and shantytowns that both sap and sustain the world's emerging megacities. The pattern suggests an implicit acknowledgment that each half of the freedom/control binary contains and requires the other.

At the same time, the dichotomy between freedom and control creates an impression of overall completeness that is warranted neither descriptively nor normatively. The choice between dreams of unlimited freedom to order one's own dealings and dreams of perfect control over permissible orderings is a choice between extremes, and therefore profoundly unsatisfactory. It is people in real space who want and need information, and for whom neither perfect freedom nor perfect control holds sustained attraction. Here the scholarly debate over the proper regulatory approach to cyberspace reflects not richness but poverty of imagination. Part IV of this book takes up the evolving relationship between law and architecture, or code, considering why legal scholarship has not supplied a theory that matches the lived experiences of network users and what such a theory ought to contain.

Looking for the Self in the Network: The Question of Method

Before considering the problems of culture, subjectivity, and architecture in greater depth, some table setting is order. Each of the debates about freedom and control that I have described suggests powerfully that the conceptual tool kit that legal scholars have brought to bear on information law and policy is inadequate. This section lays the foundation for a different approach, which Chapter 2 will develop. I begin by exploring some of the ways in which the ideological commitments of liberal political theory have constrained legal scholarship's investigations of copyright, privacy, and code, imposing overly narrow criteria of methodological adequacy. Too often, those criteria have prevented legal theorists from asking, and sometimes even recognizing, questions about culture, subjectivity, and social ordering that are enormously important to thinking about the problems that we now confront.

An alternative normative foundation for analysis of the networked self is supplied by the theory of capabilities for human flourishing, which advances an affirmative conception of human freedom. The capabilities approach has suffered, however, from the efforts of its leading exponents to distance themselves from a set of methodologies often lumped together under the heading of "postmodernism." Those methodologies offer tools for exploring precisely the questions about culture, subjectivity, and social ordering that have assumed critical importance for information law and policy. Provision of the core capabilities for human flourishing in the networked information society requires careful attention to the interplay between systems of knowledge and systems of power and to the ways in which embodiment, spatiality, and the material realities of everyday practice mediate the production of culture and identity. The methodology developed here pairs the capabilities approach with disciplines that emphasize the mutually constitutive interactions between self and culture, the social construction of systems of knowledge, and the irreducible materiality of experience.

The Limits of Liberal Individualism

Within the tradition of liberal political theory, the legal subject—the self who possesses rights and is subject to regulation—has three principal attributes. He is, first and foremost, a definitionally autonomous being, possessed of abstract liberty rights that are presumed capable of exercise regardless of context. Second, the legal subject possesses at least the capacity for rational deliberation, and this capacity too is detached from context. In these respects, the legal subject is situated within a tradition of Enlightenment rationalism extending from Kant to Hegel to Habermas and Rawls. Whatever their internal disagreements, works within this tradition presume the existence of universal truths amenable to rational discourse and analysis. Finally, the selfhood that the legal subject possesses is transcendent and immaterial; it is distinct from the body in which the legal subject resides. As Katherine Hayles puts it, the liberal self has a body, but is not understood as being a body.[14]

The tradition of Enlightenment rationalism translates into templates for ascertaining schemes of legal right and obligation within which the forms of analysis that are most highly prized are the most abstract and decontextualized. Within the contemporary legal academy, the parameters of theoretical debate are shaped by the fault lines between economic analysis and theories of rights. Consistent with Kant's categorical impera-

tive, rights theorists focus predominantly on specifying, via logical derivation, the sort of treatment that the legal subject should have a right to
expect from a regime of legal rights and obligations. Economic theorists
profess themselves to be concerned primarily with overall efficiency in
the production and distribution of social resources, and with factors that
might produce distortions from the optimum production and distribution. Within economic analysis, however, the engine of production and
distribution is the liberty possessed by the legal subjects of whom society
is constituted.

Proponents of these approaches vigorously debate among themselves whether one approach or the other is better; for my purposes,
however, the similarities are more important than the differences. Their
normative heft derives from a small number of formal principles and
purports to concern questions that are a step or two removed from the
particular question of policy to be decided. The purported advantage of
both approaches is neither precisely that they are normative nor precisely
that they are scientific, but that they do normative work in a scientific
way. With respect to copyright and privacy in particular, neither rights
nor utility functions need be specified directly in terms of the content of
culture or the nature of socially embedded subjectivity. The theories
manifest a quasi-scientific neutrality as to law that consists precisely in
the high degree of abstraction with which they facilitate thinking about
processes of cultural transmission.

Within the mainstream of copyright scholarship, most scholars
have assumed that a grand theory of the field must be grounded either
in a theory of rights or in a theory of economic analysis. Within both approaches, a theory of "authorship" as internal and essentially unknowable
derives straightforwardly from the liberal individualist paradigm. When
pressed on the question of engagement with the particulars of creative
processes, scholars of both persuasions sometimes respond that richer
descriptive and theoretical models of creativity do not themselves dictate
any particular arrangement of legal rules. Deriving such rules requires a
theory of the good that we are trying to pursue; that theory, or so we are
told, can come only from rights-based theories or from economics.[15]
Each side then claims that the other really lacks normative sufficiency.
Rights theorists note that economic analysis requires a priori specification of some utility function, while economic theorists observe that
rights theorists are equally dependent on unproved and unprovable preconceptions about natural rights. This disagreement, however, reveals
broader agreement on the importance of identifying a small set of first

principles encoding first-order normative choices, from which a normatively compelling framework for copyright can then be derived in relatively neutral fashion.

For the most part, both copyright scholarship and copyright policy making persistently overlook other (nonphilosophical, noneconomic) literatures that study artistic and intellectual cultures as phenomena that emerge at the intersections between self and society. This is not the result of ignorance; important work in copyright theory has considered these literatures and the opportunities that they offer to scholars interested in understanding creativity and creative practice. The mainstream of debate about copyright theory and policy, however, tends to ignore or discount the well-established humanities and social science methodologies that are available for investigating the origins of artistic and cultural innovation. The best explanation that I have seen for this aversion highlights an assumption about first principles shared by copyright theorists on both sides of the rights/economics divide: to emphasize the endogenous relationship of self to culture is to introduce a large set of unruly complications that undermine foundational premises about individual autonomy and that threaten to undo policy analysis entirely.[16]

Similar commitments are evident in privacy theory, but in privacy theory, the cracks in the foundation of the liberal edifice have been harder to conceal. Efforts to define privacy as an individual right cognizable within the parameters of liberal rights theories have been dogged by incompleteness. Scholars have advanced a number of different formulations, including accessibility, control, and intimacy. As Daniel Solove demonstrates, however, such formulations are always too broad or too narrow.[17] It is impossible to identify a single, overarching principle that applies in all situations—which, in turn, means that nonneutral, context-specific rules of decision must be employed to decide when a "privacy" interest is triggered. While this is not necessarily a problem in any absolute sense, it is an enormous problem within the framework of liberal rights theory, which demands that formulations of fundamental rights be both abstract and complete.

These problems of over- and underbreadth lead other scholars to conclude that what we refer to as rights of privacy are really property rights or liberty interests in disguise. In the domain of rights theory, that result is consistent with Anglo-American legal theory's Lockean roots; it recasts privacy as a corollary to self-ownership and ownership of private property. Concepts of "property" and "liberty" map more directly to the perceived boundaries of things, places, and persons, and therefore seem analytically crisper. In the domain of economic analysis, meanwhile, reducing privacy rights to liberty interests aligns with the commitment to presumptively efficient social ordering through markets. Within a utilitarian framework, private-sector practices that devalue privacy do not represent a failure of liberty, but rather the efficient aggregation of preferences. A consequence of both approaches is that "privacy" makes most sense as a derivative or second-order concept, to be honored only to the extent that it is consistent with other, more fundamental principles.[18] It becomes easy to see both why privacy must be "balanced" against other interests and why the balancing should be less rigorous than when more fundamental rights are directly implicated.

Comparative and sociological theories of privacy abound, but to most U.S. legal scholars, such theories seem only to confirm privacy's status as a second-class right. Both the Continental European privacy tradition and work by some U.S. moral philosophers ground privacy rights in considerations of human dignity and personhood that are not readily amenable to analytic reduction. Other U.S. scholars have tried to fashion a relational vision of privacy by drawing on sociological research on human interaction.[19] For the most part, liberal privacy theory's answer to these recurrent intellectual assaults has been to play one off against the other. Emphasizing the ways in which privacy is socially constructed poses immense conceptual problems for efforts to theorize privacy as a right cognizable within the parameters of liberal theory. Accordingly, legal theorists of privacy have tended to read the sociologically informed theories of privacy as fatally undermining privacy's claims to status as a fundamental right. Dignity-based theories of privacy rights, meanwhile, are faulted not only for failing the threshold requirement of analytical simplicity, but also for sociological reasons. Cultural conceptions of dignity are not uniform, and therefore (or so the reasoning goes) dignity cannot serve as the foundation for a rigorous, analytically coherent conception of privacy. The conclusion is clear: if privacy is a fundamental right, it cannot be socially constructed; if privacy is socially constructed, it cannot be a fundamental right.

More recently, some privacy scholars have begun to push against the constraints of abstraction and analytic reduction. Helen Nissenbaum's important work on privacy as shaped by "contextual norms of appropriateness and flow" seeks to force rights-based conceptions of privacy to engage the collective and contextual dimensions of privacy interests. According to Nissenbaum, one does not need a single theory of privacy to explore how privacy works in practice. To similar effect, Daniel Solove offers a conceptualization of privacy that is based on pragmatist moral philosophy and that therefore does not depend on identifying privacy's essence; in this account, privacy interests emerge from expectations generated by everyday experience. Both scholars, however, appear content to address context while holding the self constant, thereby ignoring the problem of evolving subjectivity and its relationship to contextual change. Theorists who articulate a "constitutive" conception of privacy, in which group I include myself, have attempted to relate privacy to the construction of subjectivity. Even so, thinkers in this group have continued to rely heavily on the rhetoric of liberal selfhood and its foundational presumption of autonomy.[20]

In legal scholarship on code, the rights/economics binary is subordinated to the related preoccupation with the dichotomy between liberty and constraint. Some scholars worry that code-based constraints threaten fundamental liberties of expression and association. Others think that code is simply a tool for the unproblematic reinforcement of private choices about the management of commercial activity. Both sides of this divide invoke a quintessentially liberal anxiety about the origin of regulatory authority. Whether code violates rights or impinges on the exercise of market liberties comes to depend centrally on whether it is viewed as an exercise of public or private power. Questions about the way that code regulates, and about its role within systems of social ordering more generally, are systematically overlooked. Most legal scholars who have attempted to address those questions seem to be methodologically adrift, casting about for tools that legal theory cannot itself supply.

Finally and importantly, in each of these literatures, the analytical constructs generated by liberal individualism are particularly seductive because the problems they address play out in the realm of "information." Information appears to be the ultimate disembodied good, yielding itself seamlessly to abstract, rational analysis. The networked information society appears to be the autonomous, rational, disembodied self's natural milieu, transcending the particularities of bodies, cultures, and spaces with equal ease. That view of the networked information society, though, is a nirvana fallacy—and not, when all is said and done, an especially attractive one. As we will see throughout the book, liberal individualism's commitments to immateriality and disembodiment make for both a very poor model of culture and a very poor model of self-formation, online as well as offline. Theorizing the networked information society requires systematic attention to the bodies and spaces within which individuals and groups reside and to the materiality of artifacts and architectures. That, in turn, requires perspectives drawn from outside the liberal tradition.

Information Rights and Human Flourishing

An adequate theoretical framework for information law and policy must allow the definition of rights without insisting that they be amenable to neutral, quasi-scientific reduction, and must permit formulation and discussion of instrumental goals without imposing the Procrustean requirements of utilitarianism. The theory of capabilities for human flourishing satisfies both requirements, and supplies the underlying normative orientation for the analysis developed in this book.

Let us begin by returning to the argument that deriving a normative model—of copyright, privacy rights, or anything else—requires a theory of rights or a theory of economics. It is important, first, to understand precisely what this argument claims. For rights theorists, the claim appears to be a relatively straightforward one about the importance of having a (deontological) political philosophy in which normative arguments can be grounded. In the case of economics, the parallel claim is not nearly as clear. Many practitioners of "law and economics" seem to think that they are doing (social) science as opposed to mere philosophy. But by that measure, the argument about the normative superiority of economics is a very odd one. If "economics" is understood to denote a social science methodology, then its normative valence is no greater than that of, say, sociology or anthropology. If the claimed superiority of economics is to have any basis, it must rest on a link to political philosophy that those other disciplines lack. Within the framework of liberal political philosophy in which legal scholars are trained, the obvious candidate is utilitarianism, and so that is the political philosophy with which law and economics has become identified.

The contention, then, is that even if rights-based theories and utilitarian theories are lacking in descriptive power, together they cover the normative waterfront. Within economic reasoning, this move operates as a naked form of intellectual irredentism, which holds that any consequentialist theory of the good must be amenable to reformulation in the language of economics. Here the linked anxieties about neutrality and abstraction come bubbling to the surface; the idea seems to be that utilitarian analysis is the prototype case of consequentialism, a position which it claims both by virtue of its high degree of abstraction and its ability to define away problems of judgment. Rights theorists subscribe to these assumptions largely out of uninterest in and dissatisfaction with consequentialist reasoning generally; for rights theorists, all consequentialist theories are normatively indeterminate. But the underlying assumption (on both sides) that any consequentialist theory must be grounded in economics is false. The universe of consequentialist theories is not coextensive with the universe of utilitarian ones.

In particular, the tendency to conflate consequentialism with utilitarianism ignores versions of consequentialism that use rules other than utility maximization to decide on good outcomes. Rule consequentialism enables formulation of instrumental goals without imposing the artificial constraint that the resulting improvements in human well-being be amenable to expression in terms of utility, and therefore perfectly or even approximately commensurable. And it enables the discussion and definition of the rights that human beings should be entitled to expect without imposing the artificial constraint that these rights be logically derivable from a small handful of first principles. More generally, rule-consequentialist theories of the good need not assume, and do not require, the autonomous, rational, disembodied liberal subject.

One such theory is the capabilities approach developed (in different ways but along parallel paths) by Amartya Sen and Martha Nussbaum.[21] The capabilities approach takes as its lodestar the fulfillment of human freedom, as some theories of legal rights do, but it defines freedom in terms of the development of affirmative capabilities for flourishing. Thus defined, freedom is not simply a function of the absence of restraint (or negative liberty), but also depends critically on access to resources and on the availability of a sufficient variety of real opportunities. Because of those requirements, moreover, freedom and equality are integrally connected within the capabilities approach. Equality is not simply a matter of making distributive adjustments here and there once the basic structure of entitlements is decided according to some other set of criteria. Substantive equality is a fundamental concern, and a normative constraint on both rule structures and policy recommendations.

Specifically, the capabilities approach diverges from the prevailing modes of theorizing about human rights and human welfare in four important respects. First, it holds normative commitments closer to the surface and, consequently, more available for interrogation. In this, it compares favorably with economic theories, which tend to skip over the task of specifying initial utility functions. Second, the capabilities approach resists abstraction from the conditions of everyday life and demands instead that claimed rights be defined to include the conditions necessary for real people to take full advantage of them. It therefore both demands resort to and provides a clear point of entry for the messy social science methodologies that legal scholars of information policy have resisted. Third, the capabilities approach embraces complexity and ambiguity; it does not expect the resolution of large policy questions to be easy. Accordingly, it is more capable of encompassing and articulating a framework for resolving the competing claims of incommensurable goods. Finally, because it emphasizes substantive equality as a condition of human freedom, the capabilities approach is especially well suited to theorizing about the linkages between rights, enabling conditions, and social justice.

Within the legal literature on information policy, there is evidence of a recent turn toward explicit adoption of the capabilities approach. Leading works include Yochai Benkler's treatment of the linkages between information policy, information markets, and human freedom; Margaret Chon's work on intellectual property and development; and Madhavi Sunder's exploration of the intersections between intellectual property, the Internet protocol, and identity politics. The theories advanced by these scholars differ in many respects, but are consistent in their commitment to at least the principles just described.

Application of the capabilities approach to matters of information policy is complicated, however, by two sets of considerations that relate to broader crosscurrents in twentieth-century intellectual history. The first is the relationship between the capabilities approach and liberal political theory. Both Sen and Nussbaum are firmly committed to locating the capabilities approach within the evolving traditions of liberal political economy and philosophy. Benkler likewise situates his work squarely within those traditions. Chon, and Sunder to an extent, think that a deeper and more rigorous engagement with postmodernist explorations of culture is essential to evaluating the effects of copyright on human flourishing in the way that the capabilities approach requires, but theirs is clearly a minority position. Nussbaum and Sen, and Benkler to a lesser degree, appear concerned to show that their approaches do not derive from, or require endorsement of, a standardless postmodernism.[22] Yet (as the next section will discuss) that stance rejects rather a large amount of recent thinking on the topics of culture and subjectivity, and on their relationship to the questions of freedom and equality with which the capabilities approach is centrally concerned.

Second, the capabilities approach has been criticized as lacking in analytical rigor. Some scholars charge that it generates an endless list of wants and elevates them all to the status of rights.[23] It should be noted, first, that this argument is a variant of the view, discussed above, that equates analytical rigor with quasi-scientific reductionism. It is not obvious why a theory of human flourishing that generates simpler insights should automatically be more right than one with prescriptions that are complex. Assuming for the sake of argument, however, that some amenability to analytical reduction is useful, it is precisely here that looking beyond the liberal canon becomes essential; examining the individual experience of the networked information environment can supply empirical and theoretical perspectives on the structural conditions for human flourishing that the logical methods of liberal theory cannot.

Interrogating Complexity: Culture, Materiality, Geography

Elaborating a rigorous, empirically grounded theory of capabilities for human flourishing in the networked information society demands attention to an array of social science methodologies that provide both descriptive tools for constructing ethnographies of cultural processes and theoretical tools for modeling them. These methodologies are diverse, but share a number of common attributes. They prize empiricism above logical derivation from so-called first principles, and the forms of empiricism that are prized most highly tend to be qualitative and ethnographic rather than quantitative and abstract. They generate theoretical models of social and cultural processes that are subtle and complex, and that tend not to be amenable to mathematical reduction. They recognize that because cultural practices and institutions are evolving and endogenously constituted, scholars wishing to understand them must pay careful attention not only to the forces of rational self-interest but also to practices of rhetoric, representation, and classification. Finally, they emphasize the importance of the material realities of everyday practice.

Recall, first, the problem of the "cultural environment." The project of establishing descriptive and normative foundations for cultural environmentalism has been hampered by legal scholars' reluctance to engage culture in its own right, without the filters supplied by simplistic economic models or by more complex models derived from the life sciences. The resistance to culture is itself culturally determined; it is a product of a particular liberal worldview that understands "culture" as a superfluous overlay that autonomous reason can transcend.[24] Assigning individuals and communities an "autonomy" that exists outside of culture is a mistake at the most basic level, however. Individuals and communities are constituted by the social and political cultures that surround them, and those cultural contexts in turn shape the forms of self-determination and participation that emerge.

Throughout this book I will canvass a variety of literatures that address the "culture" question. The approaches that I identify as most pertinent have in common an orientation that is broadly postmodernist, or in Bruno Latour's preferred terminology, nonmodernist: they reject fixed distinctions between culture and nature, between culture and self, and between culture and deeper social structure. Instead, they focus careful, critical attention on the "hybrid" assemblages that emerge where politics, economics, technology, ideology, and discourse intersect.[25] On this understanding, culture is not a fixed collection of texts and practices, but rather an emergent, historically and materially contingent process through which understandings of self and society are formed and re-formed. The process of culture is shaped by the self-interested actions of powerful institutional actors, by the everyday practices of individuals and communities, and by ways of understanding and describing the world that have complex histories of their own.[26] The lack of fixity at the core of this conception of culture does not undermine its explanatory utility; to the contrary, it is the origin of culture's power. As Terry Eagleton puts it, "cultures 'work' exactly because they are porous, fuzzy-edged, indeterminate, intrinsically inconsistent, never quite identical with themselves, their boundaries continually modulating into horizons."[27]

A few caveats are in order here. First, I do not mean to suggest by this cavalier juxtaposition of Latour and Eagleton—two very different scholars—that social and cultural theorists offer a single account of "culture." Questions about the nature and origins of culture and the patterns of cultural change are hotly debated. My goal is not to take sides in those debates, but rather to identify and pursue common threads. What literatures that investigate the question of culture offer is something far more valuable than a universally agreed definition: they provide a tool kit for exploring questions about culture in ways that liberal political theory does not allow. That tool kit is an indispensable prerequisite for understanding and evaluating the cultural work that information law and policy do. Second, it is important to stress that culture is broader than the universe of artistic and intellectual activities with which copyright in particular is concerned. On occasion, however, I will use the terms "culture" and "cultural goods" as a simpler shorthand for the universe of artistic, intellectual, and informational artifacts and practices. Sometimes one simply needs a word to use.

Next, recall the contradictions between openness and privacy that have bedeviled legal scholars and open-access advocates. If we replace the autonomous, rational, disembodied self with the subject who exists within and is constituted by culture, the contradiction diminishes. Policies restricting information flow become, at the very least, a legitimate subject for public discussion. So too with policies and practices regarding the collection and processing of information about individuals and communities. Raw information, especially in great quantity, is not terribly useful to anyone. Information must be sorted, categorized, and processed, and those activities impose particular, culturally determined categories and values. Concepts like "surveillance" and "privacy" cannot be understood without exploring the origins, purposes, and effects of socially situated processes of sorting and categorization. Throughout the book and particularly in the discussions of privacy, I will draw on literatures in information studies and surveillance studies that investigate those questions.[28]

Attention to patterns of everyday experience within the emerging networked information society suggests, however, that focusing simply on the cultural meanings of information, and on the categories developed by information-processing practices, is not enough to illuminate either culture or subject formation. The information society is not simply an abstract collection of categories and privileges; its inhabitants exist within real spaces and experience artifacts and architectures as having material properties. Understanding how networked information technologies affect cultural processes requires attention to the material and geographic effects of network protocols and networked processes.

As we have already seen, legal scholarship on these issues traces its roots to the analytic framework self-styled as the New Chicago School and extended into cyberlaw studies by Lessig. As elaborated in *Code*, that framework recognizes four primary "modalities of regulation": the market, norms, law, and architecture (or "code"), and holds that regulation inheres in the interactions among them.[29] In particular, cyberlaw's distinctive contribution to the legal literatures on regulation and governance has been to establish the central importance of technical sites for the production and extension of power.

The irony in this parallel is that the field of cyberlaw has developed in near complete isolation from several other fields whose literatures might shed useful light on those issues. One is the umbrella field known as science and technology studies (STS). The insight that artifacts constrain ("regulate") behavior has a long history within STS, and is mined within that literature in far subtler ways. STS scholars reject the assumption that technologies and artifacts have fixed forms and predetermined, neutral trajectories. They argue that this analytical "black boxing" of technologies and artifacts conceals the extent to which they are socially shaped. In Carolyn Marvin's words, new technologies in particular have no "natural edges," but instead serve as focal points around which the self-interested behaviors of existing groups coalesce.[30] As power struggles are resolved, or confined within narrower parameters, artifacts and protocols assume a more definite form that both embodies and conceals the terms of resolution.

One cannot explain how code regulates—and, critically, how it comes to regulate in one way rather than another—without harnessing the insights of STS. In particular, one cannot make sense of developments in either surveillance or network architecture more generally without interrogating the ways that information protocols and networked devices are reshaping our spaces and practices, encoding new path-dependencies and new habits of behavior. The credo that "code is law" recognizes that Internet technologies encode an especially powerful and peculiarly invisible form of behavioral discipline, but it does not acknowledge that these technologies also form the material substrate within which complex social patterns take root. Throughout the book, I will draw on the various literatures in STS to explore the emergence of networked information architectures and associated social and institutional practices. One of the foundational texts in STS is Langdon Winner's meditation on whether particular artifacts can be said to have a politics that has more definite consequences for the organization of society.[31] I will consider that question in the context of emerging architectures for implementing surveillance and regulating access to networked information resources.

In addition, the literatures in both STS and cultural studies explore the roles that bodies and embodiment play in processes of socio-technical ordering. Both the possibilities offered by emerging technologies and the path-dependencies encoded within relatively hardened technologies and artifacts are experienced in ways that are mediated by embodied perception. As we struggle to shape our technologies and configure our artifacts, they also and quite literally configure us, guiding us toward the well-worn paths that render the material a matter of habit.[32] As we will see throughout the book, processes of configuration play important roles in the construction of the emerging information society, shaping not only understandings of privacy, but also and more generally the experience of agency within cultural, material, and social realms.

Finally, recall the assumption that cyberspace is a separate, malleable space, an assumption that has united otherwise different approaches to the regulation of information networks. The literatures in cultural geography and urban planning, which explore the ways that spaces function within cultures, complicate that assumption. Spaces are not preexisting, natural entities, but rather are produced by human activity in patterns that bear the imprint of political, institutional, and ideological influence. Surveillance practices have spatial dynamics of their own, and there is a sizable literature devoted to exploring and understanding those dynamics and their effects on individuals and communities. Literatures that explore the production of space and the patterns of spatial practice have important implications for our understanding of what cyberspace is (and is not), and I will draw on them throughout the book.[33]

The literatures on space and spatiality return us, finally, to the question of culture. Spaces and spatially situated practices play important roles in the construction of narratives about communities and nations, becoming concrete vehicles for the emergence of what Benedict Anderson has described as "imagined communities" organized around visions of shared cultural identity. On a more particularized level, social spaces can also serve as sites for experimentation with alternative models of social ordering. Michel Foucault called such spaces "heterotopia" and argued that they play important roles in the constitution of distinct societies.[34] Literatures that explore the spatially situated processes of cultural imagination inform my project in the most basic way: this book is about the imagined community of legal liberalism and about the ways in which that community has harnessed information technology and information policy to advance its own foundational narratives. My goal throughout the book is to draw attention to the processes of construction now underway and to place them in critical perspective.

The Power of Hybridity

Most legal academics are disciplinary magpies, collecting alluring bits of this and that and cobbling them together. Reasonable people can and do differ on whether that tendency is an asset or a liability. Rigid disciplinary loyalties have no place in the study of information rights and information networks, however. Scholarly fields like STS, cultural studies, information studies, and communications studies are themselves "interdisciplines"—fields that necessarily operate at the intersections between more sharply defined areas of inquiry.[35] In any serious study of the role of law in the networked information society, methodological eclecticism is not an indulgence; it is a necessity.

Since this book articulates a theoretical stance that is broadly postmodernist in orientation, and will concentrate on questions that legal liberalism has encouraged us to overlook, it is important to stress three additional caveats. First, postmodernist thought about the information society incorporates its own brand of purist myopia. Academic work in social theory often lacks law's resolute pragmatism. Too many such works find power everywhere and hope nowhere, and seem to offer well-meaning policy makers little more than a prescription for despair. One purpose of this book is to turn theory to pragmatic ends, exploring how postmodernist critique might produce an agenda for meaningful reform in our information policy. Power is inevitable and language slippery, but that should not mean that we have nothing to say.

Second, the approach that I have outlined necessarily entails some sacrifice of intradisciplinary nuance, yet I think that is all to the good. Often, postmodernism's love affair with convoluted academic terminology and its visible struggles with its own anxieties about fixity of meaning have made it easier to parody than to understand. That result is unfortunate, and one that scholars who hope to make a difference should seek to avoid. To the extent feasible, I have sought to avoid delving into relatively narrow scholarly disagreements about terminology and emphasis, and have sought instead to identify broadly shared insights about the ways that culture moves and the ways that artifacts evolve within society. My aim in this book is explain how paying attention to those core insights can further the goal of designing a just system of information policy and an architecture to match.

Finally, and perhaps most importantly, I do not intend to argue that liberalism's aspirations are necessarily either irrelevant or undesirable. Many of those aspirations—particularly those of fostering a critical, engaged citizenry and a dynamic, innovative culture—are important and well worth pursuing. My argument is that we will approach those goals, if at all, only by discarding some of liberalism's more problematic assumptions in favor of a larger and more eclectic tool kit, and only by developing a more satisfactory framework for making normative judgments about the consequences of our choices.

I do not pretend to be an expert in any of the fields upon which this book draws. I do claim to be something that is perhaps more useful: a committed skeptic and a determined resister of rigid disciplinary boundaries. The intellectual stance that I have in mind is neither strictly liberal nor strictly postmodernist, nor is it simply interdisciplinary, since the boundaries it crosses do not divide merely disciplines. At least as applied to problems of information policy, it offers legal scholarship the richness and concreteness that it has too often lacked.

Structure of the Book

The remainder of Part I takes up the project of reconceptualizing information policy in a way that puts the networked self at its core. Synthesizing strands from the disciplinary approaches identified above, Chapter 2 develops the elements of a framework for understanding the ordinary behaviors of embodied, networked inhabitants of the emerging information society. Within that framework, the world both off- and online is apprehended through the lens of *embodied perception*. Networked information technologies *mediate* both our embodied interactions and our perceptions, affecting the ways in which we understand our own capabilities, our relative boundedness, and the properties of the surrounding world. To understand the behaviors and motivations of networked, embodied selves, legal scholarship on the networked information society should largely abandon simplified theoretical constructs like "freedom of expression" and "freedom of choice," and instead focus on the ordinary routines and rhythms of *everyday practice*. In particular, scholars concerned with the domains of creativity and subject formation should pay careful attention to the connections between everyday practice and *play*, including both the patterns of play by situated subjects and the ways in which culture and subjectivity emerge from the interactions between the ordinary and the unexpected.

The middle three parts of the book then investigate more systematically legal theory's failure to generate convincing accounts of the relationships between copyright and culture (Part II), privacy and subjectivity (Part III), and network architecture and social ordering (Part IV). Each part begins with a chapter exploring the ways in which commitment to the core tenets of liberal political theory has stymied efforts to generate convincing descriptive and normative frameworks for information law and policy. The critiques developed in Chapters 3, 5, and 7 also highlight some of the ways in which our habitual discourses about copyright, privacy, and network architecture signal the importance of bodies and spaces to understanding and formulating information law and policy.

Chapters 4, 6, and 8 situate the problems of creativity and culture production, subjectivity and subject formation, and network architecture and social ordering within the framework developed in Chapter 2. Chapter 4 argues that creativity is centrally dependent on the freedom to appropriate and experiment with artifacts and techniques encountered within the cultural landscape. A copyright regime that wishes to promote cultural progress cannot simply seek to promote stability in the economic organization of cultural production; it also must foster the cultural mobility on which progress depends. Laws and policies about "privacy" promote a different kind of mobility; as Chapter 6 explains, privacy preserves room for individuals and communities to engage in the contextually situated processes of boundary management by which subjectivity is formed. Critical subjectivity in particular requires breathing room within the interstices of social shaping. A society that wishes to foster critical subjectivity must cabin the informational and spatial logics of surveillance. Chapter 8 considers the interplay between mobility and fixity in the context of evolving network architectures, focusing both on the emergence of institutional and technical regimes for authorizing access to resources and spaces and on the increasingly seamless, invisible design of networked artifacts and processes. A society that wishes to preserve room for the mobility of everyday material practice should not automatically validate such developments, but instead should explore strategies for counteracting them.

Building from these subject-specific inquiries, Part V of the book considers the lessons that they suggest for information policy reform. Chapter 9 develops a set of structural principles that should inform the legal and technical construction of the emerging networked information society. *Access to knowledge* plays an important role within that vision, but access alone is not enough. To promote the well-being of the situated, embodied individuals and communities who inhabit the networked information society, a regime of information law and policy also should guarantee an adequate level of *operational transparency* about the ways that networked information processes and devices mediate access to information and services. In addition, it should promote regulatory architectures that are characterized by *semantic discontinuity*—by an interstitial complexity that prevents the imposition of a highly articulated grid of rationality on human behavior and instead creates spaces within which the play of everyday practice can move. Chapter 10 concludes with some thoughts on strategies for putting this thicker and more complex vision of cultural environmentalism into practice.

From the Virtual to the Ordinary: Networked Space, Networked Bodies, and the Play of Everyday Practice

Before exploring the questions about creativity, subjectivity, and sociotechnical ordering raised in Chapter 1, it is useful to establish a general framework for those inquiries. I have promised an account of the "networked self," related in some way to something called the "play of everyday practice." Those terms are not usual in legal scholarship about information policy. For most legal scholars, the most salient aspect of the networked information society is the network itself and the new patterns of cultural participation that it enables. As we have seen, legal scholars have used theoretical frameworks derived from liberal political theory—most notably, frameworks organized around expressive liberty and market exchange—to impute overarching structure and purpose to those patterns. For the most part, they have conceptualized the activities of network users as occurring in an abstract, disembodied plane, detached from material and geographic contexts.

The vision of the networked information society and its citizens as transcending bodies and spaces, and as moving inexorably within patterns dictated by the overarching values of speech and market exchange, is terribly incomplete. Without question, digital information networks have radically altered the horizons for human communication and collaboration. But cultural resources are not only digital, and creativity does not occur only online. Digital information networks are perceived as creating privacy problems precisely because of the ways in which information may be aggregated and brought to bear on people living in the real world. Architectures of control shape patterns of social ordering both online and offline. Networked information technologies change some of the problems with which law must grapple, but still a book about information policy in the networked information society cannot be only a book about the Internet. And the autonomous, rational, disembodied liberal self is as much a fiction as it ever was. To understand the architectural and regulatory challenges that confront our emerging information society, we must consider all of the ways that situated, embodied selves encounter information in a real world that is increasingly networked.

This chapter offers two sets of organizing concepts to structure that inquiry. The first set of concepts relates to the way that people and communities experience networked information technologies. Real, embodied people do not experience "information" in the abstract; rather, the world both off- and online is apprehended through the lens of *embodied perception*. The primacy of embodied perception has two important consequences. First, networked information technologies do not call into being a new, virtual space that is separate from real space. Instead, they have catalyzed the emergence of a new kind of social space, which I will call *networked space*. Flows of information through networked space alter social patterns of interaction and resource allocation in important ways. Even so, networked space remains real space inhabited by real people. Second, the people who inhabit networked space have not disappeared into a virtual world, but their embodied experience of the real world is not the same as it was before. Networked information technologies *mediate* our interactions and our perceptions, affecting the ways in which we understand our own capabilities, our relative boundedness, and the properties of the surrounding world.

The second set of concepts relates to the way that networked, embodied selves and communities use networked information technologies. To understand the behaviors and motivations of networked, embodied selves, legal scholarship on the networked information society should largely abandon simplified theoretical constructs like "freedom of expression" and "freedom of choice," and instead examine the experiences of network users through the lens supplied by literatures that focus on the ordinary routines and rhythms of *everyday practice*. In particular, scholars concerned with the domains of creativity and subject formation should pay careful attention to the connections between everyday practice and *play*, including both the patterns of play by situated subjects and the ways in which culture and subjectivity emerge from the interactions between the ordinary and the unexpected.

Myths of Digital Transcendence

Within U.S. legal and policy discourse about information rights, the terms "information society" and "cyberspace" function as powerful imaginaries. They connote a world increasingly liberated from the mundane considerations of space and time, and peopled by citizens who are increasingly liberated from the constraints of location, materiality, and physical embodiment. Information policy documents often acknowledge a "digital divide" that separates the technological haves from the have-nots and propose measures to bring the have-nots into the digital age. That formulation tends to suggest that the most important thing about the digital divide is the ability to cross it, thereby "becoming" digital. Meanwhile, Fortune 500 companies, technology start-ups, experts in "human-computer interaction," and others who cater to the desires of the technological haves pour increasing effort into designing network interfaces so seamless that one barely need stop to register their existence.

For historians, all this likely has a familiar ring. Placed in historical context, scholarly and popular fascination with the Internet is but the latest instance of what David Nye calls the "American technological sublime"—a belief in the power of technology to subdue nature and usher in an age of transcendent reason. Since the nineteenth century, new communications and media technologies have been portrayed as forerunners of utopia. Earlier thinkers expected electric communication technologies to annihilate space and time; today, we call upon networked digital technologies to finish that task, accomplishing what mere electricity could not. The Internet, in particular, represents the "digital sublime": a plateau on which physical limitations cease to exist.[1]

Closely intertwined with myths of digital transcendence is a vision of networked information technologies as enabling freedom from bodily constraints. The official story of the transition to the information economy is the story of a slow but inexorable shift to the virtual that continues a process of commodification tracing back to the industrial revolution. In the transition to the information economy, property, labor, and money become not only commodified but also dematerialized. Intangible property, intellectual labor, and human capital flow effortlessly around the world, constrained here and there by regulatory "speed bumps," but largely unmoored from physical constraints.[2]

To the extent that the embodied self appears within this narrative, it is as a placeholder for more abstract values: a site of autonomous choice, democratic deliberation, or deconstructionist liberation. Indeed, for many thinkers about "cyberspace" and information policy, the advent of the Internet seems to seal the body's ultimate irrelevance to questions of social theory and social ordering, although different groups read that irrelevance differently. Thus, libertarian social critics see in cyberspace the eventual apotheosis of enlightened social and economic individualism, while liberal theorists of a more communitarian bent envision processes of reasoned, collective deliberation. For cultural critics of a deconstructionist bent, who see the world as a collection of texts, cyberspace—the space of the pseudonymous avatar, the writerly reader, and readerly writer—confirms the primacy of signs and exposes their infinite pliability.

As Katherine Hayles has shown, the understanding of the digital body as fundamentally immaterial traces its intellectual roots to the field of cybernetics, which began as an interdisciplinary effort to understand the properties of information and came to understand information as possessing constant properties regardless of the medium in which it is contained. The cybernetic worldview powerfully shapes the contemporary understanding of materiality as a mere substrate for meaning. Some philosophers of information posit that in the networked information age, all meaningful attributes of bodies and selves can be expressed as flows of information. That approach, however, forecloses precisely the inquiry that we need to make; it brings the body into theory only to dispose of it at the first convenient opportunity.[3]

Popular and artistic imaginings of networked space, meanwhile, assert the continuing importance of the body in networked digital culture. Within science fiction, William Gibson's and Neal Stephenson's protagonists rely on digital doppelgangers to negotiate provisional, improvised survival strategies within the interstices of real-world structures of power. To escape rigidly deterministic social control, Ethan Hawke's character in the film *Gattaca* and Tom Cruise's in the film *Minority Report* effectively rewrite portions of their own biological code so that their real, embodied selves can avoid detection, while the disaffected rebels of the *Matrix* series seek refuge in a gritty analog underworld. On television, joyful, consumerist visions of the networked body jostle for elbow room with their more dystopian cousins, iPod ads sandwiched between pitches for spam-filtering services and identity-theft protection.

Who is right about the network and the body, our philosophers or our artists? The lessons of experience suggest that the truth is more complicated: technology does not erase embodiment; it alters aspects of embodied experience. This dynamic is not unique to networked information technologies. Consider the passenger automobile, which radically transformed the ways that ordinary people live, work, shop, and play. A world with cars and roads is experienced differently than a world without them: it is smaller and more easily configured to individual preferences. Similarly, the emergence of networked space catalyzes perceptions of and relations to the body's immediate surroundings in "real" space that are hard to pigeonhole within preexisting theoretical frames. For example, mobile personal communication devices enable the sensation of continuous contact, but also intensify a phenomenon that social theorists of communication describe variously as "absent presence" or "present absence": a distanced and distancing relation to people physically present and events currently unfolding in real space. Embodied experience remains important even in contexts that seem to be entirely virtual. Although popular and academic literatures on virtual worlds celebrate escape from bodies, participants in virtual worlds continually supply reminders of how important they consider bodies and body images to be.[4]

Legal scholarship about the networked information society needs tools for thinking and talking about the relationships between the experiences of network users and the bodies and spaces that those users inhabit. This chapter seeks to begin that conversation by identifying a set of factors to consider.

The Primacy of Embodied Perception

To understand the continuing centrality of bodies and spaces in the emerging networked information society, it is useful to begin by reconsidering some core assumptions that have dominated legal thought about the body and its relation to experience and knowledge. Recall, once again, that legal theorists' commitment to disembodiment stands in a long intellectual tradition. The mainstream of Western philosophical thought is founded on presumed dichotomies between mind and body, self and container, transcendent truth and immanent, contingent matter. These foundational dualisms in turn have structured theories about the relations between self and society and the mechanisms of social ordering. Within philosophy more generally, however, the possibility of a more direct and fundamental relation between embodiment and knowledge has long been a recurring theme. Today that theme has become a steady drumbeat. The foundational dualisms of rationalist thought are increasingly questioned by scholars in fields ranging from philosophy to cognitive science, who offer a robust vision of embodied perception and cognition. Within these theories, the self does not merely *have* a body; the self *is* a body, and that body is embedded in social and material environments that mediate experience and perception.

In sociology, connections between embodiment and social ordering have long been apparent. Pioneering studies by Erving Goffman and Clifford Geertz highlighted the role of performance in the development and negotiation of social conventions. Pierre Bourdieu argued that the faculty of distinction, or critical judgment, emerges out of a matrix of embodied, socially situated behaviors that vary with class and social domain. Each of these approaches recognizes that individuals and communities are not "cultural dopes" but rather "practical sociologists," expertly negotiating matters of social ordering via thousands of clues embedded in the everyday actions of others.[5] Critically, the everyday processes of practical sociology proceed using the only clues available: embodied, observable behaviors situated in real contexts.

Embodiment has also figured importantly in critical theory. Foucault's historical analyses of the ways that the body has functioned as a site of social discipline have inspired a diverse array of work on what we might call the flip side of practical sociology: the social construction of conformity, hierarchy, and difference. In particular, critical theorists of race and gender have used Foucauldian theory to inform arguments about the ways that race and gender differences are produced by the gaze of others. Melding poststructuralism with theories about the performative and deconstructive powers of speech and language, scholars such as Judith Butler argue that embodied, purportedly "natural" attributes such as gender and race are to an overwhelming degree products of social construction. Yet other gender theorists, such as Susan Bordo, Iris Young, and Kenji Yoshino, challenge this erasure of bodily difference, arguing that bodies are important sources of knowledge in their own right.[6]

Within the past two decades, each of these intellectual approaches has intersected productively with a third that focuses on the phenomenology of knowledge. Phenomenological thinkers, including most prominently Maurice Merleau-Ponty, reject the distinction between absolute truth and ephemeral experience that underlies so much of Western philosophical thought. Instead, they argue that our only route to apprehending reality is the physical means that we all possess: our bodies, which mediate our perceptions of the world around us.[7] Phenomenological theorists have been criticized for offering an essentialized and romanticized vision of human perception that leaves no room for the sorts of constructed differences that have preoccupied sociologists and critical theorists. However, in recent years phenomenology has experienced a makeover of sorts.

Work by a diverse group of contemporary scholars harnesses these seemingly disparate intellectual traditions, seeking to reposition bodies and embodiment as central to perception of both the self and the surrounding world while avoiding the trap of naturalism. The visions of embodied perception advanced by these scholars differ in many respects, but for my purposes the similarities are more important: within these new theories of the body, embodiment is central to the development of both individual perception and social consciousness, or intersubjectivity. The philosopher and critical theorist Elizabeth Grosz likens the body to a Möbius strip, a continually twisting interface along which perceptions of the internal and natural are constantly in flux. In Grosz's vision of embodiedness, bodies emerge as both vehicles for social shaping and tools for the rejection of social shaping and the assertion of critical knowledge. Standing in counterpoint to Grosz's work are works by sociologists Nick Crossley and Chris Shilling that place relatively greater emphasis on the role of embodied perception in mediating productive relations among social groups. All these scholars agree that the body has been too long neglected (or rejected) in social thought, that knowledge cannot be disentangled from embodied perception, and that embodied perception and performance belong at the center of the self-society relation. On a more abstract level, they agree that a hybrid theoretical stance is essential to grasping the elusive connections between and among embodiment, perception, and knowledge.[8]

The turn to embodiment in contemporary critical theory finds support in the emerging science of human cognition. Thus, for example, George Lakoff and Mark Johnson's work on the use of concrete referents as metaphors for more abstract concepts—ideas as containers, thinking as seeing, and so on—suggests that the physical structures the conceptual powerfully and inevitably. Their understanding of embodied cognition as the product of a continuous interplay between concrete and abstract conceptual schema aligns nicely with Grosz's metaphor of the Möbius strip. It suggests a model of the relation between the physical and the conceptual—and so between body and mind—as dynamically intertwined. Notably, Lakoff and Johnson identify Merleau-Ponty and John Dewey, who stressed the connection between knowledge and experience, as the two philosophers whose perspectives align most closely with their project of developing a "philosophy in the flesh."[9]

Critically, the cognitive-theoretic understanding of metaphor is distinct from the term's use in literary criticism and its offshoots. Within literary disciplines, metaphor is understood as consciously chosen ornamentation, even as it is analyzed for the unintended messages it might convey. Similarly, legal scholarship about the networked information society, like the long tradition of legal rationalism within which it is situated, often relies heavily on an understanding of metaphor as fundamentally superfluous to reason. But the metaphoric structuring with which cognitive theory is concerned operates at a deeper and often unnoticed level. When I say that someone's argument "rests on quicksand," I am consciously deploying metaphor as rhetoric; when I describe the same argument as being "grounded in solid fact," neither I nor my intended audience may recognize that I am speaking metaphorically. The two sorts of metaphor are related—both use one concept to describe another that is more abstract, in the process appropriating a complex web of associative meaning—but they are distinct. The latter mediates language and reason alike and cannot so easily be cast aside. Embodied perception supplies the ready-to-hand models of concreteness that render abstractions intelligible to people seeking to communicate with one another.

Within cognitive theory, the primacy of embodied perception in turn has important implications for our understanding of spaces. It suggests that space as experienced differs radically from space as conventionally theorized within the Western philosophical tradition. Within that tradition, space is understood as an inert, neutral container for human activity, an emptiness to be "filled up" by people and things. That understanding is formalized by modeling empty space as a grid defined by x, y, and z coordinates: an absolute (non)entity structured by abstract mathematical laws. But one does not and cannot apprehend abstract, mathematical space experientially. Space is experienced, instead, in terms of situatedness and orientation, and the vehicle for apprehending space in this way is embodied perception. The human cognitive apparatus is structured to apprehend the immediate environment as three-dimensional and to organize object perception and depth perception accordingly. The process of cognition is "egocentric rather than geocentric"; we orient objects with respect to ourselves, not the reverse.[10] Space in this sense is relative and mutable; it is simultaneously apprehended through embodied perception and produced by our own actions.

That insight too converges substantially with those produced by critical theory. Critical theorists of space have rejected the "empty container" model of space and have asserted that space does not exist in any such absolute, a priori form; it is not something that human activity fills up, but rather something that human activity produces. In particular, they seek to draw attention to the ways in which the social production of space is structured by power, experience, desire, and representation, and to illuminate the complex relation between the social production of space and the social production of knowledge. They argue that particular features of constructed space (including both singularities, such as the Champs-Élysées or the twin towers of New York's World Trade Center, and more general categories, such as the mental institution, the marketplace, and the home) take on powerful metaphoric, and ultimately metonymic, significance, coming over time to stand for the societies that produced them.[11]

The convergence between critical theory and cognitive science tells us something extraordinarily important about the way we both experience and produce the world around us. The primacy of embodied perception requires rejection of both the conventional distinction between absolute truth and ephemeral experience, on one hand, and deconstructionist claims about the arbitrariness of purportedly natural categories, on the other. Fixed reality exists, but it isn't external and a priori; instead, it is internal and dependent on innate cognitive structures. For all intents and purposes, only the phenomenal world exists. Just as critical theorists point to a simultaneous disconnect and interconnect between the perceived (or real) and the conceived (or imagined), so cognitive theorists argue that even the conceived is structured by the perceived in deeply determined ways. Yet the structurings themselves are not fixed; for example, Lakoff and Johnson show that different cultures interpret and express spatial orientations differently.[12] Both the metaphoric mappings and the abstract, conceptual structures that they support are contingent and subject to change. Similarly, the social spaces produced by embodied beings are both real (in the only sense that matters) and contingent.

The lessons for information theory and policy are striking. Bodies are not simply inert matter that we all happen to possess; rather, the world that we experience is an inevitable perceptual byproduct of the human cognitive apparatus. And spaces are not arbitrary fictions that can be jettisoned or assumed away. If bodies and embodied spatiality mediate cognition and social ordering in complex and interdependent ways, then we cannot simply leave bodies and spaces behind as we enter the networked information age. The transition to the virtual is always partial, equivocal, and unstable. To understand the emerging networked information society, we must take bodies and embodiment seriously and inquire how networked information technologies reshape our embodied perceptions and experiences.

Networks and Bodies, Part 1: Networked Space

The primacy of embodied perception points the way toward a very different approach to understanding the spatiality of the networked information society. We do not need to decide what kind of (separate) space "cyberspace" is or should be, but rather to investigate the ways that networked information technologies change experienced space. Networked information technologies catalyze the emergence of networked space: the real geography produced by the extension of networked information technologies throughout preexisting geographies. Networked space is not a unitary phenomenon or place; it can and does include a multiplicity of places and experiences, which in turn are connected to experienced, "egocentric" space in many different ways.

From a social perspective, space is produced by the elaboration and path-dependent cumulation of networks for the movement of goods, communication, and people. Each network changes the character of existing space; for example, once an interstate highway is built or air travel developed, some places are more accessible and others less so. In 1950, Houston, Texas, was closer to Paris, Texas, than to Paris, France; today, the reverse is true for many people. In Henri Lefebvre's evocative metaphor, the social space that results from the gradual accretion of networks is "reminiscent of flaky *mille-feuille* pastry":

> Considered in isolation, [social] spaces are mere abstractions. As concrete abstractions, however, they attain "real" existence by virtue of networks and pathways, by virtue of bunches or clusters of relationships. Instances of this are the worldwide networks of communication, exchange and information. It is important to note that such newly developed networks do not eradicate from their social context those earlier ones, superimposed upon one another over the years, which constitute the various markets: local, regional, national and international markets; the market in commodities, the money or capital market, the labour market, and the market in works, symbols, and signs. . . . Each market, over the centuries, has been consolidated and has attained concrete form by means of a network: a network of buying- and selling-points in the case of the exchange of commodities, of banks and stock exchanges in the case of the circu-

lation of capital, of labour exchanges in the case of the labour market, and so on. . . . Thus social space . . . emerged in all its diversity.[13]

Networked information technologies contribute to the production of social space by enabling new markets, relationships, and practices, which are layered over the markets, relationships, and practices that previously existed. One way to understand this process is by exploring the products of efforts to map cyberspace. Historians who study practices of mapping understand that maps do not simply depict fixed reality. Mapping is an exercise in both representation and conceptualization. Maps and mapping practices change over time in response to changed understandings of geography and sovereignty, and understandings of geography and sovereignty are produced, in part, by prevailing practices of mapping.[14] It is thus not surprising that efforts to map cyberspace have emerged as a site of contestation among scholars.

Some efforts to map cyberspace have subscribed to the assumption of experiential separateness that has dogged legal theorists of cyberspace. Perhaps the most influential of these was the conceptual mapping performed in William Mitchell's *City of Bits*, which focused on identifying places and functions "within" cyberspace. At the same time, however, Mitchell's choice of the city metaphor and his careful insistence on describing cyberplaces functionally relative to parallel places in real space undermined the notion of separateness. Mitchell's treatment suggested powerfully that cyberspace is not a place, but a conglomeration of places, many with quite prosaic functions connected directly to the activities of real people in real spaces.

Other mapmakers have sought to map "the Internet" as a network of communication infrastructure within real space. These efforts have produced overlay maps showing the real-world geographic distribution of quantifiable network components such as backbone cables and routers, major nodes, and numbers of Web sites organized by hosting domain. To a degree that should not have been surprising to anyone, the early overlay maps revealed that Internet activity corresponded substantially to the real-world organization of geopolitical and economic activity, thereby further undermining the metaphoric construct of cyberspace as separate space. Over time, however, the network overlay maps have suggested shifts in relations among existing sites of real-space activity and have traced the growth of new high-tech enterprise zones in developing countries, suggesting a dynamic relationship between the network and the production of social space.[15]

Taken cumulatively, these mappings highlight the importance of conceptualizing a networked space that is both real and emergent. This approach finds broad support in the work of social scientists who study the emergence of the "information society." As many scholars have recognized, social and economic activities are shaped by the uses of information and communication technologies to control flows of information. Those technologies in turn presuppose and require concrete, material infrastructures and organizational logics that are tightly linked to real-space geographies. The sociologist Manuel Castells argues that the space of the twenty-first century is a "space of flows": networked space that includes and is produced by activities both real and virtual, and by the interconnections between the virtual and the real.[16]

Concurrently, the seductive image of cyberspace as empty space filled up with virtual activity has come under challenge from scientists who study the ontology of complex networks. This work identifies the Internet as one example of a "scale-free" network: a network in which the distribution and connectivity of nodes follow a power-law distribution — "a continuous hierarchy of nodes spanning from rare hubs to the numerous tiny nodes" — rather than a bell curve.[17] Although scale-free networks can appear infinitely plastic to their users, they are not so in practice. The patterns of flow between nodes and to and from hubs follow predictable mathematical laws and so inscribe path-dependencies that affect the direction and volume of later flows. Traffic to prominent nodes follows a "rich get richer" pattern, and their dominance within the network — think, for example, of eBay or YouTube — is relatively durable and difficult to displace.

Together, the insights from geography, sociology, and network science point the way toward a theory of networked space as itself produced by and producing flows of information, interaction, and development. Moreover, the convergence between the sociology of networked society and the science of complex networks suggests powerfully that perceived differences between cyberspace and real space are differences in degree rather than differences in kind. Both the sociological theory of a space of flows and the mathematics of scale-free networks apply to any complex human activity structured by interconnection, from the development of markets to the spread of infectious diseases to the propagation of fashions and cultural memes. We might say then that the emergence of networked space makes these latent characteristics of real space manifest, forcing an appreciation of the extent to which social space is constituted by flows of information, by the material infrastructures and

43

organizational logics constructed to support the flows, and by the path-dependence of flows, infrastructures, and organizational logics.

If we return to the topics of expressive and market liberty, which have preoccupied legal theorists of "cyberspace," we can see that the legal literature on these topics described both new patterns of flow and new patterns of the production of experienced space. Turning first to freedom of expression, an essential insight of legal scholarship has been that flows of speech in networked space are different from flows in real space. There is substantially less agreement on the precise nature of the difference. For some scholars, networked space is a space of expanded communicative opportunity, defined by the distributed peer production of cultural goods ranging from software to wikis and blogs to fan fiction. For others, the more salient feature of networked space is the enhanced control over communication exerted by intellectual-property owners and online intermediaries, or self-imposed by individuals. Taken together, those arguments support a more moderate (and much more interesting) position: networked space's difference is neither fixed nor unidirectional, but manifests as an ongoing tension between communicative expansion and communicative closure.

Turning next to markets, we see that changes in connectivity are pervasively remaking national and global transaction patterns. In manufacturing, networked communication technologies compress time and collapse linear distance. Reshaped by global connectivity and just-in-time delivery, commodity markets increasingly mirror the efficiencies of capital markets. At the same time, however, these shifts render supply chains more vulnerable to short-term disruptions, and capital markets more vulnerable to dramatic price swings. Both types of markets also manifest a "dynamic of simultaneous geographic dispersal and concentration" in emerging "global cities."[18] On a more personal scale, global connectivity promotes personalized trade within virtual marketplaces such as eBay and Craigslist.org, but simultaneously fosters increasing alienation as both personal information and cultural goods become more thoroughly commodified. Here again, then, networked space's difference manifests as an ongoing dialectic between increased opportunity and enhanced risk, and between personalization and standardization.[19]

Some critical theorists who study the rise of the networked society have questioned whether the shift to networked space is a conceit of the global elites. But when we expand our focus from the experience of being "in" cyberspace to the effects produced by the emergence of networked space, it becomes easier to see that the consequences extend much more broadly. This is most evident in the linked realms of marketing and surveillance. Radio-frequency identification (RFID) tags in smart cards and consumer goods can be activated and linked to information networks, as can geolocation devices in mobile phones and cars. This dimension of the "always on" experience affects everyone who transacts and travels, not just those who deliberately connect to cyberspace. Other consequences flow from the behavior of network users. People who do not have, and do not want, a Facebook page can be "tagged" in posted photographs and identified for the benefit of strangers living thousands of miles away. In each of these examples, the shift to networked space changes the character of existing space as experienced by ordinary people.

Changes in the structure of networked space also have other social consequences. There is reason to think that the rise of networked space may broadly affect the distribution of social resources. A digital divide is never only digital; its consequences play out wherever political and economic decisions are made and wherever their results are felt. Legal scholars have long worried about the structure of speech markets for exactly this reason, but most legal discourse about the structure of speech markets is highly abstract. Changes in speech markets are experienced locally, in the spatial distribution of bookstores, libraries, newsstands, broadcast franchises, protests, collaborations, and innumerable other activities. It is important to consider how a digital divide might alter those markets and also other resource distributions that inhere in social space. If the haves increasingly shop online while the have-nots shop in real space, the real-space distribution of goods, services, and employment patterns likely will change, and with it the real-space distribution of all the activities that make up the commerce of daily life. At the same time, the shift to networked space produces new juxtapositions between different groups of haves and have-nots. As one example, the practice of outsourcing customer service operations to developing countries creates new patterns of communication that over time may alter the way that developing-world employees and developed-world customers understand both one another and themselves.[20]

The essential point is that all the changes catalyzed by networked information technologies do not simply make cyberspace a different place. Changes in the ways that information is experienced and the ways that economic, political, and personal interactions are structured alter the character of experienced space. The emerging networked space is both new and old, both real and virtual, both the same and different. As we will see next, the same is true of the networked selves/bodies who inhabit it.

Networks and Bodies, Part 2: Mediated Perception

So far, I have argued that networked information and communication technologies are experienced by subjects who remain fundamentally embodied and located within real geographies. Here I want to broaden and extend that claim: networked information and communication technologies play an increasingly significant role in constructing embodied experience. The relationship between the embodied self and networked digital technologies is not a one-way street, in which "technology" is an object of "experience." Rather, the relationship between the embodied self and technology is a mutually constituting one. Technologies and artifacts are incorporated into everyday life by situated, embodied beings and are experienced as altering, extending, or limiting capabilities that we already possess. At the same time, technologies and artifacts mediate our embodied perception of reality; over time, we come to experience them as constituting and defining the world around us. Reality is in part a function of what our technologies and artifacts do. Networked information technologies do not simply empower the networked self; they configure it.

Consider, first, the ways that the Internet and its information resources reshape the experienced geography of the networked information society. The long list of spatial metaphors—"Web site," "navigate," "go to," "go back," "download," "upload"—formulated to describe the experience of Internet use suggests a process experienced in terms of distances, landmarks, and juxtapositions, exactly as the theory of embodied cognition would predict. Cyberspace distances are measured differently, in clicks or retrieval times rather than in walking or driving times, but they are distances nonetheless. Many educated Internet users resist this characterization, but this is chiefly because they have been trained to conceive of distance in Cartesian terms; experientially, distance is time. (How far from your office do you live?) To the extent that the online distance to a particular resource makes its real-space location seem closer or farther away, perceptions of networked space shift accordingly. Internet use does not make geography irrelevant; it reconfigures our understanding of it.

Networked information technologies do not alter only our perceptions of spatial proximity, however. Their mediating effects are far more intimate. The networked information age is increasingly experienced via the pervasive interpolation of networked information technologies into the spaces of the body. Data flows have escaped the obvious bounds of the networked computer and cross into and out of homes, cars, personal accessories, and public spaces by many avenues. To an increasing extent, the production of networked space is characterized not by disembodiment, but by the dissolution and reconfiguration of personal boundaries that we have long regarded as fixed and natural. Networked space is neither empty nor abstract, and is certainly not separate; it is a network of connections wrapped around every artifact and human being.

Work in STS provides important resources for theorizing this process of dissolution and reconfiguration. Once again, there are important differences among the various approaches, but for my purposes what is more important is the way in which they converge: together, they suggest a networked self that is both irreducibly embodied and constituted partly by and through the technologies and artifacts that surround it. Networked information technologies define the processes by which bodily boundaries and flows of information across those boundaries are formed, re-formed, and naturalized.

Donna Haraway frames the relationship between embodied self and networked society in terms of a constantly threatened disintegration of boundaries between network and self. In Haraway's evocative term, networked space is the space of the cyborg, who is placed in circuits of information but not simply reduced to information.[21] For some purposes—the use of heat sensors to modulate lighting and climate controls in an office building, or the deployment of vaccination to control disease—the cyborg is simply a node in the network. For others—the maintenance of population-wide biometric databases accessible to law enforcement, or the deployment of vaccination to control fertility—it is a discrete entity with (at least for now) a legal right to maintain and defend its own boundedness. At many points—for example, the use of RFID transmissions to verify identity or detect location—the nature and existence of boundaries between cyborg and network is hotly contested. As distinct from the cybernetic subject, the cyborg body is both flesh and information, both particle and wave. Such an entity must continually negotiate both the conditions of connectedness and the consequences of disconnection.

Importantly, Haraway refuses to posit an ontological or experiential separation between the body and technology. She cautions that cyborg space cannot be avoided or evaded by retreat to an imaginary and finally mythological naturalism. Instead, the self and the networked world must come to some rapprochement, the terms of which will continually be opened for renegotiation. The important questions do not concern the boundaries of the unitary self, but rather the relation between networked space and embodied space, and the patterns of flow between them. Relevant patterns include flows of information to, from, and about the self and flows of information that link the self to and enable the constitution of groups and communities. As critics have noted, however, this is where Haraway's account of the cyborg body stops short. Haraway urges the development of new languages with which to talk about self and network, but does not talk directly about what roles might remain for the cyborg as body.[22]

A different strand of STS scholarship, which adopts a phenomenological perspective, usefully complements Haraway's approach. Like Haraway, these scholars reject the idea of an essential, pretechnical self. Instead, they argue that technology and embodied cognition have always been mutually constituting. Don Ihde characterizes this approach as "postphenomenology"—a critical phenomenology focused on probing existing human-technology relations rather than on drawing absolute conclusions about the essence of embodied experience. In Peter-Paul Verbeek's terminology, artifacts mediate both our experience of the world and our perception of it: embodied perception works to naturalize the technological landscape, even as changing technologies and artifacts reshape embodied perception and embodied capability.[23]

Importantly within this account of mediated perception, the shaping relation between artifacts and perception runs both ways. Consider, for example, changes in techniques of mapping and geolocation. Twenty years ago, if you wanted to drive to visit a friend in another town, you needed a map. To get from point A to point B, you studied the map, figured out the lay of the land, and plotted a route along major or minor roads and through or around intervening cities and towns. Internet mapping technologies changed that process, making it possible to get from point A to point B without needing to plot a route or to take the lay of the land at all. Because a printout from MapQuest or Google shows a complete route, however, you might still glean a general sense of the surrounding geography. Sometimes, you might be offered a choice of routes, along with contextual details such as whether travel will maximize or minimize the use of highways. Portable GPS technologies change the process of getting from point A to point B yet again. Now, you can simply follow directions as they are given, one at a time. Armed with GPS capability, you can go anywhere without getting lost, but also without needing to figure out where you are. By altering both the representation of real geographies and the manner of our habitual interaction with them, geolocation techniques enable a deeper reshaping of both our geographic agency and our geographic understanding.

Equally important, the shaping relation between artifacts and perception is experienced via the only route possible, the body and its perceptual organs and capabilities. Consider again the emergence of mobile communication technologies and the phenomenon of "present absence"/"absent presence" that they create. We have become accustomed to speaking about our growing reliance on mobile devices in the language of addiction. That metaphor, which invokes a physiological process, acknowledges a truth that we have been reluctant to confront more directly. But perhaps a more appropriate comparison is to the phenomenon of proprioception. Mobile devices augment the senses, connecting us to remote family, friends, and cultural resources. To one accustomed to this extended spatial and temporal reach, the lost Blackberry is experienced in a way more akin to temporary loss of sight or hearing than to the withdrawal effects of a withheld narcotic. Without our communications prosthetics, we are all disabled.

As the mapping example suggests, networked information technologies differ from other technologies in the extent to which the technological mediation of embodied perception is not simply functional, but also representational. The effects extend to our own self-perception. Juxtaposing postphenomenological theory with the culture of the digital image, Mark Hansen argues that "body schema"—which correspond more or less to what Verbeek would call the hermeneutic dimension of embodied perception—are informed by perceptions of body appearance that are themselves technologically mediated. This process does not originate with digital technologies—think, for example, of the understandings of bodies and embodiment brought about by the emergence and standardization of ready-to-wear clothing sizes or by the development of film-based photography. But networked information technologies and the various forms of virtuality that they allow enable continually changing representations of the body and its capabilities and limitations.[24]

Last but not least, technologies and artifacts are used in contexts and communities, and so they mediate embodied perception in ways that are irreducibly social. Studies of online environments ranging from gaming to open-source programming to the blogosphere have shown that those environments produce some effects that align with critical theorists' account of the body as a site of social shaping. For example, the Geek Feminism Wiki maintains an eye-opening archive of incidents of sexism and harassment in technical communities, many of which involve body schema of the sort that Hansen describes.[25] At the same time, however, technologies and artifacts empower users and user communities to further shared goals. Social shaping and empowerment are not mutually exclusive conditions, but rather overlap and coexist in a variety of combinations. As Hayles puts it, digital technologies are simultaneously inscribed upon the body and incorporated into embodied practice.[26] As we will see next, the resulting agency exercised by embodied users and user communities is very different than the reigning liberal models of free speech and market choice suggest.

The Play of Everyday Practice

Mediated perception notwithstanding, the networked self is not simply the passive product of technological shaping. Embodied, situated users interact with networked information technologies on a day-to-day basis, often turning those technologies to new purposes and adapting them in unexpected ways. Similarly, embodied beings both experience and produce networked space in the course of going about their daily lives. Many of these behaviors do not fit neatly into the overarching paradigms of expressive and market liberty that predominate in the legal literature. Understanding them requires a conceptual framework that treats them as ordinary rather than anomalous. The term "everyday practice" is both broader and less definite than the models of user behavior conventionally employed by legal theorists, but both its breadth and its openness are crucial to understanding the legal and regulatory challenges that networked information technologies present. As distinct from the sort of agency commonly attributed to the rational, disembodied self of liberal theory, the social and political agency that manifests in everyday practice is constrained and contingent in myriad ways. It is also, however, enormously powerful for precisely the same reason that it is resistant to theory: its connection to play.

As we will see throughout the book, legal theorists have had difficulty constructing a believable account of the ordinary, everyday ways that people use information, participate in culture, and experience networked technologies. The preferred modes of analysis within liberal legal theory tend to support idealized accounts of human activity organized around the exercise of liberty in different domains, most notably market exchange and self-expression. Theorists of technology sometimes have seemed equally wedded to idealized models of human conduct.

Some, like William Mitchell, describe the construction of a permission-based cyborg space that is largely benign, full of freely flowing information and structured by voluntary participation. Donna Haraway, meanwhile, envisions an unceasing struggle between an "informatics of domination" and an informatics of resistance.[27] Dichotomies between commerce and speech, or between utopian bliss and revolutionary struggle, are useful for expository purposes, but they can become crutches. The two-dimensional models that they offer are too stark to capture the full range of human motivations, choices, behaviors, and experiences, or the protean way in which one set of motivations and behaviors can flow into another.

Scholars who study everydayness, in contrast, emphasize its elusive, improvisational quality. In what has become the leading theoretical treatment of the everyday, Michel de Certeau argues that theory can have pernicious consequences for the study of everyday life because it privileges one set of behaviors and explanations while requiring us to ignore all others. Nonhuman actors such as large market or government institutions may be expected to conform their actions more closely to prevailing theoretical models (though this is far from universally true). The resulting patterns of conduct, which Certeau characterizes as "strategies," are relatively easy to systematize. People, however, do not so readily conform their behavior to theoretical models and the strategies that they suggest; instead, individual behavior comprises an ad hoc, diverse mix of practices that Certeau calls "tactics." Tactical behavior is reactive but not always predictable; like water around boulders in a streambed, everyday practice flows around the structures established by institutional frameworks, producing unpredicted and unpredictable results. Understanding the patterns of everyday practice requires less structure and more storytelling, or what Anglophone cultural theorists like Clifford Geertz would call "thick description." In particular, both Certeau and Geertz urged more careful attention to the spatial practices employed by ordinary people and to their uses of language.[28]

As an example of how attention to the tactical, reactive quality of everyday practice might change our understanding of information-policy problems, consider the problem of privacy and autonomy introduced in Chapter 1: how should we understand the evolution of subjectivity under surveillance? As we will see in Part III, many scholars argue that frameworks based on simple dichotomies between public and private, or between domination and resistance, are inadequate to describe many of the voluntary behaviors of individuals in public places, or to describe how the same individuals react when placed under video surveillance. Attention to everyday practice allows us to explore some of the reasons this might be so. Public spaces function as sites for cultural exploration and participation, but also for experiencing the anonymity of crowds or for signaling membership in subcultures by performing behaviors recognizable to other members. These practices, which evolved within undifferentiated, unsurveilled public space, create a kind of partial privacy out in the open.

When confronted with surveillance, these everyday practices change in complicated ways. Some individuals try to avoid the cameras, while others carry on as though nothing had changed. Some resolve to move straight from point A to point B while blending in unremarkably, while others engage in more transgressive performances, "acting out" for the cameras. Video surveillance may also inspire more coordinated responses. The NYC Surveillance Camera Project documents camera locations and maintains Web-based maps that help people plot circuitous routes around them. Still other individuals have appropriated surveillance tactics for their own purposes. Users of mobile communication devices in New York City created a Web forum, Hollabacknyc, on which to post photos of men sexually harassing women passersby. By representing male bodies and a particular set of male behaviors as diminished and ridiculous, the photos implicitly position female bodies as more powerful and public spaces as more safe.[29]

As these examples suggest, everyday practice is more than just a gap filler; tactical behavior can also be creative and may lead to productive innovation. As users react to the constraints imposed by new technologies, they also adapt those technologies to their own ends. This realization has already reshaped the study of human-computer interaction, as scholars and technologists have come to recognize that patterns of work flow are shaped by contextually determined needs rather than by grand plans.[30] It is also beginning to reshape the philosophy of technology. Here the postphenomenological approach to human-technology relations resonates with a strand of philosophical thought that critical theory has tended to overlook. The American pragmatist philosopher John Dewey developed a theory of experience as central both to understanding the world and to the exercise of social and political agency. Several contemporary pragmatist philosophers have explicitly extended Dewey's theories about experience to the realm of technologies and artifacts. They characterize human-technology interactions as manifesting a situated creativity that is local, contingent, and democratic.[31] The processes of situated creativity are not always technologically sophisticated. When they succeed, however, they produce systems far better adapted to the everyday needs of those who use them.

Within the last decade, legal scholars have come to recognize the importance of user-directed innovation but have stumbled when seeking to theorize its essence in political or economic terms. Yochai Benkler identifies numerous examples of user-directed innovation spanning every conceivable domain, from software to genetic information to reference works to cultural mash-ups. Benkler refers to these practices as examples of "commons-based peer production," a term intended to denote both a nonhierarchical production structure and a lack of proprietary control over the results.[32] The media studies scholar Axel Bruns has coined the term "produsage," which melds "production" and "usage," to signal the erasure of the dichotomy between industrial production and passive consumption, which has long defined the mass-culture industries, and the emergence of a hybrid model combining active, engaged usage with collective, iterative improvement.[33] I do not want to deny the value of economic modeling of collective production; Benkler in particular has powerfully demonstrated that without such a model, the existing economic understanding of information production is incomplete. For my purposes, however, both terms remain too narrow. Attempts to identify the essence of the new relations of production have produced useful insights, but they also risk obscuring what is most fundamental about everyday practice: its connection to play.

What distinguishes everyday practice from the predicted behaviors generated by top-down theoretical constructs is not an economic relation or a governance relation, but rather the element of play. Within our culture, play is a term most often associated with frivolity or childhood innocence, or both. So framed, play contrasts with the seriousness of purpose that liberal political theory imputes to mature adults. Alternatively, play is sometimes invoked in the legal literature in ways that align it with internal, unknowable creativity, and that refer back to the liberal ideal of the autonomous subject. Play is both more serious and less purposive than those framings suggest, and it is far more fundamental to human activity.

Social scientists who study play have concluded that its developmental functions extend into adulthood and remain centrally implicated in the processes by which individuals orient themselves in relation to the world. Particularly relevant to the domains with which this book is concerned are play with objects and narratives, which locates the individual in relation to material and intellectual culture, and play with conceptions of empathy and morality, which enables individuals to form and pursue conceptions of the good. Play is both the keystone of individual moral and intellectual development and a mode of world making, the pathway by which transformative innovation and synthetic understanding emerge. It is neither inherently frivolous nor essentially single-minded, but rather a process of open-ended encounter. Play also has other attributes that run orthogonally to the dichotomy between frivolity and seriousness of purpose, including desire, pleasure, and release.[34]

Social science perspectives on play have tended to connect individual play to social structures in ways that emphasize the linkages between performance and conformity. Johan Huizinga considered the "play-element" so fundamental to cultural development more generally that he believed the human species ought to be called *homo ludens*—man who does not merely think, but plays. Building on Huizinga's initial work on the role of mimesis in reproducing cultural structures, scholars from a number of disciplines have advanced a variety of theories about the social function of play—developing identity within the parameters established by community roles and norms, cultivating social and workplace skills or entrepreneurial instincts, constituting social narratives and mythologies, rehearsing social power. Brian Sutton-Smith's important synthetic study of literatures that investigate the various roles of play within society concludes that the principal function of deliberate play is the adaptive one of fitting us to live in an unpredictable world.[35] In the shorter term, however, play's goals are often rather more specific, tied to the production and reproduction of specific cultural forms.

Critical theorists remind us that play is also an important modality for challenging dominant cultural forms. The core insight here is the deconstructionist one that language conceals ambiguity, which play uncovers and exploits. Play involves transgression of the boundaries that language and cultural practice establish, and transgressive play may ripen into a more conscious challenge to cultural and political forms. On this understanding, the domain of play is not coextensive with that of games, which involve both play and the observance of boundaries. So, for example, Jean-François Lyotard argues that in the information age, politics becomes a game that consists of the appropriation and organization of language to justify and conceal the distribution of power, and that can be challenged only by other, incommensurable language games. But play represents a different kind of disruptive power, which can occur within the framework of the dominant game or outside and around it, and which does not require the conscious formulation of a political purpose.[36]

Yet to debate whether play is more fundamentally hegemonic or transgressive and transformative is to miss the central point about play: play is in-between in two distinct and equally important senses. The first of these senses is political. Play defies easy characterization precisely because it arises and operates in the space between (re)production and resistance. Play originates in the everyday practice of situated individuals and communities—in ad hoc, tactical responses to institutional structures and cultural patterns. It is neither wholly circumscribed by culturally determined rules nor the same thing as the negative liberty or freedom that the autonomous, rational, disembodied self is presumed to enjoy. Andrew Pickering characterizes scientific practice as a "mangle" shaped by a "dialectic of resistance and accommodation": as materials and technologies resist user efforts, user efforts shift direction to accommodate the resistance.[37] The play of everyday practice follows a similar pattern. In the ongoing dialectic between ad hoc, reactive tactics and situated creativity, the most salient aspect is not one or the other, but the continual interplay between them. Play's ambiguous status—shaped by cultural constraints, but not wholly dictated by them—is the source of its potentially transformative power.

Emerging networked communities of practice illustrate this quality of political in-betweenness, developing and articulating a relationship to overarching social institutions that partakes of both resistance and cultural reproduction. The open-source programmer who participates in online discussions about technology policy is helping build a community organized, in part, around rejection of the ownership regime established by copyright law, but he is also performing classically liberal commitments to rational deliberation as a mode of politics. The person who contributes to a mass media fandom participates in a community organized around resistance to the copyright rules that give copyright owners control of most adaptations, but also around appreciation for the mass commercial culture that copyright plays a central role in enabling. The Hollabacknyc project described above seeks to alter the ways that gender is performed and understood, but it does so by deploying the discipline of surveillance. Traditions originating in these communities of practice in turn can provoke reexamination of the law: many practices of attribution within online fan-fiction communities respond directly to pressures originating in the world of copyrighted culture in that they are explicitly designed to forestall litigation by authors and copyright owners. Over time, however, the prevalence of norms of attribution within fandoms and other communities of practice has spurred debate about whether the copyright system itself should incorporate attribution rules.[38]

Play also refers to a phenomenological in-betweenness that is not studied by most play theorists at all (although it is implicit in Sutton-Smith's evolutionary account). This is play in the sense that Gadamer described as "to and fro" and that I will call the play-of-circumstances: a pattern of events that is neither entirely random nor wholly ordered, and that generates continual change.[39] The play-of-circumstances is an (anti-) hermeneutic conception: it describes a particular sort of relationship between situated subjects and contexts, within which predictability and explanation are continually subject to disruption. As a result of the play-of-circumstances, individual conduct is simultaneously under- and over-determined—overdetermined because many environmental variables could explain the particular behavior pattern that actually occurs, but under-determined because that explanation is not, and cannot be, available to us in predictive form.

From the perspective of the autonomous liberal subject, constant vulnerability to environmental disruption is most readily understood as disempowering; from the standpoint of everyday practice, it is a potent source of cultural and political power. Recall, again, that everyday practice originates in a tactical posture; it is shaped from the outset by institutional and material constraints. From that perspective, environmental disruption may pose a threat, but it is just as likely to present an opportunity. Everyday practice takes what it can get, and so it responds to the play-of-circumstances in ways that are robustly opportunistic. Situated subjects and communities are quick to appropriate unexpected juxtapositions of spaces and resources and deploy those unlooked-for gifts toward their own particular ends. As they do so, they alter both the geography of networked space and the technical mediation of embodied perception. The Web sites, wikis, and blogrolls of emergent communities organized around open-source programming or fan fiction or resisting harassment join the private clubs, coffeehouses, book groups, and other semiprivate gathering places scattered throughout physical space; they become both means by which the geography of networked space is differentiated and sources of experienced power.

Throughout the rest of the book, I will refer to the play of everyday practice to signal play's twofold in-betweenness—in between reproduction and resistance, and in between predictability and contingency. As we are about to see, the play of everyday practice is the critical ingredient in each of the processes that Chapter 1 identified as requiring exploration. It is the motivating force behind creative practice, subject formation, and material practice. More generally, and linking back to the larger inquiry about information policy and human flourishing with which this book began, the play of everyday practice is the means by which human beings flourish. It is the modality through which situated subjects advance their own contingent goals, constitute their communities, and imagine their possible futures. It therefore must be a central consideration in evaluating the constellations of legal, institutional, and technical developments with which this book is concerned.

Cyberlaw's Project Reconceived

Equipped with a provisional understanding of embodied perception, a heightened sensitivity to the ways that networked information technologies are reshaping social and personal geographies, and a renewed appreciation for the play of everyday practice, we can set aside utopian theorizing about networked information technologies as instrumentalities of transcendence and approach problems of information law and policy with a set of more mundane and far more important questions in mind: How do processes of creativity play out in the networked spaces inhabited by real, embodied individuals and communities, and how do expansive copyright laws affect the scope for the play of everyday creative practice? How are processes of evolving subjectivity affected by the emergence of networked space, and by surveillance practices that reconfigure personal boundaries? How do emerging governance regimes organized around architectures of control affect the play of everyday material practice, and how should legal theorists evaluate the disputes about openness and unauthorized access that have arisen within those regimes? Finally, how might the rules that govern information flow in the networked information society, and that establish the structure of networked space, preserve breathing room for the play of everyday practice? The remainder of the book addresses these questions.

PART II

Copyright and the Play of Culture

CHAPTER 3

Copyright, Creativity, and Cultural Progress

Both in the U.S. and globally, the past few decades have witnessed a significant expansion of legally-conferred control over copyrighted content. Copyright attaches to a bewildering variety of human creations, ranging from novels and paintings to blog posts and snapshots. In the wake of recent term extensions, copyright also lasts longer than ever before. The rights conferred by copyright have become inexorably broader, encompassing nearly all secondary uses and adaptations of copyrighted content. Meanwhile, the exceptions and limitations to copyright that previously existed within national laws have been progressively narrowed.

One especially noteworthy casualty of copyright expansion is copyright's traditional but largely implicit public-private distinction, which historically shielded many individual uses of copyrighted works from liability. Today, copyright policy makers are increasingly disinclined to think that the law should privilege personal acts of copying, performance, or adaptation of someone else's copyrighted content. According to the former U.S. Register of Copyrights, digital communication networks and technologies "seamlessly" transform acts of private copying into acts of public distribution—acts, that is, in public and with public consequences.[1] This perspective suggests that in the digital age, copyright-infringement liability should extend broadly.

Copyright scholars vehemently disagree on whether current copyright laws strike the right balance between authors and the public. Even so, Anglo-American copyright is premised on a set of assumptions about the relationship between copyright and creativity that most scholars largely accept: copyright supplies incentives for authors to produce creative work, but the creative process is essentially internal and unknowable. Because of the incentives it supplies to authors, copyright promotes the widespread dissemination of knowledge and learning to the public, and that process runs largely one way; authors produce knowledge and the public receives it. Copyright's incentive scheme also promotes the continual forward march of creative and intellectual progress. Because copyright attaches only to creative expression and not to underlying ideas, functional principles, and the like, properly tailored copyright protection can avoid frustrating the needs of future authors. And because ideas and other noncopyrightable subject matter exist in the public domain, they are freely accessible to everyone.

This account of cultural development is incomplete in every critical respect. First, copyright scholars have not been particularly interested in understanding creative practice—in what it is that the people we call authors actually do on a day-to-day basis. Creativity is constantly invoked by copyright lawyers, lobbyists, judges, and scholars to explain their arguments and decisions, but it is never really explored. Second and relatedly, although users of copyrighted works play important roles both as audiences and as future authors, copyright theory and jurisprudence have evinced little interest in understanding how users assimilate culture and whether that process is as passive as copyright's incentive story supposes. Third, despite equally obligatory invocations of "progress," we know very little about how cultural progress actually proceeds or about how copyright law affects its direction and content. Fourth, copyright's model of the process of cultural transmission, which depends centrally on the abstract concept of the idea-expression distinction, is highly artificial and conflicts with a large body of evidence about the way that cultural transmission actually works. The equally abstract concept of the public domain suggests a distribution of cultural resources that corresponds poorly to the cultural reality that users and authors alike must negotiate.

This chapter explores the gaps in copyright's implicit account of creativity and cultural development, and links them to a set of core commitments that unite copyright maximalists and minimalists alike. Copyright theory and jurisprudence are powerfully structured by the tenets of liberal political theory, which generate a set of presumptions about the appropriate tools for understanding the interactions between copyright and culture. Those presumptions define the boundaries of copyright's epistemological universe in a way that excludes many other approaches to investigating and theorizing about creative processes. The result is that copyright theory remains impoverished in important and outcome-determining ways.

The Subject of Copyright: The Creativity Paradox

Within most accounts of copyright, the phenomenon of human creativity is central to copyright's project of promoting artistic and intellectual progress. Creativity is the fuel that powers the copyright system; without it, there would be nothing to which copyright's incentives could attach. But both copyright scholarship and copyright policy making have proceeded largely on the basis of assumptions about what creativity is and how the fruits of creativity are transmitted. Those assumptions take the form of stylized, oversimplified models of authors and users, and of the presumptively separate roles that each group plays within the copyright system. Within the framework of liberal individualism that Chapter 1 described, that approach is unsurprising. Probing the relationships between authors, users, and culture more carefully might uncover relationships and patterns of influence inconsistent with liberalism's foundational presumption of separation between self and society. As a result of its failure to ask such questions, however, legal talk about creativity is trapped in Plato's cave; it purports to have divined creativity's ideal institutional form, but captures only its shadow.

Within contemporary copyright jurisprudence, the copyrightability of a "work of authorship" is determined in the first instance by evaluating the "originality" of the work itself—that is, by focusing on the end product rather than on the process that led to its creation.[2] There are good historical reasons for this rule. As both Justin Hughes and Oren Bracha have observed, copyright law's focus on the work enables the copyright system to assign rights without relying on problematic eighteenth-century concepts of romantic authorship. Bracha notes, as well, that the doctrinal emphasis on works of authorship that emerged within late nineteenth-century copyright law accorded with the nineteenth-century liberal ideology of propertization, and that, historically speaking, it is well-suited to an age in which much authorship is corporate.[3]

The turn away from authorship in copyright doctrine is only partial, however. To resolve copyright disputes, courts and commentators return over and over again to concepts of authorship. In cases involving competing claimants to authorship status, such concepts often function as tiebreakers, enabling courts to determine which claimant is the "real" author. Carys Craig shows that in infringement cases, courts implicitly contrast what the defendant did—imitation, improvement, or criticism—with the actions of a "true" author.[4] Those categories, by necessary implication, say something about what an author does not do: she does not *merely* consume; she does not *simply* copy; she does not *just* improve; she does not *only* deconstruct. But the categories themselves bring us no closer to understanding what an author does and how she does it. Quite the opposite: a doctrinal stance that holds romantic authorship to be irrelevant to copyrightability, all the while admitting preconceptions about authorship through the back door, operates to prevent systematic attention to the ways that authorship works in practice.

Theoretical accounts of authorial entitlement do little to clear up the confusion about the nature of authorship and how it relates to creativity. Rights theorists of all varieties have generally described creativity in terms of an individual liberty whose form remains largely unspecified. For these scholars, the chief worry is that some legal feature of an author's environment—overly restrictive copyright or some form of official censorship—will constrain creativity in a way that leaves society the poorer.[5] Some scholars working within the domain of rights theory consult self-reports by artists about the nature of the creative process. When asked to discuss the sources of their inspiration, individual artists tend to describe a process that is intrinsically unknowable. When legal scholars invoke these self-reports, however, they add something: they characterize creative motivation as both intrinsically unknowable and essentially internal. Roberta Kwall characterizes creativity as a gift of self, closely akin to and often intended as an act of religious expression.[6] By directing scholarly attention to the literature on gifts, Kwall's account usefully enlarges the prevailing conception of authorial motivation, but it does little to help situate creativity in the world from which it arises. Justin Hughes relates creativity to real-world experience using a rich set of anecdotes drawn from artistic and scientific history, but his focus remains the individual creator rather than the community in which the creator is situated. He concludes that creativity is "a set of black boxes, one within each of us," that enables the transformation of experience into expression.[7]

Economic theorists of copyright prefer to work from the opposite end of the creative process, seeking to divine optimal rules for promoting creativity by measuring its marketable by-products.[8] As a general rule, economic analysis infers motivation from conduct; it is not interested in, and lacks tools to explore, the problem of what creates motivation—and more precisely, inspiration—in the first place. Put differently, economics is fundamentally the study of production rather than creation. Although the force of this distinction is blunted slightly in the age of mass-produced cultural works created for mass audiences, it is still a difference that matters; the initial inspiration must come from somewhere. Practitioners of economic analysis treat creative motivation as both internal and exogenous—a preexisting preference that matters only to the extent that it is presumptively enhanced by the possibility of an economic reward. The details—why someone creates at all and why she creates this rather than that—are irrelevant; it is assumed that market signals will take care of those. As a result, while economic tools may help explain shifts in larger patterns of supply and demand, or the institutional structures that evolve to enable exploitation of particular types of creative resources, they are not very useful for exploring creativity itself. The problem is especially acute in cases of large creative leaps, which by their very nature cannot be predicted from existing patterns.

Some economically inclined critics of maximalist economic models challenge the argument that copyright invariably supplies an incentive to produce creative work. Scholars like James Boyle and Yochai Benkler argue persuasively that sometimes creative motivation has non-market origins. But they tend to agree with the maximalists that the specifics of creative motivation are irrelevant. As Boyle puts it, it doesn't matter why people create, only that they do it.[9] But if creativity is not purely internal—if it is a function of what authors are looking at, reading, and listening to—the details of the creative process matter a great deal.

A great deal of evidence suggests that scholarly assumptions about the intrinsic quality of creativity are too hasty. To begin with, that assumption does not match the experience that artists describe at all. Artists may not be able to tell us why they create, but they can tell us a lot about the where, what, who, and how of particular creative processes—where they were in space and time; what they were looking at, reading, and listening to; who they were talking to; and what insights or experiments sprang from those interactions. And social scientists who study the creative process have found unequivocally that these things matter.[10] Even if inspiration is every bit as unknowable as artists say it is, then, it still ought to be possible to say a lot more about the everyday practice of creative work. It ought to be possible, moreover, to engage in that inquiry while recognizing and bracketing objections to "authorship" as an ontological category. In other words, rather than asking what authorship is, we should be asking what those who work in domains of artistic and intellectual endeavor do on a day-to-day basis. What practices do they engage in while creating? Critically, how do interactions both with other people and with existing cultural artifacts inform creative practice?

Asking those sorts of questions requires us to consider authors as users of cultural works first and creators only second. Here, though, we reach another impasse. The copyright system's account of cultural development is relatively incurious about users and their behavior. It is commonly understood that users of copyrighted works play two important roles within the copyright system: they receive copyrighted works of authorship, and some of them become authors. Both roles further the copyright system's larger project of promoting cultural progress. But neither copyright jurisprudence nor copyright theory has evinced much curiosity about how users perform these functions and about what they might need in order to do so. If copyright concerns the private, internal relationships between authors and their works, then it makes sense not to think much about users of copyrighted works. But if creative practice arises out of the interactions between authors and cultural environments—if authors are users first—failure to explore the place of the user in copyright law is a critical omission.

Consider two important questions about how users envision and perform their own roles within the copyright system. First, why do users engage in so-called private consumptive copying of copyrighted works? For the most part, copyright doctrine and copyright scholarship answer that question in a way that is resolutely economic (and that the terminology of "private" and "consumptive" presumes): users are motivated by their own personal, private benefit as consumers of artistic and information goods. They copy because getting something for free is better than having to pay for it.[11] According to the narrative of this user, whom I will call the "economic user," it makes sense that private copying should be infringing or should become so as new abilities to exploit markets develop. Because the economic user is not himself an author, and because he is situated within a theoretical framework inclined to view unremunerated appropriation of common resources as tragic, he is generally oblivious to the long-term effects of such copying on authorial incentives.[12] A legal rule defining all copying as infringement (unless excused by a fact-specific defense) solves the incentive problem in a way that benefits the economic user: it keeps prices low and enables information providers to develop product offerings to satisfy user-consumers at different price points.

Second, how do transformative fair uses arise? Judicial and scholarly explorations of transformative fair use posit a very different sort of user than the economic user who informs discussions about private consumptive copying: this user is a dedicated and perceptive cultural critic. To the extent that he copies, he does so in a deliberate way that relates solely to communication of a critical or parodic message.[13] This user, whom I will call the "romantic user," is author-like, and so it makes sense that copyright should privilege his creations. While a broad rule privileging transformative fair use might appear to conflict with the incentive principle, judges and scholars all agree that shelter for cultural criticism promotes the progress of knowledge, and that absent such shelter, many copyright owners would not license transformative critical copying. Shelter for transformative fair uses thus serves copyright's ultimate goals.

There are several curious things about these answers. First, the users they posit are very different from each other—so different that they seem to be completely different people, and to have little to say about behavior outside their home domains. The romantic user cannot point the law toward a different answer to the question why users engage in private consumptive copying, and this is so by choice. The romantic user's interests lie in the realm of transformation, so he has little to say about either the costs or the benefits that other sorts of private copying might generate. The economic user's approach to the problem of transformative use is equally unsatisfying. It is widely acknowledged that some fair uses, including many transformative uses, create positive externalities from which society as a whole benefits greatly, and that many such uses would not be made if the users who make them were required to internalize all of the costs. This insight justifies having a fair use doctrine, but it does not tell us how to decide particular cases. Because of the clear mismatch between individual and social utility, economically inclined judges and scholars have repeatedly stumbled in their efforts to theorize an economic basis for identifying those uses that are worth privileging.[14]

Perhaps the differences between the economic user and the romantic user follow straightforwardly from the fact that activities within the two domains are so different. There are two ways in which this could be true. First, perhaps there are simply two different kinds of people in the world, those who transform copyrighted works and those who consume them. But that hypothesis is both theoretically implausible—how can one transform something without having first consumed it?—and inconsistent with experience. Transformative fair use requires enough consumption for a critical perspective to emerge, and in the Internet age, experiments with transformative use by ordinary consumers are all around us. Alternatively, perhaps users who engage in both types of activities simply approach them quite differently. Perhaps we are romantic about transformation and economic about acts of copying that are unconnected to transformation. But that assumption begs a large and enormously important question about the relationship between consumption and creation, one that the characters of the economic user and the romantic user themselves cannot answer.

In fact, the narrative of the romantic user tells us very little about how and why the users who make fair uses do what they do. In most fair use cases, the identity of the user is known, the use has already been made, and the only question is whether it passes muster. Perhaps for these reasons, courts and commentators evaluating fair use cases tend to talk about uses as faits accomplis. Although the fair use analysis requires nods to abstract and general qualities such as commerciality, the question of lawfulness is rarely related in any systematic way to the process that led to the use. Scholarly accounts of the romantic user similarly are more concerned with ends than with means. The romantic user's life is an endless cycle of sophisticated debates about current events, discerning quests for the most freedom-enhancing media technologies, and home production of high-quality music, movies, and open-source software. He knows exactly which works he wants to use and what message he wants to convey. The romantic user therefore is poorly positioned to explain the processes by which access and use become transformation.

The narrative of the economic user tells us equally little about why users copy. We are given to understand that the economic user enters the market with a given set of tastes in search of the best deal. That assumption does not reckon with users themselves or with their reasons for copying in any meaningful way; instead, it obviates the need to ask questions that might reveal a more complex relationship between copying and motivation. Scholarly and judicial discussions of private copying approach user behavior as an aggregate phenomenon to be molded and disciplined. That stance precludes consideration of whether private copying serves other purposes, what those purposes might be, and how we should value them. In particular, we are foreclosed from considering whether there might be a more continuous relationship between the activities of copying and transformation, and whether the midpoints on that continuum might be interesting in their own right.

Ultimately, then, the narratives of the romantic user and the economic user rest on the same assumptions that have animated scholarly discussions about the nature of authorship. The narrative of the romantic user, which insistently decouples process from end result, returns us to the conception of creativity as fundamentally internal and unknowable. It is that conception, rather than any inevitable reality, that explains why the connections between access and (fair) use, or between copying and transformation, are seemingly opaque and undiscoverable. The narrative of the economic user, meanwhile, returns us by a different route to the assumption that the details of creative motivation are exogenous and therefore irrelevant. In casting users as passive recipients of culture, it ignores critical dimensions of the user's response to creative works. As before, this is a methodological limitation of economics generally. Because it measures sales rather than the communication of ideas, economics lacks the tools to distinguish between the world-changing and the merely popular, on the one hand, and between the avant-garde and the simply unappealing, on the other. Economics can model aggregate demand, but demand is a poor metric for gauging the extent to which a work captures the imagination. Lacking a window into the imagination, economics cannot illuminate the processes of cultural participation.

Not coincidentally, neither the romantic nor the economic user offers much guidance in resolving some difficult questions that contemporary copyright law must confront. Many contemporary copyright disputes involve fan responses to popular works of mass culture, ranging from fan fiction and videos to user-generated trivia guides to illustrated histories. These works all involve significant components of both copying and creation, and they often can be difficult to characterize as works of criticism. Because copyright's user narratives frame a binary distinction between consumptive and transformative copying, both courts and scholars have had difficulty deciding how to characterize such works. A related set of questions concerns whether and to what extent users should have a right to circumvent technical protection measures, such as the copy-protection system used for commercially produced DVDs, in order to make lawful uses of the underlying copyrighted content. Lacking good models that relate process to end result, courts have cheerfully decreed that the availability of tools for making fair uses is irrelevant, and scholars who think the result should be different have stumbled in trying to explain why.

In short, to develop an understanding of creativity, what is needed is not a better definition of authorship, nor an airtight conception of usership that is distinct from authorship, but rather a good understanding of the complicated interrelationship between authorship and usership, and the ways in which that interrelationship plays out in the cultural environments where creative practice occurs. The task has been so difficult for legal thinkers precisely because the path from access to manipulation to transformation depends in part on considerations that the prevailing models of author and user behavior do not admit. A more useful model would abandon preconceptions about romantic vision and consumptive utility and focus on the related processes of cultural participation and creative practice.

The Social Value (or Cost?) of Copyright

Copyright theory's account of cultural development also depends centrally on the assumption that progress has a single, merit-based trajectory and that a well-designed copyright system simply moves society along that trajectory faster and more effectively. Although some copyright scholars have urged a more critical perspective, most copyright scholars and policymakers strenuously avoid casting doubt on this account of copyright's relation to progress. In particular, although they may disagree on the optimal scope of copyright, most copyright scholars and policy makers are inclined to think that a properly tailored scheme of rights and limitations will produce markets for copyrighted expression that are more or less value neutral. They are deeply suspicious of the role of value judgments about artistic merit in justifying the recognition and allocation of rights, and equally suspicious of postmodernist theoretical perspectives that characterize artistic and intellectual knowledge as historically and culturally contingent. That stance exposes a shared epistemological universe that is relatively narrow and that forecloses potentially fruitful avenues of inquiry into the process of cultural production.

Copyright judges and scholars have struggled mightily to articulate neutral, process-based models of progress that manage both to avoid enshrining particular criteria of artistic and intellectual merit and to ensure that the "best" artistic and intellectual outputs will succeed. The canonical statement of the copyright lawyer's anxiety about the twin dangers of judgment and relativism is Justice Holmes's warning that:

> It would be a dangerous undertaking for persons trained only to the law to constitute themselves final judges of the worth of pictorial illustrations. . . . At the one extreme some works of genius would be sure to miss appreciation. Their very novelty would make them repulsive until the public had learned the new language in which their author spoke. . . . At the other end, copyright would be denied to pictures which appealed to a public less educated than the judge.[15]

On its face, this statement works hard to avoid recognizing particular criteria of artistic and intellectual merit. But it presumes that they exist and that appropriate judgments will be made by audiences competent to do so as long as copyright does not attempt to choose winners in the marketplace of ideas. Copyright scholarship routinely both echoes Holmes's warning and adopts its implicit premises.

In the last two decades, the reigning account of copyright's role in facilitating cultural progress has come under challenge from scholars grounded in contemporary social theory. Peter Jaszi, David Lange, and Martha Woodmansee explored the modernist narrative's implicit dependence upon a vision of the solitary, romantic author, while Margaret Chon interrogated the implicit presumption of singular, teleological progress. James Boyle illustrated the ways in which the construct of the romantic author is deployed to legitimate practices of economic domination, while Rosemary Coombe sought to rehabilitate those marginalized as passive consumers of the fruits of others' romantic authorship. Niva Elkin-Koren extended the critiques of romantic authorship and teleological progress into the realm of political theory, offering an account of progress as inhering in widely distributed, participatory acts of social meaning making. In addition, work by a number of scholars has explored ways in which copyright's facially neutral categories privilege some forms of artistic expression over others.[16]

Rather than treating these critiques of authorship, originality, and progress as an invitation to inquire more closely into the cultural production of knowledge, the mainstream of copyright scholarship has tended to marginalize them. The process sometimes begins with an act of misclassification, in which the emerging corpus of critical copyright theory is identified with "postmodernist literary criticism."[17] That characterization vastly oversimplifies the range of literatures on which the critical copyright theorists rely. It also ignores the fact that scholarly criticism of the modernist model of cultural production includes other, less overtly theoretical strands within the copyright literature, including most notably the important work by David Lange and Jessica Litman on the relation of the public domain to cultural production and by Michael Madison on the ways in which patterns of social and cultural organization shape prevailing understandings of fair use.[18] Misclassification is followed by misreading. Postmodernist literary criticism (or more generally, postmodernism) is taken as holding that texts have no authors and no meaning whatsoever, and the critical theorists are read as adopting a similar stance.[19] The allegation that doctrinal overbreadth stifles productive borrowing is taken as stating a claim about the requirements of "postmodern art" (or "appropriation art"), which is assumed to differ in fundamental ways from art more generally.

Thus characterized, the challenge from critical copyright theory is interpreted as setting up an either/or choice between merit and a pernicious cultural and intellectual relativism. To avoid relativism, one must choose merit. But that choice creates enormous methodological difficulties of its own. In particular, to avoid the tension that endorsement of a substantive vision of progress would create with principles of value neutrality and negative liberty, copyright scholars retreat to a process-based vision of merit. They presume that, under conditions of fair competition, personal decisions about information consumption will produce results that make sense—that the truest and most beautiful works will be the ones that appeal most strongly to the citizen's deliberative faculty or to the consumer's enlightened self-interest. Since it is far from obvious that the real world actually works this way, the turn to process rapidly generates its own anxieties, which revolve around whether the communicative marketplace actually will work as the models predict and what exactly fair competition is.

The resulting disagreements over the optimal structure of copyright rules and markets conceal a broader agreement on first principles, which goes generally unremarked. The unspoken and increasingly frantic dialectic between fidelity to and distrust of the marketplace model of communication that animates so much of copyright scholarship is ideologically motivated at the most fundamental level: it reflects a shared adherence to a rationalist philosophy that conceives of knowledge as transcendent and absolute rather than contingent and evolving. Copyright scholars subscribe to the assumption that a neutral, progress-promoting structure for copyright is achievable because the first-order commitments of liberal theory require it. They disagree chiefly on comparatively trifling questions about which market signals are accurate and which mere distortions.

Within the wider landscape of contemporary social theory, however, copyright's internal narrative about the nature of progress and the possibility of value-neutral copyright markets is anachronistic. The understanding of knowledge as transcendent and absolute and the accompanying vision of progress as linear forward motion toward enlightenment have been thoroughly discredited. Contemporary (or postmodernist) views of the evolution of knowledge, and of artistic and intellectual culture, draw attention to the ways in which beliefs about truth and beauty are socially and culturally situated, and shaped by historical, geographic, and material contingencies. Scholars trace the ways that culture emerges from practice and discourse, and that practice and discourse are themselves shaped by cultural and institutional power. Studies of art and science have explored the dialectic between settled truths and disruptive upheavals and have sought to illumine the ways that particular innovations become accepted as truth or enshrined as artistically valid.

Social and cultural theories that emphasize the contingent, iterative, socially situated development of knowledge are rooted in philosophical traditions that liberalism has resisted, and so copyright scholars' reluctance to embrace those theories is unsurprising. But deeper engagement with postmodernist approaches need not lead to the debilitating relativism that copyright scholars fear. In particular, none of those literatures has as its stated purpose the trashing of cultural conventions. To the contrary, they recognize and acknowledge that shared premises generating predictable rhythms are essential to the operation of a functioning society. Bringing critical perspectives to bear on those premises and rhythms is also essential, however. What is most important is that settled modes of knowing not become entrenched and calcified. That concern resonates deeply with copyright law's imperative to foster progress. For that reason, these scholarly approaches are better understood as opening the way for an account of the relationship between copyright and culture that is both far more robust and far more nuanced than anything that liberal political philosophy has to offer.

So understood, the insights of contemporary social theory do not negate copyright's progress imperative, but instead demand two important modifications to it. First, they require that progress be assigned a more open-ended interpretation. Stripped of its association with modernist teleologies, progress consists, simply, in that which causes knowledge systems to come under challenge and sometimes to shift. Second, and precisely because this understanding of progress abandons the comforting fiction of modernist teleologies, a postmodernist approach to knowledge demands careful attention to the ways that law and culture evaluate and reward (or penalize) artistic and intellectual production. Recognizing that those processes cannot help but reflect normative judgments, it directs our attention to the value judgments that they enact. It thereby foregrounds the complex linkages between and among progress, power, and cultural participation.

Copyright's system of incentives and rules is not, and could not be, neutral about the content of progress. A useful model of copyright

would take that proposition as the starting point and interrogate culturally situated conceptions of merit more directly. Rather than indulging in
elaborate fictions about the value neutrality of well-functioning copyright institutions, copyright theory and policy should pay attention to the
sorts of content that real copyright institutions work to privilege and to
the kinds of challenges that they work to suppress.

The Nature of Copyrightable Content

The structure of copyright law reflects not only assumptions about the
nature of progress writ large, but also assumptions about the ways that
artistic and intellectual culture develops on a case-by-case basis. Copyright scholars of all persuasions articulate a vision of the process of cultural
transmission from author to author—of cultural progress writ small—
within which abstraction is prized highly and the most valuable aspects
of artistic and intellectual culture are those that are most amenable to
abstraction. The foundational abstractions within copyright discourse
concern the primacy of idea over expression, the primacy of the work over
the copy, and the universal accessibility of the public domain. Each abstraction powerfully shapes the legal understanding of the ways that creative practitioners work and the resources that they require.

The commitment to abstraction in modeling cultural transmission is a direct outgrowth of the liberal rationalist tradition and its commitments to the autonomous, disembodied self and the possibility of
transcendent knowledge. Within that vision, the concrete forms of cultural artifacts and practices do not matter very much, nor do the spaces
within which cultural practices occur. What I want to describe in this
section is a process analogous to what Katherine Hayles characterizes as
the "platonic backhand," which "constitute[s] the abstraction as the orig-
inary form from which the world's multiplicity derives," followed by the
"platonic forehand," which derives from the foundational abstraction "a
multiplicity sufficiently complex that it can be seen as a world of its own."[20]
Building from its own foundational abstractions, copyright theory derived from within the liberal tradition constructs a model of creative practice that obviates any need to interrogate creative practice more directly.

As every student in the basic copyright course learns, copyright
does not protect ideas, and that is because ideas are thought to be the
shared raw material of progress. Ideas are what enable subsequent authors to build on the works of past authors, even if the expression in those
works is the subject of exclusive rights. The idea-expression distinction

74

establishes the relative value of abstract and concrete components of artistic and intellectual culture and enshrines an assumption, implicit in that privileging, that the two can be neatly distinguished.

When ideas are assumed to be the basic units of cultural transmission, disputes about copyright scope become disputes about identifying those expressions that should be treated like ideas. The "substantial similarity" test for infringement adopts precisely this approach, separating protected from unprotected attributes based on their place within a "series of abstractions."[21] The doctrines of merger and *scènes à faire*, which explicitly permit copying of some expression, are justified in the same terms: they identify situations in which copying must be permitted to the extent "necessary" to enable the exchange of ideas.[22] Not coincidentally, the necessity formulation shifts the focus away from both authors and users—from both the particulars of creative practice and the patterns of ordinary use.

In cases involving musical compositions and visual works, the abstractions-based approach creates special difficulties for judges and juries unaccustomed to parsing nonverbal expression in these terms. Judges sometimes resolve these difficulties by decreeing either infringement or noninfringement on an "I know it when I see it" basis.[23] What juries do is anyone's guess. In other cases, most notably those involving computer software and databases, the term "idea" also encodes a second process of abstraction. As used in copyright case law and within copyright theory, that term denotes not only ideas per se, but also facts, processes, procedures, and methods of operation. Many of these entities are substantially less amenable to abstraction; in particular, procedures and methods of operation expressed in computer microcode and judgments about utility expressed in databases are very difficult to separate from their concrete instantiations. Calling these things ideas makes their concreteness easier to overlook; conversely, emphasizing their concreteness makes it easier to claim that they are not ideas.[24]

One might think that the cumulative weight of these difficulties would cause copyright scholars to question the value of the abstractions heuristic. In fact, broad agreement as to the separability of idea and expression extends across copyright's internal methodological divide. To the extent that both rights theorists and economic theorists advocate expanded privileges to copy, they do so by reference to the importance of the free circulation of ideas. Lockean theorists argue that copying is justified to the extent required by the proviso that "enough, and as good" remain for others to use; the idea-expression distinction accomplishes this goal in most (though not all) cases. Free speech theorists link copyright's goals directly to participation in the exchange of and deliberation about ideas. Economic theorists assume that the freedom to copy ideas minimizes the "deadweight loss" that results from recognizing exclusive rights in expressive works. In particular, economic theorists can reconcile price discrimination with expressive competition only by relying on the free circulation of ideas as the principal vehicle for cultural transmission.[25]

The problem with all these stories about the primacy of ideas is that they conflict with everything else we know about the processes of cultural transmission. Like copyright scholars, other scholars who study cultural texts (including both conventional literary texts and all other forms of artistic expression) understand those texts as performing a cultural-transmission function. That function, however, resides in the text itself, including idea and expression together. Texts reflect context-dependent meanings rather than invariant ideas, and this means that text and meaning are both inseparably intertwined and continually evolving.[26] Secure in their knowledge that the cultural-transmission function performed by artistic and intellectual works resides principally in the ideas conveyed by such works rather than in the particular form of their expression, many copyright scholars scoff at the seeming mushiness of literary theory, art criticism, and the like. But copyright's model of cultural transmission is created out of whole cloth, based on nothing more than assumptions about the relationship between culture and true knowledge.

Identification of expression divorced from animating ideas as the appropriate subject of ownership reinforces a second process of abstraction, which identifies the work as the locus in which rights reside. This process of abstraction generates broad rights that negate defenses based on the transposition of expression into different forms. Thus it makes sense to conclude, for example, that the copyrightable expression in a film inheres in its characters in a way that transcends the particular actions scripted for them, or that the copyrightable expression in a novel or television series encompasses the incontrovertible fact that particular lines of dialogue were uttered by particular characters.[27] The initial form of creative expression becomes merely an exemplar; even expression is abstracted from itself.

Concrete instantiations of works figure in this analysis primarily as sites of control; the law can focus on regulating the preparation and distribution of copies or the physical rendering of works as performances without worrying much about the form of the copying or the circumstances of the performance. Abstraction from the particularities of format thus leads, paradoxically, toward ever more complete control of things embodying works. At the same time, the concept of the work systematically excludes forms of expression that do not fit the definition. For example, the contributions supplied by an editor or a dramaturge, which may mean the difference between success and failure in the marketplace, typically do not count as manifestations of authorship.[28] In other cases, emphasis on the work causes courts to overlook particularities of form that the author claims as expressive, as when a musical composition is deemed to consist solely of its notes divorced from scripted performance elements.[29]

The third foundational abstraction in copyright doctrine concerns the availability of common cultural resources. The standard account of resource availability within copyright doctrine and theory holds that creators may draw freely from a public domain of old and otherwise uncopyrightable material. In recent years, the public domain has become the object of considerable scholarly attention. Even so, relatively little attention has been devoted to the way that the term "public domain" functions metaphorically to describe the geographic and practical accessibility of the cultural commons.

There are two competing models of the public domain in contemporary copyright law. Both models are dynamic; that is, they attempt to describe changes in the universe of publicly available content over time and to evaluate the effects of these changes for cultural progress and for society more generally. They differ in their normative assessment of the public domain and its role within the overall copyright system. The first, which I will call the conservancy model, holds that expansion of copyright threatens the continued viability of a robust public domain, with adverse consequences for cultural progress. Conservancy theorists view recent expansions of copyright as damaging to patterns of information flow within the copyright system generally. According to these scholars, recent legislative expansions of copyright are best described as series of unprincipled enclosures, or land grabs, by powerful domestic industries.[30] The second model, which I will call the cultural stewardship model, paints these changes in quite a different light. According to this model, continued ownership of copyright enables the productive management of artistic and cultural subject matter. Passage into the public domain should occur only after the productive life of a cultural good has ended. Adherents of the cultural stewardship model acknowledge the important role that public-domain building blocks play in the ongoing development of artistic culture. They argue, however, that the idea-expression distinction adequately performs that function and will continue to perform it even if copyright is lengthened and expanded to cover new forms of creative expression.[31]

In the heated back-and-forth over what the public domain does or should contain, both groups of scholars have paid surprisingly little attention to the way that the public domain functions metaphorically to position common cultural resources within a wholly imaginary geography. The space that is the public domain has the Heisenbergian property of being both discretely constituted and instantly accessible to all users everywhere. The metaphoric construction of the public domain as a universally accessible space in turn tends to obscure questions about the practical availability of common cultural resources; it is easy to assume that metaphoric availability and practical availability are one and the same. This enables copyright jurisprudence to avoid coming to grips with the need for affirmative rights of access to expressive resources within the spaces where people actually live. If everyone always has access to the public domain, then broad exclusive rights for copyright owners threaten neither access to the common elements of culture nor use of those elements as the substrate for future creation.

At the same time, scholarly and judicial discussions of the public domain have largely overlooked another spatial metaphor—that of "breathing room" or "breathing space"—that recurs increasingly often in debates about copyright policy, on topics ranging from the nature of authorship to the scope of fair use. In a variety of contexts, both judges and scholars invoke breathing room to refer to the leeway that follow-on creators require to access and reuse creative materials, whether or not those materials enjoy public-domain status. The idea of breathing room for follow-on creativity suggests a very different conceptualization of the relationship between the proprietary and the publicly available, one that is not tied to a particular domain, but rather is defined by the needs of creative practice more generally. For the most part, however, courts and scholars invoke breathing space without interrogating its spatial connotations and without considering what it suggests about the needs of authors and users alike.[32]

And so the problem of the public domain links back to the other defects in copyright theory, which relate to the particulars of the creative process. Because the public domain is a construct intended to foster the ongoing development of artistic and intellectual culture, a theory of the public domain should make sense when measured against the ways that creative practice works. As used in copyright cases, the metaphoric model of the public domain both relies on and encourages a sort of magical thinking in which neither the particulars of creative practice nor the needs of users matter much. Like the idea-expression distinction and the work-copy distinction, copyright's model of the public domain privileges abstraction over concrete, materially embedded reality.

Each component of copyright's abstraction-based model of cultural production tends to marginalize more concrete questions about how people use culture and produce knowledge and about the conditions that lead to and nurture creative experimentation. The result is a doctrinal framework that obstructs careful examination of creative processes and makes grappling with difficult policy choices in copyright even more difficult than it ought to be. If we are to change direction, exploring the ways that real people located in real spaces experience and use copyrighted works is essential. Understanding the processes that generate artistic and intellectual change requires careful attention to the ways in which processes of cultural production and transmission are mediated by and through texts, artifacts, bodies, and spaces.

The Challenge for Copyright Theory

If copyright scholars want to know whether copyright doctrines intended to guarantee the continued creation of cultural resources actually do their job—and we should—we should begin by exploring the ways in which copyright's internal model of creativity, its modernist understanding of progress, and its abstractions-based model of cultural transmission have created blind spots in legal thinking about copyright and culture. It is important to recognize, moreover, that this is not simply a tempest in an academic teapot. Copyright's theoretical deficit has concrete political and practical implications. Commitments to internalized, unknowable authorship, teleological progress, and abstract, modular culture shape copyright's rules about scope and infringement and invest those rules with an air of inevitability. Interrogating creative processes and practices more directly would produce a more robust and believable account of creativity and of the pathways of artistic and cultural progress. Chapter 4 takes up that project.

CHAPTER 4

Decentering Creativity

Conceptualizing copyright's role in processes of cultural development requires a model of creativity that faces outward: that recognizes the inseparable relationship between authorship and use of cultural works. Such a model must acknowledge the multiple ways in which users and user-authors interact with cultural works, and must recognize that those interactions cannot be explained by telling a story about linear, value-neutral progress, the separability of idea and expression, and the continuous availability of the public domain.

This chapter develops an account of creativity and cultural progress as emergent properties of social and cultural systems. Within preexisting cultural networks, individuals and communities appropriate cultural goods for interrelated purposes of consumption, communication, self-development, and creative play. From each user's situated perspective, the experienced cultural landscape determines the resources that are available to that user. The cultural landscape includes both public and proprietary content, and is shaped both by established conventions of artistic and intellectual production and by the spatial distribution of cultural resources. Both creativity and cultural progress emerge contingently out of interactions between situated users and cultural landscapes. A critical ingredient in this process is the play that cultural landscapes afford, including the extent to which they not only permit purposive creative experimentation but also facilitate serendipitous access and unexpected juxtapositions.

The emergence of networked space alters the cultural landscapes of situated users in important ways, but it does not change the fundamental patterns that this chapter describes. Networked information technologies make available new resources and create new patterns of information flow, but cultural path-dependencies remain important in structuring creative practice. The emergence of networked space also does not diminish the central importance of mass culture within cultural landscapes. Networked information technologies reconfigure patterns of interaction with mass culture, simultaneously empowering users and extending the culture industries' reach.

Understanding cultural progress as decentered, always emergent, and shaped by the contingent particularities of cultural landscapes suggests both a more modest conception of the role that copyright plays in stimulating progress and a more rigorous explanation of the systemic harms that too-expansive copyright can produce. Copyright's role in the contemporary creative ecology is essential but limited: it provides an economic foundation for the organization of cultural production. It must perform that role with self-restraint, lest it impair the mobility that is the indispensable ingredient in creative practice.

A Decentered Model of Creativity

In accounting for creative practice by individual authors, it is instructive to recall where Chapter 3 began: with commonly held assumptions about the essentially internal, unknowable nature of creativity. There is broad agreement among creative individuals of all types that creativity is characterized pervasively by an unpredictability that encompasses both inspiration and production. Neither creative inputs nor creative outputs are known in advance, and copyright scholars have taken that fact as evidence of creativity's internal, individual nature. Yet it is possible to be far more precise about both what is not known and what is. Researchers in psychology and education have produced a vibrant literature on the social, cultural, and psychological factors that shape creativity. In addition, social theory tells us a great deal about the processes and practices of cultural production: about how cultural resources are encountered and used and how systems of cultural knowledge evolve.

Together, the evidence from creativity studies and the insights and resources of social theory argue for an account of artistic and intellectual creativity that is decentered: that incorporates multiple contributing factors and makes none primary, and that situates creative practice within the social, cultural, material, and spatial realities that shape and constrain it. Here I will attempt to develop a preliminary description of creativity that satisfies these criteria. I will proceed by developing three interlinked accounts. The first begins with the self and builds outward; it explores "where creativity comes from" at the individual level. The second begins with context and builds in; it inquires how the conventions and forms of artistic and intellectual culture shape the creative practice of individuals and groups. The third interrogates the boundary conditions between the individual and the social, with particular regard to the essential and desirable unpredictability of creative practice.

Situated Users

Because everyone is a user of artistic and cultural goods first and a creator second (if at all), an account of creative practice must begin with users. As we saw in Chapter 3, copyright law and theory rely on highly artificial models of users and user behavior: the economic user, who is interested only in consumption, and the romantic user, who is interested only in expressing an already-formed critical perspective. A model of creativity must replace these one-dimensional figures with a more believable construct that offers a basis for understanding how creative practice emerges and develops. That construct must be capable of explaining why users copy and how access and use become transformation and authorship. In particular, it must shed light on the process by which individual user-authors arrive at unanticipated inspiration and generate unpredicted and unpredictable outputs.

Let us begin by focusing on something that may seem, at first, to be a contradiction in terms: the ubiquity of constraint in the creative process. I do not mean constraint in the sense of coercion or limitation, but rather in the sense of situatedness within one's own culture. Situatedness, in turn, does not refer to a "situation" in the prescriptive sense (that is, one that might give rise to a legal defense or to an ethical obligation), but more minimally and descriptively to the fact that individuals and groups are located within particular cultural contexts. Each situated self encounters path-dependencies that shape both the content and the material forms of cultural knowledge, and thus shape creative opportunity. Recognizing situatedness does not require submerging the individual irretrievably within the social; creativity has idiosyncratic, internal dimensions as well as external ones. But what is distinct about each individual in relation to the surrounding culture will include differences in situation and the different path-dependencies that result.

Cultural situatedness supplies the framework for a more believable model of the user, one that foregrounds the path-dependencies that all users and user-authors experience. I will call this user the "situated user." Sources ranging from biographies of creators to studies of mass-culture fans reveal that situated users of copyrighted works appropriate preexisting cultural goods for a variety of interrelated purposes: They consume cultural products, including both those that they deliberately seek out and those that they serendipitously encounter or are motivated to try for some other reason. They appropriate cultural goods in order to communicate with one another in a common vernacular. They appropriate cultural goods for purposes of self-development, shaping and reshaping their own intellectual, aesthetic, and hedonic tastes. Finally, situated users appropriate cultural goods for purposes of creative play. Through these processes, some situated users become authors: they create works that are intended to be shared with others, and some of those works attain wider fame and influence.

There are four important points to appreciate about these activities by situated users, which together frame a model of cultural participation that is very different from the one framed by the conventional dichotomies between author and consumer, author and imitator, author and improver, and author and critic that pervade the copyright literature. The first point is that although the activities of situated users can be listed separately for analytical purposes, in practice they often cannot be disentangled. Each feeds into the others in ways that are difficult to identify and impossible to predict. A teenager who enjoys listening to music does so in a way that is never purely consumptive; music becomes both a focal point for interactions with her peers and a source of knowledge about the content of her culture and her relation to it. Acting on suggestions from peers, family members, and teachers and on other environmental clues, she will seek out music that accords with her developing self-image. Eventually, some teenagers will experiment by creating music of their own, and that music will be influenced by the tastes and affinities that they have developed as consumers and fans.

The second point, which follows from the fact of situatedness, is that the cultural activities of situated users take place within a web of semantic entailments. One cannot simply step out of or around the resources, values, and absences within one's own culture, but must negotiate one's way through them, following the pathways or links that connect one resource to the next. Music lovers begin with the tastes cultivated by their immediate surroundings and then sample the offerings recommended by peers, schools, and purveyors of mass culture en route to developing and pursuing their own particular inclinations. A host of cultural and personal factors explains why Alison Krauss became a bluegrass musician but Sarah Chang became a classical violinist and Stefani Germanotta became Lady Gaga, why Joshua Redman became a jazz bandleader rather than a symphony oboist, why Edward Burtynski photographs epic industrial landscapes but Cindy Sherman stages pulp fiction tableaux, and why Barbara Kingsolver's fiction draws on Native American culture but that of Ian McEwan mines the disaffections of the British upper-middle class.

The process of negotiating cultural pathways, which I will call "working through culture," bears little resemblance to models of progress flowing in value-neutral fashion from continual improvement upon the corpus of established knowledge. Instead, it moves in patterns that are both (and sometimes simultaneously) recursive and opportunistic. Creative practice and cultural progress emerge gradually out of complex patterns of imitation and appropriation. A young boy inspired by the fictional universe of *Star Wars* may be moved to try his hand at drawing robots, starships, and alien worlds. As he shares his interest with others, or browses other science fiction and fantasy video-rental offerings, he may discover other stories with similar characteristics, and imitate and experiment with other styles of artistic illustration. Upon enrolling in art classes, he will encounter other artists and illustrators and experiment by imitating their styles en route to developing a style that is recognizably and consistently his own. Even as his technique matures, imitation and reworking will remain central in his day-to-day creative practice.

On this understanding, creative practice is relational at its core. Carys Craig argues that authorship should be reconceptualized as a dialogic process consisting of "an *intra*personal dialogue (developing a form of personal narrative by drawing upon experience, situation, and critical reflection) and an *inter*personal dialogue (drawing upon the texts and discourses around her to communicate meaning to an anticipated audience)."[1] As Craig recognizes, this is an argument not only about the nature of authorship but also and more fundamentally about the nature of the interaction between emergent self and evolving culture; it is an account of where creativity comes from that locates creativity in the process of working through culture alongside others who are always already similarly engaged.

The third important point about the activities of situated users, which follows from creativity's relational nature, is that the process of working through culture is closely tied not only to semantic links between content but also to the spatial distribution of cultural resources. As Chapter 3 discussed, copyright theorists have tended to offer accounts of creative processes that are highly abstract and seem to presume access to extant cultural resources regardless of their location in space and time. For individuals situated in the real world, questions of access are inextricably bound up with the real-world distribution of artistic and intellectual culture and cultural artifacts. Those resources are distributed spatially in ways that make any particular resource more or less proximate, and therefore more or less relevant, to any given individual.

The set of cultural resources accessible within the cultural landscape that surrounds each situated user is neither geographically discrete nor composed entirely of resources that are publicly owned; therefore, it does not map neatly to the legal category of public-domain expression. Many user-authors will develop their interests and talents primarily through interaction with proprietary, non-public-domain works—the fictional universe of *Star Wars*, for example, is under copyright and will remain that way for a very long time. The cultural landscape is what supplies the elements in culture that are experienced as common, regardless of their ownership status. It is defined by the ways in which artistic and intellectual goods are accessible to individuals in the spaces where they live, and by the forms of interaction with preexisting expression that are possible and permitted.

Fourth and finally, the process of working through culture involves physical interactions among embodied users and between embodied users and material artifacts. Scholars in STS and cultural studies have documented the ways that users employ their bodies to explore the powers and limits of new technologies, new media, and technological and cultural artifacts.[2] Accounts of artistic creativity within copyright scholarship tend to ignore the ways in which culture is similarly apprehended, assimilated, and performed through the body. Copyright scholars may be uniquely predisposed to overlook the importance of embodiedness and materiality because for most of us, the preferred medium of expression is text and the coin of reputation is the idea. If we look beyond the limits of our own assumptions about creativity, however, the body is everywhere around us.

Bodies and embodied perception play central roles in interpretation of and communication about cultural resources. The role of embodied perception in mediating the experience of cultural goods is more readily evident in the performing and visual arts, for which both academic and lay reviewers alike emphasize attributes such as rhythm and flow. But embodied perception informs the experience of literary works as well. Textual works were initially recited rather than read, and many byproducts of orality have persisted in the print era, including both enduring conventions such as poetic meter and avant-garde literary expressions that self-consciously disregard established narrative conventions in favor of other, more discursive rhythms.[3] In the domain of mass culture, singing and moving to music and repeating lines of dialogue or action sequences from favorite television shows and movies are all practices that employ the body as the mediator of cultural experience. Teenagers swap lip-synching videos with friends and acquaintances not only to share the music, but also and more importantly to share an experience that is fundamentally an embodied one. Francesca Coppa shows that textual reworkings by mass-media fans, which focus on plot and character, are forms of dramatic storytelling that reflect embodiedness, "relying on the audience's shared extratextual knowledge of sets and wardrobes, of the actors' bodies and their smiles and movements . . . to direct a living theatre in the mind."[4] A young girl captivated by Star Wars may imagine and write her own stories about the characters; eventually, she may write "Mary Sue" stories that create leading female characters and place them in central roles.[5] In either case, she will rely on her accumulated understanding of bodies and embodied behaviors to get the details right.

As might perhaps be expected given our occupational preoccupation with dissent, copyright scholars who have confronted the "remixing" of cultural artifacts have tended to emphasize the manipulation of texts and artifacts embodying others' expression in the service of what Sonia Katyal calls "semiotic disobedience."[6] Within the broader context of situated, embodied interaction, however, the framework of dissent seems incomplete and strained. It seems both simpler and more accurate to recognize that situated users' interactions with cultural resources are ubiquitous and protean. In particular, many processes of cultural participation occur not via consumption or communication in the abstract, but rather by literally inserting the self into the work, and those processes can be celebratory as well as critical. The writer of critical fan fiction was not born a critic; she was a fan first and still is.

Both physical engagement with artifacts and embodied interpretation of texts remain important as consumption and communication shade into creative play. In the visual and performing arts, the body is an indispensable tool for accessing and mastering prevailing creative conventions; imitation of the masters perfects technique and inscribes glossaries of form. Imitation is the way would-be artists discover and nurture their interest in visual expression, and the way would-be musicians discover and nurture their interest in composition and performance. In literature and film, it is conventional to say that intergenerational dialogue manifests through the interpretation and reworking of texts. But texts are not abstractions; they are manifested through voices and rhythms, characters and settings. Regardless of artistic field or genre, creative outputs do not simply spring forth from the minds of their creators, but emerge through processes that are iterative and literally hands-on, rooted in embodied experience.

The situated user—who copies because copying is inextricably bound up with cultural participation, and for whom the copying of encountered artifacts and expressions is integral to creative play and creative practice—has important implications for copyright's understanding of creativity. As we saw in Chapter 3, that model casts copying, reworking, and derivation as peripheral and inauthentic activities. In recent years, copyright scholarship has puzzled over contemporary cultural practices such as hip-hop sampling, appropriation art, and fan fiction, which more directly foreground their reliance on reworking. As Richard Schur describes, these are practices that invert the traditional abstraction-based hierarchy of copyright law entirely. Within these forms of cultural expression, the relation between idea and expression is not "one idea, many expressions" but rather "one expression, many ideas."[7] The temptation, then, is to cast these works as new challenges for copyright. The key point to appreciate, however, and one that is often lost in discussions celebrating the novelty of "appropriation art," is that appropriation itself is not new. In their reliance on copying, these new creative practices are not fundamentally different from older ones.

To the contrary, the well-known history of both classical and contemporary art forms illustrates the centrality of copying within creative practice. In the visual arts, copying has been considered an essential part of artistic development at least since the Renaissance.[8] Identification and critical analysis of borrowing and reworking are standard fare in contemporary museum exhibits. Thus, for example, the 2003 *Manet/Velasquez* exhibition at New York's Metropolitan Museum of Art celebrated Velasquez as a source of inspiration for the impressionist movement, and featured several Velasquez works side by side with Manet's reinterpretations of those works. The Met's 2010 *Picasso* exhibition, on view at the time of this writing, identifies a number of instances in which Picasso copied images and techniques from others. In music, it is well understood that popular genres such as blues and jazz are created by a ceaseless process of borrowing. But musicologists who study the classical form now enshrined as elite culture have documented the fact that classical composers were equally dependent on borrowing and reworking. They filled their symphonies and overtures with sound samples ranging from hunting horns to bird calls to carnival music, all sounds heard in the background of their own lives. Sometimes, the borrowings were far more central. The third movement of Mahler's powerful first symphony is based on the French children's song "Bruder Martin" ("Frere Jacques" in the French version); there are countless other examples.[9]

Shifting the focus to literature, drama, and film, the list of borrowings continues. In literature and drama, borrowing and reworking are both conventional and critically prized. Consider some twentieth-century examples: George Bernard Shaw's *Pygmalion* (followed by Lerner and Loewe's *My Fair Lady*), Thornton Wilder's *The Skin of Our Teeth*, James Joyce's *Ulysses* (followed by Charles Frazier's *Cold Mountain*), John Gardner's *Grendel*, David Henry Hwang's *M. Butterfly*, and Gregory Maguire's *Wicked*. Last but hardly least, audiovisual works of mass culture routinely generate both box-office momentum and critical acclaim by reworking existing materials. *Star Wars*, for example, contains elements derived from Akira Kurosawa's *The Hidden Fortress* and other elements derived from the pulp comic-book series *Buck Rogers in the 25th Century*. Charlie Chaplin's iconic *Modern Times* reworks themes and imagery from Fritz Lang's dystopian *Metropolis*. And so on.

All these examples would be beside the point if there were any plausible basis for thinking that when we as a society make claims about the intrinsic worth of art, these are not the sorts of art that we mean. But we do mean these examples, and thousands of others like them, and we routinely invoke them as justification both for having copyright laws and for deciding particular cases in particular ways. Creativity is remix, and always has been.

Returning to the question with which this section began—about the process by which creative practice emerges and develops—we see that creative practice emerges from interactions with cultural landscapes via processes of juxtaposition, iteration, dialogue, and experimentation that are both conceptual and physical. Situated users begin with situatedness and work through culture to arrive at the unexpected. They derive inspiration from the culture within which they are situated, and develop their interests and skills through a continual process of dialogue with peers, with preexisting cultural artifacts, and with one another.

Networks of Culture, Networks of Practice

Emphasizing the path-dependence of cultural participation and creative practice reminds us that creativity has a significant external dimension that is worth examining more systematically. From an outside-in perspective, artistic and intellectual culture is most usefully understood not as a set of end products, such as movies, songs, drawings, and novels, but rather as a set of interconnected, relational networks of actors, resources, and emergent creative practices. Within those networks, creative practice is shaped by all that is culture, including the demands and established practices of knowledge communities and the conventions that crystallize around particular artifacts, techniques, and materials. It is shaped, as well, by contests over prevailing conventions that arise both within and across cultural boundaries.

The points that I want to make here are informed substantially by methodologies in critical theory and STS that are themselves contested. The strand of critical theory known as deconstructionism and the strand of STS scholarship known as social constructivist theory of technology (SCOT) hold that texts/technologies have no fixed meanings but rather take on meanings ascribed by their readers/users.[10] These theories in turn have engendered two powerful critiques. First, both deconstructionism and SCOT have been criticized for ascribing a version of autonomy to human-generated artifacts. Second and more seriously, they have been criticized for rendering meaningful discussion about larger social and cultural processes impossible. The second critique in particular is compelling for its sheer entertainment value; at times the aversion to fixity within these scholarly literatures smacks of self-parody. It is tempting to conclude that the medium is the message. I think, though, that this is a mistake, and that legal scholars (or at least copyright scholars) have made the further mistake of being too inclined to assume that these substrands stand for their disciplines more generally.

The methodologies of critical theory and STS are most usefully understood as offering points of entry from which to explore the creation of meaning within complex cultural systems. Here the autonomy critique is a red herring; a central tenet of both critical theory and STS is that texts and technologies, and the social practices that cohere around them, are sites of evolving and contested meaning. The STS literature in particular emphasizes that a technology is in fact a "heterogeneous assemblage" of elements that together shape the particularities of its form and use.[11] Over time, these assemblages can shift in response to changing practices, discourses, and institutional alignments. This approach has potentially fruitful applications to the arts and intellectual pursuits that are the traditional subject matter of copyright, which develop within networks of cultural production. In this section, I use the term "networks" not to suggest that the study of culture is reducible to the study of network science, but instead to denote sets of interactions that are simultaneously fluid and constrained and that lack fixed, distinct borders of their own. Networks of cultural production are, of course, both situated within and constitutive of culture more broadly, but these networks also can overlap other sorts of cultural boundaries, and indeed the opportunism that characterizes working through culture makes some such overlaps inevitable. Both boundaries and boundary crossings play important roles in catalyzing cultural progress.

If creative practice is a heterogeneous assemblage of knowledge, materials, and institutions, what are its constituent elements? With respect to the accumulated knowledge that animates creative practice, the approach to the development of scientific knowledge developed by Thomas Kuhn suggests an analogous, multipart model of creativity. Kuhn distinguished between "normal science" and "paradigm shifts" in generally accepted scientific understanding. During periods of normal science, there is general agreement on the fundamental principles that are thought to structure physical or biological systems; during paradigm shifts, that general understanding undergoes radical, discontinuous change. Studies of artistic culture suggest a process that loosely parallels the one Kuhn described: iteration within established conventions, punctuated by larger "representational shifts." In "normal science" mode, creative practice is more strongly constrained by existing institutions. At moments of representational shift, this is less true. Representational shifts in artistic practice do not inevitably disrupt artistic understanding the way that paradigm shifts in science do, because artistic practice does not require the same sort of grounding in fact that scientific practice does. In artistic and intellectual culture, different ways of seeing, hearing, and conceptualizing the world can more easily coexist. Occasionally, however, representational shifts can inaugurate powerful social narratives that are more closely equivalent to paradigm shifts. A good example of the latter is Adam Smith's "invisible hand," which fundamentally changed the way Western civilization understood economics by endowing the market with an independent, metaphorically embodied existence.

Processes of artistic and intellectual production are mediated by validating institutions, which propagate the established conventions of "normal science" and serve as the first line of reception for (or defense against) representational shifts. Networks of cultural production create particular fields and domains of expertise—for example, twentieth-century poetry or documentary street photography.[12] To an extent, the demarcation of fields and domains is created and maintained by the entities that traditionally have been the concerns of sociology: the communities and institutions that make up "art worlds."[13] Established taste-making institutions within art worlds play important roles in determining the fate of innovations, although new validating institutions will sometimes emerge.

The linked institutions of art worlds are not the sole custodians of "normal science," however. The processes of demarcation and definition extend beyond particular institutions (museums, critics, academic disciplines, and so on) to encompass more deeply embedded conventions. For example, as Chapter 3 discussed, scholars have explored the ways in which a particular understanding of authorship structures copyright's discourses about creativity, authenticity, and meaning. Another example is the distinction, difficult to pinpoint but nonetheless widely agreed to exist, between pornography and art. These and other conventions about the nature of authorship and art are maintained and reproduced by a broad and heterogeneous array of social institutions. In addition, as the Frankfurt School of cultural theory argued and as contemporary media scholars have shown, capitalist models of cultural production and distribution exert enormous influence on the form and content of creative expression. Corporate employers in the creative industries, corporate channels of media distribution, and providers of advertising all shape tastes and conventions in a variety of ways.

The simplistic, content-neutral "marketplace of ideas" model discussed in Chapter 3, in which innovations succeed or fail based on their merit, usefully draws our attention to audience response but does not consider or attempt to describe these overlapping fields of institutional, cultural, and material influence. It therefore cannot explain why some innovations capture the imagination of the relevant public and others fade away unnoticed, nor why the innovations that catch hold take the particular forms that they do. For example, the debate at the start of the twentieth century about whether photography was an art form or merely a technical endeavor required the generation and embrace of a new narrative about art and authorship. That narrative, which emerged as practitioners of photography built an art world of their own, privileged some aspects of photographic technique over others. A similar process of discursive construction has been underway as practitioners of hip-hop attempt to define both an aesthetic and an art world for themselves and struggle with some of the contradictions that process has entailed.[14]

Social groups also mediate creative practice, functioning both as users and as immediate cultural environments for their members. Such groups can play important roles in determining both conceptions of artistic and intellectual merit and conceptions of the appropriate social domains of creative practice. Moreover, social groups and validating institutions may be interrelated in complex ways. In the case of indigenous or so-called traditional cultures, validating institution and social group are closely linked, so that conceptions of merit are closely bound up with perceptions of cultural identity. As Madhavi Sunder has described, in these circumstances contests over cultural authority can become contests over the meaning of cultural membership. In other cases, as the example of hip-hop illustrates, the relationship between social groups and (traditional or majority) validating institutions may be more nearly disjunctive, and contests over cultural authority can become a defining condition of subcultural identity.[15]

In addition, because creative practice involves physical action by embodied human beings, it is shaped not only by the patterns of knowledge and discourse that crystallize around content in the abstract, but also by the patterns of behavior and discourse that crystallize around artifacts, materials, and social spaces. Representational shifts can result from the opportunities generated by new artifacts and materials and by new spatial configurations. For example, the chemical and physical requirements of traditional, film-based photography emphasize skill in "seeing," "capturing," and printmaking; in digital photography, the potential for manipulation of the initial image shifts the focus to reenvisioning and altering observed reality in an infinite number of ways. The built environment of the concert hall, the home stereo system, the personal digital-music player, and the home digital-recording studio all encourage some forms of interaction with music and some techniques of composition to a greater degree than others. Processes of artistic bricolage are similarly both conceptual and physical. The genre of world music does not simply combine abstract compositional technique from different musical traditions, but also combines disparate rhythms, instruments, and performance configurations. Judges deciding copyright disputes over music sampling have wondered why defendants did not simply make their own recordings of the desired excerpts, but the practice of sampling derives its meaning as intracultural dialogue precisely from using the original recording. In these cases and in countless others, creative practice coalesces around the material and artifactual resources available within cultural landscapes.

Critically, each of the dynamics described above infuses creative processes and practices with a species of path-dependence characterized not by a rigid determinism but by a more fruitful complexity. Creative practice sits at the intersection of struggles between and among elite, corporate, and popular tastemakers over the division of cultural authority, which in turn affect prevailing interpretations of what counts as "normal science," and for whom. To a significant degree, especially in periods of "normal science," creative practice is constrained in matters of both form and substance. At the same time, creative practice is opportunistic, indiscriminate, and centrally dependent on the borrowing, appropriation, and reworking of whatever it encounters. Situated users have multiple, overlapping affiliations with taste-making institutions and social groups, rendering patterns of cultural influence more complex. And to the extent that cultural artifacts and practices permit a variety of uses and interpretations, their developmental paths are never wholly within anyone's control. Both their origins and their continuing relevance are determined by negotiation and renegotiation at the boundary crossings between overlapping cultural and social networks.

The Play of Culture

The foregoing discussion suggests, as it is meant to, that creative practice is substantially determined by cultural context. At the same time, it is equally clear that creative practice is not fully determined by cultural context; if it were, creative outputs would be easy to predict and we could all move on to other problems. Culture does not function in the same way that chemistry or physics or electricity functions. If you mix gaseous hydrogen with gaseous oxygen, you will get an explosion and a few drops of water, in exactly predictable amounts, every time. If you mix Homeric epics with the history and folk traditions of the American South, you may get *O Brother, Where Art Thou?* or *Cold Mountain* or any number of other possible results. The question thus remains: what, if anything, is it possible to say about all that is unpredictable in artistic and intellectual expression? What increases the likelihood that someone will see, hear, or conceptualize the world differently in the first place? A critical ingredient is the scope that networks of cultural production afford for the play of everyday practice, including not only the extent to which they permit purposive creative experimentation but also the extent to which they enable serendipitous access to cultural resources and facilitate unexpected juxtapositions of those resources.

Some copyright scholars have challenged the presumption of deliberate authorial purpose that undergirds both rights theories and economic theories of copyright, arguing that artistic and intellectual innovation flow in more open-ended fashion from processes of creative play.[16] Play theorists caution that art and play are not one and the same; art involves a type of symbolic mastery that play need not involve. At the same time, they underscore the recurring and inevitable linkages between play and playfulness in creative enterprise. Research in the psychology of creativity supports this position and suggests that a certain kind of unstructured freedom to "see what happens" is an important determinant of creative success.[17]

Yet other social science research also suggests that new pathways of artistic and intellectual exploration are opened partly by types of serendipity that are even further removed from individual control. Just as fields of study and domains of expertise are important determinants of creative practice, so disruption and cross-fertilization between extant fields and domains are important conditions of creative possibility. In science, important paradigm-shifting theories have been generated by scientists who migrated to one field after being trained in another. Others, such as Einstein's theory of relativity, appear to have been stimulated by fortuitous encounters with concrete, practical problems that previous theoreticians had not considered. In art, representational shifts often have emerged following serendipitous encounters with artifacts, techniques, and assumptions originating within different creative traditions.[18]

Scholars who point to the importance of the chance encounter that yields unexpected fruit are describing both creative play and a different sort of play that is most closely analogous to the play-of-circumstances described in Chapter 2. Like the play-of-circumstances more generally, this sort of play—call it the "play of culture"—has a distinct phenomenology that revolves around the unexpected encounter. Logically and chronologically antecedent to the creative play performed by individuals and groups, the play of culture supplies the unexpected inputs to creative processes. Creative practice appropriates the unexpected and puts it to use; the results of this process, iterated over and over, yield what we name, and prize, as progress.

Together, the play of culture and the processes of creative play that it sustains are what prevent established ways of seeing, hearing, and conceptualizing the world from becoming calcified. The play of culture also fuels serendipitous consumption by situated users and inclines audiences toward the new. For both users and user-authors, the chance encounters it generates are sources of dissonance, provocation, meaning, and unexpected beauty. Sustaining the conditions for those encounters should be a central goal of any system of copyright law.

Mass Culture and Popular Culture in Networked Space

Some copyright scholars and cultural commentators argue that an unregulated global communications network spells doom for the entire enterprise of for-profit cultural production. Commentators who take this position disagree on whether that result should be mourned or celebrated. According to some, in an age of uncontrolled copying, no one will want to invest in the creation of new music, movies, television shows, or books, and we will return to a predigital dark age. Others rejoice at the prospect of mass culture's imminent demise. Freed from the dominance of the culture industries, they claim, we will enter a golden age of amateurism and unfettered creative play in which every individual will have access to cultural resources and collaborators from around the globe. So far, at least, the reality is more complicated than either description suggests. Mass culture is not dead, nor is it likely to be—and that fact should be cause for celebration among advocates of mass culture and advocates of amateur culture alike.

Let us begin by returning to Chapter 2's characterization of networked space as offering a simultaneous opening out and closing in of communicative opportunity. We can trace this dynamic emerging in the realm of artistic and intellectual culture. The emergence of networked space expands the universe of cultural resources available to network users, both by making many existing resources more accessible and by introducing new ones. As existing networks of cultural and institutional influence extend more broadly, they encounter and overlap with a larger number of other networks, and their boundaries become more porous. This in turn increases the likelihood of the unplanned, fortuitous discovery and the unforeseen juxtaposition. Global communication networks offer more effective access to a wider variety of cultural products, and create a correspondingly greater potential for fruitful cultural hybridization.

Global communications networks also enable new patterns of creative practice. The practices of distributed peer production and "produsage" described in Chapter 2 rely on networked information and communication technologies for both the economies of scale they enable and the social and geographic fluidity that they create. As Yochai Benkler explains, abundant connectivity and excess computing capacity create the conditions for new kinds of collaborative production, such as open-source software and *Wikipedia*, that otherwise would not be feasible economically or socially. In the networked information society as it has developed thus far, artistic and intellectual culture also is less dependent on established channels of production and distribution. For both these reasons, in networked space, artistic and intellectual culture is not only more accessible, but also more diverse, vibrant, and eclectic.

That, however, is only half of the story. Users are still situated within real communities, geographies, and cultures. Networked information technologies alter patterns of information access in important ways, but they do not eradicate the particularities of cultural landscapes or change the culturally contingent nature of creative practice. The process of engaging with networked information resources is still a process of working through culture, node by node and link by link.

Networked information technologies also do not displace mass culture from its privileged position within the cultural landscapes of situated users. The same network effects that contribute to the success of distributed peer production work to ensure the continuing relevance and even dominance of mass culture. Scholars allied with the "free culture" movement have argued that a wide variety of intermediaries will spring up to match the needs and desires of Internet users, and they have been right. Within the "rich get richer" ecology of the network, however, the intermediaries that supply authorized access to works of mass culture continue to enjoy considerable power. As global information networks increase the penetration of mass culture through all major media and to all corners of the globe, alternative cultural resources require more effort to find. And to the extent that the profusion of intermediaries creates more potential for confusion, mainstream intermediaries that offer familiar interfaces and reliable quality likely will continue to enjoy reliable market share.

Yet the continuing dominance of mass culture should not be an occasion for gloom. Disdain for mass culture is fashionable among copyright scholars, but it is shortsighted. Mass culture is, for better or worse, a vital part of the cultural landscapes that situated users inhabit. Works of mass culture unite global networks of fans, creating communities organized around shared experience. Economically minded scholarship addressing the so-called solidarity goods phenomenon recognizes this, but then misses the point by complaining about the very attributes that make solidarity goods valuable: their standardization and their unregenerately middlebrow appeal.[19]

Mass culture also forms the substrate for much that is proudly labeled alternative culture. Many of the new forms of expression that commentators cite as representatively amateur—musical and video mashups, fan fiction and fanvids, compilations of information about popular entertainment franchises, blog commentary on articles culled from the mainstream media, and the like—build from a foundation laid by mass commercial culture. All this adds up to the conclusion that some degree of shared orientation to mass commercial culture is both inevitable and good, for amateurs as well as information plutocrats, and should be distinguished from the relative lock-in produced by copyright rules that place large sectors of the cultural landscape off limits to would-be borrowers.

At the same time, much of what looks like change is really continuity; remix culture has always existed. Creative practitioners have always drawn inspiration from myth, legend, and celebrity. Shakespeare, for example, often used the device of a play-within-a-play to retell the stories of classical mythology, as when the hapless tradesmen of *A Midsummer Night's Dream* perform the tragedy of Pyramus and Thisbe for the royal court. That performance and others like it are the original fan fiction, a practice of participatory and critical engagement with cultural works that stretches back hundreds (even thousands) of years. Renaissance painters clothed their noble patrons in togas and placed them in biblical tableaux. Jumping forward to the twentieth century, one can think of no more omnipresent visual icons of the Pop art movement than Andy Warhol's monumental Campbell's soup cans or his silk-screened portraits of celebrities such as Jacqueline Kennedy Onassis and Marilyn Monroe. Among the works of the twentieth-century painter Larry Rivers is a series of portraits of great artists and performers in the settings that inspired them. In one, the impressionist painter Henri Matisse stares out from within a papier-mâché reproduction of his celebrated *Red Room*; in another, Charlie Chaplin climbs the assembly line in the film *Modern Times*. Only the Matisse work was then in the public domain, but it is hard to see why different conventions should govern the two works, each of which portrays an icon of cultural modernism.

In the space between the middlebrow and the avant-garde, mass culture catalyzes processes of cultural hybridization that arise as creative practice exploits what is ready to hand in the cultural landscape. Today, pop culture rather than Greek mythology or Catholic hagiography is the primary source of new material. That change was only to be expected and should be celebrated by the culture industries, since it underscores mass culture's central importance in the cultural lives of situated subjects. What is most firmly rooted in the public consciousness is not Shakespeare or Homer, but the products of culture industries ranging from Disney and Warner Bros. to Bollywood and Hong Kong.

The benefits of this cultural hybridization do not run only one way. As Naomi Mezey and Mark Niles explain, mass culture benefits from "an interdependence, even a circulation, between mass and popular culture," since "popular culture makes use of the mass cultural resources that capitalism provides, and mass culture often co-opts and markets pop cultural practices."[20] The mass-culture industries borrow indiscriminately from popular, indigenous, and elite cultural forms. Big-budget films adapt fairy tales and traditional legends from around the globe; entrepreneurs bring traditional African music to Western recording studios and the Broadway stage. And as films from *Amadeus* to *Pollock* to *Basquiat* to *Shine* to *Shakespeare in Love* demonstrate, Hollywood has found endless creative fodder in the lives of artists from all eras.

Networked information technologies do mediate processes of cultural hybridization in new and often unprecedented ways. Yet this too was only to be expected; as we saw in Chapter 2, evolving artifacts and technologies mediate and re-mediate experienced reality, altering users' capabilities and simultaneously reshaping users' perceptions of the world around them. This is as true for the cultural world as it is for the natural, physical one. Consider, once again, the example of photography. As the historical record expanded to encompass photographic documentation, the scope of historically inspired borrowings expanded correspondingly. The most-cited example of this point is probably the big-budget film *Forrest Gump*, which applied the techniques of collage to document its eponymous hero's involvement in various important twentieth-century events, but the documentary form predates *Forrest Gump* by many decades. And once again, the point goes far beyond Hollywood and far beyond collage. I have a friend who paints stunning, fauvist portraits of great jazz musicians, most of whom are no longer living. Because she can no longer see her subjects in person, she works from old photographs. To call this infringement, or derivative in the pejorative sense, would be to misconstrue completely the deeply creative nature of her enterprise. Shepard Fairey created his iconic portrait of Democratic presidential candidate Barack Obama by working from photographs that were his only means of access to his subject. In each case, the photographic record has offered situated users a different way of perceiving history and celebrity, and a new entry point for the reworking of cultural narratives.

Most significantly, networked information technologies heighten situated users' perceptions of the malleability of culture. The boundaries of creative works seem less fixed and more readily amenable to revision, and this creates new fluidity in the cultural environment. As Yochai Benkler, Jack Balkin, Niva Elkin-Koren, and many others have argued, the enhanced malleability of texts, images, and sounds also has important democratic consequences. Widespread, relatively inexpensive access to technologies for manipulating and distributing creative content has democratized cultural production, providing tools for more people to participate in the processes of appropriation, reworking, and cultural dialogue in which creative people have always engaged.

Once again, however, the mass-culture industries also benefit from both the dissolution of boundaries and the adaptive flexibility that digital technologies enable. Successful cultural properties can be versioned in innumerable ways, sliding with ease from the big screen to the home theater to more immersive and participatory gaming environments. Movies on DVD offer deleted scenes, alternate endings, "director's cut" versions, and behind-the-scenes commentary on the production process. These offerings acknowledge that the boundaries of creative works are fluid and that reworking of sounds, images, and texts continues to lie at the heart of the creative process as it is understood by practitioners ranging from the iconoclastic to the mainstream. And the malleability of mass-culture products in turn deepens their cultural power, creating the conditions for their pervasive embedding within the cultural landscapes of situated users around the globe.

In sum, reports of the death of mass culture in the era of global information networks have been greatly exaggerated. There is every reason to expect that in the emerging networked information society, mass culture will continue to enjoy and even to increase its global dominance, and that its ubiquitous offerings will continue to supply inspiration for remix culture, both high and low. It will do so, however, in a cultural ecology that is more diverse, more democratic, and more volatile. Sustaining this cultural ecology is where the copyright system's core mission lies.

Copyright and Cultural Mobility

This approach to theorizing creative practice and to understanding the relationship between mass culture and popular culture has direct implications for copyright policy and doctrine. Decentering creativity disrupts the tight linkage between copyright and individual, internal creativity that has come to dominate public debate about copyright issues, and that pervades legislative and policy processes. That disruption, in turn, enables an account of the oft-invoked "copyright balance" that emphasizes the process of working through culture and the importance of play within cultural landscapes, and that underscores the connections between cultural mobility and human flourishing. This twofold reframing dictates a very different approach to questions of optimal copyright scope.

Lobbyists for the copyright industries are in the habit of asserting that copyright is the single most critical prerequisite for a vibrant artistic and intellectual culture. Some of this is theater driven by political expediency. No one wants to be against creativity, and if copyright equals creativity, then no one wants to be against copyright. Yet beneath the rhetoric, both copyright lawyers and copyright scholars tend to assume that copyright law is centrally important in stimulating a high level of creativity. Since copyright theory and jurisprudence persistently devalue the role of context in shaping culture, that assumption is unsurprising. The tight linkage between copyright and creativity in turn fuels romantic author narratives and justifies drawing firm distinctions between authors, on the one hand, and consumers, imitators, and improvers on the other. Those distinctions dominate the current landscape of copyright law; they undergird broad rights to control copies, public renderings, and derivations of copyrighted works, as well as expansive readings of the rules that create liability for technology providers.

Decentering creativity challenges the widespread assumption about the nature and direction of copyright's influence on creativity in two ways. First and most obviously, it tends to suggest a much more modest conception of the role that copyright plays in stimulating creative processes and practices. Copyright fulfills some important economic functions (of which more shortly), and therefore plays an important role in organizing cultural production, but it is hardly ever the direct cause of a representational shift in creative practice, nor does it appear to play a direct role in motivating much that is "normal science." Scholars who ask how deploying copyright might stimulate creativity (as opposed to production) are asking the wrong question. Neither creative inspiration nor the creative outputs that follow from it are so easily engineered.

Questions remain, however, about the extent to which the contextual factors that are more important in stimulating creativity are amenable to social engineering. Arguably, the dynamic that I have described would exist in any social and economic system that is sufficiently complex. And if creativity is not especially amenable to social engineering, perhaps both those whose primary concern is social engineering and those whose primary concern is strong copyright can simply take it as a given. At the very least, then, one might posit that strong copyright does no harm. Put differently, if copyright is not the most important factor in stimulating creativity, it still may be the most important factor within our control. If copyright serves other important functions, such as the organization of cultural production and the distribution of artistic and intellectual goods, perhaps strong copyright is good policy.

Here the decentered model of creativity makes its second contribution: it provides a firmer foundation for arguments about the systemic harms that a regime of copyright can produce. Critics of copyright maximalism have long argued that overly rigid control of access to and manipulation of cultural goods stifles artistic and cultural innovation, and a growing body of anecdotal evidence suggests that copyright's "permission culture" does exert a substantial constraining influence on creative practice.[21] Similarly, research in the psychology of creativity suggests that attempts to impose a rigid structure on the creative process quickly become counterproductive and that the success of the creative process hinges in part on the ability to avoid externally imposed distractions.[22] A model of creativity grounded in the methods of contemporary social theory supplies both a rigorous analytical underpinning for those arguments and observations and a discourse in which to frame them. Within this framework, a regime of copyright that aims to promote cultural progress must be assessed on its effects on creative practice by situated users, and on the extent to which it renders elements of the cultural landscape more or less accessible. And within this framework, those who advocate more limited copyright can be "for" rather than "against" creativity.

What legal regime, though, does the decentered model of copyright recommend? It might be argued that copyright and play are definitionally incompatible. There is an inevitable tension between social theorists' emphasis on mobility, emergence, and decentering and the legal system's need for fixity, clarity, and predictability. Some theorists from both sides of the law/social science divide argue that legal recognition of particular kinds of claims—to specific forms of cultural property or to particular formulations of human rights—itself works a form of imperialism in which the law's need for doctrinal and definitional certainty is inimical to the demands of emergent social processes.[23] To an important extent, though, this social science critique of law's possibility ignores its own most powerful disciplinary insight: law is not separate from social systems. As Naomi Mezey explains, the relationship between law and culture is an interdependent one characterized by cycles of definition, slippage, and redefinition.[24] Within this general pattern, law and culture evolve together; the fixity that law imposes on culture is a matter of degree and may be a defensible means of pursuing other social goals that are themselves evolving.

In designing a good system of copyright, then, we also must consider the other social goals that a system of copyright serves. Here economic theorists' emphasis on the production and distribution of cultural goods becomes important and can be restated more accurately: copyright is a means of creating economic fixity, and thus predictability, in the organization of cultural production. Control of copying, manipulation, and derivation enables the organization of entire sectors of economic activity in ways that produce a variety of concrete benefits, ranging from jobs and exports to independence from patronage to cultural solidarity goods. Those are desirable goods: a society characterized by complete lack of economic certainty would be unstable; state control of cultural production would be undesirable; and a culture without shared expressive referents would be far less enjoyable. But these arguments too have been pushed to extremes in the copyright wars. Lobbyists for the copyright industries argue that because copyright enables economic and cultural productivity, truncating copyright entitlements would be disastrous not only for their employers but also for the country more generally. Neither conclusion follows. In the real world, which is the world that creative communities have always inhabited, play and economic stability are not mutually exclusive. And it is well recognized that economic fixity is not an unmitigated good.

It is therefore correct to say that copyright requires a balancing act, but the decentered model of creativity prompts us to redescribe what copyright balances. What is required is not a balance between present authors and the abstract "public," nor between valuable entitlement and ephemeral "deadweight loss," both formulations that encourage would-be balancers to equate relative concreteness with relative importance. Balance also does not refer merely to a process by which the claims of competing interest groups are aired en route to striking a deal. As Robert Burrell and Allison Coleman have trenchantly observed, references to balancing in copyright rhetoric contain a "semantic ambiguity" that results in a slippage between notions of balance as process and notions of balance as correct result.[25] The notion of balance that I mean to invoke is substantive and concerns the ways in which copyright's goal of creating economic fixity must accommodate its mission to foster cultural play.

Economic analysis can help us understand some of the considerations relevant to the balance between economic fixity and cultural mobility, but both valuation and incommensurability problems prevent a comprehensive summing of the relevant costs and benefits. Modeling the benefits of artistic and intellectual flux is hard to do, and comparing those benefits with the more tangible, predictable gains from existing models of creative production is even harder. The emphasis on "creative destruction" now popular among copyright scholars invokes a historical theory, not an economic theorem.[26] Moreover, creative destruction is nicest for those who do not have to undergo it. It is hardly surprising, then, that economic theorists can't agree on how to model the optimal regime for promoting improvements. No one is against creativity, but that apparent unanimity conceals rather large disagreements about how wholeheartedly and unreservedly we are for it. Modeling the opportunity costs of cultural fixity is equally difficult. Although we can say with some confidence that cultural fixity affects individual behavior, it is hard to assess its cumulative effect on unknown future behavior. To the extent that economic modeling focuses on what is known (or assumed) about benefits and costs, moreover, it tends to crowd out the unknown and unpredictable, with the result that play remains a peripheral consideration, when it should be central.

To grapple with these problems, a larger tool kit and a different attitude toward social engineering are required. Methodologically, the distinction is one between a social theory of creativity that embraces an eclectic range of methods, including economic methods, and an economic model of creativity that has room only for its own methods and that consequently distorts in predictable and predictably damaging ways. Substantively, the distinction is one between deploying known cost-benefit calculations in an attempt to generate predictable results and deliberately leaving room for unpredictable results to emerge. Creativity requires breathing room and thrives on play in the system of culture. Copyright law should be judged based on how well it advances those goals.

Rights theories, meanwhile, can help us articulate some of the aspirations that a good regime of copyright should promote, but furthering those aspirations requires moving beyond abstract ideals to concrete guarantees. Yochai Benkler powerfully advances the cause of a robust vision of liberal humanism that "is concerned first and foremost with the claims of human beings as human beings."[27] Within that vision, it makes sense to talk about liberal ideals of autonomy and self-determination and to understand those ideals as bound up with a larger commitment to human flourishing. But a commitment to human flourishing also requires more direct engagement with patterns of cultural progress and with the material and spatial realities of cultural processes. Autonomy is exercised, and self-determination pursued, by working through culture. Laws granting rights in artistic and intellectual expression should be designed with that process in mind.

PART III

Privacy and the Play of Subjectivity

CHAPTER 5

Privacy, Autonomy, and Information

In the last two decades, the environmental and social determinants of privacy have undergone rapid change. The amount of information collected about both individuals and social groups has grown exponentially and covers an astonishing range of subject matter, from purchasing history to browsing behavior to intellectual preferences to genetic predispositions. This information lasts longer and travels farther than ever before; it is stored in digital databases, exchanged in markets, and "mined" by both government and private actors for insights into individual and group behavior. The increase in data-processing activity coincides with the rapid spread of identity-linked authentication regimes for controlling access to spaces and resources, both real and digital. Authentication data are added to the other information stored in digital databases, creating comprehensive, persistent records of individual activity. The last two decades also have witnessed a dramatic upswing in real-time monitoring—by camera, satellite, and electronic pattern-recognition tools—of public spaces, privately owned spaces, and traffic across communication networks.

Government entities are involved in many of these activities, but the vast majority of data-mining, authentication, and monitoring initiatives do not originate with government. They originate in private-sector desires to learn more about current and prospective customers, to administer access to real and virtual resources, and to manage communication traffic over networks. Moreover, the increasingly widespread diffusion of cameras, networked personal devices, and social-networking platforms means that individuals and social groups themselves actively participate in many of these activities.

107

What all this signifies for people's understandings and expectations of privacy is hard to understand. Surveys report that ordinary people experience a relatively high generalized concern about privacy but a relatively low level of concern about the data generated by specific transactions, movements, and communications. Some policy makers interpret the surveys as indicating either a low commitment to privacy or a general readiness to trade privacy for other goods. Others argue that the various "markets" for privacy have informational and structural defects that prevent them from generating privacy-friendly choices. They argue, as well, that inconsistencies between reported preferences and revealed behavior reflect a combination of resignation and befuddlement; most Internet users do not understand how the technologies work, what privacy policies mean, or how the information generated about them will actually be used.[1]

Confronted with these developments and struggling to make sense of them, courts increasingly throw up their hands, concluding that constitutional guarantees of privacy simply do not speak to many of the new technologies, business models, and behaviors, and that privacy policy is best left to legislators. Legislators are quick to hold hearings but increasingly slow to take action; in many cases, they prefer to delegate day-to-day authority to regulators. Regulators, for their part, rely heavily on principles of notice, consent, reasonable expectation, and implied waiver to define the scope of individual rights with respect to the practices that fall within their jurisdiction.

Legal scholars also have struggled to respond to these social, technological, and legal trends. There is widespread (though not unanimous) scholarly consensus on the continuing importance of privacy in the networked information economy, but little consensus about what privacy is or should be. Among other things, legal scholars differ on whether privacy is a fundamental human right, what circumstances would justify pervasive government monitoring of movements and communications, whether guarantees of notice and informed consent are good or even effective safeguards against private-sector practices that implicate privacy, and what to make of the inconsistency between expressed preferences for more privacy and revealed behavior that suggests a relatively low level of concern.

Despite the voluminous amount of scholarship now being published on privacy issues, however, scholarly accounts of privacy within U.S. legal theory are incomplete in three ways that go to the most fundamental questions about what privacy interests encompass. First, privacy scholars generally have assumed that the self that privacy protects is characterized by its autonomy. This formulation does not withstand close scrutiny—scholars cannot agree on whether "autonomy" denotes an absolute condition or a matter of degree, and neither understanding makes sense taken on its own terms—and the policy recommendations it generates are incoherent. Yet privacy theory clings to it nonetheless. Privacy scholars have seemed both unable and unwilling to generate a different theory of the self that privacy protects. Second, although privacy theorists have articulated a variety of collective interests that privacy serves, they have avoided digging too close to the root of the asserted social interest in denying privacy—in gathering information, imposing identity-linked authentication procedures, and monitoring spaces and networks. Scholarly reluctance to confront the case against privacy weakens the case for privacy; collective-interest justifications that seem incomplete are more easily swept aside. Finally, privacy theory offers a very poor account of the metaphors used to describe privacy interests and harms. Most privacy theorists disdain spatial metaphors for privacy as ill-suited to the networked information age, but have not explored why spatial metaphors continually recur in privacy discourse or what that recurrence might mean for privacy law. At the same time, they have seemed not to notice the dominance of visual metaphors in privacy discourse, and have not considered the ways in which the implicit equation of privacy with invisibility structures the legal understanding of privacy interests and harms.

As in the case of copyright, the deficiencies in privacy theory can be traced to the methodologies that legal scholars of privacy commonly employ and the assumptions on which those methodologies are based. Like legal scholarship about copyright, legal scholarship about privacy is infused with the commitments of liberal political theory. As we saw in Chapter 3, those commitments do not function well at the self/culture intersection. Privacy concerns the boundary conditions between self and society and the ways that those conditions mediate processes of self-formation. In U.S. legal scholarship about privacy, resistance to examining the complex relationship between self and society works systematically to undermine efforts at reconceptualizing privacy and to steer privacy theorists away from literatures that might help in that task.

Some privacy scholars argue that privacy is itself an artifact of liberal political theory. According to Peter Galison and Martha Minow, rights of privacy are inseparably tied to the liberal conception of the autonomous, prepolitical self. They argue that privacy as we know it (in advanced Western societies) ultimately will not withstand the dissolution of the liberal self diagnosed by contemporary social theory.[2] Privacy and liberal political theory are closely intertwined, but the problem of privacy is more complicated than that argument suggests. The understanding of privacy as tied to autonomy represents only one possible conception of privacy's relation to selfhood. More fundamentally, although privacy is often linked to the liberal values of dignity and autonomy within our political discourse, it also conflicts with other liberal values. In the networked information society, protection for privacy compromises the liberal commitments to free flows of information, to the presumed equivalence between information and truth, and to the essential immateriality of personality. The conceptual gaps within privacy theory therefore reflect not only tensions between liberalism and critical theory, but also tensions internal to liberalism. As we will see, the gaps within privacy theory have very real consequences for the content of privacy law and policy.

The Subject of Privacy: The Autonomy Paradox

The first defect in privacy theory is the most fundamental, and concerns the relation between privacy and selfhood. Privacy rights attach to individuals, but how and why? Exactly who is the self that privacy is supposed to benefit? Within U.S. privacy theory, answers to those questions often invoke concepts of autonomy. But autonomy-based formulations of privacy interests raise more questions than they answer. Different strands of privacy doctrine suggest very different accounts of the way that privacy and autonomy are related, and those accounts are inconsistent both internally and with one another. The commitment to autonomy becomes even odder when it is situated in historical context. For nearly a century, the notion of the self-sufficient, autonomous individual has been under attack. Within social theory on both sides of the Atlantic, the autonomous self has given way to the socially constructed subject. Unlike their European and Canadian counterparts, however, most U.S. privacy theorists have resisted or avoided engaging with the insights and methods of contemporary social theory, and have interpreted those insights as undermining not only the idea of separation between self and society, but also the very idea of a self that might have privacy claims to assert.

It is instructive to begin our exploration of the "autonomy paradox" in privacy theory by considering accounts of the individual privacy claimant that emerge from privacy jurisprudence. As Neil Richards has demonstrated, strands of U.S. constitutional jurisprudence establish robust privacy protection for thought, belief, and association; the asserted purpose of this protection is to nurture unconventional or dissenting thought that otherwise might be stifled by social disapproval.[3] Constitutional privacy jurisprudence also protects certain decisions that are viewed as intimately bound up with the definition of self, and again it does so to shield individuals making such decisions from the chill of majoritarian displeasure.[4] By way of parallel to the nomenclature developed in Chapter 3, I will call the presumed beneficiary of these doctrines the "romantic dissenter." The romantic dissenter is not, on the whole, a fragile figure; among other things, when she chooses to participate in the rough-and-tumble of the marketplace of ideas she will not be able to demand protection against those who disagree with her or against ad feminam attacks on her character. But her claim to privacy protection for her beliefs, associations, and intimate decisions is widely acknowledged. And if she chooses to speak anonymously, she often can invoke constitutional protection for that decision as well.[5]

The romantic dissenter also animates the strand of constitutional privacy doctrine that establishes privacy protection for homes and personal papers. Here too privacy functions as a safeguard against majoritarian tyranny. The home is conceptualized as a retreat from public life, affording shelter from public scrutiny of one's activities; in this respect, it complements the doctrines that protect intellectual privacy.[6] In addition, privacy protection for the home shelters activities that simply have no place in the public sphere.

The emerging U.S. legal framework for information privacy, which revolves primarily around the design of procedures for opting into or out of data collection, seems to contemplate a very different beneficiary of privacy protection.[7] This individual is concerned above all with maximizing his surplus in the marketplace. He may have preferences for privacy, but he regards those preferences and any formal entitlements to privacy as tradeable for other benefits that he might value more highly. I will call this privacy claimant the "rational chooser"; as with the economic user of copyrighted works, the rational chooser's implicit theoretical allegiance is to economic models of behavior and decision making.

As in the case of copyright, the first thing to notice about these characters is that they seem to exist only within their home domains. One can easily imagine the rational chooser consenting to have his communications or reading decisions monitored and to have trouble comprehending the chill that supposedly would result from allowing information about intimate decisions to be disclosed. Yet that view of appropriate privacy rules for belief, association, and the like is decidedly a minority one. Expressive and associational privacy, and to a lesser extent residential privacy, are the domains of the romantic dissenter. The romantic dissenter, meanwhile, might complain that the collection, use, and sale of information about her grocery purchases or her rental history chill her opportunities for self-development. Should she do so, she would have trouble finding a sympathetic audience. Within the structure of U.S. privacy law, commercial transactions are the domain of the rational chooser. The banal, de minimis nature of most such transactions has repeatedly frustrated efforts to reframe information privacy problems as implicating profound self-development concerns. Within common-law privacy doctrine, some uses of information do trigger higher levels of legal protection, but they involve falsity or particularly intimate facts linked to the romantic dissenter's traditional concerns.

One explanation for the inconsistency might simply be that people have different expectations in different domains of activity and that those domains therefore demand different degrees of legal solicitude. If so, then arguably there is nothing inconsistent about protecting communications and associations to a greater extent than commercial transactions. Yet underlying the different sorts of rules for different kinds of privacy are some very different assumptions about the sorts of autonomy that individual privacy claimants exercise. Both the romantic dissenter and the rational chooser exercise autonomy, but the autonomy exercised by each is different. The rational chooser is a definitionally autonomous being who experiences unbroken continuity between preference and action; his choices are relatively impervious to outside influence, and so he neither wants nor needs privacy protection for them. The romantic dissenter requires privacy protection for her autonomy to flourish; as a practical matter, then, she exercises autonomy only to the degree that her environment enables it. If the rational chooser and the romantic dissenter were actually two different people, this might not be especially troubling. Since they are supposed to be the same person, the divergent conceptions of autonomy are worrisome.

The two different visions of the autonomy exercised by privacy claimants map to two different schools of thought about the nature of autonomy more generally. Within the framework of liberal political theory, the rational chooser corresponds to the conventional understanding of negative liberty as the absence of overt constraint. At any point in time, the autonomous self is definitionally capable of both choice and consent, and so we can say that autonomy subsists both in those choices and in the overall pattern that they establish. For other privacy theorists, however, this understanding of autonomy sets up an "autonomy trap."[8] These theorists argue that sometimes moment-to-moment choices need to be constrained so that people can become free to make better long-term choices than they otherwise might make. This position on autonomy corresponds to the conventional understanding of positive liberty as a freedom to choose wisely that cannot exist without some sort of environmental enablement. The romantic dissenter corresponds to this latter position; she requires rules that guarantee privacy of thought, belief, and association in order to develop her capacities to the fullest.[9]

The problem with the negative liberty framework is that when it is taken as a description of human capability, it is self-evidently false. Autonomous adults do not spring full-blown from the womb. Children and young adults must grow into their autonomy, and this complication introduces the problem of dynamic self-formation that the negative-liberty framework seeks to avoid. To know when an individual has attained the capacity for autonomous choice, we need to decide how much nurture is enough.

Within a positive-liberty framework, though, the search for the dividing line between "autonomy" and external influence presents a problem of infinite regress. Some privacy scholars, myself included, have attempted to finesse this problem by characterizing information-collection practices and privacy rules as intimately involved in the ongoing constitution of selfhood. Even as they highlight the dynamic nature of self-formation, however, these "constitutive privacy" scholars continue to insist on the existence of an autonomous core—an essential self identifiable after the residue of influence has been subtracted.[10] The problem, however, is not simply that autonomy is constituted over time and by circumstances; it is that including autonomy in the definition of the ultimate good to be achieved invokes a set of presumptions about the separateness of self and society that begs the very question we are trying to answer.

The debate about underlying conceptions of autonomy in privacy law is a theoretical one, but its consequences are not. First, the divide between the different domains of privacy, and between the corresponding conceptions of autonomy, doesn't tell us what to do when those domains collide. These days, such collisions are more the rule than the exception. Is use of a computer system in the privacy of one's home to be governed by the rules that establish stringent privacy protection for activities at home or by the rather less stringent rules that govern privacy in commercial transactions with the providers of licensed software and communication networks? If the former, does taking one's laptop (or smart phone or personal digital assistant) outside one's home change the rules that apply? What privacy rules should apply to records showing purchases of intellectual goods? The romantic dissenter and the rational chooser can't answer these questions; we have no rules of encounter that might tell us how to reconcile their incompatible demands.

The figures of the romantic dissenter and the rational chooser, and the underlying conceptions of autonomy that they represent, also don't map to an assortment of other problems that are experienced by ordinary people as implicating privacy concerns. To begin with the most banal, they don't explain the desire for privacy for ordinary bodily functions. Activities such as excretion and sex are neither secret (everyone does them) nor romantic in their anatomical essentials, yet the view of them as private is strongly held. The romantic dissenter and the rational chooser also don't help us understand why most people assume that sharing personal details with one's airplane seatmate or one's circle of friends does not automatically equal sharing them with one's employer. Nor do they tell us why many people tend to feel that being subject to regularized surveillance in a public place is qualitatively different from simply being visible to others present there. In other words, they don't explain why most people understand privacy as a quality subject to an enormous amount of contextual variation.[11] Not coincidentally, privacy theory lacks good frameworks for understanding why these problems, none of which appears to implicate autonomy in any obvious way, nonetheless implicate (and often violate) the affected individuals' sense of self.

Ultimately, the autonomy paradox illustrates the ways in which the commitments of liberal political theory have constrained scholarly approaches to the self-society relation. Interrogating the conceptions of autonomy that exist in privacy theory exposes a deep conceptual poverty about what selves are made of. Straining to identify the point at which autonomy ends and influence begins does not take us very far toward answering that question. Within contemporary social theory, the separation between self and society that lies at the root of the autonomy paradox does not exist. From that perspective, a robust theory of privacy requires an understanding of the processes by which selfhood comes into being and is negotiated through contexts and over time. It is not obvious why that understanding should be attainable only by interrogating the conditions of true independence. And yet privacy theory remains preoccupied with the latter inquiry.

In general, U.S. privacy scholars are deeply resistant, even hostile, to the idea of the socially constructed self. The aversion is so strong that many privacy theorists are unwilling to entertain even the more modest argument for "constitutive privacy"—which, as we have seen, manages at most a partial engagement with the problem of evolving subjectivity. Those scholars read the constitutive-privacy argument as completely inconsistent with liberty of choice and of belief. As Jeffrey Rosen puts it, "I'm free to think whatever I like even if the state or the phone company knows what I read."[12] That argument, which elides the distinction between social shaping and choice, is a product of the liberal conception of autonomy, pure and simple; social shaping negates choice only if choice is understood as requiring a perfect absence of influence.

That understanding of theories of social shaping is far too crude; social shaping need not entail the negation of self. One can choose to understand the autonomous liberal self and the dominated postmodernist subject as irreconcilable opposites, or one can understand them as two (equally implausible) endpoints on a continuum along which social shaping and individual liberty combine in varying proportions. By taking the latter perspective, moreover, it is possible to meld contemporary critiques of the origins and evolution of subjectivity with the more traditionally liberal concerns that have preoccupied American privacy theorists. Postmodernist social theory seeks to cultivate a critical stance toward claims to knowledge and self-knowledge. In a society committed at least to the desirability of the liberal ideal of self-determination, that perspective should be an appealing one. A theory of privacy for the information age should engage it and should explain what function privacy performs in a world where social shaping is everywhere and liberty is always a matter of degree.

The Social Value (or Cost?) of Privacy

Perhaps motivated by the autonomy paradox, some privacy theorists seek to formulate the value of privacy in purely social terms. That approach, however, leads rapidly to the second defect in privacy theory, which concerns the way in which accounts of the collective interest in privacy traditionally have been formulated. Arguments from collective interests typically do not engage directly with the asserted social justifications for seeking more information and so for denying privacy in specific cases. Instead, they advocate privacy by describing some other, incommensurable good that privacy advances. Arguing about whether a general preference for privacy should overcome instances of specific societal need passes over a critical moment in which the specific social need is effectively conceded and linked to a powerful general imperative that relates to the value of information and information processing: more information is better. Failure to challenge the information-processing imperative leaves privacy theory in an epistemological double bind. When it accedes to unrestricted flows of personal information, privacy theory betrays its own deepest commitments. When it proposes to restrict flows of information, privacy theory exposes itself to charges of Luddism and censorship. Failure to confront the assumptions on which those charges are founded amounts to an effective concession that privacy is at odds not only with markets but also and more fundamentally with innovation and truth.

Many privacy theorists have approached the problem of the collective interest in privacy by defining it away. Some argue that the collective interest in privacy is a mirror of the individual interest, whatever that may be. On this interpretation, society's interest in privacy is reduced to ensuring that the individual's interest is fulfilled.[13] One obvious difficulty with this approach is that it succeeds only to the extent that we understand the nature of the individual interest. But presuming a perfect identity of social and individual interests also begs a question that deserves to be considered more carefully. It makes sense to think that society should want to promote individual flourishing, but a societal definition of human flourishing might include interpersonal goods and might value those goods differently than the affected individuals would. Other scholars position collective interests as inevitably opposed to individual ones. This oppositional understanding of privacy emerges most powerfully in communitarian political theory, which holds that the welfare of the community must take precedence over the welfare of the individual. A similar position is implicit in the work of other scholars who argue that security should be privileged over privacy in most cases.[14] Yet the oppositional understanding of privacy does not consider that society may have something to gain as well as something to lose by protecting privacy.

Within the last two decades, a number of scholars have made a more sustained effort to define privacy-related goods that are truly collective in nature. Although there are a number of differences in background and approach among these scholars, they are united in insisting that a just society is more than simply the aggregate of its individual members and that collective goods are more than simply the aggregate of individual goods. According to Robert Post and Ferdinand Schoeman, privacy promotes the formation and maintenance of civil society. Priscilla Regan, Radhika Rao, and Colin Bennett and Charles Raab argue that privacy protection promotes equality. Daniel Solove takes a different, avowedly pragmatist tack, arguing that privacy serves multiple goods, both individual and collective, that are intimately bound up with everyday experience.[15]

None of these theories about privacy's collective value, however, tells us what to do differently when it is time to balance privacy interests against other interests. Here Bennett and Raab look to process. Political scientists by training, they focus on the design of privacy institutions and on getting privacy and privacy advocates a seat at the bargaining table. But getting privacy onto the table brings us no closer to understanding how to balance the collective and individual interests in privacy against privacy's asserted costs. Instead, generalized concerns for privacy tend to give way to countervailing interests that are more crisply articulated.[16] Privacy theorists sometimes explain this outcome by using a version of the availability heuristic: it can be difficult to see how relaxing privacy standards in a particular case would jeopardize the value placed on civility or equality more generally. Overcoming this problem, they argue, requires even stronger, more compelling normative arguments about the social values that privacy serves.

While privacy theorists are right about the central role of normative judgment in privacy policy making (a question that I take up in more detail below), they are wrong about where that normative judgment needs to kick in, and also wrong to blame the availability heuristic for breakdowns in the policy process. On the whole, privacy scholars do not interrogate the information-processing imperative on which the case against privacy rests. They do worry about error costs in privacy decision making; to oversimplify only slightly, privacy skeptics worry about false negatives in the realm of security (for example, overlooked terrorists) and false positives in the realm of commerce (for example, bad hiring decisions), while for privacy advocates, the problems are reversed (for example, innocent citizens unjustly detained and trustworthy job candidates mistakenly rejected). But debate about the magnitude and direction of the error rate elides important threshold questions about the validity of the challenged practices as information-processing practices.

On its face, this reluctance to dig more deeply is very odd. In other legal contexts, it is well recognized that information-processing practices reflect, and often create, social value judgments. In particular, historians and theorists of discrimination have drawn attention to the social construction of purportedly objective statistical "truths" about race, religion, and gender. As Frederick Schauer demonstrates at length, opposition to entrenched societal discrimination is hard to reconcile with commitment to the truth-value of information; the line between useful heuristics and invidious stereotypes is vanishingly thin. Effective antidiscrimination policy therefore requires the exercise of moral judgment about the value of information.[17]

Privacy scholars have strenuously resisted generalizing these conclusions from antidiscrimination theory to information processing more generally. More often, a sort of reverse generalization occurs: privacy theorists tend to think that the solution is better (information-based) metrics for separating the invidious frameworks from the truthful ones. Thus, for example, Lior Strahilevitz contrasts valuable "information" with wasteful "signals," and argues that privacy policy should encourage use of the former rather than the latter.[18] That seems reasonable enough, but it assumes an ontological distinction between the two categories that does not exist. Jeffrey Rosen worries about the risk of "being misdefined and judged out of context in a world of short attention spans."[19] That statement expresses a commendable doubt about the human capacity to judge, but it sidesteps the question of information value. The worry about any particular piece of information is that we will not take the time and effort to weigh it properly, not that the information is somehow wrong "in itself." Still other privacy scholars argue that flows of personal information are best understood as speech protected by constitutional guarantees of expressive liberty. On that view, laws protecting privacy can prohibit trade only in information that is provably false.

When privacy scholars' reluctance to confront the information-processing imperative is situated within the tradition of liberal political theory, it becomes much less mysterious. The information-processing imperative comes to us directly from the Enlightenment; it is grounded in a view of information gathering as knowledge discovery along a single, inevitable trajectory of forward progress. Within that philosophical framework, the interest in getting and using more complete information is presumptively rational and entitled to deference. The truth-value of "more information" is assumed and elevated to a level beyond ideology; as a result, the other work that information processing does goes unaddressed and usually unacknowledged. The free-speech argument against privacy invokes a related ideology about knowledge discovery in the "marketplace of ideas": even if some speech is wrong or irrelevant, truth will emerge victorious so long as the flow of information is allowed to proceed unimpeded.

Faith in the ultimate truth-value of information, however, leads in both theory and policy to a series of rapidly cascading failures to hold back an inevitable tide. If information is always true but only sometimes relevant, where should the law draw lines? Unsurprisingly, attempts to isolate neutral rules of decision have been singularly unsuccessful. Within a liberal market economy, it is an article of faith that both firms and individuals should be able to seek and use information that (they believe) will make them economically better off. Businesses, in particular, want consumer personal information both to minimize foreseeable losses and to structure expected gains. Information reduces the uncertainty that accompanies any new venture because it affords access to a set of conventions for evaluating risk and profit potential. In disciplines ranging from marketing to actuarial science to finance, information processing transforms guesses into their more respectable cousins, estimates and projections, which in turn support the development of new products and industries.[20] Information also is bound up with discussions of risk and security in the public policy arena. In those discussions, every piece of information is presumptively relevant to the task of identifying and countering national security threats.

Faith in the truth-value of information reaches its zenith in processes of risk management, but the information-processing imperative also pervades other areas of activity. In legal disputes, in which uncertainty complicates questions of responsibility and remedy, every piece of information is presumptively relevant to the calculus of liability or guilt. For the modern welfare state, complete information is important to the determination of benefits. In many of these latter contexts, beliefs about the relationships between information and truth are also rooted in another foundational principle of the liberal tradition: the notion that respect for individual autonomy requires individualized treatment. Yet that argument too militates in favor of more information, not less. Whether the starting point is truth or dignity, the rationale for considering particular items of personal information rapidly becomes an argument in favor of collecting and using every piece of information that can be obtained.

Once again, many intellectual resources that might prove helpful to the project of interrogating the information-processing imperative have been placed off limits by liberal legal theorists' profound distrust of contemporary social theory. In particular, legal theorists' perception of postmodernism's deep commitment to moral and epistemological relativism tends to foreclose the possibility that its insights about the social construction of knowledge might prove useful. If, for example, postmodernism cannot claim to help privacy theory make moral judgments about the appropriate content of antidiscrimination law, or offer concrete policy recommendations that might provide comforting certainty to businesses and governments, then what good is it?

Again, though, that understanding of postmodernism's lessons is too simple. Systems of knowledge can be both contingent and deeply rooted, arbitrary in an absolute sense and yet deeply intertwined with norms and ways of living. What literatures about the construction of knowledge afford, and liberal political theory typically does not, is access to the genealogy of a society's moral and intellectual commitments—to the ontological relationship between knowledge and moral, legal, and economic power. This in turn affords a vantage point of partial separation, a position of skepticism from which to interrogate existing presumptions and practices.

Specifically, literatures outside the liberal canon bear on three large and interlocking sets of problems that privacy theory needs to confront. First, they expose the ways in which practices and policies about information processing construct knowledge, including knowledge about the subjects of the emerging information society. Second, they provide resources with which to engage social and institutional preoccupations with risk and security. Third, they enable investigation and description of the ways in which categorization comes to support elaborate social, technical, and institutional infrastructures. In each of these areas, a more skeptical stance toward the information-processing imperative would enable privacy scholars and policy makers to interrogate claims about necessity and efficacy more effectively. In addition, it would enable privacy theorists to offer a more coherent account of the collective interest in limiting information processing and of the ways in which that interest intersects with the problem of self-formation.

The Nature of Privacy Harms

The final conceptual defect in scholarly accounts of privacy concerns the ways that the metaphoric structuring of privacy discourse affects our understanding of privacy and privacy harms. Unlike copyright scholars, privacy scholars are acutely sensitive to the recurrence of spatial metaphors in privacy discourse. Most have reacted negatively to the spatial metaphorization of privacy expectations and interests. For the most part, however, privacy scholars have not carefully investigated the roles that spatial metaphors play in privacy discourse. At the same time, they do not seem to notice the extent to which legal conceptions of privacy interests and harms are structured predominantly by visual metaphors.

Since the U.S. legal system purports to recognize an interest in spatial privacy, it is useful to begin there. Doctrinally, whether surveillance invades a legally recognized interest in spatial privacy depends in the first instance on background rules of property ownership. Generally speaking, surveillance is fair game within public space, and also within spaces owned by third parties, but not within spaces owned by the targets of surveillance. Those baseline rules, however, do not invariably determine the outcomes of privacy disputes. Expectations deemed objectively reasonable can trump the rules that otherwise would apply in a particular space. Thus, for example, a residential tenant is entitled to protection against direct visual observation by the landlord even though she does not own the premises, and a homeowner is not necessarily entitled to protection against direct visual observation by airplane overflight, nor to privacy in items left out for garbage collection.[21] Employees sometimes can assert privacy interests against undisclosed workplace surveillance.[22]

For my purposes here, the interesting thing about the reasonable-expectations test is that it is fundamentally concerned not with expectations about the nature of particular *spaces*, but rather with expectations about the accessibility of *information* about activities taking place in those spaces. Even the exceptions prove the rule: *Kyllo v. United States* (2001), which involved the use of heat-sensing technologies to detect indoor marijuana cultivation, was styled as a ringing reaffirmation of the traditional privacy interest in the home, but in fact upholds that interest only against information-gathering technologies "not in general public use."[23] Similarly, although legal scholars disagree about the precise nature of the privacy interest, they seem to agree that cognizable injury would require the involvement of a human observer who perceives or receives information.[24] Focusing on the accessibility of information also explains why no privacy interest attaches to most activities in public spaces and nonresidential spaces owned by third parties: persons who voluntarily enter such premises have impliedly consented to being seen there.

In short, and paradoxically, prevailing legal understandings of spatial privacy do not recognize a harm that is distinctively spatial: that flows from the ways in which surveillance, whether visual or data-based, alters the spaces and places of everyday life. Instead, both courts and scholars are enormously critical of spatial metaphors in privacy discourse. The Supreme Court has expressed reluctance to extend spatial conceptions of privacy outside the physical space of the home. In *United States v. Orito* (1973), the majority characterized the dissenters' formulation of the privacy interest as a "sphere" that accompanies each individual as lacking any limiting principle. In fact, that conclusion does not necessarily follow — or rather, it follows only if the privacy interest, once recognized, must be absolute, and that is what the Court read the "sphere" metaphor to imply.[25]

Like the *Orito* Court, many privacy theorists are deeply uncomfortable with spatial metaphors in privacy discourse. These scholars tend to offer four principal reasons for their resistance to spatialization. First, some scholars object that the spatialization of privacy interests reinforces doctrinal links between privacy and property. This undermines claims to privacy in public spaces and also undermines claims to privacy in spaces and across communication networks owned by third parties. *Kyllo* has been roundly criticized precisely for seeming to make the physical space of the private home a preeminent consideration. Second and relatedly, some scholars assert that links between privacy and property reinforce and perpetuate social and economic relations of inequality. They note that historically, privacy linked to property has insulated domestic abuse and corporate discrimination from public scrutiny. Third, some scholars assert that spatial metaphors in privacy discourse are too imprecise to be useful. Thus, for example, Lloyd Weinreb observes that spatial metaphors for privacy "do[] not specify at all the shape or dimensions of the space or what it contains."[26] Finally, many privacy scholars argue that spatial metaphors are unhelpful in the networked information society because the greatest threats to privacy arise from the pervasive collection and sharing of information.

And yet spatial metaphors continue to recur in privacy discourse. Even in contexts that are not thought to involve spatial privacy at all, judges routinely and unselfconsciously refer to "spheres" and "zones" to describe privacy interests. Spatial metaphors for privacy appear particularly often in concurring and dissenting opinions in which judges are attempting to explain their understanding of the privacy to which individuals ought to be entitled and that the law should attempt to guarantee.[27] Despite the insistent drumbeat of scholarly criticism, spatial metaphors also populate the scholarly literature on privacy. Articles on information privacy contain numerous references to "zones" and "spheres" of privacy, and these terms do not refer only to defined physical spaces. Instead, they position privacy more generally as a sort of metaphorical shelter for the self.[28]

Even as they criticize spatial metaphorization, privacy theorists often seem oblivious to the predominance of visual metaphors in privacy discourse. An implicit linkage between privacy and visibility is deeply embedded in privacy doctrine. The body of constitutional privacy doctrine that defines unlawful searches regulates tools that enable law enforcement to "see" activities as they are taking place inside the home more strictly than tools for discovering information about those activities after they have occurred. *Kyllo* was deemed worthy of Supreme Court consideration precisely because it seemed to lie on the boundary between those categories. Within the common law of privacy, harms to visual privacy and harms to information privacy are subject to different requirements of proof. Of the four privacy torts, two are primarily visual and two primarily informational. The visual torts, intrusion upon seclusion and unauthorized appropriation of name or likeness, require only a showing that the conduct (the intrusion or appropriation) violated generally accepted standards for appropriate behavior. The informational torts, unauthorized publication and false light, are far more stringently limited (to "embarrassing" private facts and to falsity).[29] Efforts to develop a more robust informational privacy tort have confronted great skepticism, for reasons that seem closely linked to conventions about visibility. Litigants have tried to characterize collections of personally identified data visually, likening them to "portraits" or "images," but courts have resisted the conflation of facts with faces.[30] Information-privacy skeptics, meanwhile, have argued that privacy interests cannot attach to information voluntarily made "visible" as part of an otherwise consensual transaction.[31]

Over the last decade, the principal contribution of what has been dubbed the "information privacy law project" has been to refocus both scholarly and popular attention on the ways in which techniques of information collection operate to render individuals and their behaviors accessible in the networked information age. Many contemporary legal and philosophical theories of privacy are organized explicitly around problems of information privacy and "privacy in public." These theories might be read to suggest that the persistent theme of visibility in privacy discourse is a distraction from the more fundamental problem of informational accessibility. Although the theories differ from one another in important respects, an implicit premise of all of them is that databases and personal profiles can communicate as much as or more than images. Visibility is an important determinant of accessibility, but threats to privacy from visual surveillance become most acute when visual surveillance and data-based surveillance are integrated, enabling both real-time identification of visual-surveillance subjects and subsequent searches of stored visual and data-based surveillance records.[32]

Yet the information privacy law project remains more closely tied to visibility than this description would suggest; its principal concern has been with data trails made visible to others. Solove, for example, argues that for the most part, informational accessibility does not result from a conscious decision to target particular individuals; instead, accessibility is embedded in the design of social and technical institutions. Even so, he uses the term "digital dossier" to describe the threat that institutions insufficiently protective of privacy create. The digital dossier is a form of "unauthorized biography"; a way of representing the individual to the gaze of the world.[33]

Even as information-privacy theorists have sought to shift the focus of the discussion about privacy interests, moreover, the terms of both academic and public debate continue to return inexorably to visibility, and more particularly to an understanding of surveillance as direct visual observation by centralized authority figures. Within popular privacy discourse, this metaphoric mapping tends to be organized around the anthropomorphic figure of Big Brother. Academic privacy theorists have tended to favor the motif of the Panopticon, a model prison proposed by Jeremy Bentham that consisted of cells concentrically arranged around a central guard tower, from which the prison authority might see but not be seen. Architecturally and also etymologically, Bentham's conception suggests that direct visual observation by a centralized authority is the best exemplar of surveillance for social control. Important work in information privacy often invokes the Panopticon and other visual metaphors to drive home arguments about information-based risk.[34] Although Solove critiques Big Brother, his preferred metaphor of a hidden, dehumanized bureaucracy also is heavily reliant on visuality—the problem is precisely that privacy invasion lacks a "face" of its own.[35]

Why do privacy theorists find spatial metaphors for privacy so troubling and visual metaphors so compelling? Situating privacy theory within liberalism's legacy of mind-body dualism goes a long way toward explaining the mismatch between the official privacy discourse of visibility and the unofficial privacy discourse of spaces, zones, and spheres. The understanding of privacy and privacy invasion as transcending space and physicality resonates powerfully with the liberal understanding of the self as abstract and disembodied. Bodies exist in spaces that are concrete and particular; vision is general and abstract, linked metaphorically with the transcendent power of reason.

From this perspective, it is not particularly surprising that the paradigm cases of privacy invasion should be conceptualized in terms of sight. Within Western culture, vision is linked metaphorically with both knowledge and power. The eye has served throughout history as a symbol of both secular and religious authority. The Judeo-Christian God is described as all-seeing, and worldly leaders as exercising "oversight" or "supervision." Cartesian philosophy of mind posits that objects and ideas exist "in the field of mental vision," where truth is "illuminated" by the "'light of Reason.'"[36] In the language of everyday conversation, someone who understands is one who "sees"; someone who doesn't get it is "blind." Claims of privacy invasion are claims about unwanted subjection to the knowledge or power of others. Within this metaphoric framework, it makes sense for such claims to be conceptualized in terms of seeing and being seen and for that process to operate relatively unselfconsciously.

Yet that way of understanding privacy carries significant intellectual and political costs. If it makes sense to conceptualize privacy problems in terms of visibility, it also makes sense to conclude that problems that cannot be so conceptualized are not privacy problems. As Solove observes, if privacy invasion consists in being visible to Big Brother, then identifying privacy problems becomes analytically more difficult when there is no single Big Brother at which to point.[37] And if visibility is linked to truth, it makes sense that privacy claimants often lose in the courts and before Congress. But knowledge, power, and sight are not the same. If "privacy" really is meant to denote an effective barrier to knowledge or to the exercise of power by others, equating privacy invasion with visibility assumes what ought to be carefully considered.

Privacy theory lacks a good account of either the official privacy discourse of visibility or the unofficial privacy discourse of spaces, zones, and spheres, and it needs both if it is to accomplish the task it has set for itself. The way that we talk about privacy shapes our understanding of what it is—and what it is not. Without careful consideration of the work that visual and spatial metaphors do in privacy discourse, it is impossible to have a rigorous discussion about why privacy matters and what kind(s) of privacy the law ought to protect. More concretely, a theory of privacy for the networked information society must address privacy problems in a way that corresponds to the experiences and expectations of real people. Perhaps we should understand the persistent recurrence of privacy concerns around bodies and spaces as telling us something important about the nature of privacy and privacy invasion as experienced. As we saw in Chapter 2, rich and vibrant literatures across a wide range of disciplines suggest that the relation between self and society is not, and never has been, a purely informational one, but rather is materially and spatially mediated. Privacy law and theory need to recognize the importance of bodies and spaces before the account of privacy interests can be complete.

Challenges for Privacy Theory

Finding a viable way forward for privacy theory and policy will require an approach that is temperamentally postliberal and methodologically eclectic. Liberal ideals of selfhood may furnish important aspirational guideposts for that inquiry, but access to the full range of contemporary thinking on the social and cultural aspects of the human condition is essential. Conceptualizing the subject of privacy requires a theory of socially situated subjectivity—a theory of the subject that is less unitary than liberalism's account of the separate self, but more robust than a mere subject position. In addition, it requires a set of disciplinary resources that interrogate the value of information-processing practices and that situate ongoing processes of self-formation in the concrete cultural and material contexts inhabited by real, embodied people. Chapter 6 considers what such a theory of privacy might contain.

CHAPTER 6

Reimagining Privacy

As we saw in Chapter 5, a viable understanding of privacy for the networked information society must consider the complexities of the self-society relation and must confront the assumptions that underlie the information-processing imperative—the culturally determined urge to collect more and more information. At the same time, it must avoid conceiving of either subjectivity or privacy in purely informational terms; both subjectivity and privacy have important spatial and material dimensions. Building on those insights, this chapter develops an alternative account of privacy interests and harms that is based on the emergent, relational development of subjectivity within social spaces that are increasingly networked.

As in Chapter 4, I begin by developing a decentered model of subjectivity organized around three sets of considerations: the evolution of experienced "selfhood" from the situated subject's perspective, the collective dimension of subjectivity, and the play that overlapping social and cultural networks afford. Next, I consider the ways in which the emergence of networked space and the development of surveillance practices within that space affect the processes of evolving subjectivity. In particular, I draw attention to some informational, spatial, and normative dynamics of the networked information society that U.S. privacy jurisprudence and theory have tended to overlook. Finally, I offer a working definition of "privacy" as room for socially situated processes and practices of boundary management.

A Decentered Model of Subjectivity

A comprehensive and robust formulation of the interests that privacy protects requires an account of subjectivity that does not avoid the interactions between self and culture but instead embraces them. Important recent work in privacy theory asserts the importance of context in structuring privacy expectations and interests.[1] Yet that mode of recognizing context also marginalizes it. Context is not simply the background against which separate, autonomous subjects' expectations about privacy emerge; rather, subjectivity is intrinsically marginal, a phenomenon that emerges at the interface between individual and culture. The real danger for privacy theory is not that it might lose the individual irretrievably within the social, but that it might fail to appreciate the ways in which evolving subjectivity subsists in a continual intermingling of external and internal factors.

Situated Subjects

Models of experienced selfhood within U.S. privacy theory typically have emphasized purposive, often solitary activities. Within that scholarly tradition, one way to explore experienced selfhood from the individual perspective might be to list the activities that U.S. constitutional jurisprudence identifies as central to self-development: expression, secluded contemplation, and voluntary association. Without question, those activities are vitally important to the sense of self. Beginning with them, however, returns us to the vision of the autonomous, solitary, disembodied individual that has animated the mainstream of U.S. privacy theory and that has proved to be a theoretical dead end.

If we return, instead, to the framework developed in Chapters 2 and 4, a very different baseline emerges, rooted in the everyday world that situated, embodied individuals and communities inhabit and in the patterns of everyday practice. As in the case of creative practice, the everyday practice of selfhood is constrained and channeled by the fact of situatedness within one's own culture. The contingencies and path-dependencies that shape the content and material forms of cultural knowledge also shape the content and material manifestations of evolving subjectivity. Like creative processes, the processes of individuation that mark the development of experienced selfhood are processes of working through culture; they cannot work in any other way. In examining evolving, socially situated subjectivity, however, we must pay even greater attention to interpersonal behaviors and relationships.

From a baseline of situated, embodied practice, each component of the constitutional model of self-development is incomplete. Equally important is what each leaves out: the culturally specific learning that informs expression; the embodied, socially embedded behaviors that together with contemplation produce identity; and the affiliations that precede and inform voluntary associational decisions. So read, the constitutionally privileged forms of purposive self-development function as markers for larger categories, each of which denotes a different mode of interaction between self and culture. These categories are not mutually exclusive; rather, they represent different dimensions along which the processes of evolving subjectivity can be described.

The first category consists of activities involving the intake, processing, and outflow of cultural goods. Although constitutional jurisprudence treats self-expression as the leading indicator of individuality in this category, the formation of opinions and expressions requires a preexisting cultural substrate. To account for that substrate, we need to include in the culture category all the various interactions with artistic and intellectual goods described in Chapter 4—consumption, communication, self-development, and cultural play—as well as interactions with the artifacts and practices that make up society more generally. Just as artistic and intellectual creativity develops within a web of preexisting semantic entailments, so subjectivity is infused with the ways of knowing embodied in the texts, artifacts, and practices of the culture(s) into which an individual is born. A child born in Boston will come to believe some very different things than a child born on the same day in Beijing or another born in a mountain village in Pakistan. Culture—informational, material, and social—structures what we know and how we come to know it.

Activities in the second category relate to the development and performance of identity. Privacy theorists tend to advance accounts of a selfhood that is solidified through solitary cultivation. Without a doubt, one's sense of self is inextricably intertwined with one's considered intellectual and moral commitments. What I want to emphasize here, however, is the equally foundational importance of performance and performativity. Studies of performance in everyday life meld the methodologies of speech act theory, which emphasizes the performative force of utterances; cultural anthropology, which describes culture as arising through embodied behaviors; and deconstruction, which regards language as encoding multiple texts rather than universal truths.[2] According to performance theorists, identity in a social world exists only insofar as it is performed to and for others. Opinions, commitments, habits, and dispositions solidify over time through the trial and error of performance, just as styles of dress do. This is true whether or not anyone else is present to witness particular actions and whether the actions are intended to demonstrate conformity or difference; all performances of identity, from conduct on the job to behavior at a nightclub to written entries in a private diary, imagine a public of some sort.[3]

Importantly, identity development through performance is multivalent, constituted through and by performances that are directed at different audiences for different purposes. Each of us exploits the inherent ambiguity of language to fine-tune the performances that we enact. What Erving Goffman called the "presentation of self in everyday life" is a more variable phenomenon than Goffman himself appeared to recognize. And for that reason, identity play is both more and less serious than contemporary privacy theory generally tends to suppose. It is less serious because assumption of a particular identity need not entail full-on commitment to that identity to the exclusion of all others, but it is more serious precisely because it enables the trying-on of multiple subjectivities.

The third category consists of activities of individuation and affiliation. While the constitutional model seems to presume associations created ex nihilo by voluntary choice, critical constituents of evolving subjectivity are the networks of relationships within which individuals are born and grow to adulthood. Some feminist critics of the liberal model of isolated individualism argue that we are constituted predominantly by our relationships and only incidentally by our (nominally) separate choices. Yet the feminist model of the relational self is also incomplete. Research in cognitive theory indicates that an important part of early childhood development is the process of differentiating oneself from surrounding objects and processes.[4] This literature suggests that boundaries and boundedness are as important to the development of subjectivity as care and affiliation are.

The answer to this seeming contradiction lies in the processes of social psychology. Socially, interpersonal boundaries of various sorts function to enable differential control over flows of information and affiliation. Alan Westin's pathbreaking discussion of privacy interests, which identified "reserve" as a critical aspect of privacy, implicitly recognized as much.[5] Ultimately, however, reserve is too one-dimensional and intel-

lectual a notion to be useful in characterizing the range of social processes that result from selective withholding and selective disclosure. A
richer conceptualization of the differential control that social processes
entail is the social psychologist Irwin Altman's model of privacy as a dialectical process of boundary regulation by embodied subjects. Although
roughly contemporaneous with Westin's work, Altman's model—a product of the University of Utah rather than the Ivy League, and of the young
field of "environmental psychology" rather than the august discipline of
law—has not received nearly as much attention in legal and policy circles.

While Westin presented a relatively static taxonomy of types of
interpersonal separation, Altman crafted a dynamic model designed to
encompass the range of behavioral processes by which privacy in its various forms is created and maintained. Altman characterized privacy as "a
central regulatory process by which a person (or group) makes himself
more or less accessible and open to others," and identified "the concepts
of personal space and territorial behavior" as the principal regulatory
mechanisms in the process.[6] He observed that the concepts of personal
space and territorial behavior inform a range of privacy-regulating behaviors; together, those behaviors constitute a coherent system for personal
boundary management that responds dynamically to changing circumstances, needs, and desires.

Altman's work showed that privacy-regulating behaviors mediate
human interaction both physically and conceptually; our understandings of selfhood are shaped by the embodied habits of boundary management that we develop. Importantly, moreover, while the term "privacy"
carries with it specific cultural baggage, the processes he described have
a more universal character. Although different cultures have different
conventions about personal space and territory, people in every culture
use personal space and territory to manage interpersonal boundaries.[7]

In sum, when experienced selfhood is examined through the lenses
of culture, identity, and affiliation, it encompasses much more than the
effort to leave one's intellectual imprint on the world through the force
of disembodied will. Experienced selfhood is more accurately described
as evolving subjectivity, formed and re-formed out of productive tensions
between intake and outflow, performance and reflection, contact and
separation. The processes of evolving subjectivity are mediated by the
space-making mechanisms, both literal and metaphorical, that enable situated, embodied individuals to create connections and separations between themselves and others.

Networks of Knowledge, Networks of Performance

Emphasizing the culturally situated nature of experienced selfhood reminds us that subjectivity has a significant collective dimension. Situated subjects grow to adulthood and develop what they experience as selfhood within extended networks of collective knowledge. Consequently, much of what passes for subjectivity is more properly understood as a sort of collective subjectivity, or collectivity—the cultural consciousness within which individual subjects are located. Put differently, the subjectivity that results from the processes described above is predominantly intersubjective, informed by existing, socially situated conventions, practices, and ways of knowing.[8]

In developed Western societies, and particularly in the United States, conceptions of the self derived from liberal political theory play an important role in constructing our socially situated notions of both selfhood and privacy. Although liberal theorists resist describing liberalism at the level of culture, liberalism is itself a cultural construct. In particular, the understanding of selfhood as autonomous, fully individuated, and essentially immaterial is a product of the collective culture of liberal individualism.[9] That culture supplies the components of the constitutional model of self-development discussed above. It also informs the collective discourse about selfhood more generally by providing reference points against which the evolution of knowledge, the development of identity, and the formation of networks of affiliation are evaluated.

The social and material practices that express selfhood also supply situated users with important information about the nature of both selfhood and privacy. Important strands in contemporary social theory examine the ways in which culturally and historically situated practices of self-improvement—or what Foucault called "technologies of the self"— have emerged and disappeared, shaping understandings of what selfhood means and how it is best developed.[10] Practices of self-improvement are diverse, ranging from reading to fashion and grooming to diet and exercise. Some of these practices are undertaken in public and others in private; even private practices of self-improvement, however, reshape the self for an imagined audience. Shared assumptions about which practices belong where inform collective notions of how selfhood is best fulfilled and how privacy is appropriately asserted.

Both public and private processes of self-construction are geographically mediated. In contemporary Western societies, practices of self-improvement and identity play are situated in particular places. Different places, such as the public square, the shopping mall, the fitness club, or the place of worship, figure differently in relation to both subjectivity and privacy. The confessional affords great scope for privacy, but does so in the service of molding subjectivity along a prescribed path; the shopping mall provides little privacy but great scope for identity play. Each place also functions as a situs for the development of collective identity; we are, after all, a nation of church-going shoppers. The objects that we purchase (or worship) and the bodies that we improve and adorn express and reinforce the collective sense of the well-appointed self.

Finally and importantly, collective culture is neither monolithic nor singular. Individuals may claim membership in multiple, often overlapping groups and communities, and those memberships inform the sense of selfhood at the most basic level. Different groups will have different understandings of the appropriate modes of self-improvement and the appropriate boundaries between self and community, and their practices will embody different norms of identity performance and relational obligation. Not all groups will embrace to the same extent the assumptions that inform the liberal model. In addition, information about members will flow differently within a community than outside it. These differences introduce fruitful tension into the ongoing collective conversations about self and privacy. They make collective understandings of the self, and of the types of privacy to which the self is or should be entitled, more fluid.

Acknowledging the informational and material frameworks that define collectivity need not negate the reality of experienced selfhood. Instead, it complements that perspective in a way that is particularly useful for the project of theorizing privacy. It reminds us that surveillance technologies and the expectations (or fears) that they generate are not the only source of privacy norms and practices. Privacy norms and practices are complex and dynamic, and we should pay careful attention to the social patterns and values they express. Locating subjectivity as a cultural construct that has ascriptive and normative dimensions makes it easier to have a conversation about the kinds of subjectivity that we value and about the extent to which privacy and privacy-promoting behaviors play a role in producing it.

The Play of Subjectivity

As in the case of creativity, subjectivity is both substantially determined and incompletely determined by cultural context. A model of subjectivity therefore must consider not only the ways in which subjectivity is culturally determined, but also the ways in which the evolution of sub-jectivity and collectivity eludes prediction. That question returns us to everyday practice and to play. Just as it does in the context of artistic and intellectual culture, play figures importantly in the production of subjec-tivity and of collective culture more generally.

In general, the legal literature on privacy has not considered selfhood as a function of play, but rather has preferred to speak more so-berly of "experimentation" and its connection to the values of liberal in-dividualism. Thus, for example, both theories of constitutive privacy and theories of intellectual privacy advanced by legal scholars stress the im-portance of freedom to experiment with commitments and affiliations.[11] The notion of carefully considered personal experimentation as opening new possibilities for individual development is important, but it only in-completely apprehends the connection between collective culture and the production of self. As we saw in Chapter 2, play does not occur only within the realms of artistic and intellectual culture; it pervades all human activity. Play with texts, artifacts, personae, and social conventions can be serious or frivolous, conformist or perverse, and its consequences extend far beyond purposive self-development. Play is both an agent of cultural production and the means by which membership in social networks is learned and claimed.

Here again, moreover, focusing only on deliberate play yields too narrow a perspective on the ways that play shapes the development of sub-jectivity. Deliberate play moves within a universe of already-contemplated possibilities. Despite their differences, play theorists agree that a distin-guishing characteristic of play is its dual character; play is open ended but also constrained. Equally important for the development of subjec-tivity are the possibilities that are not already contemplated by either the individual players or the rules of the game.

As before, we can round out our understanding of the relation-ship between subjectivity and play by drawing on the concept of the play-of-circumstances. From the standpoint of the solitary, autonomous subject, the Gadamerian conception of circumstantial play described in Chapter 2 might seem wholly external, and even alien, to subjectivity. Certainly, to the extent that play moves collective culture in ways that were neither intended nor anticipated, subjectivity plays a more modest role in that process than some accounts suggest. But circumstantial play coincides with the absence of subjectivity only if one understands subjec-tivity as a fixed point around which play occurs. If one understands sub-jectivity as itself an emergent quality, the idea of circumstantial play co-existing with (rather than negating or subsuming) subjectivity becomes more tenable. On this view, an important function of play is the opening of spaces or gaps into which evolving subjectivity (and so evolving collectivity) might move. Evolving subjectivity, or the everyday practice of self, responds to the play-of-circumstances in unanticipated and fundamentally unpredictable ways. As it does in the domain of artistic and intellectual culture, the play-of-circumstances operates as a potent engine of cultural dynamism, mediating both evolving subjectivity and evolving collectivity, and channeling them in unexpected ways.

Linking evolving subjectivity with the play of everyday practice suggests a complex relationship between subjectivity and surveillance. Because the play of everyday practice is unpredictable, the processes of evolving subjectivity are robust in a way not envisioned by the most dystopian models of surveillance. It does not necessarily follow, however, that evolving subjectivity is impervious to constraint. Surveillance alters the playing field; whether and to what extent it also alters evolving subjectivity remain to be considered.

Surveillance and Subjectivity in the Networked Information Society

The increasingly dense web of interconnections in the networked information society has three interlinked effects on the processes of evolving subjectivity described above. These effects are, respectively, informational, spatial, and normative. First, the information collected from and about people is used to constitute individuals and communities as transparent objects of others' knowledge. Second, surveillance practices reorder the spaces of everyday life in ways that channel embodied behavior and foreclose unexpected behavior. The resulting norm of exposure alters the capacity of places to function as contexts within which subjectivity is developed and identity performed. Third, norms of transparency and exposure are deployed to legitimate and reward practices of self-exposure and peer exposure. These practices are the morality plays of contemporary networked life; they operate as both spectacle and discipline.

This section draws on the emerging field of surveillance studies to explore the informational, spatial, and normative effects of pervasive surveillance. Scholars in that field have brought a variety of allied disciplines—including sociology, urban geography, communication theory, and cultural studies—to bear on the institutions and subjects of surveillance. Their work enables a richer understanding of how surveillance functions, and a correspondingly richer understanding of what privacy interests in the networked information society might include.

Transparency

As we saw in Chapter 5, developing a viable conceptual framework for privacy interests requires more than a decentered model of subjectivity; it also requires rethinking the information-processing imperative, which drives the collection of ever greater amounts of personal information and which conceives of such information as disclosing ever more precise truth. Exploring "information privacy" issues through the theoretical and empirical lenses supplied by surveillance studies reveals the ways that information collection and processing operate as socially situated practices of truth construction, which in turn mediate evolving subjectivity. The privacy interest in information processing encompasses not only the individualized information that surveillance collects but also the informational frameworks that it imposes.

Much work in surveillance studies builds upon Foucault's landmark study of the prison and its role in the emergence of modern techniques of social discipline. U.S. privacy theorists have drawn on that work primarily for its discussion of Bentham's Panopticon; as we saw in Chapter 5, they have understood the Panopticon as reinforcing the conceptualization of privacy in terms linked to visibility. They have tended not to notice that Foucault offered the Panopticon as a metaphor for a different and more comprehensive sort of discipline, which is concerned more fundamentally with normalization. One of his central insights was that in modern societies, social discipline is accomplished by statistical methods: "[W]hereas the juridical systems define juridical subjects according to universal norms, the disciplines characterize, classify, specialize; they distribute along a scale, around a norm, hierarchize individuals in relation to one another and, if necessary, disqualify and invalidate."[12] These processes do not require a centralized authority to administer them; instead, they are most powerful when they are most widely dispersed among the civil institutions that regulate everyday life. These observations, which have obvious application to a wide variety of statistical and actuarial practices performed in both government and private sectors, have served as the foundation for elaboration of the work of modern "surveillance societies."[13]

Surveillance in the panoptic sense functions both descriptively and normatively. It does not simply render personal information accessible—

a trivial extension of the privacy-as-visibility metaphor—but rather seeks to render individual behaviors and preferences transparent by conforming them to preexisting categories. Panoptic surveillance simultaneously illuminates individual attributes and constitutes the framework within which those attributes are located and rendered intelligible. For this reason, the logics of transparency and discrimination are inseparable. Surveillance functions precisely to create distinctions and hierarchies among surveilled populations.[14] Surveillance theorists also identify another inequality embedded in the logic of informational transparency. Transparency within surveillance society typically runs only one way; there is little public transparency about the algorithms and benchmarks by which people living in surveillance societies are categorized and sorted.

Within modern surveillance societies, panoptic surveillance functions both prospectively and retrospectively. From a prospective standpoint, panoptic surveillance enables the formation of statistically based public policy, informing everything from early childhood education to the delivery of health care to the structure of the criminal justice system. But in seeking to mold the future, surveillance also shapes the past. In creating fixed records of presence, appearance, and behavior at particular places and times, surveillance constitutes institutional and social memory.

Importantly, however, surveillance in postindustrial, digitally networked societies is more radically decentralized and resilient than Foucault's work suggests. Building on Gilles Deleuze's and Felix Guattari's work on systems of social control, Kevin Haggerty and Richard Ericson describe the prevailing modality of surveillance as the "surveillant assemblage": a heterogeneous set of public and private processes that are interlinked and seek to harness the raw power of information by fixing flows of information cognitively and spatially. Surveillant assemblages grow rhizomatically, "across a series of interconnected roots which throw up shoots in different locations," and for this reason they are extraordinarily resistant to localized disruption.[15] Of critical importance within Haggerty and Ericson's framework, the surveillant assemblage operates upon its subjects not only by the "normalized soul training" of Foucauldian theory, but also by seduction. Its flows of information promise a cornucopia of benefits and pleasures, including price discounts, enhanced services, social status, and entertainment. The surveillance society is not the grim dystopia that privacy advocates have assumed—and that privacy skeptics argue has failed to materialize. In return for its benefits and pleasures, however, the surveillant assemblage demands full enrollment.

Some scholars use performance theory to interrogate the effects of networked databases and cameras on the performance of identity. Recall that according to performance theorists, "identity" develops through performance and varies contextually. From this perspective, the problem with surveillance is that it seeks to constitute individuals as fixed texts upon which invariant meanings can be imposed. The struggle for privacy is recast as the individual's effort to assert multiplicity and resist "norming."[16] This account emphasizes agency to a far greater degree than the Foucauldian and Deleuzian accounts. It too is concerned with normalization and transparency, but it argues that human nature is much more impervious to normalization and transparency than those literatures suggest, and that the subjects of surveillance are knowing and only partially compliant participants in their own seduction.

These accounts of the effects of informational transparency differ from each other in some respects, but the overlap is substantial. Together, they address many of the difficulties with privacy theory identified in Chapter 5. They recognize, first, that subjectivity evolves as a function of socially situated practices, including information-processing practices. They also recognize that the truth conveyed by personal information can be simultaneously accurate and contingent, constituted in significant part by the logics that inform the enterprises of sorting and classification. To an extent, therefore, they might be read to support the argument that the principal threats to privacy in the networked information society are informational in nature.

The account of privacy as consisting in relative informational opacity runs into difficulty, however, when we consider the problem of visual surveillance in public places. An informational-transparency framework for conceptualizing privacy harms suggests that purely localized visual surveillance is relatively innocuous. The real danger to privacy comes from databases; visual surveillance creates pressing privacy threats only when it is digital, networked, and combined with other sources of information. Yet the theory doesn't align with the practice: surveillance cameras produce effects that are experienced by real people as altering levels of experienced privacy. This suggests that the informational-transparency framework is incomplete.

Exposure

Linking privacy exclusively to informational transparency tends to mask a conceptually distinct privacy harm that is spatial and concerns the nature of the spaces constituted by and for pervasive, continual observation.

Those spaces are characterized by a condition of exposure. Exposure is not an invariant feature of either real or digital geographies, but rather a design principle that can be deployed to constrain the range of available behaviors and norms. Neither privacy law nor privacy theory has recognized an interest in limiting exposure uncoupled from the generally acknowledged interest in limiting observation, and in general we lack a vocabulary for conceptualizing and evaluating such an interest. I will characterize the spatial dimension of the privacy interest as an interest in limiting or controlling the conditions of exposure. This terminology is intended to move the discussion beyond both visibility and transparency to capture the linked effects of architecture and power as experienced by embodied, situated subjects.

Consider an individual who is reading a newspaper at a plaza café in front of a downtown office building. The building's owner has installed surveillance cameras that monitor the plaza continuously. Let's assume the cameras in this example are clearly visible, and clearly low-tech and analog. It would be reasonable for the individual to assume that they probably are not connected to anything other than the building's own private security system. Most likely, tapes are stored for a short period of time and then reused. The consensus view in U.S. privacy theory tends to be that there is essentially no legitimate expectation of privacy under these circumstances and that the surveillance therefore should not trouble us. But those surveilled often feel quite differently. Even localized, uncoordinated surveillance may be experienced as intrusive in ways that have nothing to do with whether data trails are captured.

Because information-based analytical frameworks don't recognize these dimensions of the spatial privacy interest, commentators operating within those frameworks tend to question whether they are real. Yet that conclusion denies the logic of embodied, situated experience. Surveillance infrastructures alter the experience of places in ways that do not depend entirely on whether anyone is actually watching. Governments know this well; that is part of the point of deploying surveillance infrastructures within public spaces. Recall also the ways in which spatial metaphors continually recur in discussions of privacy. As we saw in Chapter 5, even in contexts that are not thought to involve spatial privacy at all, judges and scholars refer to "spheres" and "zones" to describe the privacy that the law should attempt to guarantee. The insistent recurrence of spatial metaphors in privacy talk suggests that something about the experience of privacy, and that of privacy invasion, is fundamentally and irreducibly spatial. It seems sounder to conclude that the information-based frameworks are incomplete. Conceptualizing the privacy interest as having an independently significant spatial dimension explains aspects of surveillance that neither visibility nor informational transparency can explain.

Work in surveillance studies suggests that direct visual surveillance affects the experience of space and place in two ways. First, surveillance fosters a kind of passivity that is best described as a ceding of power over space. As the geographer Hille Koskela puts it, visual surveillance constitutes space as a "container" for passive objects.[17] She distinguishes the spatial shaping that produces "container-space" from the "power-space" constituted by panoptic strategies of normalization, which depend on access to particularized information. But the "containerization" of space is itself a panoptic strategy. Panopticism in the Foucauldian sense is architectural as well as statistical; it entails the rearrangement of space to obviate the need for continual surveillance and to instill tractability in those who enter the space. Our newspaper-reading individual cannot see whether anyone is watching her, but she can see that the plaza has been reconfigured to allow observation secretly and at will, and that there is no obvious source of information about the surveillance and no evident method of recourse if she wishes to lodge a complaint. The reconfiguration places individuals under a twofold disability: the targets of surveillance cannot entirely avoid the gaze (except by avoiding the place) and also cannot identify the watchers. We can say, therefore, that surveillance alters the balance of powers and disabilities that obtains in public places. It instills an expectation of being surveilled, and contrary to the conventional legal wisdom, this reasonable expectation and the passivity that it instills are precisely the problem.

Performance theory reminds us that individuals surveilled are not only passive bodies, and this leads us to the second way in which surveillance affects the experience of space and place. Like identities, places are dynamic and relational; they are constructed over time through everyday practice. Surveillance alters important parameters of both processes. Koskela argues that surveillance alters a sense of space that she calls "emotional space." She observes that "[t]o be under surveillance is an ambivalent emotional event" because "[a] surveillance camera . . . can at the same time represent safety and danger."[18] This point contrasts usefully with U.S. privacy theorists' comparatively single-minded focus on the "chilling effect"; it reminds us that surveillance changes the affective dimension of space in ways that that formulation doesn't address.

One may feel safer from crime, but also more vulnerable to other unpredictable actions.

Marc Augé has argued that the defining feature of contemporary geography is the "non-place": places are historical and relational; non-places exist in the present and are characterized by a sense of temporariness, openness, and solitariness. Augé does not discuss surveillance, but the distinction between places and nonplaces maps well to the affective dimension of space that Koskela identifies. Augé's critics observe that "placeness" is a matter of perspective; for example, airports may be places to those who work there, while wealthy residential enclaves may be nonplaces to those whose entry incites automatic suspicion.[19] It may be most accurate to conceptualize "placeness" both as a matter of degree and as an attribute that may be experienced differently by different groups. Along this continuum, surveillance makes places more like nonplaces.

In short, spaces exposed by surveillance function differently from spaces that are not so exposed. With respect to space, surveillance employs a twofold dynamic of containerization and affective modulation in order to pursue large-scale behavioral modification. Koskela observes that surveillance makes public spaces less predictable for the watched. The relation is reciprocal: surveillance also attempts to make those spaces more predictable for the watchers. By altering the balance of powers and disabilities, exposure changes the conditions that shape the ongoing construction and performance of identity, community, and place.

The effects of exposure and transparency are complementary, and the genius of surveillance appears most clearly when one considers them together. Transparency alters the parameters of evolving subjectivity by imposing normalizing categories and distinctions; exposure alters the capacity of places to function as contexts within which identity is developed and performed. Surveillance directed at transparency seeks to systematize, predict, and channel difference; surveillance directed at exposure seeks to prevent unsystematized, unpredictable difference from emerging.

This understanding of the spatial dimension of privacy is relevant not only to physical spaces, but also to the ongoing debate about privacy interests in online conduct. Recall that the mismatch between online conduct and fixed physical place is one of the principal reasons that privacy theorists have resisted spatial formulations of privacy interests and have supported a purely information-based understanding of privacy interests. Privacy skeptics, meanwhile, assert that whether or not online forums correspond to physical places, online conduct that is visible to others is not private in any meaningful sense. Both arguments overlook the extent to which online conduct and online surveillance are experienced spatially.

Let us now zoom in on our café-sitting individual as she uses her laptop computer to explore the Web, view and download content, write pseudonymous blog posts, and send e-mail. Privacy rules derived from ownership and expectation suggest that she can have no legally cognizable expectation of privacy in most of those activities. The software is licensed, the communication networks are owned by third parties, and it is increasingly common knowledge that online activities are potentially subject to pervasive surveillance by governments and commercial interests. Federal statutes carve out limited zones of privacy, but as their definitional frameworks are challenged by rapid technological change, those statutes more often serve to highlight the absence of a generally applicable privacy interest in online activity.

Here again, the reasonable-expectation standard begs the question: when does surveillance of online activities change expectations in a way that we as a society should find objectionable? As the hypothetical suggests, the question cannot be answered simply by invoking an expanded conception of the privacy of the home. Information-privacy theorists have objected, rightly, that this move tethers spatial privacy interests to a fixed physical space and ignores the fact that many online activities occur outside the home. A privacy analysis for the information age must focus on something other than physical location. The question also cannot be answered by reifying communication networks as separate "spaces." As we saw in Chapter 2, online space is not separate from real space. Communication networks are layered over and throughout real space, producing a social space that in totality is more accurately understood as networked space. Actions taken in physical space have important consequences online, and vice versa. In ways that real space does not, online space contains material traces of intellectual, emotional, and relational movement, but privacy law and policy must be crafted for those who live in the real world.

A viable theory of privacy for the networked information age must consider the extent to which the "privacy of the home" has served as a sort of cultural shorthand for a broader privacy interest against exposure. The home affords a freedom of movement that is both literal and metaphorical and that has physical, intellectual, and emotional dimensions: we can move from room to room, we can speak our minds and read whatever interests us, we can pursue intimacy in relationships. The advent of networked space challenges privacy theorists to articulate a more general account of the spatial entailments of intellectual, emotional, and relational activities. By analogy to what Altman described as the "invisible bubble" that surrounds each embodied individual, we might envision a zone of personal space that permits (degrees of) unconstrained, unobserved physical and intellectual movement.[20] That zone furnishes room for a critical, playful subjectivity to develop. This account of spatial privacy matches the experience of privacy in ways that the purely informational conception does not.

When the spatial dimension of privacy is understood in this way, it becomes easier to see that surveillance of online activities alters the experience of space in the same ways that surveillance of real places does. From the standpoint of Foucauldian theory, surveillance of online activities is a logical extension of the panoptic gaze, and not only for purposes of imposing transparency and normalization. To be most effective, the "containerization" of space must extend to intellectual, emotional, and relational processes conducted online. As in physical space, the exposure of online activities alters the affective dimension of online conduct. From the standpoint of Deleuzian theory, surveillance of online activities furthers the goals of the surveillant assemblage; it hastens the conversion of bodies and behaviors into flows of data. These processes in turn affect the ongoing construction of self, place, and community within networked space more generally.

Coveillance, Self-Exposure, and the Culture of the Spectacle

Other social and technological changes also can alter the balance of powers and disabilities that exists in networked space. Imagine now that our café-sitting individual engages in some embarrassing and unsavory behavior—perhaps she throws her used paper cup and napkin into the bushes, or coughs on the milk dispenser. Another patron of the café photographs her with his mobile phone and posts the photographs on an Internet site dedicated to shaming the behavior. This example reminds us that being in public entails a degree of exposure, and that (like informational transparency) sometimes exposure can have beneficial consequences. (It also reminds us, again, that online space and real space are not separate.) Maybe we don't want people to litter or spread germs, and if the potential for exposure reduces the incidence of those behaviors, so much the better.[21] Or suppose our café-sitter posts her own location on an Internet site that lets its members log their whereabouts and activities. This example reminds us that exposure may be desired and eagerly pursued; in such cases, worries about privacy seem entirely off the mark. But the problem of exposure in networked space is more complicated than these examples suggest.

The sort of conduct in the first example, which the antisurveillance activist Steve Mann calls "coveillance," figures prominently in two different claims about diminished expectations of privacy in public. Privacy critics argue that when technologies for surveillance are in common use, their availability can eliminate expectations of privacy that might previously have existed. Mann argues that because coveillance involves observation by equals, it avoids the troubling political implications of surveillance.[22] But if the café-sitter's photograph had been posted on a site that collects photographs of "hot chicks," many women would understand the photographer's conduct as an act of subordination. And the argument that coveillance eliminates expectations of privacy vis-à-vis surveillance is a non sequitur. This is so whether or not one accepts the argument that coveillance and surveillance are meaningfully different. If they are different, then coveillance doesn't justify or excuse the exercise of power that surveillance represents. If they are the same, then the interest against exposure applies equally to both.

In practice, the relation between surveillance and coveillance is more mutually constituting than either of these arguments acknowledges. Many employers now routinely search the Internet for information about prospective hires, so what began as "ordinary" coveillance can become the basis for a probabilistic judgment about attributes, abilities, and aptitudes. At other times, public authorities seek to harness the distributed power of coveillance for their own purposes—for example, by requesting the identification of people photographed at protest rallies.[23] Here what began as surveillance becomes an exercise of distributed moral and political power, but it is power called forth for a particular purpose.

Self-exposure is the subject of a parallel set of claims about voyeurism and agency. Some commentators celebrate the emerging culture of self-exposure. They assert that in today's culture of the electronic image, power over one's own image resides not in secrecy or effective data protection, which in any case are unattainable, but rather in the endless play of images and digital personae. We should revel in our multiplicity, and if we are successful in our efforts to be many different selves, the institutions of the surveillant assemblage will never be quite sure who is who and what is what. Conveniently in some accounts, this simplified, pop-culture politics of the performative also links up with the celebration of subaltern identities and affiliations. Performance, we are told, is something women and members of racial and sexual minorities are especially good at; most of us are used to playing different roles for different audiences. But this view of the social meaning of performance should give us pause.

First, interpreting self-exposure either as a blanket waiver of privacy or as an exercise in personal empowerment would be far too simple. Surveillance and self-exposure bleed into each other in the same ways that surveillance and coveillance do. As millions of subscribers to social-networking sites are now beginning to learn, the ability to control the terms of self-exposure in networked space is largely illusory: body images intended to assert feminist self-ownership are remixed as pornography, while revelations intended for particular social networks are accessed with relative ease by employers, police, and other authority figures.[24] These examples, and thousands of others like them, argue for more careful exploration of the individual and systemic consequences of exposure within networked space, however it is caused.

Other scholars raise important questions about the origins of the desire for exposure. In an increasing number of contexts, the images generated by surveillance have fetish value. As Kirstie Ball puts it, surveillance creates a "political economy of interiority" organized around "the 'authenticity' of the captured experience." Within this political economy, self-exposure "may represent patriotic or participative values to the individual," but it also may be a behavior called forth by surveillance and implicated in its informational and spatial logics.[25] In the electronic age, performances circulate in emergent, twinned economies of authenticity and perversity in which the value of the experiences offered up for gift, barter, or sale is based on their purported normalcy or touted outlandishness. These economies of performance do not resist the surveillant assemblage; they feed it. Under those circumstances, the recasting of the performative in the liberal legal language of self-help seems more than a little bit unfair. In celebrating voluntary self-exposure, we have not left the individualistic, consent-based structure of liberal privacy theory all that far behind. And while one can comfortably theorize that if teenagers, women, minorities, and gays choose to expose themselves, that is their business, it is likely that the burden of this newly liberatory self-commodification doesn't fall equally on everyone.

The relation between surveillance and self-exposure is complex because accessibility to others is a critical enabler of interpersonal association and social participation. From this perspective, the argument that privacy functions principally to enable interpersonal intimacy gets it only half right.[26] Intimate relationships, community relationships, and more casual relationships all derive from the ability to control the presentation of self in different ways and to differing extents. It is this recognition that underlies the different levels of "privacy" enabled (at least in theory) by some—though not all—social-networking sites. Accessibility to others is also a critical enabler of challenges to entrenched perceptions of identity. Self-exposure using networked information technologies can operate as resistance to narratives imposed by others. Here the performative impulse introduces static into the circuits of the surveillant assemblage; it seeks to reclaim bodies and reappropriate spaces.

Recall, however, that self-exposure derives its relational power partly and importantly from its selectivity. Surveillance changes the dynamic of selectivity in unpredictable and often disorienting ways. When words and images voluntarily shared in one context reappear unexpectedly in another, the resulting sense of unwanted exposure and loss of control can be highly disturbing. To similar effect, Altman noted that loss of control over the space-making mechanisms of personal space and territory produced sensations of physical and emotional distress.[27] These effects argue for more explicitly normative evaluation of the emerging culture of performance and coveillance, and of the legal and architectural decisions on which it relies.

Thus understood, the problems of coveillance and self-exposure also illustrate a more fundamental proposition about the value of openness in the information environment: openness is neither neutral nor univalent, but is itself the subject of a complex politics. Some kinds of openness serve as antidotes to falsehood and corruption; others serve merely to titillate or to deepen entrenched inequalities. Still other kinds of openness operate as self-defense; if anyone can take your child's picture with his mobile phone without you being any the wiser, why shouldn't you know where all of the local sex offenders live and what they look like? But the resulting "information arms races" may have broader consequences than their participants recognize. Some kinds of openness foster thriving, broadly shared education and public debate. Other, equally important varieties of openness are contextual; they derive their value precisely from the fact that they are limited in scope and duration. Certainly, the kinds of value that a society places on openness, both in theory and in practice, reveal much about that society. There are valid questions to be discussed regarding what the emerging culture of performance and coveillance reveals about ours.

It is exactly this conversation that the liberal credo of "more information is better" has disabled us from having. Jodi Dean argues that the credo of openness drives a political economy of "communicative capitalism" organized around the tension between secrets and publicity. That political economy figures importantly in the emergence of a media culture that prizes exposure and a punditocracy that assigns that culture independent normative value because of the greater "openness" it fosters.[28] Importantly, this reading of our public discourse problematizes both secrecy and openness. It suggests both that there is more secrecy than we acknowledge and that certain types of public investiture in openness for its own sake create large political deficits.

It seems reasonable to posit that the shift to an information-rich, publicity-oriented environment would affect the collective understanding of selfhood. Many theorists of the networked information society argue that the relationship between self and society is undergoing fundamental change. Although there is no consensus on the best description of these changes, several themes persistently recur. One is the emergence and increasing primacy of forms of collective consciousness that are "tribal," or essentialized and politicized. These forms of collective consciousness collide with others that are hivelike, dictated by the technical and institutional matrices within which they are embedded. Both of these collectivities respond in inchoate, visceral ways to media imagery and content.[29]

I do not mean here to endorse any of these theories, but only to make the comparatively modest point that in all of them, public discourse in an era of abundant information bears little resemblance to the utopian predictions of universal enlightenment that heralded the dawn of the Internet age. Moreover, considerable evidence supports the hypothesis that more information does not inevitably produce a more rational public. As we saw in Chapter 2, information flows in networked space follow a "rich get richer" pattern that channels ever-increasing traffic to already-popular sites. Public opinion markets are multiple and often dichotomous, subject to wild swings and abrupt corrections. Quite likely, information abundance produces a public that is differently rational—and differently irrational—than it was under conditions of information scarcity. On that account, however, utopia still lies elsewhere.

The lesson for privacy theory, and for information policy more generally, is that scholars and policy makers should avoid investing emerging norms of exposure with positive value just because they are "open." Information abundance does not eliminate the need for normative judgments about the institutional, social, and technical parameters of openness. On the contrary, it intensifies the need for careful thinking, wise policy making, and creative norm entrepreneurship around the problems of exposure, self-exposure, and coveillance. In privacy theory, and in other areas of information policy, the syllogism "if open, then good" should be interrogated rather than assumed.

Privacy as Room for Boundary Management

Reimagining privacy for the networked information age requires that we take account of both the processes of evolving subjectivity and the ways in which the emergence of networked space enables practices of surveillance and self-exposure to intensify. Subjectivity evolves as individuals and communities engage in practices of self-definition that are both culturally embedded and open ended. Surveillance presses against those practices and against the play of subjectivity, in ways both metaphorical and literal. The interest in privacy, which operates at the interface between evolving subjectivity and surveillance, should be understood as an interest in preserving room for socially situated processes of boundary management to operate.

The mainstream public debate about privacy typically portrays privacy as a good infinitely amenable to being traded off against other goods. That debate reflects the powerful influence of Westin's taxonomy of individual preferences about privacy. According to the taxonomy, the production of which was funded in part by businesses that engage in direct marketing, the U.S. population consists of three groups of people: the "privacy unconcerned," "privacy pragmatists," and "privacy fundamentalists."[30] On Westin's account, the privacy unconcerned do not care what happens to information about them, while privacy fundamentalists will not be satisfied with anything but the most stringent, and therefore unrealistic, level of privacy protection. That leaves privacy pragmatists—those willing to make reasonable compromises when the gains outweigh the costs—as the group to whom privacy policy should be targeted. The taxonomy sounds innocuous, but it does important normative work. To be a Westin-style pragmatist is to consent to the continual erosion of privacy in the name of convenience. To want more privacy than the "pragmatists" want is to be a "fundamentalist," a term tarred with myriad negative connotations.

The exploration undertaken in this chapter allows us to formulate a revised conception of what privacy is about and what purposes it serves. As in the case of copyright, the law of privacy must balance a type of fixity against a type of mobility, and the nature of that balance is widely misunderstood. Privacy law does not exist to protect fixed, exogenously constituted selves from the effects of technological and social dynamism; it exists to shelter dynamic, emergent subjectivity from informational and spatial constraint. Both sides of the balance are valuable. Subjectivity requires some stability and predictability; similarly, the development of relationships and communities requires the ability to know and remember certain facts about one another and to coexist in defined spaces. But a society that wishes to remain democratic, vibrant, and innovative cannot hope to do so based solely on practices and architectures directed toward transparency and exposure.

Choices about privacy are choices about the scope for self-articulation. They are, therefore, choices about room to pursue the (unattainable, yet vitally important) liberal ideals of autonomy and critical independence. By this, I do not intend either to romanticize privacy or to readmit the liberal conception of privacy for fixed, autonomous selves through the back door. I mean only to make a narrower claim about the importance of some of liberalism's cultural and political aspirations. In a society committed at least to the desirability of the liberal ideal of self-determination, pervasive transparency and exposure are troubling because they constrain the range of motion for the development of subjectivity through both criticism and performance, and these conditions do not automatically cease to be troubling when the subjects of surveillance have indicated their willing surrender. Such a society values neither the docile bodies of Foucauldian theory, the assimilated denizens of Deleuzian systems of social control, nor the fragmentary, infinitely protean selves posited by performance theorists.

It follows that choices about privacy are constitutive not simply of civil society, as some privacy theorists would have it, but of a particular type of civil society that prizes particular types of activities and particular types of subjects. In this respect, privacy functions as a sort of social Rorschach test, and not simply because norms about acceptable levels of privacy vary from culture to culture. Privacy exemplifies a culture's normative, collective commitments regarding the scope of movement, both literal and metaphorical, accorded to its members.

The privacy that emerges as most important for fulfilling these commitments is best described as an interest in breathing room to engage in socially situated processes of boundary management. Privacy is not only about refusing access, visibility, or interference with particular decisions. It is also and more generally about preventing the seamless imposition of patterns predetermined by others. The privacy embedded in social practices of boundary management by situated subjects preserves room for the development of a critical, playful subjectivity that is always-already intersubjective—informed by the values of families, confidants, communities, and cultures. In a world with effective boundary management, however, there is play in the joints, and that is better than the alternative. And on this understanding, privacy implicates not only individual interests, but also collective interests in human flourishing and in the ongoing development of a vibrant culture. Privacy's goal, simply put, is to ensure that the development of subjectivity and the development of communal values do not proceed in lockstep.

This understanding of the relationship between subjectivity and boundary management dovetails well with Foucault's later statements positioning subjectivity as a sort of critical-ethics-in-operation.[31] To the extent that the subject exists outside the framework of social shaping, it exists precisely in the possibility of change through the problematization of existing subjectivities and collectivities. That possibility always exists in the interstices of the informational and material architectures of social discipline, but it exists more fully to the extent that the interstices are larger and the linkages less complete.

Some intriguing new strands in the scholarly literature on privacy lend additional support to a definition of privacy as room for boundary management in the service of always-emergent subjectivity. Jonathan Kahn's provocative reading of the Georgia Supreme Court's decision in *Pavesich v. New England Life* (1905) against *Plessy v. Ferguson*, decided by the U.S. Supreme Court nine years earlier, shows that for the turn-of-the-century legal thinkers who developed the quintessentially American understanding of privacy as a right to be let alone, privacy and slavery were conceptual opposites. To similar effect, scholars in surveillance studies have documented the use of surveillance systems to control underprivileged populations. A conception of privacy as the opposite of subordination also underlies David Matheson's argument that privacy invasion is a "wrongful relational interference" with one's person, liberty, or property, a species of informational assault on the self.[32]

Implicit in all these scholarly treatments of privacy, moreover, is a recognition that processes of boundary management operate along dimensions that are spatial and material as well as informational. Slavery operates by control of bodies and spaces. Modern social welfare systems operate via similar principles, albeit for rather different purposes. The systems are alike in their casual abrogation of the physical, spatial, and emotional boundary principles that ought to prevail in the state's inter-action with its citizens. In Matheson's treatment, the idea of a wrong-ful relational interference suggests the absence of breathing space, in both the informational and the spatial sense, that deprivations of privacy can produce.

It is worth noting that the understanding of privacy as a set of boundary-management practices is intimately related to the cluster of values that I have argued should inform our understanding of copyright law. The play of culture and the play of subjectivity are inextricably inter-twined; each feeds into the other. Creativity and cultural play foster the ongoing development of subjectivity. Educators in particular have long recognized that engagement with the arts promotes both cognitive devel-opment and transformative learning. Evolving subjectivity, meanwhile, fuels the ongoing production of artistic and intellectual culture, and the interactions among multiple, competing self-conceptions create cultural dynamism.

But the enabling relation between privacy and creativity is even more fundamental. Privacy is an indispensable enabler of processes of creative engagement. Creative workers self-report that the ability to cre-ate boundaries and separations is an essential one at all stages of the process.[33] Freedom of intellectual exploration similarly presupposes and requires the ability to exact a degree of intellectual privacy from one's surroundings. My intent here is not to reintroduce the model of solitary romantic authorship that Chapter 4 took pains to discredit; rather, my claim is the comparatively modest one that boundaries matter in creative practice as they do elsewhere, and perhaps more so. Creativity thrives on a mixture of connection and disconnection; for both creative individuals and creative collaborations, bringing creative practice to fruition requires breathing space.

To restate privacy's role in terms of ongoing processes of bound-ary management is to confront, once again, the insuperable difficulties of expressing privacy interests in the abstract language of rights theories. But this should not trouble scholars nearly as much as it has done. Rights theories help us articulate important aspirations that privacy serves, in-cluding the Millian liberty to develop one's convictions without fear of social tyranny. Those aspirations do not become irrelevant simply be-cause the background assumptions of liberal political theory fail to hold. At the same time, rights theories fail privacy advocates and privacy policy in at least two ways. First, the abstract language of rights without contexts establishes an implicit baseline that is manifestly inaccurate. As we have seen, there are good reasons that privacy is so resistant to the abstractions that dominate most rights theories; it cannot be separated from the contexts and places that give it meaning. Second, "privacy" is itself an abstraction, and a potentially dangerous one. The protections necessary to safeguard processes of boundary management within the systematic, rhizomatic architectures of the surveillance society need to be conceptualized systemically and concretely if they are to be effective.

Economics and behavioral approaches to privacy, meanwhile, risk mistaking satisficing behavior for normative judgments about the socially appropriate extent of transparency and exposure. Those approaches are therefore extraordinarily useful for predicting the directions that surveillant assemblages will take, but at the same time extraordinarily useless in countering them. Measuring the costs and benefits of privacy within a framework that takes satisficing behavior as the baseline tends to elide the systemic externalities that the loss of privacy imposes. Economic insights are valuable, but only to the extent that they might inform a hybrid methodological stance. The challenge for a law and politics of privacy is to ensure that collective practices of surveillance and information processing cohere with other collective aspirations for self-development.

Finally, the conflation of human flourishing with open access to information in all its forms is far too simple and needs to be carefully reconsidered. In some contexts, human flourishing demands reduced openness; in particular, human flourishing requires a reversal of the dynamic of one-way transparency, a rethinking of the principle of exposure, and a critical, revisionist stance toward the normative underpinnings of the culture of exposure. Human flourishing requires both boundedness and some ability to manage boundedness. Respect for privacy does not require absolute secrecy for personal matters. Rather, it entails something easier to imagine but more difficult to achieve: more openness about some things and less openness about others.

PART IV

Code, Control, and the Play of Material Practice

CHAPTER 7

"Piracy," "Security," and Architectures of Control

The changes produced by the ongoing expansion of copyright and the broadening and deepening of surveillance are not just legal changes. The perceived imperatives of piracy and security are catalyzing major realignments in the structure of the networked information society. In an effort to control flows of unauthorized information, the major copyright industries have pursued a range of strategies designed to distribute copyright enforcement functions across a wide range of actors and to embed those functions within communication networks, protocols, and devices. Meanwhile, in an effort to provide security against a variety of perceived threats, ranging from terrorism to fraud to identity theft, governments and private actors have moved to extend surveillance and authentication capabilities across an equally wide range of actors and instrumentalities. In aggregate, these realignments seek to produce architectures of control: configurations that define in a highly granular fashion ranges of permitted conduct.

Legal scholars have analyzed the emergence of digital architectures of control primarily through the prism supplied by Lawrence Lessig in *Code and Other Laws of Cyberspace*. Lessig sought to draw attention to the ways in which code shapes behavior across a variety of domains; to underscore the point, he asserted that code "is" law. Importantly, however, Lessig did not characterize code as the only or most important regulator of online behavior, but rather described it as one of four regulatory "modalities"—law, code, norms, and the market—that can work singly or in combination. In a diagram that forms the theoretical backbone of *Code*, he depicted the four modalities as Newtonian "forces" acting to shift individual behavior this way or that.[1] Most legal scholars who write about the networked information society have adopted this taxonomy and overall approach, and have focused on elaborating the interactions of the vectors that Lessig specified.

Scholarly responses to emerging architectures of control fall into three general categories. Scholarship in the first category takes seriously Lessig's metaphoric equation of code with law, and attempts to assess emerging digital architectures of control using the standards that would be applied to proposed legal regulation, particularly laws affecting freedom of expression. Scholarship in the second category rejects the metaphoric equation of code with law because of code's origin in private behavior. These scholars analyze code as an exercise of economic liberty; code is not law, they argue, but rather the market in action. Scholarship in the third category argues that code is different enough from law that we should consider it unique. On this view, regulation by code raises new possibilities, challenges, and dangers.

Each of these approaches has produced important insights, but each also suffers from the same general defect identified in Chapters 3 and 5: constrained by the commitments of liberal political theory, legal scholars frame code's origins and effects in simplistic and unrealistic ways. To the extent that it offers the vectors of law, code, market, and norms as ontologically distinct tools capable of deployment by disinterested, autonomous regulators, the *Code* framework lends itself to precisely this sort of oversimplification. The architectures of control now emerging within information networks are embedded within broader changes in patterns of social ordering in the emerging information society. *Code's* four regulatory modalities are resources available to be harnessed, sometimes singly but more often in combination, in the service of particular agendas advanced by socially embedded actors.[2] Moreover, those actors deploy additional resources that the *Code* framework does not encompass.

The Emergence of Architectures of Control

We do not live—yet—in an information society thoroughly pervaded by architectures of control. Architectures of control are emerging gradually, in a piecemeal, uncoordinated fashion, at points where the interests of powerful institutional actors align. Nor are architectures of control the result of any grand, sinister master plan; this will not be a conspiracy story. Where such architectures are emerging, they reflect an inclination that is far more deeply rooted and mundane: the desire to use information and information technologies to manage risk and structure risk taking.

Prologue: "Computer Fraud and Abuse"

The story of the emergence of architectures of control begins in the 1980s, with the first efforts to develop laws regulating access to computers and computerized information. For centuries, information about people and about corporate and government operations was maintained on paper and processed by hand. The 1970s and 1980s saw the rise of large computer systems capable of maintaining, sorting, and processing large repositories of information, controlling industrial machinery, and directing the operation of communication networks. This "control revolution" created new challenges for law- and policy makers unaccustomed to thinking about information and information processing as subjects of regulation beyond the limited framework provided by intellectual property laws.[3]

To an extent, existing law supplied templates for allocating rights in the information stored on computer systems. By analogy to existing common-law privacy protections, some types of information about identified individuals might be the subject of a cognizable privacy interest. Many important pieces of privacy legislation, including the federal Privacy Act, date from this period. Alternatively, some (though not all) data or algorithms stored on a computer might be protected as trade secrets.

In many cases, however, whether or not a trade-secrecy claim or a privacy claim might be made, there was a problem that existing laws did not address: the threat of unauthorized access that might compromise the security of the system. By the 1980s, Congress concluded that the time had come for legislation addressing unauthorized access. The Computer Fraud and Abuse Act of 1984 (CFAA) set forth a variety of prohibitions targeting unauthorized access to computer systems designated as "protected." Initially, the CFAA's most stringent protections applied to computers used by the federal government or by financial institutions. Subsequent amendments prohibited unauthorized access to other computers where such access was undertaken knowingly and with intent to defraud or was undertaken intentionally and resulted in the destruction or alteration of information. In 1994, Congress expanded the CFAA's scope substantially, criminalizing a variety of additional actions with respect to nongovernment computers, including unauthorized access that results only in the use of computer time (above a minimum dollar value) and the knowing transmission of viruses and other programs that cause damage.[4]

The CFAA's core criminal prohibitions—those targeting malicious or knowing damage to computer systems and networks—have enabled the federal prosecution and conviction of individuals who deliberately compromise the technical security of information systems or who use their insider status to violate rules of confidentiality. But the post-1994 CFAA also criminalizes a much broader range of conduct on a much thinner showing of intent. In addition, courts have defined the evidence of harm needed to satisfy the statute's $5,000 minimum in a way that enables nearly any violation to be charged as a felony.[5]

In addition, the CFAA's civil provisions have been invoked in cases involving a variety of Web-based activities that the drafters did not contemplate at all. Typically, defendants in such cases have gained access to information that is publicly available on the Internet in ways that the site proprietor dislikes—by using "deep linking" to extract information rather than proceeding through the "front page," or by using automated tools to crawl a site repeatedly in search of up-to-the-minute pricing information. Often, the site proprietor has posted notices, in English or in computer code, indicating that it prohibits the conduct in question. In such cases, the CFAA is deployed as a species of unfair-competition regulation, defining the limits of appropriate behavior with respect to publicly available data according to the data provider's dictates.

Within less than a decade, however, it became apparent that the CFAA had almost nothing to say about many other situations involving online conduct, and nothing at all to say about the appropriate uses of networked information technologies as tools for regulation of individual behavior. Those situations have engendered different and far more complicated sets of regulatory responses.

Pervasively Distributed Copyright Enforcement

In an effort to prevent online copyright infringement, the major copyright industries have developed and aggressively pursued a portfolio of strategies designed to enforce control of copyrighted content at multiple points in the network. This regulatory regime relies on a range of tools, including technologies that restrict the range of permitted information use, contractual regimes for authorizing "compliant" implementations of those technologies, legal prohibitions against interfering with the resulting technical-contractual regimes, other legal rules broadly distributing responsibility for policing communication networks, and publicly inculcated norms of appropriate user behavior. I classify these strategies into six groups according to the behaviors that each group primarily targets.

The earliest strategies for protection of digital content revolved around "surface level" implementation of automated restrictions on digital content.[6] Surface-level restrictions—variously known as copy-protection technologies, technical protection measures (TPMs), and digital rights management (DRM)—operate at the level of individual media files and restrict the actions that users may take with the files. They are developed and implemented at the application level and in freestanding consumer electronics equipment, via licensing processes coordinated by copyright interests and their designated technology partners. Within these technical-contractual regimes, the relevant technical standards are held as trade secrets. Licensees recruited into the regimes must agree to preserve secrecy, and their implementations of the standards must satisfy associated criteria of robustness.

Surface-level protection strategies have produced some notable failures, but also some notable successes. The most highly publicized and widely criticized efforts to implement surface-level technological restrictions occurred within the recording industry. Users, accustomed to unrestricted recording and copying, resented the experiments. New copy-protection systems for recorded music were hacked almost as rapidly as they appeared, and industry efforts to develop a universal, more robust standard for the technical protection of digital audio files failed. A more successful example of surface-level technological restriction is the encryption system built into DVD players and incorporated in all prerecorded DVDs. Technical rules blocking copying are enforced by other technical rules that prohibit play on any noncompliant media player. The system was developed by a consortium of the major studios and is currently administered and enforced by a private membership association, the DVD Copy Control Association (DVD-CCA), which licenses the technology. This regime's success is not due to its technical efficacy in any absolute sense. The copy-protection algorithm, known as the Content Scramble System (CSS), has been broken, and the decryption algorithm, known as DeCSS, is widely available on the Internet if one knows where to look. Most people don't do this, though, and this appears to be a function of two related factors: the technology's universality and its perceived normalcy. Because the deliberately designed limitations have been in place from the moment that DVD players were first marketed to consumers, the operation of the regime administered by the DVD-CCA is effectively invisible; to most end users, it is "just the way things are."[7]

A second, more durable set of strategies for pervasively distributed copyright enforcement has targeted third-party technology companies whose products and services are perceived to facilitate particularly high levels of infringement. In broad brush, this campaign has two complementary goals. First, it seeks to keep protected content protected. In the United States, the primary vehicle for accomplishing that goal is the Digital Millennium Copyright Act (DMCA), which penalizes circumvention of technological measures that effectively control access to copyrighted works and bans the manufacture and distribution of technologies that might enable copyrighted content to be stripped free of its protective wrapping.[8] Second, the campaign targeting third-party technology companies seeks to minimize the availability of tools for reproducing, distributing, and manipulating unprotected content. Equipment and services that give users that freedom—including digital video recorders, digital music players, and CD and DVD burners—work at cross-purposes with the effort to shift the market toward protected content. In an effort to assert control over these segments of the technological marketplace, copyright proprietors have invoked a set of doctrines within copyright law that create secondary liability for facilitating copyright infringement. For many years, the doctrinal structure governing secondary copyright liability effectively shielded providers of multipurpose technologies, but the entertainment industries have deployed a carefully designed litigation strategy to erode the certainty that the law formerly provided.[9]

Legal prohibitions do not physically or electronically prevent the spread of unprotected content or circumvention tools, and for that reason some consider them ineffective. For example, the DMCA did not prevent the development and widespread Internet distribution of DeCSS, the unauthorized algorithm that decrypts prerecorded DVDs. For would-be legitimate providers of digital media equipment and services, however, the potential costs of violating the prohibitions are significant. The content industries have filed a steady progression of lawsuits against technology companies for facilitating infringement or interfering with technological protection measures. Such litigation is widely perceived as deterring both innovation by technology developers and investment by venture capitalists. The potential costs of litigation also have affected independent researchers who study the technological systems that the DMCA protects; many such researchers report having changed their research programs to avoid legal conflict.[10]

The third set of strategies for pervasively distributed copyright enforcement seeks to move automated enforcement functions progressively deeper into the logical and physical layers of the user's electronic environment. Such "trusted system" efforts are, and are designed to be, far more impervious to hacker workarounds. They are also far more inhospitable to unauthorized technologies that an independent third party might seek to market. They are, however, far more complicated to implement. Successfully operationalizing trusted-system functionality across the broad range of personal computing and consumer electronic equipment now in use requires the cooperation of major sectors of the software, computer, and communication industries. So far, the track record of these initiatives is mixed.

The most hotly debated aspect of trusted-system strategies for pervasively distributed copyright enforcement has concerned the role of government in coordinating their implementation. For example, after early efforts to secure a private consensus on trusted-system standards derailed, the entertainment industries requested that government enact new laws mandating the development and adoption of content-protection standards. In the United States, an initial effort to secure a broad mandate covering all computing and consumer electronics equipment failed when the technology industries refused to support it. In the wake of that failure, both content and technology industries advanced narrower proposals, including a "broadcast flag" for digital television content, a parallel regime for digital audio broadcasts, and a proposal that would mandate the watermarking of broadcast content to prevent broadcasts recorded using analog technologies from being digitized. No proposal has yet become law, but new bills are regularly introduced in Congress, and the Federal Communications Commission (FCC) has issued a trusted-system rule that covers the set-top boxes supplied by cable companies.[11] The European Commission also has signaled its desire to encourage the development of trusted-system technologies.[12]

Exclusive focus on the question of technology mandates, however, ignores the extent to which trusted-system initiatives continue to move forward in the private sector. Some focus on implementing controls at the operating-system layer, while others seek to hard-wire trusted-system functionality into every kind of equipment that users might employ to access copyrighted content. Some are offered by a single firm, such as Intel's Trusted Execution Technology, which provides "a highly versatile set of hardware extensions to Intel® processors and chipsets that, with appropriate software, enhance the platform security capabilities."[13] Other efforts to develop and implement trusted-system controls are more collaborative, such as the Trusted Computing Group (TCG), an organization that focuses on personal-computing platforms; the Digital Media Project, which seeks to develop standards for moving protected content across different consumer platforms; and the Copy Protection Technical

Working Group, a broad-based industry effort to coordinate the develop-ment of standards for digital broadcasting. The most recent generation of trusted-system initiatives incorporate cloud-based storage of digital media content. An example is Sony's Digital Entertainment Content Ecosys-tem, a set of protocols for delivering stored content to users via authenti-cated devices and platforms.

The fourth set of strategies for pervasively distributed copyright enforcement targets third-party providers of network services, such as In-ternet service providers (ISPs) and search engines, that play a vital role in the distribution of online communications, including both protected and unprotected content. ISPs serve as gatekeepers for most online conduct by users, while search engines, social-networking platforms, and other sites that host user-generated content play an analogous gatekeeping role in the processes of online search and retrieval. In 1998, as part of the DMCA, the U.S. copyright industries won passage of legislation estab-lishing a "notice and takedown" procedure under which online service providers may maintain immunity from monetary liability by promptly removing material called to their attention by copyright owners.[14] The content industries have made aggressive use of the notice-and-takedown procedure, using automated detection tools to comb the network for un-protected content and generate large numbers of takedown notices. Both the legal merit and the accuracy of the notices are hotly disputed; one recent study found that more than 30 percent of notices presented ques-tionable claims of infringement and many more were technically flawed.[15] Generally, however, online service providers comply with takedown no-tices in order to avoid litigation; this shifts the burden to users to show lawful use before the material can be restored.

The DMCA's notice-and-takedown provisions do not apply to service providers based outside the United States, nor do they apply to entities that merely serve as passive conduits for Internet traffic routed from non-U.S. locations. Nonetheless, the statute contains a separate, little-discussed provision authorizing injunctive relief against a service provider to block access to a specific location outside the United States. In at least one case, the entertainment industries have successfully in-voked this provision to encourage "conduit" service providers to close national borders to allegedly infringing traffic. In 2002, the recording in-dustry sued to require providers of Internet backbone service to block access to Listen4Ever, a China-based Web site offering copyrighted music files for download. The Listen4Ever site "disappeared" shortly thereafter, and the industry dismissed the suit.[16]

The DMCA also does not require automatic filtering, but the copyright industries have leaned heavily on Internet intermediaries to adopt protocols designed to screen out infringing content. They have pressured popular content aggregators like YouTube and MySpace to implement automated filtering protocols for "user-generated content," and have pressured ISPs to identify and block traffic over popular peer-to-peer (P2P) networks. The actions of users at a nonprofit educational institution may not be attributed to the institution unless it is on notice of a pattern of infringing conduct, but the copyright industries have stepped up efforts to provide such notice and have provided universities with automated tools for processing takedown notices and disabling student access to P2P networks. In 2008, copyright interests secured passage of legislation conditioning the availability of federal financial aid on an institution's development of "plans to effectively combat the unauthorized distribution of copyrighted material, including through the use of a variety of technology-based deterrents."[17] All these efforts have borne fruit; although neither for-profit entities nor universities have filtered as aggressively as the content industries might wish, some amount of automated filtering is fast becoming the norm.

More recently, the copyright industries have begun pressuring ISPs to adopt so-called three-strikes programs for terminating users' Internet access. In France, entertainment interests won enactment of legislation that authorizes judges to issue termination-of-service orders. Parallel efforts on the European Union level, however, have not succeeded.[18] In the United States, the Recording Industry Association of America (RIAA) has focused principally on seeking private agreements with ISPs. In 2008, it announced a formal program to pursue the consensual implementation of three-strikes policies. The details of that program and any ensuing agreements are still unknown.[19]

The fifth set of strategies for pervasively distributed copyright enforcement consists of efforts directed at changing end-user behavior. Between 2003 and 2008, the RIAA and the Motion Picture Association of America (MPAA) filed thousands of so-called John Doe lawsuits against anonymous file traders. This procedural tactic enabled them to request the issuance of subpoenas to the ISPs whose services were used to access the Internet. The subpoenas requested identification of the subscribers to whom particular Internet Protocol addresses were assigned at the specified times. The RIAA established a settlement service center to process claims against identified users, offering them a choice between a confidential, relatively small monetary settlement and public financial ruin.

Most defendants quickly settled, but the RIAA eventually concluded that the campaign's costs, including harm to consumer goodwill, outweighed its benefits. In 2008, it announced that it would suspend its end-user litigation campaign to focus on ISP-level initiatives.[20] Motion picture copyright owners have continued to sue individual users.[21]

The sixth and final set of strategies for pervasively distributed copyright enforcement operates entirely on the rhetorical level and seeks to mold public awareness of copyright issues. Entertainment industry representatives have deployed a variety of rhetorical tropes designed to position online copyright infringement, and particularly P2P file sharing, as morally objectionable and socially insidious. In a blizzard of press releases and media interviews, and in more formal settings ranging from conference addresses to congressional testimony, they have equated online copyright infringement with theft, piracy, communism, plague, pandemic, and terrorism. In an effort both to boost demand for trusted-system functionality and to shore up support for government-imposed technology mandates, they have also linked P2P file sharing with the spread of pornography and with increased risk of exposure to viruses and spyware.[22] Meanwhile, they have created and distributed (free of charge) curriculum materials for grades K–12 to introduce students to copyright rules.[23]

Pervasively distributed copyright enforcement is a work in progress; its constituent strategies are evolving and hotly contested. It is worth careful study, nonetheless, both in itself and for what it may come to represent. In aggregate, it works systematically to shift the locus of control over intellectual consumption and communication away from individuals and independent technology vendors and toward purveyors of copyrighted entertainment goods. This shift has consequences for information policy that are as large as any dictated by copyright law's system of entitlements and exceptions. More broadly, pervasively distributed copyright enforcement also suggests a template for architectural and legal realignment to serve other imperatives. In fact, such a shift is also underway, catalyzed by perceived threats to national and commercial security.

(In)Security Everywhere

Although the strategies of pervasively distributed copyright enforcement are diverse, they have a common purpose. This section, in contrast, considers regulatory strategies directed toward a heterogeneous group of issues that are perceived as falling under the general heading of "security." These strategies involve a larger group of actors, and some can appear to work at cross-purposes with others. When they are considered as a group, however, common themes emerge. Architectures designed to promote security are driven by a shared logic. According to that logic, security is promoted by pervasively embedding technologies and protocols for identification and authentication; by cross-linking those capabilities with pervasive, large-scale information collection and processing; and by promoting related (though arguably inconsistent) norms of ready disclosure and unceasing vigilance.

The first set of strategies concerns the monitoring of movement in physical space. State sovereigns have always taken an interest in traffic across their borders, but the development of networked information technologies has enabled them to exercise that interest much more systematically. For decades, border officials have cross-referenced international travelers' identification documents against database records of known or suspected criminal activity. Most recently, those records also include biometric information, collected from all travelers to the United States under the auspices of the United States Visitor and Immigrant Status Indicator Technology (US-VISIT) program. A similar program is used in Japan, and several other countries are moving toward implementation of biometric screening programs.[24]

Within the last decade, and in the United States more particularly after the terrorist attacks of September 11, 2001, government entities have extended their interest in mobility to encompass movement within public spaces. Annual reports on privacy and human rights prepared by the Electronic Privacy Information Center and Privacy International document the use of video surveillance systems in countries around the world.[25] In major U.S. cities and at government buildings and mass transit hubs, surveillance cameras maintained by federal, state, and local authorities are increasingly an ordinary feature of the landscape. In addition, the U.S. Department of Homeland Security funds the installation of surveillance cameras along national borders and in many rural communities that have requested them.[26]

The extension of video surveillance throughout public spaces intersects with a trend toward the privatization of gathering places. Many spaces that appear public—ranging from courtyards in downtown business districts to suburban shopping malls—are in fact privately owned. To an increasing extent, those spaces are subject to video surveillance by their owners. Although the fact of surveillance is often disclosed, private surveillance networks generally are not subject to due process or disclosure requirements. Private does not equal secret, however. Video records held by private operators are subject to production via the legal process and to compulsion by government investigators. More generally, the combined reach of private and public cameras creates many areas in which visual surveillance becomes difficult to avoid.[27]

A second set of strategies seeks to extend and routinize surveillance of networked digital communications. Governments have long been able to monitor telephone conversations, but the basic architecture of the Internet made e-mail much more difficult to intercept. That has changed. Sophisticated tools now exist for inspecting data packets in transit, for monitoring wireless transmissions, and for locating wireless users. Other legal changes enlist network intermediaries in communications monitoring. The Communications Assistance to Law Enforcement Act of 1994 (CALEA) required telecommunications carriers to implement surveillance capabilities that could be activated "expeditiously" following receipt of a properly authorized request from law enforcement. By FCC ruling, CALEA's requirements were subsequently extended to wireless carriers, broadband pager-service providers, and voice-over-Internet providers.[28] The Foreign Intelligence Surveillance Act (FISA) grants the government surveillance authority beyond that conferred by CALEA, and proceedings under FISA are conducted in secret. As is now well known, in the years following the September 11 attacks, the government conducted additional, extensive warrantless wiretapping without resort to FISA.[29] Last but hardly least, numerous sources suggest that agencies within the federal government, including the National Security Agency and the Central Intelligence Agency, engage in large-scale pattern analysis of telephone, e-mail, and World Wide Web traffic.[30]

Yet the push toward surveillance of networked communications is not entirely government directed. ISPs have shown increased interest in examining their own traffic for a variety of reasons—pressure from content owners seeking to enforce copyrights, desire to monetize and prioritize their own proprietary services, and heightened sensitivity to bandwidth usage. A steady stream of incidents suggests that ISPs are actively experimenting with various network surveillance techniques.[31] For many years, the telecommunications industry successfully exerted its lobbying and litigation power to block the issuance of "net neutrality" regulation that would prevent Internet access providers from implementing methods of discriminating among different types of network traffic; as of this writing, it is pressing Congress to prevent a partial neutrality mandate issued by the FCC from taking effect.[32]

The third set of strategies relates to the processing of information about individuals and groups. Within the United States, both federal and state governments now routinely use data mining and profiling technologies to identify suspected threats. Heightened public awareness of racial and ethnic profiling has put pressure on law enforcement to explain and justify the ways that it assesses potential threats to safety. For the most part, the official response to complaints about profiling's discriminatory effects has been a push toward "better" profiling with more precise information. Data-mining initiatives gain added momentum as they become linked to strategies in the first two groups; it is logical to think that surveillance of movement across borders, within public spaces, and across communication networks enhances security more effectively when it is supplemented by good information about risks. Some government data-mining efforts, such as those used to identify potential threats to airline safety, have engendered widespread public opposition. Others, such as a series of recent initiatives to enhance networking and data sharing among state law enforcement agencies by establishing so-called fusion centers, have drawn less attention.[33]

Although government data-mining activities are extensive, they are dwarfed in both scale and scope by data-processing activities occurring in the private sector. Because U.S. data-privacy law is relatively permissive, the United States has become the center of a large and growing market for personal information, encompassing all kinds of data about individual attributes, activities, and preferences. Trade in some information, such as financial and health information, is subject to legal restrictions, but most other types of information flow freely among participants ranging from large financial institutions to search engines to divorce attorneys and private detectives. Flows of data are facilitated by corporate data brokers like ChoicePoint, Experian, and Axiom. To help companies (and governments) make the most of the information they purchase, an industry devoted to data mining and "behavioral advertising" has arisen; firms in this industry compete with one another to develop more profitable methods of sorting and classifying individual consumers. In Europe, where data-protection laws are stricter, there is less private-sector trade in personal information, but also more government freedom to collect and store data about citizens.

Government and private-sector record-keeping and data-mining activities are increasingly intertwined. In the United States, a number of federal agencies have awarded multimillion-dollar contracts to corporate data brokers to supply them with personal information about both citizens and foreign nationals.[34] In addition, the government routinely uses subpoenas to acquire particularized information about named individuals from private-sector entities. Personal voice and e-mail communications are subject to statutory protections against routine disclosure, but governments in the United States and Europe have imposed data-retention mandates on telecommunications providers so that communication information is preserved for later, particularized acquisition.[35]

The fourth set of strategies seeks to distribute protocols for real-time identification and authentication of individuals across a wide range of devices, and to make their use both widespread and routine. This strategy gains added momentum as it becomes linked with strategies in the first three groups; information about real or perceived risks generated through data mining or through the monitoring of movement and communications is most useful when it can be linked to its subjects in real time. Here again, the lion's share of public attention has been devoted to federal initiatives to impose uniform identification and authentication protocols. The track record of such efforts is mixed. In the United States, efforts to move toward a universal identification framework seem, for now, to be failing. Despite repeated extensions of the federal deadline to comply with so-called Real ID requirements (mandated by the Real ID Act of 2005), few states have taken meaningful steps to comply.[36] More narrowly targeted identification requirements have enjoyed greater success. Since 2006, all newly issued U.S. passports include RFID chips that can be scanned by border officials to authenticate the passport and view information about the holder's identity. Worldwide, many countries have universal identification systems, and use government identity numbers for a variety of purposes ranging from tax administration to the provision of welfare benefits.

As before, the focus on government identification initiatives has caused many to overlook the considerable advances of private-sector technologies for authenticating identities and matching them to locations and activities. Global-positioning-system technologies in cars and networked personal devices enable users to locate themselves, but also enable them to be located. Highway toll transponders and transit-system smart cards create records of individual movement. Biometric identifiers are used in many corporate facilities, and have become a popular feature in laptop computers and data-storage devices. PIN codes are ubiquitous and create persistent records of individual transactions. The widespread use of information-based authentication and the resulting heightened risk of identity theft create pressures for even more identification and authentication. With respect to information exchanged across digital networks, the demand for authentication-based security against viruses, spyware, and spam has become a powerful force driving the development of trusted-system functionality. Many innovations in the trusted-system domain are directed principally toward threats from malware and only secondarily toward copyright enforcement. For example, the newest version of the Internet Protocol, IPv6, includes a so-called stateless mode that facilitates persistent identification of Internet users, and was designed to enable secure transactions.[37]

Although strategies for real-time identification and authentication dovetail with the push toward expanded surveillance of border traffic, public spaces, and traffic across communication networks, many private-sector authentication tools have been positioned in the marketplace as serving goals and desires beyond security. In an increasing number of contexts ranging from online shopping sites to intercity highways to airport-security screening lines, "preferred customer" authentication has become a commodity that can be purchased. Data from such authentications feeds back into the data-mining economy, enabling detailed analysis of preferred customers' desires. Technical developments in trusted-system functionality, such as Microsoft's new program of server-level authentication for popular software applications, are positioned as vehicles for portability in an age of mobile networked devices.[38] By making authentication a condition of access to resources stored on the network, such programs can generate detailed profiles of information use.

The fifth set of strategies is directed at the ordinary people who are the subjects of enhanced security measures. While user-directed strategies in the copyright context simply seek to deter unauthorized file sharing, those in the security context are far more complex, reflecting the fact that every person is simultaneously the target of, a necessary participant in, and a potential consumer of enhanced security measures. Some user-directed strategies are straightforwardly hortatory, directed toward recruiting individual citizens to join the corps of watchers seeking to prevent acts of terrorism. Although efforts to fund a formal program aimed at enlisting the general public as the government's eyes and ears have failed, other, more informal initiatives remain in effect. Metro transit authorities in New York City and Washington, D.C., exhort their riders, "If you see something, say something." An eclectic assortment of state and local law enforcement initiatives has enlisted members of the public in surveillance efforts that range from trolling Internet chat rooms for child predators to monitoring illegal border crossings.[39]

Other user-directed strategies seek to inculcate appropriate beliefs about personal information management. The emerging regimes of pervasively distributed security and authentication depend on the ready availability of large quantities of personal information. It is important, therefore, that individuals continue to provide those regimes with the information that they require. Nurturing the optimal blend of vigilance and compliance requires educating members of the public to understand their own disclosures as essential to the purchase of both security and convenience. Thus, for example, one can protect one's credit rating by laboriously gathering reports from each credit agency and navigating the complex processes the agencies make available to resolve discrepancies, or one can subscribe to a third-party monitoring service simply by giving that service carte blanche access to information about one's credit history. The inevitable and often spectacular failures of systems put in place to ensure commercial security tend to be understood as demonstrating the need for still more disclosure so that more tightly controlled authentication can succeed.

As in the copyright context, the sixth and final set of strategies involves the use of rhetoric to shape public opinion on issues related to terrorism, identity theft, and other security threats. Rhetoric about terrorism also invokes threats to the health of the body politic; if copyright infringement is a pandemic, global terrorism is a "cancer" or "virus" that demands comprehensive, drastic immunotherapy.[40] The color-coded threat-alert system promulgated by the Homeland Security Department, modeled on air-quality alert systems that have become commonplace in most major U.S. cities, works to foster continual background awareness of looming, deadly dangers.[41] Notably, comparable metaphors are largely absent from the official discourse about data protection and identity theft, which proceed chiefly in the language of consumer protection and risk management. Panic about the security of personal information would work at cross-purposes with norms of disclosure that feed the operation of security-related technologies and protocols. Private-sector and nonprofit data-security advocates, however, sometimes use the "epidemic" metaphor as a way of emphasizing the magnitude of these problems.

Like pervasively distributed copyright enforcement, pervasively distributed security protocols are a work in progress. What is notable, though, is the extent to which different kinds of protocols emerging in different market and government sectors tend to overlap and reinforce one another, creating a broadly distributed web of authentication points for authorizing transactions and communications and deep reservoirs of information about the behaviors of individuals and groups. As the protocols and associated business models and legal regimes continue to evolve, coming into increased alignment with one another, the gaps in that web become progressively smaller.

Technology as/and Regulation: Is *Code* the Answer?

Within legal scholarship, theoretical frameworks for understanding the emergence of architectures of control all begin with Lessig's *Code*, which has organized legal thinking about the regulatory impact of networked information technologies for the past decade. *Code* was and remains a visionary statement—an effort to name a potent force that legal theory had failed to recognize. Drawing together and systematizing a set of insights that had gradually been emerging within the legal literature, Lessig sought to emphasize both the importance of materiality—of the architecture of the built world—and the regulatory complexity that results from taking materiality into account. At the same time, however, the regulatory framework outlined in *Code* remains situated squarely within the conceptual landscape of liberal political theory. In Lessig's diagram of regulatory modalities, the subject of regulation is the liberal subject: a solitary, undifferentiated dot who interacts with regulatory forces that stand out in sharp relief against an empty background.[42] That framing usefully drew legal scholars' attention to the regulatory significance of digital architectures, but it has hindered efforts to describe and theorize the relationship between code and governance.

Within the framework that *Code* established, the two dominant strands within liberal legal theory seem to offer two principal choices for evaluating the regulatory effects of emerging digital architectures. If code is "like" law, then liberal rights theories suggest that its legitimacy should be assessed by interrogating its effects on the various liberties that traditionally have concerned legal scholars and policy makers. Alternatively, if code is more fundamentally the product of private innovation—a creature of the market and of market-driven standards processes—then perhaps its legitimacy should be assessed in the same ways the law typically evaluates other market processes. Within the tradition of liberal legal theory, and particularly within economic theory, that approach requires a default posture of deference to market processes and a suspicious stance toward government intervention.

Under either approach, however, the precise nature of the relationship between code and human freedom has proved elusive, in large part because of the way that liberty is understood within liberal theory.

The prevailing conception of liberty as the absence of constraint is not particularly useful for describing the ways in which different digital architectures affect the experiences of network users. The foundational assumptions underlying arguments from market liberty, meanwhile, do not describe the conditions that actually exist in markets for the technologies that constitute architectures of control.

A few scholars argue that code is not like either law or markets. Their work usefully draws our attention to the ways that code differs from regulatory tools more familiar to legal scholars. At the same time, however, scholars who analyze code as unique give insufficient attention to code's socially embedded nature—to the institutions and actors seeking implementation of architectures of control and to the mechanisms by which those architectures gain market share and popular legitimacy. As a result, they oversimplify the sort of governance that code represents.

Code, Law, and Liberty

If code is like law, then within the framework of liberal rights theory, the most important questions to be asked about it concern its effects on protected liberties. Civil libertarian analyses of code have a variety of starting points; some scholars focus on property rights, while others are more concerned with code's effects on expression and other personal liberties. Lessig himself takes the latter approach, posing repeated questions about how code affects the freedoms traditionally guaranteed by the Bill of Rights. In general, however, the conceptions of liberty and constraint on which these analyses rely are too binary and abstract to be helpful in assessing what architectures of control actually do. Meanwhile, the metaphors used to discuss architectures of control suggest that those architectures structure experienced space in ways that the liberty/constraint binary does not capture.

Liberal theorists who stress the sanctity of property rights argue that architectures of control simply reinforce prerogatives of ownership.[43] On this account, circumventing a copy-protection device is no different from breaking into a locked house, and owners of digital property may legitimately impose terms that involve collection, retention, use, and sale of personal information as conditions of licensed access. Within a property-rights framework, moreover, personal information floating unclaimed in the public domain is there for the taking. Other property scholars argue that these arguments reserve to the property owner a despotic dominion that is absent in the real world. In the real world, property rights

172

are complicated, interdependent creatures, hedged about with exceptions and conventions. To take one small example, we knock on one another's front doors all the time without invoking or even thinking of legal rules about trespass.[44] So too, they argue, with technological self-help; invoking property interests does not inevitably lead to the conclusion that a property owner can do anything it pleases to protect those interests. But theorists who advance a more moderate conception of digital property rights struggle to locate within the boundaries of property theory principles that can explain exactly when such behavior becomes objectionable.

Scholars who focus on expressive liberty argue that emerging architectures of control stifle individual freedom of expression. This is so, they claim, because architectures of control artificially restrict uses of digital content and foreclose the possibility of anonymous self-expression.[45] Freedom of expression also has become the conceptual fulcrum of a litigation campaign challenging the DMCA's prohibition on devices for circumventing technical protection measures applied to copyrighted works. Neither scholars nor litigators, though, can easily explain what types of architectural constraint would be legitimate within a freedom-of-expression framework. The argument from property rights cuts the other way, moreover. In the real world, private property rights frequently trump speech rights, and copyright owners assert that this rule should apply in disputes about digital property as well.

As this brief summary suggests, both property and speech arguments about digital architectures share some peculiar characteristics, beginning with the confident assumption that one or the other discourse can be made to generate definitive rules for resolving disputes about how much control is too much. Neither property theory nor speech theory definitively resolves questions about the permissible extent of architectural control. More fundamentally, both property-based and speech-based arguments about architectural effects on liberty take as their baseline a conception of liberty that is foundational to liberal political theory, but that maps poorly to the reality of the networked information environment: the conception of liberty as consisting in the absence of constraint, exercised by the autonomous self that remains after social shaping is stripped away. To say that code constrains that sort of liberty is not, in the end, to say very much at all. Physical architectures and human-designed artifacts constrain that sort of liberty, too. Autonomy-based conceptions of liberty therefore cannot help us determine what makes particular architectural configurations desirable or undesirable.

Some scholars, whom I will call the "code libertarians," attempt to avoid the problem of liberty and constraint altogether. They agree that the decentralized, loosely coordinated strategies that I have described evidence intent to restrict freedom of expression, but argue that individual liberty will prove impervious to architectural control. The crux of this argument is the gap between regulatory ambition and technical feasibility. Surely, argue these scholars, it is going a bit far to say that these developments strip people of whatever agency they possess. If we are to take individual freedom seriously, we also must take seriously the individual capacity to resist control that seems unjust. Working from that premise, the code libertarians reason that if new architectural obstacles to resistance and appropriation appear, people will find ways around them. If the new order is this bad, people will refuse to accept it, and if it is foisted upon them, they will sabotage it.[46]

In the literal sense, the code-libertarian argument about the effect of digital architectures on individual liberty is quite right. Technically sophisticated observers agree that a certain amount of uncontrolled copying of unprotected content will always evade the content industries' reach. That argument traces its roots to an important paper advancing what has become known as the "darknet hypothesis," which posits that "any widely distributed object will be available to some fraction of users in a form that permits copying."[47] While it may be a mistake to assume that copy protection on all works will be broken, the darknet hypothesis suggests at minimum that some copy protection will be.[48] For similar reasons, technically sophisticated commentators also tend to believe that efforts to impose perfect surveillance are doomed to failure. Well versed in techniques for withholding personal information, they argue that such techniques are available to anyone who wants them and will become widely used if people come to perceive demands for personal information as oppressive or risky. And the same assumptions that underlie the darknet hypothesis suggest that at least some security protocols will be broken.

Rather than avoiding the problem of liberty and constraint, however, the code-libertarian argument merely relocates that problem within a familiar set of implicit claims about what liberty is. Superficially, the claim that liberty inheres in the capacity for hacking and other forms of self-help sits within a long tradition of civil disobedience to unjust laws (and it has been framed that way, albeit unsuccessfully, in litigation over the scope of the DMCA's anticircumvention provisions). Yet it is potentially far more absolute, premised on a right to defy not only unjust architectures, but any code-based restrictions at all.

Ultimately, focusing on the incompatibility of technical constraints with absolute conceptions of liberty obscures more important questions about what is at stake in the legal and technical realignments that I have described. It does not follow that because architectures of control cannot eliminate residual liberty, they will have no effect on the everyday lives of network users. Exploring those effects, however, requires tools that legal theorists are unaccustomed to using. If we pay attention to some other terms that tend to crop up in debates about digital architectures, they suggest avenues of inquiry that have little to do with abstract liberty or freedom of expression.

First, consider the speed with which the darknet hypothesis has captured the imaginations of academics and policy makers. We saw in Chapter 5 that the debate about how far privacy rights extend in the networked information society is structured in important and largely unacknowledged ways by visual and spatial metaphors. The debate about the darknet hypothesis reveals a similar process at work in the domain of network architecture. Public discourse about the threats of digital piracy, terrorism, and cybercrime positions uncontrolled spaces and networks as sources of chaos and danger. In the darknet hypothesis, that danger is expressed metaphorically as the negation of visibility. Reasserting control over these spaces entails making visible what occurs within them—enabling those in authority to "see" activities formerly shrouded in darkness. Although no single metaphor comparable in power to the darknet hypothesis has emerged in public debate about security and surveillance, members of the data-processing industries sometimes describe their activities in terms of a need to minimize "black space" around individuals and groups.

Meanwhile, despite the negative connotations with which they are burdened, metaphors like "darknet" and "black space" suggest something important about the relationship between the architecture of information networks and the structural conditions of human flourishing. Like the concepts of "breathing room" and "breathing space" that we encountered in Chapters 3 and 5, the metaphors suggest that ordinary people experience freedom spatially, as affording a type of shelter that is important to their own well-being. The possibility of obtaining shelter through hacking and tinkering does not undercut, but instead reinforces, this point, which concerns the baseline held out to the ordinary network user as the alternative to lawlessness. Users who have the technical capability to do so may retreat to darknets or take refuge in black spaces not because they are up to no good but rather because architectures of control allow no other refuge. A society divided between controlled nets and darknets, however, is not the same as one in which a broader variety of authorized spaces are subject to less rigid control. Likewise, a society in which the struggle to retain black space around one's everyday activities is cause for suspicion is different from one in which it is not.

Finally, consider participants' own descriptions of the conduct at issue in legal disputes about architectures of control. In the copyright context, many defendants characterize their conduct neither as trespass nor as speech, but rather as "tinkering"—taking something apart to see how it works or to make it work better.[49] In other contexts, tinkering may enable network users to alter their presentation of identity in some way, enabling them to use information resources without generating data trails. Advocates for expressive freedom have tried to reframe tinkering as itself expressive, or at least innovative (and therefore deserving greater deference by intellectual property laws). But that reframing is both awkward and unhelpful; when all speech is conduct and all conduct speech, the attribute of expressiveness ceases to be useful in informing thinking about the structure of information rights. Taken at face value, the term "tinkering" is a reference to the material environment, not the information environment. It describes the exercise of tactical, situated creativity with respect to the artifacts encountered in everyday life.

The terms "darknet," "black space," and "tinkering" all suggest powerfully that legal explorations of the ways that architectures of control affect human freedom should be proceeding down very different paths. In particular, they suggest that legal scholars should pay more careful attention to literatures that explore how artifacts and architectures shape the experiences of their users and how material culture and social ordering are intertwined.

Code and Markets

Perhaps, though, legal theorists who take seriously Lessig's equation of code and law have simply been pursuing the wrong analogy. Since code is produced, for the most part, via market-driven processes, then maybe regulation by code is most appropriately understood as a variant of regulation by the market. Some legal scholars argue that in a decentralized market economy, whatever modes of social ordering emerge from the market will be modes that are chosen by market participants, including both information vendors and information consumers.[50] Arguably, it is a mistake to regard orderings imposed in this fashion as anything other than voluntary, and if they are voluntary, it is a waste of time to worry about whether they are coercive of individual users in a more abstract, theoretical sense. The problem with this argument, which I will call the "market libertarian" argument, is that markets for the technologies that make up architectures of control persistently violate its most fundamental assumptions about how market processes work. The dynamics of marketplace acceptance and rejection are much more complicated than the market-libertarian model would have us believe. They are intimately bound up with the actions of government acting as both regulator and customer, as well as with decisions made by large technology companies pursuing a variety of self-interested goals. The choices available in the resulting markets are not inconsistent with, and may enable, the imposition of highly restrictive regimes that many market participants experience as onerous.

The market-libertarian argument about code-based regulation is often expressed in the language of economic efficiency, but ultimately it relies on liberal political theory's foundational presumption of separation between state and market. Within the structure of liberal thought, the presumption of state-market separation operates in ways that are simultaneously normative and descriptive. Risks to liberty and social welfare are thought to arise principally from state interference with or entanglement in market processes. This means that code-based regulation is problematic when government attempts to impose technology mandates or when market actors capture regulatory processes and bend those processes to their own ends. This normative theory of state-market separation requires a descriptive model within which state-market separation is the norm and state-market entanglement the aberration. That is, however, a very poor model of the way that networked information technologies actually develop. State and private interests are deeply and inevitably intertwined, and architectures of control are emerging at the points of convergence. The complexity and path-dependence of that process makes it extremely difficult for markets to police.

In the context of copyright, both information providers and governments have powerful (though slightly different) motives for the pervasive extension of control. Information providers seek, first and foremost, to enforce what they perceive as their entitlements. Governments are in general sympathetic to the asserted need to protect private property, both for idealistic reasons related to notions of the social contract and the rule of law and for less idealistic reasons related to legislative and regulatory capture and the promotion of trade-related agendas. Thus, one might logically expect to see extensive state backing of private intellectual-property enforcement efforts undertaken by powerful domestic industries, and in fact this has been the case. Governments also seek to protect online commerce, including all the varieties of "legitimate" commerce in or enabled by the ready availability of personal information.

More fundamentally, however, state sovereigns confronting perceived security imperatives are not indifferent to the possibility of inserting control and surveillance functions into communication networks, nor to the existence of large databases of information about individual transactions and preferences. In the realm of online communication, architectural controls designed for one purpose can easily be adapted to others. Embedded controls that identify and locate information users, purchasers of goods and services, and transit and communication customers also lend themselves well to the reproduction of territorial sovereignty. Comprehensive databases linked to surveillance and authentication tools can empower sovereigns to combat a wide range of other evils—terrorism, or pornography, or hate speech, or dissent.

Devolution of surveillance capability into private hands enables greater control than government could achieve directly. Generally speaking, in democratic societies, government surveillance initiatives incur far more searching public scrutiny and meet with far more resistance than analogous private efforts deployed to enforce private bargains. Many profiling projects undertaken by the government have quickly become mired in controversy. Except among a small group of technological and legal cognoscenti, private-sector trusted-system initiatives and authentication technologies for increasing security in e-commerce have generated comparatively few ripples of alarm. Here the ideology of the marketplace itself reinforces the ongoing realignment of digital architectures. Just as privatization legitimates self-enforcing control and surveillance, so privatized control and surveillance reinforce the perception that the ordering imposed is freely chosen by arm's-length contracting parties. To the extent that such capabilities remain primarily a matter of industry initiative, information providers enjoy much greater freedom to define the scope of their entitlements and the reach of their business models. The emerging network of private enforcement and surveillance capabilities serves both private and state interests far better than more extensive official involvement might. It is unsurprising, then, that proposed bills to enhance copyright enforcement, guarantee security in e-commerce, and confer expanded surveillance powers on law enforcement have exhibited persistent overlaps.[51]

Cyberlaw scholarship lacks a compelling theoretical model of this process. Michael Birnhack and Niva Elkin-Koren come closest, characterizing the evolving relationship between public and private sectors as an "invisible handshake."[52] Yet even that account slips now and then into the practiced rhetoric of market freedom and state coercion. Critical to the emerging dynamic is that each participant in the development of digital architectures of control sees in the other's goals a window of opportunity. Private actors may be worried about the customer-relations ramifications of conducting surveillance for the state or about the imposition of costly and inflexible technological mandates; at the same time, however, they have repeatedly proved themselves willing to risk some goodwill and sacrifice some technical autonomy in return for greater freedom to pursue other goals.

The market-libertarian model of economic governance fares no better when we consider intramarket dynamics. The model posits that (assuming a competitive marketplace) if consumers do not want systems that restrict the use of digital media files or that impose onerous authentication requirements in the name of "security," they will reject them. But the actual operation of technology markets is very different from what that description suggests, in two critical ways. First, the ultimate users of information goods are by no means the most important consumers of the technologies that make up emerging architectures of control. Second, the idealized model of consumer choice that is a cornerstone of the market-libertarian argument does not account for technological and institutional path-dependence.

The primary markets for copyright-protection systems are not end-user markets but rather the markets of intermediary licensors for those technologies. In the copyright context, those markets include both content distributors and manufacturers of devices for rendering the content. Pervasively distributed copyright enforcement seeks to eliminate unsanctioned technologies and business models by recruiting technology companies into the contractual networks that implement technological restrictions. The twin threats of indirect infringement liability and DMCA liability provide strong incentives to join these networks. Increasingly, therefore, the rational strategy is to license content and build devices subject to restrictions, regardless of whether the intermediary might otherwise prefer a different strategy. Large incumbents in the consumer electronics and personal computing markets have greater resources, and they have successfully resisted some copyright-industry initiatives to impose broadly defined mandates that would disrupt existing markets and distribution systems. They have been much less inclined to resist the introduction of restrictions in newer technologies, such as DVD players, digital music and video game players, and software-based multimedia devices, for which consumer expectations are less fully formed. And they have participated in efforts to develop trusted-system functionality for digital media files and digital broadcast content.

Similarly, the primary customers for security technologies include device manufacturers and a broad array of e-commerce companies, ranging from online marketplaces to banks and brokerage firms. The government is not simply a potential source of security mandates, but also an important customer for security systems in its own right. In response to public- and private-sector demands for security and authentication, large technology companies have participated willingly in efforts to develop secure protocols for system access, data storage, and commercial transactions. Some developers of trusted systems, including most notably market leaders Microsoft and Intel, appear to believe that trusted-system capabilities mesh well with other security-related design goals, such as enhanced network, server, and file security. For Microsoft in particular, deployment of this functionality also seems bound up with a number of business-related objectives, including preservation of its market position vis-à-vis open-source platforms.

Large communication providers confront a complex calculus of legal and business considerations. Many of these companies initially resisted content-industry demands for identification of individual subscribers accused of engaging in P2P file sharing.[53] But the large telephone and cable companies that provide most residential Internet access also have other agendas of their own. Cable companies have participated in the ongoing effort to develop a regulatory framework establishing trusted-system protection for cable television content. In addition, many communications companies seek to use their newly installed high-speed fiber-optic networks to establish quality-of-service pricing and to deliver their own proprietary content to subscribers. Therefore, they are not generally averse to technologies for flagging and sorting network traffic.

The choices and practices of content intermediaries, e-commerce companies, communication providers, and technology developers do not prevent end users from resisting functionality that they find undesirable or offensive, or from demanding functionality that they would value more highly, but they make both strategies more difficult to implement and therefore less likely to be pursued. The more deeply embedded such functionality becomes, the harder it becomes to avoid by purchasing noncompliant or alternative equipment and services. This effect will intensify if, as Jonathan Zittrain predicts, users are taught to fear files and applications that the platform vendor cannot or will not authenticate.[54]

The interplay of supply and demand in the market for the technologies that make up architectures of control is further complicated by the dynamics of technical standardization. Like all networked information technologies, the technologies that constitute architectures of control are designed based on standards for formatting, exchanging, and processing information. Standards processes typically occur long before implementations surface in the consumer marketplace. Many standards processes are closed, and the subject matter is technically complex. To become involved in setting standards, users must be determined enough and informed enough to overcome a series of significant hurdles. Some consumer advocacy groups have begun to do exactly this; what remains to be seen is whether these efforts will generate enough critical mass to affect the content of the standards that are selected. Unaffiliated and academic researchers have been more inclined to cast a critical eye on standards and standards processes associated with emerging architectures of control. Perhaps even more than their colleagues at for-profit companies, however, these individuals are highly motivated to solve the difficult theoretical problems that are involved in making architectures of control work.

More generally, standardization creates technical and institutional path-dependencies that are difficult for any market participant to dislodge. Standards can be changed, but change moves slowly, and design decisions tend to have consequences for many generations of products. The licensing arrangements associated with architectures of control add to the overall inertia, creating institutional lock-ins that structure commercial relationships among content providers, technology providers, and other intermediaries. The dynamic of path-dependence is enhanced by some decidedly nontechnical factors. To the extent that draconian enforcement initiatives and heavy-handed public education efforts fuel popular resistance to architectures of control, increased popular resistance in turn fuels and legitimates the rhetoric of crisis and the extension of technologies to control it. The ratcheting-up of a crisis mentality increases the downside risks of liability for independent entrepreneurs and government oversight for standards developers. In short, even as the new control-based initiatives fail to convince end users, they strengthen their hold on the intermediaries whose products, services, and standards define the end-user marketplace.

For all of these reasons, the market-libertarian explanation for the emergence of architectures of control is far too simple. Idealized models of market choice cannot provide a useful template for evaluating the dynamic of constrained, path-dependent choice that predominates in markets for networked or network-capable information technologies. To understand why technology markets are offering particular choices rather than other conceivable choices, we must look elsewhere.

Code as Itself

A few legal scholars have sought to develop new analytical frameworks for analyzing digital architectures, frameworks that reject easy analogies to law or markets and instead ask different kinds of questions. Some argue that code represents a unique mode of governance that is wholly new. Others assert that emerging digital architectures make possible a form of regulation conceived long ago but never before realized: perfect panoptic surveillance. These theories represent important steps toward developing an understanding of how the regulation imposed by code differs from that imposed by law alone. In their confident embrace of digital exceptionalism, however, they also reflect the conceptual poverty of the models of social ordering that predominate within the mainstream cyberlaw literature.

James Grimmelmann argues that regulation by code is both uniquely plastic and uniquely inflexible. He asserts that regulation by code is different and more troubling than regulation by physical architecture because of the immediate and fine-grained control that code permits and because software regulation lacks transparency. Raising some of the same concerns, Polk Wagner argues that law should step in to regulate forms of online behavior so that code will retreat. Both scholars are right to worry that the ability to design highly granular forms of control will tempt policy makers and entrepreneurs to mischief. Within both analyses, however, law and code are the only two regulatory variables in play. The institutional and cultural factors that might lead us toward certain (worrisome) implementations of code rather than toward other possible implementations are incompletely explored.[55]

Jonathan Zittrain tackles the latter question, arguing that the move toward digital lockdown is motivated principally by fear of the unknown. He asserts that networked information technologies should be prized to the extent that they foster generativity, which he defines in terms of a technology's capacity to serve as a platform for unpredictable future innovation.[56] Zittrain's principal worry is that maintaining current levels of generativity may be incompatible with the kinds of security that

182

people want. But because he devotes little analysis to the other factors that cause the policy landscape to tilt in one direction or the other, it is hard to understand either how we got here or how to change current trajectories of technological and commercial development.

In contrast to Grimmelmann, Wagner, and Zittrain, each of whom seeks to develop an account of code's difference out of whole cloth, Sonia Katyal finds conceptual precedent for code-based regulation in Foucault's discussion of the Panopticon. Foucault characterized the Panopticon as the perfect prison, designed to ensure both complete access to those to be surveilled and complete invisibility for the watchers.[57] As we saw in Chapter 5, privacy scholars have long invoked panoptic imagery to criticize the use of networked digital technologies for surveillance and profiling purposes. In so doing, however, they read Foucault's description of the Panopticon as a lesson in the power of visual surveillance. Katyal develops her analysis of "piracy surveillance" along similar lines, arguing that the combination of P2P architectures with laws enabling access to personal information about network users is troubling because it operates to make users' activities visible.[58]

All of these thinkers are onto something important about what code does differently and why it matters, but liberalism's anxieties are also prominently on display in the answers that they offer. Code's capabilities for control do not arise in a vacuum, nor does its generativity. And visibility is only one of the considerations that code puts into play.

Let us begin by returning to the Panopticon. Foucault proffered the Panopticon not as a blueprint for a particular disciplinary institution, but rather as an organizing metaphor for a group of disciplinary strategies embedded in the operation of ordinary social institutions and coordinated by the everyday routines and interactions of a variety of public actors. He analyzed the emergence of hospitals, schools, armies, and prisons as institutions that enact social discipline by targeting marginal, abnormal, or imperfect members of society for treatment, education, socialization, or punishment. In particular, he argued that these ostensibly marginal institutions also discipline those not subject to their control, albeit indirectly. Schools, hospitals, armies, and prisons normalize by partition; by defining, segregating, and disciplining those deemed abnormal or transitional, they simultaneously define and enforce the parameters of normalcy for everyone else.[59]

So conceptualized, panoptic discipline requires neither constant visual observation nor centralization of authority; instead, it depends importantly on several other factors. First, it entails an arrangement of social space that enables but simultaneously obviates the need for continual surveillance. Second, this arrangement proceeds from and is reinforced by the ordinary operation of social institutions. Third, it is accompanied by discourses—ways of organizing and framing perceived truths—that establish parameters of normal behavior. Finally, the institutionally embedded arrangements of spaces and discourses in turn foster the widespread internalization of disciplinary norms. In contrast to the four-part taxonomy outlined in *Code*, the components of panoptic discipline meld into one another in ways that are fluid and relatively seamless. And as James Boyle explains, law that meshes with the mechanisms of panoptic discipline is far more powerful than law that simply seeks to command obedience.[60]

This is not to argue that a properly conceived panoptic model is all we need in order to understand regulation by code. That model is also incomplete in important respects. Foucault emphasized the authoritarian nature of eighteenth- and nineteenth-century social institutions, but the technology-based strategies described above are for the most part deployed and coordinated by a decentralized network of private actors. The discursive discipline embedded in the operation of contemporary market institutions also operates differently; it is not dictated by authoritarian institutions, but rather is generated within a variety of market and nonmarket settings via complex feedback processes. A good model of regulation by code must account for the ways that normalization proceeds under the conditions of constrained, path-dependent choice described above.

In addition, the core commitments of liberal theory tend to disable legal scholars who study code as code from acknowledging two central aspects of the regulatory dynamic. First, as we have seen again and again throughout this book, legal theorists tend to overlook or deemphasize the material and spatial dimensions of social processes. As Zittrain's and Grimmelmann's analyses implicitly recognize, code's normalizing effects do not flow solely from what it prohibits. They flow far more powerfully from what code permits, and how. The STS perspective in particular would insist on moving beyond a crude materialist determinism to an analysis of the mundane, material ways in which code organizes social and economic activity. Of particular interest are the unexamined ways in which code's affordances—the actions it permits and the ways it presents information—shape users' expectations and habits. Regarding architectures of control, critical questions concern the availability of breathing space and the extent of institutional tolerance for tinkering as material (not expressive) practice. For similar reasons, a cultural geographer would want to consider the ways in which code propagates new pathways and boundaries throughout the spaces in which people live, producing configurations that embody new arrangements of institutional power.

Second and relatedly, liberal commitments encourage legal scholars to overlook the ways in which prevailing conceptions of the "normal" are themselves constructed. Code is both a means and an effect of discursive normalization. The design of digital architectures reflects beliefs about rational social ordering that are not themselves givens. It also reflects beliefs about unacceptable risks and the most reliable ways of minimizing them. Legal theorists of technology have difficulty probing these issues both because they have difficulty acknowledging discourse as a substantive determinant of policy in its own right and because they have difficulty recognizing rationality as a culturally constructed norm. Thus, in responding to pervasively distributed copyright enforcement, legal scholars and public-domain advocates have tended to focus on the "theft," "piracy," and "communism" strands, all of which hinge on presuppositions about the extent to which copyright is really "property," and to ignore or ridicule the other, more hyperbolic comparisons. Privacy scholars have preferred to debate whether post-9/11 security measures actually improve security rather than to delve too deeply into the ways in which public discourse invests that term with particular, contingent meanings.

Scholars who recognize code as a modality of governance not reducible either to law or to markets are on the right track. But understanding the regulatory effects of emerging architectures of control requires a model of governance that incorporates factors that legal theorists of code have systematically overlooked. Such a model must accommodate the complex institutional dynamics of contemporary technology markets. It should acknowledge and allow examination of the ways that artifacts and architectures configure their users. Finally, it should permit interrogation of the ways that artifacts and architectures reflect and reproduce social discourses about risk and risk minimization.

Challenges for a Theory of Code and Law

While architectures of control have excited enormous interest among legal scholars, the social and institutional contexts within which they are embedded have not excited nearly enough. The ability to interrogate the assumptions underlying such architectures and, if necessary, to control their excesses depends critically on the capacity to see them as socially driven solutions to socially constructed problems. The four-part *Code* framework has been instrumental in setting legal scholarship on that path, but it cannot take us where we need to go. An account of regulation as emerging from the Newtonian interaction of code, law, market, and norms is far too simple regarding both instrumentalities and effects. The architectures of control now coalescing around issues of copyright and security signal systemic realignments in the ordering of vast sectors of activity both inside and outside markets, in response to asserted needs that are both economic and societal. Understanding the technical, social, and institutional changes now underway requires a theoretical tool kit that encompasses the regulatory functions of institutions, artifacts, and discourses.

CHAPTER 8

Rethinking "Unauthorized Access"

As we saw in Chapter 7, institutional and technological changes driven by the perceived imperatives of piracy and security are reshaping the networked information environment, leading to the emergence of architectures of control. Efforts to develop a framework for determining whether and how law should concern itself with these developments have been only partly successful, for reasons that reflect the analytical limitations of the model of regulation developed in *Code*. Meanwhile, the everyday practice of individuals and communities in the networked information society follows its own rhythms. The mismatch between institutional regimes organized around architectures of control and the tactical behaviors of situated subjects sets the stage for recurring conflict over the conditions of access to networked resources and spaces. It is not surprising, then, that such conflict has been a defining feature of the legal landscape for the past two decades.

In this chapter, I lay the groundwork for a different way of thinking about the architecture of the networked information environment: one that takes into account both emerging social and institutional patterns and the everyday practice of network users. The starting point is a deceptively simple question: what if we inverted the analysis suggested by the *Code* framework? Rather than asking what architectures of control do, what if we asked how users experience the accessibility of information networks and resources, and then considered how architectures of control reshape that experience? *Code*'s implicit orientation toward the liberal subject—the solitary, unknowable dot at the heart of the regulatory matrix—results in relative indifference to the first question. How might foregrounding the experience of situated, embodied users affect our understanding of both network architectures and the institutional and social patterns within which they are embedded?

The analysis proceeds in three parts. First, I consider the accessibility of information networks and resources from the perspective of the situated user. Although the analysis roughly follows the pattern begun in Chapters 4 and 6, it is also different. Those chapters sought to "decenter" understandings of creativity and subjectivity, detaching them from individualist and intentionalist perspectives on creativity and self-formation. In the context of disputes about access, it has become vitally important to recover an individualist perspective, albeit a reconfigured one, to provide a baseline for evaluating the institutional and technological changes now underway. Accordingly, this chapter develops a "recentered" model of accessibility that considers the ways in which networked information technologies, including both technologies of control and technologies of more general application, structure the experienced accessibility of network resources. Networked information technologies have some features that empower users and other features that create new challenges for everyday practice. We saw in Chapter 2 that technologies and artifacts mediate our perceptions of the possible; we use them to remake our world, but we also take the world they present to us as given. For some time now, networked information technologies have been evolving in a direction that reinforces the latter process, rendering the operation of the networked information environment increasingly opaque.

Next, I explore the ways in which the emergence of architectures of control alters the experienced accessibility of networked resources and spaces. Architectures of control and the institutional arrangements within which they are embedded do not simply aim to define the boundaries of legal entitlements, nor to create and rationalize information flows within markets and government information systems. They reflect a fundamental shift in our political economy, toward a system of governance based on precisely defined, continually updated authorization of access by and to actors, resources, and devices. Within the emerging regimes of authorization, discourses of national security, economic security, and technical authority work to reinforce a system of differential accessibility to information about the network's operation. Paradoxically, those discourses derive enormous power from the fact that they have taken root within an ideology of openness in which precepts about open government and open markets function both as received truths and as cardinal aspirations. Although regimes of authorization have no necessary connection to authoritarian political forms, they work to instantiate a system of governance that is authoritarian in the generic sense: one that favors compliant submission to authority. They seek to produce not only willing vendors, consumers, and citizens, but also tractable ones, and they seek these changes not merely at the behavioral level, but at the infrastructural level as well.

Finally, I consider regimes of authorization in relation to the theory of information rights and human flourishing developed in this book. The topic of accessibility presents difficult problems for law, policy, and theory. Limits on access to technical protocols and networked resources can be enormously important to social welfare; therefore, the law sometimes must reinforce such limits. But flexibility in the conditions of access to technical protocols and networked resources is also vital to human flourishing; therefore, the law should not reinforce regimes of authorization wherever they are asserted, and sometimes should seek to limit the reach of such regimes. Like the rules and institutions that confer and enforce copyright entitlements and those that confer or withhold privacy protection, the rules and institutions that regulate the network's accessibility should acknowledge and accommodate the play of everyday practice.

A Recentered Model of Accessibility

In legal theory, discussions about the conditions of accessibility tend to become discussions of ownership status. Here, however, I am not concerned with ownership, but rather with the practical accessibility of network resources. It is useful to approach that topic by jettisoning the conventional, ownership-related categories of public/private and property/commons in favor of a more open-ended conceptual analysis of the geographies now emerging within networked space. I begin by sketching some alternate formulations of the ways in which networked information technologies create, disrupt, and regulate geographies of accessibility. Next, I consider how situated users experience the accessibility of the network and its constituent resources, both informational and technical. Finally, I explore the complex relationship between the design of networked information technologies and the everyday practice of network users.

Geographies of Accessibility in Networked Space

Experientially, accessibility has spatial, material, and temporal dimensions. A given resource may be theoretically accessible but geographically remote, technically or practically difficult to acquire, or old and hard to find. Although accessibility works differently, and sometimes more easily, in networked space than it does in real space, considerations of space, materiality, and time remain important in determining whether, how, and by whom particular resources will be found. Accessibility in networked space has geographic patterns of its own. Those patterns highlight the importance of technical protocols and processes in mediating the accessibility of networked resources.

As Chapter 2 explained, networked space is constituted by flows of information and communication that are layered over real-space geographies. The geography of networked space is defined by those flows—and, importantly, by their borders. In general, the borders of networked space are not tightly linked to national borders, but this does not mean that flows of networked information are unbounded. We are accustomed to thinking of borders as signaling fixed, binary points of demarcation, but geographers and scholars of human migration have long recognized that borders depend importantly on socially constructed rules. For example, applicants for a visa to travel to the United States encounter the national "border" while still in their home countries; the duty-free section of Charles de Gaulle Airport is decreed to be borderless for some purposes while remaining subject to French law for others. Saskia Sassen argues that borders are more accurately described as analytic "borderlands," the sets of conditions that govern passage from one domain to another. Those conditions are discursive as well as physical, and derive much of their power from the extent to which their foundational assumptions—about sovereignty, legal authority, and so on—are taken for granted.[1] So too with networked space, which has analytic borderlands of its own.

Networked space makes the discursive aspect of borders manifest; even its physical boundaries derive from semantic conditions—from rules instantiated in code that could be arranged in some other way. Yet the practical operation of network borders reminds us that discursive boundaries are no less powerful than physical ones. Flows of information, communication, and commerce move in patterns structured by both technical protocols and rules of network behavior. Technical protocols such as search algorithms and automated filters determine which information is shown to particular users and how it is shown. Often, decisions about the provision of information are based on information automatically collected from and about users. The rules that determine the distance between networked resources are constituted dynamically by the linking practices of network users and the indexing practices of search engines, which together determine the paths that connect one resource to the next.[2] The resulting patterns establish the topologies that network users must negotiate.

Technical protocols determine not only the direction and boundaries of information flows, but also the scale of the economic, social, and cultural processes to which they relate. In real space, we intuitively grasp the significance of scale in shaping the patterns of everyday practice. Some processes are local, others citywide, others national, and the scale of a particular process or institution affects the way that both participants and bystanders experience it. So too with the geographies of networked space. Some processes in networked space, such as auctions for collectibles on eBay or discussion boards on CNN.com, take place on a grand scale. Others, such as dedicated members-only listservs, operate on a scale that is smaller and more intimate.

The emergence of networked space, however, has also changed the scale on which many social processes occur. The social science literature on globalization identifies the emergence of a new sense of space as simultaneously global and local, without mediating levels in between. Geographers have deployed the term "glocal" to describe this space, which simultaneously collapses some scales and renders others inconceivably large.[3] Glocal space is a by-product of the emergence of networked space: it is produced by the extension of information and communication networks throughout real space, and by the interpenetration of the real and the virtual. The space that results from this process increasingly is characterized by the technologically mediated disappearance of intermediate levels of scale between local and global.

Within legal and policy discussions about the networked information society, scale is often understood as a purely technical phenomenon, while scalability and interconnectivity are assumed to be generally beneficial. Those assumptions are far too simple. Scalability furthers some goals that are worth pursuing, such as communication and competition, but undermines others. The seamless interoperability that enables global communication also enables global data flows of personal information. The demise of "walled gardens" in social networking may enable easier networking across larger and larger communities, but also may increase the likelihood of unwanted information flows to community members and make communities too large to sustain certain types of interaction. Standardization in copyright law shapes cultural practices globally, but increasing globalization leaves less and less room for heterogeneity, contextual separation, and local variation.[4] The ostensibly technical question "Does it scale?" thus both crystallizes and masks questions that are fundamentally political. Like borders, scale depends in part on analytical constructs, this time relating to the appropriate scope of social, cultural, and economic activity.

Finally, accessibility has a temporal dimension. Other things being equal, information is more likely to be accessible to someone if it is stored in a relatively permanent, easily searchable form. With respect to both variables, a very odd dynamic is beginning to emerge. Artistic and intellectual culture is relatively inaccessible and ephemeral, while personal information is relatively ubiquitous and persistent. Those de facto policies are expressed and effectuated via the technical protocols that govern the storage, retention, and searchability of digital information, and via a wide range of associated institutional practices.

Within the domain of copyright, legal and technological developments are producing a world in which the conditions of access to cultural and informational resources are carefully controlled, and those resources are constantly at risk of disappearing. The archival practices of portals for proprietary content vary considerably, and many such portals use robot.txt files to block caching and archiving by search engines. Intermediaries such as libraries, booksellers, and search engines still play important roles in providing access to these resources, but an increasing number of copyright disputes seek to limit the types of access that intermediaries can offer. Confronted with shrinking budgets and shelf space, many libraries are dismantling their stacks and moving physical copies to remote storage. In place of physical texts, they offer patrons access to digital versions provided by proprietary subscription services that require continual payment streams. And "going digital" also creates new risks to cultural memory. Digital storage formats have proved to be far more unstable than paper over the long term. Ironically, then, there is a large risk that efforts to create comprehensive digital archives may hasten the processes of cultural forgetting that they seek to prevent.[5] In his 2006 novel, *Rainbows End*, Vernor Vinge described the spectacle of staff members at a large university library systematically ripping up physical books to scan them into a digital library. In the era of Google Book Search, Vinge's vision seems both otherworldly and mundane. Although Google does not destroy the rare books that it is archiving in partnership with university libraries, a key factor in Google's proposed settlement with the publishing industry is the effective disassembly, from the user's perspective, of archived materials as they appear in search results.[6]

Within the domain of privacy, the landscape of memory and

absence is oddly inverted. Network architectures constitute social memory along with cultural memory. In the age of "Web 2.0" social-networking technologies and real-time Internet archiving, information about individuals, communities, and groups is increasingly distributed and persistent. Internet archivists and open-access activists may deplore the absence of, say, great books in open archives, but they have been less willing to consider the privacy-related consequences of the "store everything" mentality.[7] As a practical matter, of course, the refusal to make explicit value judgments about the relative merits of different categories of information is itself a judgment—that everything is worth storing for historical reasons, and that no other considerations are relevant. Increasingly, we lack what Michael Curry and Leah Lievrouw call "ecologies of forgetting"—information environments that afford anonymity and ephemerality for those who desire it.[8]

Access to the protocols and processes that regulate geographies of accessibility and inaccessibility in networked space ought to be a subject of paramount concern both for scholars studying the network and for ordinary network users. Yet, as we will see next, a growing constellation of factors—business models, legal doctrines, and accepted design practice—operates to diminish the technical accessibility of the network, obscuring important aspects of the structure and operation of the networked information environment from those who inhabit it. This is so both for technologies that legal scholars have recognized as implicated in architectures of control and for those that they have not.

Situated Users, Reconsidered

How do network users experience the accessibility of resources within networked space? The answer to that question is oddly self-contradictory. For situated users of network resources, networked information technologies enable access to an astonishing bounty of information resources, including technical and scientific information. Often, though, the information abundance of the network contrasts with technical inscrutability in the platforms, portals, and devices that mediate access to the network. The experience of networked space is both increasingly personalized and increasingly opaque.

Information networks offer users an unprecedented wealth of information and an equally unprecedented opportunity for collaboration with like-minded others. It is an oversimplification to say the network's resources are unlimited, or that anything "on the Internet" is instantly available to anyone who connects. Any habitual Internet user knows that although information resources made available via the network are, in theory, equally accessible to all network users, some resources are more available than others. Experientially, the accessibility of those resources is structured by our own inclinations and affinities—by the various human, cultural, and geographic networks within which we are situated. Here the analysis largely duplicates that in Chapters 4 and 6; the process of working through the cultural landscape is, increasingly, a process of working through the networked landscape. The "network of networks" makes boundaries more porous, but still we must begin where we are. Even so, the end result of that process is a qualitatively enormous increase in access to both information and people.

In this chapter, however, I am concerned not only with the accessibility of information resources made available via the network, but also with the accessibility of the network itself—with the technical processes by which it operates and with the ways that those processes shape both our settled routines and our far-ranging explorations. Here the picture becomes more complicated. For some time now, networked information technologies have been evolving in directions that make them simultaneously more convenient—more intuitive, more portable, more seamlessly integrated with our lives—and less accessible in their own right.

In contemporary debates about technology policy, questions about technical accessibility are often subsumed within the rubric of "network neutrality," a term that refers to the conditions under which third-party information providers can access proprietary networks and platforms to offer their services. The network neutrality debate has for the most part proceeded on the presumption that concerns about access to information can be satisfactorily resolved via open and nondiscriminatory treatment of information service providers. Some think market competition will produce that effect; others disagree. The U.S. Federal Communications Commission has called for transparency about network-management practices that affect the treatment of third-party providers, and has attempted to mandate neutrality for some (though not all) types of network providers.[9] For the most part, however, parties to the network neutrality debate do not express a comparable level of concern about the technical transparency to users of the processes that govern access to information.

In fact, neutral provision of access to third-party information providers and technical transparency of the network to users do not necessarily go hand in hand. For the technically trained, this point can be difficult to grasp. From a technical standpoint, the network does not exist as a single entity. Layered atop the Internet's basic protocols are a hodge-podge of applications and networked devices, some understood as "open" and some embedded within emerging architectures of control. From the network perspective, accessibility is determined by the rules that operate at every layer, and those rules can be disaggregated, examined, and chosen or avoided. From the perspective of the ordinary, situated user, though, things look different. Ordinary users experience not rules but effects; together, those effects determine the affordances of the network and its constituent applications—the possibilities for action that the network creates.[10] The rules that produce the effects need not be explained or disclosed, and increasingly are not.

Consider first the regimes of "trusted computing" that the copyright industries have sought to implement. Early models of DRM envisioned a set of atomized authorization processes, but that model collided with user expectations. In an age of increasing mobility, users want to take their content with them, place- and time-shifting it to suit their needs without constantly needing to obtain reauthorization. One proposed solution to these problems is an application of trusted computing sometimes called the personal digital network (PDN) or personal digital network environment (PDNE), which would extend throughout a designated space or across a designated set of consumer electronics equipment. The most important feature of the PDN is seamless plug-and-play capability; within a successfully designed PDN, the transitions between authorized devices should be effortless from the user's point of view.[11]

The seamless PDN is still a long way from implementation, but it is clear that portability of content does not equal transparency of operation. In addition, portability likely will go hand in hand with other changes in functionality that are less appealing to users. In major content-side initiatives, portability is highly leveraged, but only across authorized equipment, while both sharing and repurposing of media files are significantly restricted. The technologies being developed to produce those effects are held as secrets; "looking under the hood" to see how they work is expressly forbidden.[12] From the user perspective, the seamless PDN thus would operate both as an extension of the embodied self and as a revision of it. Trusted-computing technologies may provide increased access to some resources, but they will do it by limiting accessibility in a variety of other ways.

Now consider a group of technologies that is fast becoming integral to a variety of processes, some expressly linked to security and others not. Imagine a typical day in the life of a commuter in a major East Coast city. To get to work in the morning, she scans a smart card to use public transit or uses the transponder installed in her car to pay for tolls and parking. After work, she meets a friend for a drink, consulting the transponder in her car or an application on her mobile phone to find the bar her friend has suggested. On her way home, she stops at a supermarket and uses her debit card to buy groceries. When she returns home, energy-saving sensors in her home detect her presence, turn on the lights, and adjust the climate controls. These technologies are rudimentary versions of "ubiquitous computing" technologies: computing technologies built into the artifacts of everyday life to manage flows of goods, services, people, and energy in the physical environment. Those who design ubiquitous-computing technologies envision trajectories toward increasing convergence. Not long from now (or so technologists hope), our commuter will manage all of her daily transactions using a single device. Sensors in refrigerators will take the guesswork out of stops at the grocery store, while embedded RFID chips will enable grocers to manage retail inventories automatically.

The organizing concept for these endeavors is the notion of "unremarkable computing": a seamless web of networked, continually communicating artifacts that users experience as natural, if indeed they pause to think about it at all.[13] Engineers and policy makers have understood the shift toward unremarkable computing as presenting two principal problems. First, for the technologies to be most useful, their designers must identify the optimal balance between ease of use and complexity of function. Researchers in human-computer interaction seek to answer this question by modeling increasingly complex problems and building interfaces that embed and then simplify the complexities. Second, unremarkable computing raises concerns about the privacy and security of personal information that the ubiquitous sensors collect and exchange. Yet there is a third problem that is not reducible to either of the other two: what if users were to want access to the ways that the technologies of unremarkable computing work? There are many legitimate reasons for wanting such access; for example, one might want to know how one's personal information is being used, or to improve the ways that one's own devices interact.[14] To the extent that existing laws address this question, they do so from a completely different perspective, that of the trade-secret owner seeking to recruit authorized licensees and exclude competitors, or of the government agency seeking to maintain the secrecy of technical information in the interest of national security. Once again, then, the technologies of unremarkable computing offer new methods of access to some resources within networked space, but they do so in a way that limits access to information about the network's operation.

Similar effects are produced by technologies that most U.S. legal theorists have understood as exemplars of openness: the technologies of search and social networking. Consider the following incidents: in 2006, AOL released a database containing tens of thousands of search queries entered by its subscribers to the public for research purposes. Before releasing the database, AOL had "anonymized" the queries, removing some information to ensure that they could not be linked to any particular user. As it happened, the database contained enough information to enable some users to be identified with some not too difficult reverse engineering. In response to widespread public outcry, AOL disabled access to the database and confessed that it had given the matter insufficient thought.[15] Similar results followed a series of ill-advised decisions by the popular social-networking site Facebook. In 2007, Facebook added data feeds that kept its members updated, in real time, on every change in the status or activities of their online "friends." Also in 2007, it joined a commercial venture, the Beacon program, that would alert members to their friends' purchases. In both cases, the user response was swift and unequivocal. Many users didn't want their friends to receive real-time notifications of every change to their profiles, and didn't want to be turned into promotional agents for products they had purchased. Facebook redesigned its menu of options to give users greater control and later ended the program as part of a settlement of legal claims filed against it.[16]

The AOL and Facebook controversies represent only the tip of a very large iceberg, and users do not always rebel against new uses of information about their activities. Google's e-mail service, Gmail, mines the subject lines and the contents of e-mail messages for keywords and serves ads related to those keywords. When Google announced the launch of Gmail, and acknowledged that it would use e-mail content to target advertising, users flocked to the service, attracted by the unprecedented amounts of storage that it provided. Privacy advocates warned that Google had provided little real information about how the targeting would be done, but for many users, the possible harms felt too remote or indefinite to matter.[17] If anything, privacy advocates likely understated the extent of Google's data-mining activities. Gmail is but one of a number of linked Google services. Google Shopping stores information about online purchases and shopping preferences; Google Maps supplies satellite imagery and travel directions; Google Desktop encompasses an array of localized information-management services, including a file manager and a shareable calendar, and so on. When you are signed in to your Google account, all the different data streams are linked. Google's acquisition of Doubleclick gave it access to a large amount of data about commercial preferences with which to enhance its profiling algorithms, and the proposed Google Book Search settlement would give Google access to data about users' intellectual interests. Recently, Google announced that it would begin behavioral targeting of advertising to all users of its search engine.[18]

Among legal scholars, these developments are not typically described or understood as raising problems of technical accessibility. Privacy advocates argue that they involve unauthorized access to users and therefore raise questions about the nature and scope of privacy interests. We have already seen that existing privacy frameworks work poorly in such contexts, but my intent here is not to recast accessibility as a privacy issue. Rather, it is to argue that the technologies of search and social networking also raise a different problem, which relates squarely to both the accessibility of information resources and to the transparency of network processes. According to Frank Pasquale, the technical opacity of search threatens the ideal of equal access to information.[19] He is exactly right, but the problem extends both far beyond equal access to information and far beyond the domain of search.

Google's official mission statement promises "to organize the world's information and make it universally accessible and useful," but when its services are considered together, that mission can be reframed in a way that is both more personal and oddly more comprehensive: the management of individuals' entire networked existence.[20] In fact, the two missions are one and the same. Google uses information about and generated by users to create and manage the world of information that it reflects back to users. Its algorithms mediate flows of information, showing subscribers what Google predicts they will want to see. That business plan is noteworthy because of Google's dominant market position, not because the plan itself is an unusual one. AOL didn't disclose why users received the search results they did, and Facebook didn't specify how the Beacon program would work. "Google Everything" is but one example of a more general trend in the networking of everyday life to produce the "semantic web"—"a Web in which machines mine mountains of metadata in order to automate a wide variety of transactions" and personalize the online experiences of network users.[21]

Like the PDN and ubiquitous computing, the semantic web promises many conveniences. Consider the notion of a "Coasean filter" for marketing-related communications. Such a filter would be tailored so precisely to individual preferences that it would admit only those offers that matched the preferences.[22] Who cannot claim to be intrigued by the promise of a networked future in which only relevant advertising will appear? Ultimately, however, the semantic web operates by separating personalization and control; information about how its constituent technologies channel content to (or away from) users is jealously guarded. Arguably, the public outrage that followed the AOL and Facebook episodes, and the lingering unease that some users feel about Gmail, is only partly about privacy and partly about the lack of operational transparency that characterizes the network as users experience it. Those controversies, and others like them, remind us that we are losing the ability to control the processes of personalized shaping or even to know much about them.

Perhaps, though, technical and cultural accessibility are not equally important. To understand why technical accessibility is important in its own right, we need to return to the accounts of embodied perception and everyday practice developed in Chapter 2 and reconsider the particularly intimate ways in which networked information technologies mediate the everyday practice of network users.

Autonomic Technologies and the Play of Everyday Practice

Chapter 2 explored the ways that networked information technologies mediate our perceptions of the world around us: we experience technologies and artifacts as altering our preexisting capabilities vis-à-vis the physical world, but technologies and artifacts also mediate our embodied perception of that world—of how it is organized and how it works. Because they are both tools for producing useful results and tools for representing the world, networked information technologies shape our perceptions of reality more comprehensively than simpler artifacts do. These points run orthogonally to the principal thrust of STS scholarship. Rejecting the cultural myth of "autonomous technology," STS scholars remind us that technologies do not have autonomous trajectories, but rather are socially shaped.[23] This important point about contingency is often assumed to mean that technologies have no power to shape us, but it should not be. Paths taken have consequences.

The technologies described above are designed to render the functioning of the networked information environment seamless by making complex processes of networked computing largely invisible to end users. Invisible does not mean neutral, though. The technologies of the PDN seek to reshape the embodied experience of the digital media environment. Ubiquitous-computing technologies seek to reorganize the relations between embodied users and their physical and social contexts. Semantic-computing technologies mediate the relations between embodied users and their (own?) preferences, organizing unruly flows of information into patterns that are more easily managed. Each of these design efforts succeeds most fully when users experience its operation as natural—as "just the way things are."

To the extent that we naturalize the built environment, the window for remaking it grows smaller. The tendency to naturalize the operation of technologies and artifacts—to take the world they present to us as given—makes it harder to formulate such a desire, much less implement it. Of course, that tendency is not itself a by-product of digital technologies; it predates the digital age. But because networked information technologies simultaneously mediate and represent the world around us, they have at least the potential to accelerate processes of naturalization. Each of the technologies described above possesses that potential. Ubiquitous computing defines an "Internet of things," DRM defines an "Internet of (proprietary) media," and the semantic web promises to define an "Internet of me"—a universe of relevant information sorted and managed by each person's personal information manager. As we incorporate these technologies more fully into the practice of everyday life, it can be increasingly difficult to identify the point where technology leaves off and the embodied self begins. From the perspective of embodied, situated users, new technological developments in the networked information society may lack visible trajectories, let alone autonomous ones.

Borrowing from biology, I will use the term "autonomic" to describe the relationships between these technologies and the networked self. IBM has used the term "autonomic computing" to refer to a philosophy of design for very complex systems. Its "Autonomic Computing Manifesto" envisions a future in which information and communication technologies mediate flows of information automatically via sophisticated feedback mechanisms. It invokes the model of the autonomic nervous system, which mediates essential biological processes automatically via feedback mechanisms that for the most part lie below the threshold of our conscious control.[24] I mean something related but slightly different, which concerns the way that networked information technologies—whether or not they have technically complex feedback mechanisms—are experienced by users. To an ever-increasing extent, networked information technologies operate automatically to mediate the activities of culture, self, and community formation. It is no coincidence that the figure of the cyborg, discussed in Chapter 2, emerged in the work of a scholar trained in the life sciences. In the arena of the biomedical, the distinction between internal and external was already problematized by advanced, internally implanted prosthetics. But flows of information across interfaces between the body and a technologically enabled society are not confined to the domain of the biomedical, and the characteristics of those flows have profound implications for both self-development and the creation of social meaning.

The play of everyday practice is important precisely because it counters the innate tendency to naturalize—to take the current technological landscape as given—with the innate tendency to tinker, repurpose, and adapt. Everyday practice is the day-to-day process of negotiating the dialectical relationship between constraint and possibility. Within networked space, information flows are defined by semantic and technical structures. The play of everyday practice pushes against those structures, sometimes conforming to them and sometimes finding ways to work around them. Some users might want, or need, to know at least in a general sense what a networked digital product does. Others might want to find out how the product or network works "behind the scenes"— what is happening to the information that it collects, for example, or how particular search results came to be displayed. Still others might want the ability to repurpose the product or network—to make it do different things. In each case, the product resists, but everyday practice persists.

We can hypothesize that, generally speaking, the process of naturalization and the play of everyday practice exist in a sort of equilibrium— sometimes one is ascendant, and sometimes the other is. It is possible that even the new autonomic technologies would not alter that overall pattern. Because they operate so invisibly, autonomic technologies threaten to tilt the balance more heavily toward naturalization. It is harder to work around a set of protocols that has been designed to disappear. But the obverse is also true: the human tendency to tinker, repurpose, and adapt artifacts—to incorporate artifacts into the play of everyday practice— increases the likelihood that interesting facts about the network and its constituent devices will be discovered. The distributed, "unfinished" nature of networked information technologies amplifies the power of everyday practice. Everyday practice leverages both the distributed, democratic nature of networked information technologies and what Jonathan Zittrain has called their generativity—their extraordinary amenability to tinkering and revision.[25] Users build new tools, develop new "places," generate new communities, and create new cultural practices. While networked information technologies present everyday practice with large challenges, they also present it with large opportunities.

But aspirations toward seamless design are not the only factor in play. The equilibrium between naturalization and everyday practice also depends on larger social and institutional factors. Here we return to the linked architectural and institutional changes introduced in Chapter 7. As autonomic technologies morph into more carefully structured governance regimes organized around architectures of control, the activities that constitute the play of everyday practice are exactly the ones that those regimes seek to prevent.

The Networked Self in the Age of Authorization

As we saw in Chapter 7, U.S. legal scholars have examined emerging architectures of control principally through the lens of liberalism's foundational dichotomy between liberty and constraint. Because that framing encourages a focus on what technologies of control prohibit, legal scholars have paid far less attention to what those technologies do in the grey area where liberty and constraint mingle: they authorize. Emerging architectures of control operate within nascent institutional regimes that span both public and private sectors and that derive their power from a reconfiguration of the meaning and significance of "unauthorized access." The vehicle for this process is not the "appliance" Internet described by Zittrain; appliances do not engage in acts of authorization, nor do they recruit individuals and technology vendors into networks of authorized, and compliant, insiders.[26] It is something different and far more powerful: a new mode of governance for the networked information society. The emerging regimes of authorization work to produce both a configuration of networked space that is increasingly opaque to its users and users who are increasingly habituated to processes of authorization and their associated requirements of technical and operational secrecy.

The Shifting Meaning of Unauthorized Access

Let us begin by reexamining Chapter 7's account of the emergence of architectures of control, this time with authorization rather than prohibition in mind. The emerging technical and institutional regimes organized around architectures of control do not function simply to prohibit certain actions. Instead, they reconfigure networked space by extending and normalizing protocols for authorization of access to network resources. In the two decades since the enactment of the Computer Fraud and Abuse Act (CFAA), the prevailing conception of unauthorized access, and so of the appropriate domains of authorization, has changed almost beyond recognition. In the 1980s, "unauthorized access" described a group of relatively narrow, stand-alone problems capable of resolution within a single statute. In the twenty-first century, managing access has become the central regulatory problem of the networked information society. The principal purpose of emerging architectures of control is to define as precisely as possible the actions that are authorized and the persons or devices authorized to take them.

The drafters of the CFAA conceived of unauthorized access as a threat to a "computer," and understood a computer to be a fixed, discrete location to which one might gain access. Once inside that location, the extent of authorized access could be differentiated, but the principal boundary to be defended was that of the computer itself. That conception implied a correlative understanding of the default rules that obtain in the world outside the computer's boundaries. In that world, no special authorization of access would be required for most ordinary actions that a "user," or ordinary person, might wish to take.

The CFAA's conceptualization of the world as a large unregulated space surrounding small zones of authorized access also shaped the conceptualization of those labeled wrongdoers under the statute. Most often, it was assumed, those wishing to gain access would be highly skilled outsiders—hackers looking for the digital equivalent of a joyride in a stolen car, or "crackers" bent on more malevolent ends. Many scholars have argued that equating hackers with wrongdoers oversimplified an emerging subculture that was far more complex, and I have no quarrel with that position. My point here is different: whether or not the view of hackers embodied in the CFAA was accurate or appropriate, it was a view that excluded most of the general population. Anxiety about computer users remained largely confined to those "superusers" possessing both atypical skill and high levels of motivation to gain entry to purportedly secure systems.[27]

The relatively simple vision of a computing world comprising isolated fortresses under threat from malevolent outsiders was complicated by the problem of the unauthorized insider. When someone hacks into a protected computer or file from outside the system, that action is unauthorized both technically and legally. The situation changes when an insider—an employee, a contractor, or a customer—abuses a position of trust to access resources that he is not supposed to use. From a technical perspective, the actions might be considered authorized; for example, perhaps the wrongdoer supplied the required password. Defining the actions as unauthorized—or, in the CFAA's terms, actions that "exceed[] authorized access"—requires resort to nontechnical standards of proper conduct. Once articulated, such standards became vehicles for the CFAA's expansion to cover a variety of "unauthorized" actions with respect to publicly available content on the internal pages of Web sites.[28] For a variety of reasons, however, most Web site owners did not choose to implement their preferences via technologies that precisely calibrated authorization of access, and so the melding of technical and normative authorization remained incomplete.

In the copyright context, the objects requiring protection against unauthorized access have no fixed location. To accommodate the idea of digital objects that carry restrictions with them, the conceptualization of unauthorized access underwent a dramatic shift. For such a system to work, authorization itself must become broadly distributed. The architectures of pervasively distributed copyright enforcement drive toward precisely that end. They seek to change the technical and legal parameters of content-related transactions, both online and offline, in a way that renders them fundamentally relational on two levels. For individual users, transactions over copyrighted content become processes characterized by the ongoing authorization of access and use. Those processes, in turn, will not work properly unless compliance by licensed equipment and service providers is mandatory and verifiable, and that necessitates realignments in the relationships between intermediaries and content providers. Effective implementation of pervasively distributed control requires ongoing authorization of intermediaries' access to and implementation of the relevant standards.

As both authorization and unauthorized access detached themselves from fixed locations, the identity of the presumed threat also shifted. The hacker remains a powerful figure in copyright's mythology because it is hackers who have the skill and (presumed) motivation to circumvent technical protections and release unprotected copies into darknets. Now, however, the figure of the hacker coexists uneasily with the idea that the real locus of distrust is the ordinary user, who cannot be relied upon to turn away from illegality when the opportunity presents itself.

At the same time, redefining "unauthorized access" to encompass circumvention of the protocols for access to widely distributed files has made it much more difficult to create legal exceptions that would shield a range of socially valuable activities. Law- and policy makers have tried several different methods of creating such exceptions. In formulating the DMCA's core prohibitions, Congress attempted to use "access" as a narrowing concept to safeguard user rights. The DMCA distinguishes between technical protection measures (TPMs) that function as access controls and those that protect against violation of the exclusive rights of copyright owners. It bans the manufacture and distribution of tools for circumventing both types of TPM, but prohibits only those individual acts of circumvention that are directed at access controls. Congress thought a ban on the circumvention of access controls appropriate and fair because otherwise users could circumvent to avoid payment. Meanwhile, Congress thought, users would remain free to devise means of their own choosing to circumvent rights controls as necessary to exercise the privileges afforded them under copyright law.[29] That strategy for safeguarding user rights, however, depended entirely on an interpretation of "access" as encompassing only a narrow domain of activity.

Litigation over the meaning of the DMCA's prohibitions has established that the new model of authorization-based access cannot be so easily cabined. Consider a TPM that allows the user to play a music or video file but prevents copying. According to the legislative rationale for the DMCA's bifurcated structure, this TPM is a rights control. Yet in litigation over circumvention of the CSS algorithm, which encrypts DVD movies to allow playback but not copying, courts acquiesced without question in the entertainment industries' classification of CSS as an access control because it prevents rendering the content on noncompliant devices.[30] That construction means that only authorized DVD *players*—as opposed to authorized *users*—may access the encrypted content. But if only authorized players can make authorized access, then two further conclusions follow. First, if every act of rendering protected content is an act of accessing the content, then the individual privilege to circumvent rights controls exists only in theory. Second, if "access" refers to devices and not to people, then the development of unauthorized media players violates the ban on tools for circumventing access controls. This rule grants far-reaching control over technology development to those who control the processes of authorization.

Efforts to define narrower legal shelters for certain types of unauthorized access have met with a similar fate. Software reverse engineering is a type of unauthorized access that copyright law allows on the grounds that it is essential to both innovation and competition. Seeking to preserve that privilege, Congress created an exception to the DMCA's prohibitions, allowing both circumvention of TPMs and the manufacture of circumvention tools "to achieve interoperability of an independently created computer program with other programs."[31] Since PC-based media players are also computer programs, in theory that exception should allow the unauthorized creation of interoperable media players. Courts have found a variety of ways to avoid reaching this result, however, and it would be hard to square with their conclusion that the statute's prohibitions encompass access to digital media content by unauthorized devices.

Taking a different approach, the Copyright Office has attempted to legitimize unauthorized access to a particular class of devices. Mobile phones released in U.S. markets typically are configured to work only on one or a few authorized networks; configuring a phone for use on another carrier's network requires an act of circumvention (or reverse engineering). The DMCA authorizes the Copyright Office to create exemptions from the rule forbidding circumvention of access controls when necessary to enable access to particular classes of works. The Copyright Office issued a rule allowing circumvention of access controls on mobile phone software that operate to restrict network access. Unlike the reverse-engineering exception, the mobile phone exemption brackets the question of what is or isn't a "computer program" and invokes consumer protection concerns.[32] But the device-based framework is no more coherent than a framework that distinguishes between computer programs and media players. Many mobile phones are also media players, and the two types of functionality can be made to intertwine. This flexibility allows the technology vendor to determine which set of rules will apply. For example, Apple Computer has used technical countermeasures to disable "liberated" iPhones, releasing firmware upgrades that turned the devices into useless "bricks."[33] If Apple released upgrades that selectively disabled iTunes, owners of hacked iPhones who attempted to fix the problem would risk violating the DMCA's access prohibition.

In the world of pervasively distributed security measures, the conceptualization of unauthorized access has begun to shift again, in a way that completely inverts the implicit presumptions that produced the CFAA. As more and more of the ordinary transactions that make up everyday life become processes characterized by the ongoing authorization of access and use, authorization becomes essential to the ordinary person's existence—necessary to get to work, pay bills, and access communication systems. Levels of access also become defining conditions of privilege; some users have more access than others, and that fact too structures the rhythms of everyday life.

In such a world, moreover, the target class is related to the class of putative wrongdoers only in the most notional sense. On their face, of course, security measures target wrongdoers. The need to catch the terrorist, the money launderer, or the identity thief is obvious and pressing. Yet when security measures are brought to bear on everyone, those individuals cannot plausibly be said to be the sole targets of the corrective measures any more than speeders can be said to be the sole intended audience for traffic signals. Pervasively distributed security measures target everyone because universal coverage is their raison d'etre. They operate on the presumption that security requires it.

As authorization of access become the norm, the ability of users to make authorized access increasingly depends on their agreeing to submit to invasive procedures for authentication. Network users have become accustomed to accepting without question automatic updates of software that, among other things, mediates authorization processes. Other security procedures may require the installation of cookies, tracking software, or biometric readers on users' devices. The outer boundaries of technology vendors' authority to install functionality for tracking, authentication, and authorization are poorly delineated. There is no generally agreed dividing line between spyware and authorized installation, and technology vendors have little to gain from drawing one.[34] In short, within the new political economics of precisely calibrated authorization, the conditions of authorized access to users do not seem to be precisely defined, or limited, at all.

The emerging regimes of authorization are not the work of some invisible, hitherto-concealed dictator or corporate cabal. They are the products of our ordinary institutions of governance: markets, property and contract rights, and legislation by democratically elected representatives. They depend for their success on two kinds of changes in our political culture. The first relates to political discourse; the second, to ingrained habits of behavior and thought.

Ideologies of Openness, Discourses of Authority

The emerging regimes of authorization require regimes of secrecy to sustain their operation. This hard reality creates insuperable difficulties for a legal system premised on an ideology of openness in government and in markets. One would expect societal commitment to an ideology of openness to prompt questions about regimes of technical secrecy, and many dedicated public-interest advocates have devoted their careers to raising such questions. Just as often, though, the process seems to work in reverse: the power of the ideology of openness operates to conceal the extent to which technical secrecy is reinforced by law. Regimes of technical secrecy derive additional force from moral panics that cast restrictions on access as a matter of social and cultural survival, and from processes of technical mystification that position decisions about network architecture as purely technical matters best handled by expert elites.

In evaluating the role of secrecy in our political discourse, it is useful to return to Jodi Dean's critique of the "political economy of communicative capitalism," which we encountered at the end of Chapter 6. Dean argues that the political economy of the modern mass-communication society is characterized by an ideology of openness and antihegemony, but driven in fact by a mix of secrecy and spectacle. Within this political economy, she argues, secrecy becomes both a locus of economic value and the object of public desire. The desire to expose secrets feeds a public culture of the spectacle, which neither satiates the desire nor dislodges the power that secrets represent.[35] Remarkably for a study of the political economy of the networked information society, however, Dean's book devotes almost no attention to the politics of openness in technical contexts. To understand the political economy of openness in the networked information society, it is necessary to consider the treatment of specifically technical information as well. Discussions of technical information are characterized by a dialectic between secrecy and spectacle, but that dialectic has a slightly different flavor than the one Dean describes.

It is well recognized that governments can leverage secrecy to create structures of differential visibility that reinforce their own power, and it is commonly believed that such secrecy threatens core principles of democratic governance. Such assertions of government secrecy are increasingly routine. For example, many law enforcement experts believe that surveillance deters crime most effectively when the fact of surveillance is visible but the details of surveillance behavior are deliberately concealed. They apply similar reasoning to technical information about surveillance practices, arguing that secrecy serves both deterrence- and enforcement-related goals. Efforts to gain access to operational information about government profiling and data-mining practices are invariably met with assertions about the ways in which secrecy serves national security and about why disclosure would jeopardize essential state secrets.[36]

How, in this context, should one interpret statutory frameworks and underlying normative principles purporting to require government accountability in data processing? The U.S. Freedom of Information Act mandates far-reaching disclosure of information about government actions and processes, but exempts classified information, trade secret information, and information about law enforcement techniques and procedures if such disclosure would "risk circumvention of the law" or create risks to physical safety.[37] Although the FOIA is widely considered to be a keystone of open government, in reality the amount of secrecy those exceptions permit is indeterminate, and may be very great. Assertions of national security interests do not always persuade courts; the process of seeking access proceeds slowly; and the extent of publicly available information about such practices remains incomplete. In particular, the operations of the vaunted Foreign Intelligence Surveillance Act (FISA) court remain almost entirely secret. Ironically, in the wake of disclosures about widespread and wholly unauthorized government wiretapping, we have come to cling to its (presumed) procedural regularity—again, a case of partial disclosure used to great effect.[38] (Better the devil who plays by secret rules than the one who follows no rules at all.)

In the private sector, secrets about the structure of privately administered components of the information society are a potent source of economic power. The basic Internet protocols remain open, but from the ordinary individual's perspective, that counts for much less than we are led to think. The individual experience of the network is shaped by a host of technical intermediaries, many of whom argue that maintaining the secrecy of technical protocols is a competitive necessity, essential to preserving robust and "open" competition. Efforts to gain access to information about the algorithms that determine the order of online search results typically have been stymied by assertions of trade secrecy, and digital content owners have used the trade-secret status of DRM protocols as one weapon in their litigation campaign against devices that enable unauthorized access.[39] Frameworks for ensuring private-sector accountability in the processing of personal data are focused principally on ensuring individuals the right of access to their "own" data—that is, data about the person, not data about the algorithms that will process it.[40]

Spectacle also plays an important role in discourses about technical secrecy in these government and private-sector processes, but the spectacles that capture public attention are not the banal tales of self-exposure that we encountered in Chapter 6. Instead, they involve a different sort of morality play, which revolves around the malevolent figures of the hacker, the "pirate," and the terrorist. Rather than rewarding the exposure of technical secrets, these morality plays tend to reinforce regimes of technical secrecy, aligning secrecy with political, economic, and cultural survival. Consider, for example, Judge Lewis Kaplan's characterization of the problem posed by the DeCSS litigation:

> In a common source epidemic, as where members of a population contract a non-contagious disease from a poisoned well, the disease spreads only by exposure to the common source. If one eliminates the source, or closes the contaminated well, the epidemic is stopped. In a propagated outbreak epidemic, on the other hand, the disease spreads from person to person. Hence, finding the initial source of the infection accomplishes little, as the disease continues to spread even if the initial source is eliminated. For obvious reasons, then, propagated outbreak epidemics, all other things beings equal, can be far more difficult to control.
>
> This disease metaphor is helpful here. The book infringement hypothetical is analogous to a common source outbreak. Shut down the printing press (poisoned well) and one ends the infringement (the disease outbreak). The spread of means of circumventing access to copyrighted works in digital form, however, is analogous to a propagated outbreak epidemic. Finding the original source of infection (e.g., the author of DeCSS or the person to misuse it) accomplishes nothing as the disease (infringement made possible by DeCSS, the resulting availability of decrypted DVDs) may continue to spread from one person who gains access to the circumvention program or decrypted DVD to another. And each is infected, i.e., each is as capable of making perfect copies of the digital file containing the copyrighted work as the author of the program or the first person to use it for improper purposes.[41]

As Chapter 7 described, Judge Kaplan's elaboration of the disease metaphor for online copyright infringement is not a solitary occurrence, but rather adopts a persistent theme sounded by the copyright industries and echoed in media coverage of digital copyright issues. The rhetoric of contagion plays an analogous role in the security context. Addressing a joint session of the U.S. Congress several months after the U.S. invasion of Iraq, British prime minister Tony Blair called terrorism "a new and

deadly virus" originating in "a fanatical strain of religious extremism . . .
that is a mutation of the true and peaceful faith of Islam." Other public
figures, including legislators from both political parties, describe terrorism as a "cancer" that must be "eradicated" before it destroys the health
of the body politic.[42]

These statements are not simply window dressing for a substance
that lies elsewhere—in reasoned debate about the nature of property
or the appropriate extent of civil liberty. When rhetorics of crisis succeed,
they create the perception of an existential threat to society that requires
an immediate and drastic response. This process, which scholars have
termed "securitization," urgently suggests that society must be reorganized
to counter the threat.[43] In casting piracy and terrorism as threats to the
health of the body politic, the metaphors of contagion and cancer work
not only to mobilize public support for secrecy, but also to signal the
range of appropriate and necessary corrective actions.

The classic societal response to an acute threat to public health
is quarantine. Foucault described the methods developed by medieval
city-states for managing outbreaks of the plague. As Foucault explained,
authorities responded to a great threat that traveled by human contact in
the only way possible—by eliminating contact. Although medieval phy-
sicians did not have the benefit of modern principles of microbiology
and epidemiology, they understood that the plague spread by human-to-
human contact. Therefore, during an outbreak, citizens were forbidden
to leave their homes. Every evening, a designated corps of inspectors
would go door-to-door and demand that each inhabitant of a household
stand at the window to prove that he or she was still alive. If the inhabitants of a home were stricken, the home remained isolated until everyone
in it had either died or shown immunity by surviving. Then the home
was scoured and its contents were burned.[44] In the networked information society, some responses to acute security threats map more or less
directly to the classic pattern; for example, antimalware programs "quarantine" infected files.

But most information-age "epidemics" are too complicated for
quarantine to be a viable strategy, for two reasons. First, the understanding of acute danger as episodic does not translate well to the contexts of
copyright infringement, terrorism, and identity theft. In the societies that
originated the techniques of plague control, emergencies were temporary. As the plague passed, so did the ability to sustain the extreme measures it was thought to justify, which required both a massive expenditure
of resources and near-complete suspension of ordinary activity. Second,

the germs that cause the plague have no positive qualities, and there is no independent reason to disseminate them. Digital economies, in contrast, thrive on endless flows of all types of information. The "propagated outbreak epidemic" to which Judge Kaplan referred is simply an example of a more general property of networks of all sorts; information must move for the network to exist.

Governance regimes predicated on technical, legal, and market strategies for separating authorized from unauthorized flows of information and communication solve both of these problems. Such regimes open up a middle ground between a state of quarantine and rules allowing the unrestricted movement of people, communications, and information. Within that middle ground, many possibilities exist for convergence between perceived security imperatives and the self-interest of information intermediaries.[45] As we saw in Chapter 5, flows of information in the emerging networked information society reflect a set of beliefs about the relationship between risk, information, and profit. For the institutions that participate in the network, information technologies promise systematized knowledge as an antidote to insecurity. At the same time, architectures designed to facilitate authorized movement may be more readily perceived by market actors as affording the potential for competitive leverage.

Understanding emerging regimes of authorization through the lens of securitization also explains the paradoxical stance toward openness exhibited by corporate and political actors. To serve both their competitive and regulatory functions, regimes of authorization must be buttressed by technical and procedural secrecy, but they also must demand more and more openness of individual citizens. The morality plays of the hacker, the pirate, and the terrorist serve both to induce more disclosure in exchange for more security and to convince network users that more security cannot be had in any other way.

Critically, the public discourse around secrecy and security is also unstable in important ways. Public interest advocates have generated a constant stream of cases in which secrecy has pernicious effects on concrete, identifiable people—people wrongly placed on the Transportation Security Administration's no-fly list and unable to clear their names, computer-ignorant grandmothers sued by the recording industry based on assertedly foolproof methods for tracking their downloads, and so on. In addition, scandals about electronic voting and identity theft have begun to generate narratives that are inconsistent with those that the morality plays seek to instill.[46]

On the other hand, as these examples suggest, technical processes also introduce a new kind of tension between ideologies of openness and discourses of secrecy, a tension revolving around technical authority and the appropriate roles of those who possess it. The emergence of technical standards as sites for the production of power constitutes new regulatory and political processes: the expert fora in which technical standards are defined and revised. In those processes, the patterns of accessibility typically associated with modern forms of democratic government are dramatically altered.

Standards processes for information networks and platforms tend to be conducted in ways that obscure network governance functions behind a veil of technical mystification. Most obviously, some standards processes are operated by private consortia of technology companies, pursuant to trade-secrecy regimes. Others are conducted by open-membership organizations or by government bodies, but even nominally open or public standards processes can be opaque and mysterious. They are conducted in complex, technical language and unfold over lengthy time periods, and both factors can operate to prevent widespread public awareness of what is at stake. This tends to obscure the political implications of network standards and protocols, along with difficult and important questions about whether governance by elites trained predominantly in technical fields is normatively desirable.[47]

The emerging regimes of authorization contribute to the climate of technical mystification by restricting participation in their standards processes to authorized professionals. The DMCA's exceptions for reverse engineering, encryption research, and security testing are crafted in ways that preclude their invocation by members of the public.[48] In other contexts, regimes of trade secrecy and state secrecy that foreclose routine public access to information about surveillance systems produce similar results, operating to professionalize innovation by restricting technical access to authorized insiders.

Moral panics and technical mystification do not displace the ideology of openness that is so central to our political discourse; they depend centrally on ideologies about the value of certain kinds of openness in certain contexts. At the same time, however, they change the prevailing understanding of how openness is supposed to work. Together, moral panics and technical mystification facilitate the normalization of institutional ecologies predicated on differential accessibility to the technical operation of the emerging networked information society. Those ecologies have profound implications for our political culture.

Configuring Tractable Users

Regimes of authorization and accompanying discourses of authority work to establish technical and market path-dependencies—patterns of accessibility and inaccessibility—that themselves come to be seen as normal and natural. This reshapes the everyday experience of networked space in ways that the liberal binary of liberty and coercion does not encompass. The thrust of these strategies is to produce tractable users who comply with the requirements of authorization protocols and refrain from behaviors that are unauthorized or simply anomalous.

Consider, again, the problem of liberty and constraint that has preoccupied cyberlaw scholars. Within liberal political theory, the evil of paramount concern is coercion by an authoritarian government. Because information networks have evolved in ways that are relatively resistant to government control, cyberlaw scholars have viewed the rise of information networks as fundamentally incompatible with the propagation of authoritarianism.

The emerging political economies of authorization are quite different from authoritarian political regimes, and that difference has operated to conceal the magnitude of the cultural and political change that they represent. Regimes of authorization have no necessary connection to authoritarian political regimes; in fact, the opposite is more nearly true. Regimes of authorization thrive in market economies, which more reliably provide both the technical know-how and entrepreneurial initiative to fill apparent security needs. In addition, regimes of authorization may or may not concern themselves directly with the sorts of dissent that matter most within the liberal paradigm and that reliably mobilize authoritarian political regimes. Architectures of control need not prevent people from setting up their own digital soapboxes, nor from purchasing access to listeners.

In place of authoritarian government, regimes of authorization offer a more generic model of authoritarian governance. Both models of regulation seek to instill habits of compliant submission to unquestioned authority, and to use their authority to generate and normalize new patterns of conduct. But authoritarian governance has a different goal and a correspondingly different modus operandi than authoritarian governments do.

Social theorists who study the networked information society argue that there is a mutually constituting relationship between the network's material affordances—the possibilities for action that it creates—and the forms of subjectivity that it enables, which I will call the network's "psychic affordances." These theorists offer different conceptions of self-formation, but each identifies a fundamental relationship between network structure and processes of self-formation. Manuel Castells argues that the emerging networked information society is constituted by a dialectical relationship between the Net, a new set of institutional arrangements organized around networked information and communication technologies, and the Self, a set of activities directed toward defining the meaning of identity. For Gilles Deleuze, the emerging "control society" provides very limited scope for self-differentiation. He characterizes the control society as signaling a shift from Foucauldian discipline via externally imposed normalizing frameworks to less crude but potentially more powerful "modulation" by continual streams of information to, from, and about individuals. Other theorists, such as Jean Baudrillard, argue that the distinguishing characteristic of the networked information society is not modulation but simulation: the networked presentation of alternate realities casts the self adrift, unable to distinguish reality from an endless series of simulacra.[49]

Although these theories are very different from one another, each directs our attention to the ways that the structure of the network mediates the formation of the networked selves who inhabit it. That process is material as well as informational. The geographies and architectures of networked space establish the material field for processes of self-constitution. Scholars of geography and urban planning have explored the ways that the design of public spaces shapes cultural and social life, and have argued that planned spaces risk achieving order at the expense of diversity, vibrancy, and social and cultural mobility. Drawing on this work, Michael Madison has observed that, just as early twentieth-century urban planning moved to eliminate visual chaos and replace it with order, so the technical and contractual mediation of information flows within information networks threatens to eliminate the diversity of textures and "feels" that flourishes under less restrictive architectures. Aesthetically and experientially, one might compare the controlled spaces that result from digitally mediated standardization to large shopping malls or gated communities.[50] This architectural shift recasts the options available to both ordinary and technically skilled network users, producing subtle but fundamental behavioral and cultural changes.

Experientially, the processes of standardization contemplated by emerging regimes of authorization work to produce a larger geography of information space that is increasingly standardized and that we increasingly come to take for granted. At the same time, the interpolation of regimes of authorization into formerly private spaces redraws the boundary between private and public, producing at the intersection a third sort of space that is neither entirely private nor conventionally public. That space combines the exposure of behavior in public spaces (but not the mobility or expressive privilege) with the isolation of private spaces (but not the security against intrusion). Regimes of authorization invade, disrupt, and casually rearrange the boundaries of personal and social spaces and of the intellectual, cultural, and relational activities played out within those spaces.

Only some of these emerging architectural and institutional changes alter the scope for individual agency as conventionally understood by legal theorists. Most obviously, direct technical constraint on behavior—for example, a digital file that cannot be shared with anyone, or a tamper-resistant biometric authentication device—substitutes rule-governed behavior for individual judgment and responsibility. In many cases, we might conclude that looseness of fit between rules and behavior is itself a social good. Where the precise contours of legal rules are unclear, or the proper application of legal rules to particular facts is contested, imperfect control of individual conduct shields a range of experimentation that involves individuals and communities in the creation of law and furthers the value-balancing goals of a sound and inclusive public policy.

The more significant effects of regimes of authorization, however, are not so easily characterized as constraints on liberty. Recall, once again, that the momentum toward regimes of authorization is so strong precisely because we are not driven to embrace them by coercion. Our relationship to these developments is ambivalent, driven in equal parts by fear and desire, and cemented by growing habituation. For individuals, networked information technologies promise more immediate, accurate, and convenient fulfillment of their desires. The networked self in the age of authorization seeks safety, to be sure, but also the convenience that authentication and personalization bring. This is, again, the difference between prohibition and authorization; the control society can claim to have won broader acceptance in the marketplace because it offers commodities that people (learn to) want.[51]

In narrowing the horizons of individual desire, regimes of authorization also narrow social and architectural tolerances for the construction of difference. As Rosemary Coombe demonstrates in the context of intellectual property and John McGrath shows in the context of surveillance, the rules that govern the uses of information can expand or constrict the scope for creative appropriation—for play with the symbolisms embedded in cultural artifacts and attached to particular, culturally identified behaviors.[52] Regimes of authorization extend these effects throughout networked space, operating upon difference and unpredictability to produce more homogeneous, more carefully modulated behavior. As Chapter 6 discussed, even newly emerging practices of self-exposure take on a standardized quality.

In sum, the networked self in the age of authorization is a different self, and the networked society a correspondingly different society. It may be that the psychic affordances of the emerging regimes of authorization are the ones we want; certainly, that is what conventional hedonic analysis would suggest. Before reaching that conclusion, though, we should take stock of their effects on a range of individual and social practices that we claim to value. In particular, we should consider more carefully the effects of regimes of authorization on the play of everyday practice.

Accessibility as Scope for Material Practice

Law plays an integral role in the emergence of regimes of authorization. With increasing frequency, legal prohibitions, incentives, and mandates are deployed unquestioningly to reinforce technical, commercial, and political regimes of differential accessibility. That is both a great mistake and a lost opportunity. Limitations on access to networked resources can be important, and even essential, for the networked information society to function in a way that promotes the well-being of its citizens. Legal rules that prohibit and punish unauthorized access to networked resources sometimes will be necessary. But only sometimes. The well-being of the networked selves who inhabit the emerging information society also depends importantly on the ability to find—or create—breathing room for everyday material practice. Regimes of authorization that operate systematically to diminish such breathing room therefore warrant careful, critical attention from law- and policy makers.

Recall the analysis of the relationship between processes of naturalization and the play of everyday practice that concluded the first half of this chapter. That discussion suggested that everyday material practice—including not only tinkering and reengineering by relatively skilled users, but also the repurposing of artifacts and spaces by ordinary users—serves both instrumental and intrinsic goals that are far broader and more momentous than those typically acknowledged by lawmakers and legal commentators. Everyday material practice is the root cause of movement in material culture, the antidote to technical, spatial, and interpretative stagnation. It is what counteracts the innate tendency to naturalize the built environment—to take the configurations of spaces and the affordances of artifacts as givens and to move obediently in the patterns they suggest. It is precisely the fluidity and unpredictability of everyday material practice that regimes of authorization treat as suspect and seek to contain. Law may side with rigidity sometimes, but to align with it always would be to jeopardize an essential dimension of cultural vibrancy.

As in the case of copyright, one might argue that attempting to define legal shelter for the play of everyday material practice would be both quixotic and unnecessary. Arguably, defined zones of legal protection are definitionally incompatible with the play of everyday practice, which by its very nature resists technical and institutional limitations. For similar reasons, we might conclude that the everyday practice of situated users is a given and therefore something with which the law need not concern itself; within any regime of governance, some amount of diffuse, tactically driven behavior will occur.

Those conclusions, however, would be too hasty. The analysis in the second half of this chapter suggests that the everyday material practice of situated users is also a quantity that is contingent and extraordinarily vulnerable to environmental modulation. To the extent that habits of tractability instilled by the emerging regimes of authorization reinforce processes of naturalization already underway in the networked digital environment, they work to insulate that environment and its constituent protocols from challenge, critique, and revision. More generally, the habits of tractability instilled by emerging regimes of authorization dampen the amplitude of everyday practice in contexts both technical and nontechnical, jeopardizing a broad range of other goals that the play of everyday practice promotes. The play of everyday practice forms the substrate out of which a mature and critical subjectivity, a vibrant artistic and intellectual culture, and a robust culture of technical innovation all emerge. If we are serious when we say that these are goals that our society values, then we need an information policy to match.

This analysis has important implications, first, for the legal treatment of hacking and tinkering by situated users. Attempts by legal theorists to justify a "right to hack" or a "freedom to tinker" have seemed unable to formulate a narrative that would capture the urgency of such a right. Attention to the play of everyday practice enables us to cast hacking and tinkering in a new and more compelling light. The process of tinkering with artifacts and tools is both mundane and extraordinary. Tinkering is an indispensable prerequisite for transformative innovation, but it is also what ordinary people do on a daily basis, and in everyday practice it is an indispensable prerequisite for the exercise of material and social agency. It enables users of technology to adapt standardized tools and interfaces to their more particular goals. That process in turn increases the likelihood that the fruits of innovation will be distributed broadly and adapted eclectically, in ways that promote the flourishing of disparately situated communities.

The constitutive importance of tinkering for human flourishing means that lawmakers cannot take the easy out by prohibiting all acts of "circumvention" or "unauthorized access" without regard to motives or consequences. Instead, the law has a dual role to play, proscribing some kinds of unauthorized access while preserving room for the acts of tactical evasion and situated creativity that make up the fabric of everyday life.

This chapter's exploration of the various dimensions of accessibility also demonstrates, however, that merely rolling back legal prohibitions on hacking and tinkering would be unlikely to guarantee all the kinds of accessibility or all the kinds of breathing room that human flourishing demands. Some problems of accessibility and breathing room — particularly those that recur in copyright disputes — are readily amenable to resolution by determined tinkering. Other problems are not. For example, it is probably shortsighted to rely on tinkering and hacking to ensure the optimal mix of openness and privacy, including both informational privacy and adequate shelter for behavior in networked spaces, or to guarantee sufficient representation in expert standards processes. In those contexts and many others, preserving scope for everyday material and spatial practice requires a broader array of regulatory options.

Notably, many of the goals that I have just listed do not require simply increased accessibility, but rather a normatively informed recalibration of the balance between "open" and "closed." Put differently, the requirements of human flourishing place nonneutral, normative constraints on the design of network architectures. Again and again throughout this book, we have seen that interstitial flexibility serves important social purposes. The value of architectural and institutional constraints lies not only in the pattern of constraint and authorization that they impose, but also in the spaces left over for activities that are neither constrained nor authorized. Networked space can be a space of dystopian domination or a space that affords breathing room for situated creativity and critical identity practice, depending significantly on the nature of its system of boundaries and permissions. Network-neutrality mandates, however they are crafted, simply do not speak to that question. We have also seen that technology markets may not—and in the current climate, likely will not—produce such a normatively informed recalibration "on their own."

It is worth emphasizing that identifying these needs is a long way from prescribing ways in which the law should attempt to pursue them. This point is too often lost in debates about information law and policy; partisans on both sides are apt to assume that calls for correction are calls for command-and-control forms of regulation. As we have seen, there are dangers in attempting to make either code or law all-powerful. The control fetishism of code-based regulation is in tension with the critical importance of indeterminacy in the linked realms of cultural creativity, evolving, socially situated subjectivity, and material practice. But law can descend into control fetishism as well. Considering how to shape information rights and associated technical architectures that promote human flourishing while avoiding the problem of control fetishism is the subject of Part V.

PART V

Human Flourishing in a Networked World

CHAPTER 9

The Structural Conditions of Human Flourishing

Within U.S. legal and policy circles, the discourse of information-policy reform has been organized principally around the themes of access to knowledge and network neutrality. Global discourses of information-policy reform are organized around parallel themes of access and connectivity. Each of those themes has contributed powerful insights to our understanding of the principles that should inform information law and policy. Human flourishing requires not only physical well-being but also psychological and social well-being, including the capacity for cultural and political participation. The access-to-knowledge movement reminds us that enjoying the latter goods requires meaningful access to the resources of a common culture. The network-neutrality movement reminds us that in the networked information age, access and architecture are inseparably intertwined, and that power over the technical conditions of access should be closely scrutinized.

This book, however, has demonstrated the need for a more comprehensive, structural understanding of the ways that the information environment can foster, or undermine, capabilities for human flourishing. Some information-policy problems cannot be solved simply by prescribing greater "openness" or more "neutrality." The everyday behaviors of situated subjects require spaces where they can be enacted, tools with which they can be pursued, and meaningful legal guarantees in which they can claim shelter. In addition, we have seen that play is a vital catalyst of creative practice, subject formation, and material and spatial practice. Those processes do not follow automatic and inevitable trajectories, nor are they equally robust under all conditions. Facilitating the play of everyday practice requires attention not only to information accessibility and network neutrality, but also to the semantic structure of the networked information environment, and more particularly to the interstices within systems of institutional and informational meaning. Both the legal specification of information rights and the design of information architectures should be guided by the need to preserve room for play in the use of cultural resources, in the performance of identity, and in the ongoing adaptation of places and artifacts to everyday needs.

Beginning with the centrality of the play of everyday practice, this chapter derives three subsidiary principles that should inform the design of legal and technical architectures. The first principle remains that of access to knowledge; without the raw materials necessary for social and cultural participation, one cannot participate meaningfully in the development of culture and community, and without access to the appropriate networks and tools, one cannot partake of the resources that the networked information society has to offer. The second and third principles, however, move beyond access to specify other structural attributes of the networked information environment that are necessary to preserve room for the play of everyday practice.

The second principle, operational transparency, seeks to render the network's geographies of accessibility and inaccessibility less opaque—to counter the trend toward seamless, inscrutable design. Operational transparency entails a set of practices designed to put users themselves in a better position to engage in processes of boundary management and to exercise situated creativity with respect to the network's constituent protocols and processes. To take full advantage of the network's potential to enable human flourishing, network users need meaningful information about how the network and its constituent artifacts and protocols work as well as access to the processes in which network standards are designed.

The final principle concerns the location of the boundaries that define the scope of copyright, privacy, and (un)authorized access to information technologies. To preserve room for play, those boundaries should afford sufficient freedom to access and repurpose cultural and technical materials, and should reserve to individuals and communities sufficient control over both personal information and the experienced boundaries of personal space. This mixture of freedom and control is achieved most effectively when regulatory architectures are characterized by a condition that I will call "semantic discontinuity." Semantic discontinuity refers to gaps and inconsistencies within systems of meaning and to a resulting interstitial complexity that leaves room for the play of everyday practice. In an increasingly networked information society,

224

maintaining those gaps requires interventions designed to counterbalance the forces that seek to close them.

On Enabling Capabilities: The Materiality of Play

Let us begin by returning to the theory of capabilities for human flourishing introduced in Chapter 1. There I asserted that moving beyond the foundational assumptions of liberal individualism would enable more precise specification of exactly what the capabilities approach requires the information environment to provide. It is time to make good on that claim. To enable capabilities for human flourishing, the material and informational infrastructures of the networked information society must afford sufficient room for creative, material, and identity play. Fulfilling this condition requires rules about information access and use that accommodate the materiality and serendipity of everyday practice.

As articulated by its leading advocates, the theory of capabilities for human flourishing begins with a positive conception of human freedom, namely, that human beings cannot attain and enjoy freedom in the truest sense unless a variety of basic needs are met. Nussbaum develops a list of ten such needs or "core capabilities": life; bodily health; bodily integrity; senses, imagination, and thought; emotions; practical reason; affiliation; care for other species and the natural world; play; and political and material control over one's environment.[1] As one might expect, some items on the list relate to the requirements for physical subsistence. Notably, however, many items address the requirements for moral, emotional, and intellectual subsistence. In particular, many move squarely into the domain with which this book has been concerned: the relationship between the information environment and the networked selves who inhabit it. According to Nussbaum, the ability to use one's senses, imagination, and thought encompasses a right to participate in culture by "experiencing and producing works and events of one's own choice." The ability to play includes the ability "to enjoy recreational activities." The ability to exercise practical reason requires the capacity "to form a conception of the good and to engage in critical reflection about the planning of one's life," and the ability to exercise control over one's environment requires the capacity for effective political participation.[2]

Within information-policy circles, the theory of capabilities for flourishing has become identified with the normative and political claims of the access-to-knowledge (A2K) movement. The importance of capabilities for cultural, moral, and political participation has inspired efforts to develop a more detailed understanding of core informational capabilities and to relate those capabilities to features of the informational and technological environment. Lea Shaver identifies "the ability to access, utilize, and contribute to knowledge" as a distinct capability with its own set of entailments.[3] Shaver develops a five-part taxonomy: education for informational literacy, access to the global knowledge commons (including both Internet access and linguistic capability), access to knowledge goods in concrete form, an enabling legal framework (including both laws about intellectual property and laws guaranteeing freedom of expression), and effective innovation systems.

In both Nussbaum's list of core capabilities and more specific efforts to theorize specifications for A2K, however, two important dimensions of the relationship between the information environment and human flourishing remain underdeveloped. The first concerns the materiality of artifacts, architectures, and spaces. We have seen that the human experience of the information environment remains fundamentally embodied and materially mediated. Nussbaum's discussion of control over the material environment presumes that such control is exercised principally through the institution of property, while her conception of practical reason stresses a moral agency that seems only indirectly connected to material practice. Scholarship within the A2K movement has been instrumental in demonstrating that cultural and technical innovation does not invariably require property incentives and that human flourishing requires broad access to the fruits of both cultural and technical innovation. That account of human flourishing, however, still contains an implicit gulf between the intellectual and the material. As we have seen, the intellectual, moral, and material practices of situated individuals and communities are inextricably intertwined. A list of core capabilities for human flourishing therefore should include a non-property-based conception of material agency directed not (only) toward innovation, but also and more fundamentally toward advancing the cultural and moral interests of situated subjects.

The second undertheorized dimension of the relationship between the networked information environment and human flourishing relates to the role of play. As we have seen, most U.S. legal theorists of intellectual property and privacy, including those affiliated with the capabilities approach, articulate conceptions of play that align with the commitments of liberal theory—that is, accounts of play as a purposive, internal, and unknowable activity. Nussbaum's description of "being able to use imagination and thought" similarly presupposes seriousness of purpose, while her definition of "play" as the ability to engage in "recreation" seems to contemplate mere frivolity. Without question, the ability to engage in deliberate play with cultural goods, identity practices, and material artifacts is important, but it is not enough. And a dichotomy between purposive play and frivolous recreation would be too simple to encompass all the modes of interaction and experimentation that people pursue. The relationship between human flourishing and play is more complex, and understanding it requires a different and less subject-centered approach.

Chapter 2 developed a broader conception of the play of everyday practice and argued that such play derives its power from its tactical, flexible quality—from its political and phenomenological in-betweenness. So framed, the play of everyday practice performs a vital role along each of the dimensions that this book has explored. Within the cultural environment, the play of everyday practice is what generates creative progress; progress emerges in a gradual, nonlinear fashion as situated users appropriate, imitate, and rework the artifacts and techniques encountered within cultural landscapes. Within the social environment, the play of everyday practice responds to continual encounters with the new and unfamiliar, and so informs the development and gradual evolution of critical subjectivity. Within technical environments, the play of everyday practice adapts and repurposes artifacts and spaces in ways that serve the tactical goals of situated subjects and communities, and this reservation of authority to shape the material conditions of everyday life promotes both innovation and psychological and social well-being.

In each of these domains, the play of everyday practice has structural entailments. The play of everyday practice flourishes in an environment characterized by both resources and opportunity. It flourishes most fully when neither the content of the resources nor the precise nature of the opportunity is fully predictable, and when there is leeway for experimentation. The play of everyday practice exploits imperfect alignment among the sets of overlapping constraints—institutional, discursive, geographic, and material—that characterize experienced reality. It is a function of the size and frequency of the interstices within grids of fixed meaning and permitted action.

To understand why play and rule structure are inextricably related, consider a hypothetical: A major provider of media content announces that henceforth it will embrace fan culture by creating a venue where fans can "play" with the characters from a variety of popular television shows and movies. It establishes a dedicated Web site, stocks the site with preselected video clips, and authorizes fans who register with the site to remix the clips (but only those clips) at will. It announces plans to add more variety—including both more video clips and greater technical capability—at some unspecified time in the future. Advocates of greater legal freedom to remix think this behavior signals a positive shift in corporate culture, but they caution that it is a poor substitute for a less constrained remix culture that allows experimentation with a broader range of images and meanings. The Copyright Office needs to decide whether to issue a rule allowing so-called vidders to circumvent technical protection measures that regulate access to audiovisual content. It has statutory authority to grant the exception if it concludes that creators of fanvids are "adversely affected . . . in their ability to make noninfringing uses" of the protected works. In other words, it must decide whether fanvidders enjoy sufficient scope for play when they enjoy only the remix privileges that creators choose to allow.[4]

Strategic decisions by corporate intellectual-property owners to establish defined zones of authorized play are becoming more common, and are not confined to the realm of cultural goods. In some industrial contexts, producers of equipment embodying valuable intellectual property have sought to harness the distributed power of user creativity by authorizing innovation within certain clearly delineated parameters. Such projects do not necessarily accommodate the full range of user interests. Meanwhile, some scholars who have begun to study the cultural dynamics of crowd-sourced innovation argue that the cynical use of play tropes in the networked information environment too often conceals the structured exploitation of unremunerated labor.[5]

These examples remind us that "play" is a term capable of multiple, often competing interpretations. Rules for play can be liberating or infantilizing, productive or stifling, depending on whether they are appropriate to the actors and to the activity. For a variety of reasons, it makes good sense to restrict very young children to playgrounds and to subject children of all ages to appropriate rules about the nature, location, and scope of play. Geographic boundaries and scope rules can become more controversial when applied to adult play. Many meaningful activities that we count as playful occur within sets of constraints—consider, for example, soccer or jazz or poetry or cryptography research. But not all constraints should be valued equally. Critically, focusing solely on whether the actor understands her own activities as playful can't lead us to a meaningful rule for evaluating the quality of the constraints. Play is related to rule structure in a way that is inverse and inherently interstitial; it is a function of the spaces that the constraints leave unoccupied.

Understanding capabilities for human flourishing as inextricably linked to the structural attributes of the networked information environment—to its semantic and physical architectures and particularly to its interstitial structure—points toward three conditions that are necessary to enable their development. Those conditions are access to knowledge, operational transparency, and semantic discontinuity. Each condition can be satisfied by a range of possible actions, but each requires action within that range. Although some features of the current information environment satisfy the conditions for human flourishing, many do not. Many of the legal and technical developments that this book has explored jeopardize precisely those attributes of the information environment that enable material agency and that facilitate the play of everyday practice. For a host of often well-intentioned and seemingly logical reasons, those developments seek to shrink the interstices of regulatory and informational regimes—to reduce the looseness of fit between individual behavior and the institutional and technical structures that operate to constrain and channel it. The remaining sections of this chapter explore each of the three conditions for human flourishing and identify types of initiatives that might reverse the trend.

Access to Knowledge

First, the development of capabilities for human flourishing requires access to information, including networked information resources. The access must be of sufficient quantity and quality to enable participation in cultural and social life for purposes ranging from the political to the "merely" recreational. In addition, the access imperative encompasses any tools and technologies that are or may become necessary to enjoy access. The access imperative is the subject of a growing body of commentary, so my discussion will be brief and will focus on highlighting major areas for reform.

As a preliminary matter, it is important to note that my formulation of the access imperative excludes several important dimensions of informational capability that are simply beyond the scope of this book. First, informational capability has social and institutional dimensions. Social literacy includes the information necessary to function as a member of a particular community. Such information is acquired by a variety of processes, only some of which involve access to intellectual goods. Institutional literacy includes, for example, market literacy—that is, knowledge about bank accounts, access to credit, and whatever else is necessary to survive and thrive in an economy that is increasingly networked and global. Second, informational capability has a political dimension that does not depend only on access to intellectual goods, but also requires legal safeguards for freedom of expression and political participation. Entire literatures are devoted to each of those topics. Here, I will focus more narrowly on access to the informational resources necessary for cultural, social, and political participation.

Both the attainment of basic literacy and the capability for ongoing cultural and political participation are powerfully shaped by the ways that intellectual property laws, and particularly copyright laws, mediate access to intellectual and cultural resources. Copyright scholars have long recognized that a system of proprietary rights in intellectual goods inevitably creates some "deadweight loss." Simply put, if authors and publishers are entitled to demand payment, users who are either unwilling or unable to pay will lose out. Scholars have justified the deadweight loss by pointing to copyright's presumed incentive function. If authors and publishers are not entitled to demand payment for their works, they reason, copyright will cease to function as a meaningful incentive for production of some important cultural goods, leaving all of us the poorer. Neither side of that equation requires perfection, however. As we saw in Chapter 6, the incentive side of the equation requires reformulation; copyright is not the primary motivator of creative practice by situated subjects, but instead is more accurately described as serving an economic-organization function. Furnishing sufficient control for copyright to serve that function does not require unconstrained control over either pricing or use, and satisfying the access imperative does not require free access to everything all of the time. Honoring the access imperative within the framework of copyright law requires only enough paid access for the market-based system of cultural intermediation to work as a practical matter and enough free or lower-cost access to satisfy basic conditions of social justice.

Although the system of global copyright expanded its reach dramatically during the twentieth century, one of the twentieth-century copyright system's signal virtues was that it left unobstructed a variety of avenues for obtaining free or lower-cost access to copyrighted materials. Resale markets afforded access to many mass-produced works at reduced prices, while public libraries provided free access to many different kinds of works. Both institutions functioned as mechanisms for implicit price discrimination, crudely sorting users based on their willingness to pay while excluding no one based on inability to pay. The inexact sorting mechanisms of analog copyright do not simply represent analog imperfection; they performed an important access-promoting function because they were inexact. In economic terms, the consumer surplus resulting from that system factored importantly into the social benefits that the system of copyright law produced. By widely distributing access to cultural resources, it created a broad and deep foundation for cultural participation, cultural production, and cultural progress. A more perfectly calibrated system of compensated access to cultural resources, which would supplant some functions traditionally performed by resale markets and libraries, would not produce the same benefits.

Consider the current controversy regarding the Google Book Search project. On one reading of the dispute, Google Book Search represents a collision between two models of full-text access to cultural works, the library and the bookstore. If we understand the bookstore as the default and the library as the exception, we might be inclined to think that a principal raison d'etre of the library is to fill unmonetized gaps in the system of access. In the era of full-text digital searches and print-on-demand availability, we might expect the two models of access to converge to a significant degree as the reach of monetized access expands. If so, we might favor sharply limiting the extent of uncompensated full-text access available to library patrons. But if libraries perform functions that are important and qualitatively different from the functions that bookstores perform—functions related to distributive justice, to cultural preservation, and to the promotion of serendipitous access—then that stance would not make nearly as much sense. If libraries are not simply gap fillers, then we ought to approach the question of full-text access very differently. Rather than asking how libraries should accommodate the interests of publishers, we should ask how the functions of libraries might best be preserved in a digital world.

A different set of problems is presented when market formation is desirable but is stymied by transaction-cost and holdout problems. In such cases, access can be promoted by regimes of automatic licensing. An example of the difference that such licensing can make comes from the realm of music copyright. In 1909, lawmakers concerned to foster widespread, affordable access to musical works instituted a system of automatic licensing for the preparation of sound recordings. That system, which remains in place today, led to the emergence of a robust, market-based system for access to copies of recorded music. By the late twentieth century, however, the political climate in the United States had become much more hostile to the concept of automatic licensing. Legislation creating a digital public-performance right in sound recordings sharply limited the availability of automatic licensing and also created new legal obstacles to the formation of collective licensing organizations. In part because of the reluctance to embrace automatic licensing more fully, the market for access to digitally streamed music has developed haltingly, and innovative start-up models are rightly perceived by all parties as creating large litigation risks. The irony, of course, is that the major record labels that play the role of market obstructionists in today's music-copyright dramas owe their privileged legal status in considerable part to the catalogs that automatic licensing has enabled them to amass.[6] Copyright reforms designed to promote market-based access should make automatic licensing widespread.

A just regime of copyright also must include strategies specifically designed to enable access by users located in the global South. Scholars and A2K advocates have advocated a variety of measures to address persistent global disparities in educational capabilities. Strategies for ameliorating the North-South access gap involve a range of reforms to national and international laws, and are designed to promote access to basic educational materials for free or at below-market rates.[7] As a result of pressure from established copyright interests, however, discussions of access reform within the conceptual framework of the General Agreement on Tariffs and Trade have placed great emphasis on safeguarding private bargaining processes and have generally ignored the question whether some markets may require baseline levels of information flow in order to form at all.

The copyright industries of the global North are right to assert that the development of thriving markets for copyrighted content is a desirable goal, but their resistance to access reforms designed to promote educational capability is shortsighted. As Margaret Chon puts it, "Education is fundamental to the capacity-building upon which all further progress is made."[8] And as Ruth Okediji notes, in developing countries "the capacity to infringe is significantly limited by the lack of computers to access online content."[9] The neoliberal view of the primacy of markets, which predominates within the international intellectual-property system, regards strong intellectual-property protection as an essential precondition for cultural and technological progress. For many developing economies, that theory puts the cart before the horse. Bridging the digital and educational divides that separate developing and developed counties requires sustained investments in literacy and capacity-building. Without the broadly distributed capability to participate in the development of intellectual goods, some countries simply will not develop intellectual property industries at all. Gross inequalities in resources and education levels cannot simply be assumed away; such inequalities also must be starting considerations in the design of a global copyright regime.

A final important area for access reform concerns provision of the infrastructure necessary to enable situated subjects to enjoy the fruits of copyright liberalization. In an increasingly digital world, enjoying access to cultural resources requires access to information networks. The A2K movement has been instrumental in connecting intellectual property issues to network access and architecture issues, reminding us that access to knowledge has dimensions that reach beyond intellectual property law. More specifically, the net-neutrality movement emphasizes the important role that nondiscriminatory interconnection policies play in securing access. In developed countries, the principal vehicle for addressing access and nondiscrimination issues is national broadband policy. The leading empirical study of national broadband policies, conducted by Harvard's Berkman Center for Internet and Society at the request of the U.S. Federal Communications Commission, concludes that a range of policies designed to promote open access at various stages of the communication process "are almost universally understood as having played a core role in the first generation transition to broadband in most of the high performing countries . . . [and] now play a core role in planning for the next generation transition."[10] In developing countries, where infrastructures are lean to nonexistent, and where the resources for large-scale broadband deployment typically do not exist, policy makers and entrepreneurs have experimented with an array of other mechanisms for providing network access, including satellite transmissions and mobile-communication platforms.

Access to cultural artifacts, however, does not necessarily go hand in hand with either the legal right or the technical ability to use them as creative practice requires. Some legal scholars argue that users enjoy more latitude than a reading of the copyright law would suggest. In particular, they assert that content owners' increasing acceptance of "remix culture" creates a category of "tolerated use" upon which users can safely rely.[11] That may be correct, but it is far too early to proclaim a stable equilibrium. Controlled "playgrounds" such as the one described earlier in this chapter offer corporate intellectual-property owners a new direction for tolerated use, and one that does not inevitably afford broad user freedoms. In addition, new models for cloud storage and the authenticated delivery of media content may foreclose some types of use as a technical matter. Some scholars argue that because rights of use and reuse are necessary for cultural and political participation, access should be conceptualized as including such rights.[12] These scholars are right to think that not all kinds of access are equally valuable; for exactly that reason, however, an access principle alone cannot provide a sufficient foundation for a just information policy. The need to afford latitude for situated users signals the need for a different and complementary principle, which relates to what I have called semantic discontinuity, or interstitial flexibility within the system of legal rights, institutional arrangements, and associated technical controls.

In addition, rights of access to information and information networks do not necessarily correlate with rights to privacy; indeed, they more typically function in the opposite way. As network users become habituated to trading information for information and other services, access to goods and services takes place in an environment characterized by increasing amounts of both transparency and exposure. Similarly, access to the network and to networked information artifacts can be a double-edged sword, depending on how the network and its constituent artifacts are configured. To an increasing degree, features of the networked information environment are characterized by seamless opacity and highly granular authorization processes. These changes have implications for two clusters of important social values, one relating to transparency and accountability and the other relating to informational and spatial freedom of movement. Neither set of concerns can be addressed effectively simply by mandating access to information goods and services. Instead, human flourishing in the networked information society requires additional structural safeguards.

Operational Transparency

To benefit fully from the opportunities that networked information technologies offer, network users require not only access to information delivered by networks and devices but also access to information about the way those networks and devices function. I will use the term "operational transparency" to refer to three distinct sets of transparency concerns, each of which relates in a different way to the technical and informational operation of networked processes and to the effects of those processes as experienced by situated users. Operational transparency encompasses transparency about the design and implementation of surveillance practices, transparency about the operation of the network's borders and flows, and transparency about the processes by which network standards are designed and adopted.

The rationale for identifying operational transparency as a condition of human flourishing in the networked information society is straightforward. The lives of situated subjects are increasingly shaped by decisions made and implemented using networked information technologies. Those decisions present some possibilities and foreclose others. Most people have very little understanding of the ways that such decisions are made or of the options that are not presented. In many cases, this facial inaccessibility is reinforced by regimes of secrecy that limit even technically trained outsiders to "black box" testing. We would not tolerate comparable restrictions on access to the basic laws of physics, chemistry, or biology, which govern the operation of the physical environment. The algorithms and protocols that sort and categorize situated subjects, shape information flows, and authorize or deny access to network resources are the basic operational laws of the emerging networked information society; to exercise meaningful control over their surroundings, people need access to a baseline level of information about what those algorithms and protocols do.

The first category of operational transparency issues relates to the surveillance processes employed by both public and private entities to sort and categorize individuals and groups. Existing regulatory frameworks that have attempted to ensure transparency about the collection and use of personal information do not fully address the need for operational transparency in surveillance. In the United States, most private-sector uses and transfers of personal data are regulated only by the Federal Trade Commission's general prohibition against unfair and deceptive trade practices. Most reputable firms that deal directly with consumers do disclose some information about their "privacy practices," but the incentive is to formulate disclosures about both purposes and potential recipients in the most general terms possible. This practice in turn shields secondary recipients of personal data, many of whom do not disclose information about their activities at all. In contrast, the guidelines on fair information practices adopted by the Organization for Economic Cooperation and Development (OECD) and enacted as a directive by the European Union require parties that collect personal information to provide disclosures that specify the purposes for which the information will be used and any potential recipients other than the original collector. They also must afford a meaningful opportunity to examine and correct the information.[13]

From the standpoint of operational transparency, even the more stringent regulatory regime adopted in the European Union has two major defects. First, the statement of fair information practices, which dates from the 1970s, seems to envision a series of discrete information-collection events, and is poorly suited to the reality of dynamic information collection in online environments. More fundamentally, even highly granular, dynamically updated purpose and recipient disclosures would not necessarily shed light on the operational significance of collected information. Telling someone what pieces of information were considered for the purposes of making decisions about credit or medical coverage or targeted advertising provides no information about how that information mattered, about the other assumptions used to construct the operational heuristic, or about how different information would have changed the result. Yet such operational information makes all the difference, and liberal legal thinkers should have no trouble understanding why. Operational disclosures are essential both for informed consumption of the goods and services that are offered and for open, informed debate about the processes by which individuals and groups are sorted and categorized. In some cases, such disclosures might lead the affected individuals to change their own behavior; in others, they might lend concrete support to calls for regulatory reform.

Internationally, pressure to strengthen fair-information-practice guarantees is mounting. In 2011, the OECD began considering whether the fair-information-practice guidelines require revision to reflect the realities of modern data-processing practice.[14] At minimum, such reforms should address the problems of dynamism and operational significance. For a guarantee of transparency to be meaningful, people who are the subjects of information processing need enough information to enable them to understand more accurately both how items of information in their own profiles will be used and more generally how particular types of decisions are made.

A second category of operational-transparency concerns relates to information about the network's geographies of accessibility. As we saw in Chapter 8, those geographies are increasingly opaque to network users, concealed by the seamless operation of autonomic technologies. Most ordinary network users have little understanding of how networked information processes work, yet those processes mediate access to an increasingly broad range of public and private services. Danielle Citron's important work on "technological due process" explores the use of networked information technologies to perform a variety of public functions traditionally associated with government, ranging from the tabulation of election results to eligibility assessments for benefits. Citron argues persuasively that guarantees of due process that apply to government action should be extended into the realm of network architecture.[15] A regime of technological due process would require the public provision of meaningful information about the ways that traditionally public functions are performed, and would extend that requirement to the capabilities of technical systems supplied by private contractors. In addition, it would increase accountability by imposing strict audit requirements and authorizing legal challenges to inadequate disclosures.

As we have seen, though, operational-transparency requirements that apply only to the public sector are not enough to achieve operational transparency of the network as experienced by situated users. Geographies of accessibility and inaccessibility are comprehensively mediated by proprietary platforms and algorithms. Frank Pasquale has proposed that search engines be subjected to a regime of "qualified transparency," which would mandate disclosure of their practices for filtering and displaying search results. As Pasquale explains, such a regime need not involve unrestricted public disclosure of trade-secret information in order to effectively convey to individuals the information that they need.[16] Various devices are available to protect commercially important secrets from general disclosure, including disclosure to an ombudsman or expert panel that would verify the accuracy of publicly reported operational information. By analogy, policy makers could design similar regimes of qualified transparency for the other technologies discussed in Chapter 8, such as nascent rights-management systems that pair cloud storage with plug-and-play portability, or the regimes of unremarkable computing envisioned by designers of networked artifacts.

The final category of operational-transparency concerns relates to the processes by which general network standards are developed and implemented. As we saw in Chapter 8, both secrecy and technical mystification tend to frustrate sustained public scrutiny of standards processes and their outputs. Some of those standards, such as the basic Internet Protocol, are matters of great public concern. For such standards, the public interest in operational transparency is not satisfied by providing for qualified transparency after standards have been determined. In her study of the political struggles surrounding the development of IPv6,

Laura DeNardis concludes that best practices in Internet-standards governance require commitment to a standard that is "open in its development, open in its implementation, and open in its use."[17] A policy of nominal openness toward interested and technically skilled participants is not enough to satisfy the first criterion. Even bodies like the Internet Engineering Task Force, which has maintained a strong commitment to open standards development, must confront "intrinsic barriers to participation related to technical expertise, language, funding, and culture."[18] Adequate operational transparency requires the design of participatory mechanisms that take those barriers into account. To achieve openness in implementation, DeNardis recommends open publication of and royalty-free access to general network standards. A well-designed regime of qualified transparency, tasked with identifying and disclosing departures from such standards, would work to ensure openness in use.

This preliminary analysis of operational-transparency interests leaves unanswered important questions about the dividing line between those technical protocols that should be subject to open-process requirements and those that should be subject only to the less stringent requirement of qualified transparency. Strategies for designing both types of regimes, and for generating increased commitment to open development processes, are important subjects for future research and experimentation. Ideally, a well-designed regime of qualified transparency would exert upward pressure on development practices, bringing to the public's attention the existence and capabilities of proprietary protocols that shape networked information processes and generating systemic pressures toward even greater disclosure.

Even high levels of operational transparency, however, would not necessarily equip networked individuals and communities with the resources to counter continuing interstitial shrinkage in the legal and institutional frameworks that regulate access to and use of information and information networks. Imagine that existing delivery systems for copyrighted content have been replaced by a system for cloud storage and automated delivery to users wherever they are located via a variety of fixed and mobile devices. The pricing structure is clear and uncomplicated, and the delivery mechanisms are effective and largely bug free. The delivery system incorporates clearly disclosed technical rules that authorize the consumptive use of media content for which access fees have been paid, but that do not authorize copying for other uses. Or imagine a clear rule stating that a provider of financial services may purchase whatever information it wants about individuals, may incorporate that information into its algorithms governing credit availability and pricing as it sees fit, and may sell the information to whoever it wants. Individuals are told exactly how their transactional and personal histories will affect their eligibility for various financial services and interest rates.

In both of these examples, the rules are clear and transparent—and in that respect, they represent some improvement over current practice in both areas—but the interstitial flexibility that they afford for the processes of creative practice and subject formation is minimal. These examples illustrate that, like access, operational transparency may be a necessary condition for human flourishing in the networked information society, but it is not a sufficient condition. The examples of what operational transparency does not cover point to a third structural condition for human flourishing, which relates to whether the legal and technical rules that govern access to and use of information resources contain sufficient interstitial complexity to facilitate cultural mobility, the boundary-making processes of privacy, and the play of material practice.

Semantic Discontinuity

In an age characterized by increasingly seamless and granular regulation of information access and use, and by increasingly precise efforts to monitor and predict individual behavior with comparable seamlessness and granularity, preserving adequate room for play within the domains of culture, subject formation, and material practice requires regulatory and technical interventions designed to foster what I will call "semantic discontinuity." Semantic discontinuity is the opposite of seamlessness: it is a function of interstitial complexity within the institutional and technical frameworks that define information rights and obligations and establish protocols for information collection, storage, processing, and exchange. Interstitial complexity permeates the fabric of our everyday, analog existence, where it typically goes unappreciated. Its function, however, is a vital one. It creates space for the semantic indeterminacy that is a vital and indispensable enabler of the play of everyday practice.

Systems of logical reasoning that derive from the tradition of Enlightenment rationalism have enormous difficulty in acknowledging the importance of semantic discontinuity. Instead, instances of semantic discontinuity tend to be conceptualized as imperfections that detract from the realization of legal, market, and technical ideals. More specifically, in thinking about the optimal regulatory structures for the networked information society, law- and policy makers are caught in a tug-of-war between two logical principles that together operate to deprive the networked self of the shelter afforded by interstitial complexity. The first principle holds that a system of law should neither draw nor respect lines between different types of conduct unless those lines can be justified by reference to first principles. A canonical statement of this principle is Oliver Wendell Holmes's injunction that the role of the law is to make rules for the "bad man," who will exploit semantic or technical loopholes in any way that he can.[19] The second principle holds, at times paradoxically, that a system of law governed by principles of rationalism and provided with enough information can derive the right system of rules to govern individual conduct.

To a considerable extent, it is the push and pull between the logician's skepticism and the technocrat's confidence that produces the dynamic that this book has explored. Unwilling to acknowledge a potential conflict between copyright and creativity, we demolish assertedly arbitrary boundaries that limit copyright scope while at the same time insisting on the possibility of defining properly tailored limitations and exceptions to shelter the lawful activities of users. Unwilling to acknowledge a potential conflict between unlimited flows of personal information and sound social and economic policy, we eliminate seemingly arbitrary restrictions on the collection, processing, and exchange of personal data while at the same time insisting on the possibility of protecting autonomy by means of narrowly defined zones of personal privacy in appropriate cases. In so doing, we implicitly accede to technocratic regimes of private governance organized around the processing of personal information. Together, these attitudes produce a schizophrenic approach to the design of network architectures. In some cases, we prize technical openness; in others, technical closure.

As we have seen, the continuities of information flow imposed by emerging market and legal institutions signal institutional realignments that are not simply logical or technical, but also and more fundamentally political. Those realignments enhance the power of actors and institutions that benefit from commercially continuous flows of cultural and personal information. At the same time, they diminish the ability of individual users and communities of practice to encounter and interact with flows of culture, and to pursue contextually specific practices of self-definition, in patterns that form and re-form more organically. Powerful actors that benefit from emerging regimes of authorization argue that it is unrealistic to expect the rhythms of digitally mediated life to match earlier ones; users who want the freedoms that new communication technologies bring should be prepared to make some sacrifices. But that argument confuses two kinds of inevitability: the fact that emerging patterns of information flow serve powerful economic and political interests, and thus might have been predicted by anyone paying attention to the distribution of incentives, does not make the patterns natural or just.

A commitment to human flourishing in the networked information society requires an effort to reverse, or at least cabin, the tendencies toward seamless continuity within legal, market, and technical infrastructures for information exchange. In making law for the bad man, we must not lose sight of the fact that we are also making law for the good person and for the good society more broadly. Creativity, critical subjectivity, and everyday practice flourish in conditions of (partial) unpredictability, and humans require creativity, critical subjectivity, and everyday practice to flourish. With practices this foundational at stake, freedom can consist in privileging discontinuity for its own sake.

Participation within Cultural Landscapes

Chapter 4 argued that copyright law- and policy making should foreground the everyday practice of situated users and the constrained yet open-ended process of working through culture. Copyright creates the legal foundation for capital investment in cultural production, and that function is an important one both economically and culturally. At the same time, culture requires room to move, and its movement benefits all who participate. Copyright should be understood as striking a balance not between present authors and the abstract "public" but rather between the near-term goal of creating economic fixity and the longer-term goal of fostering cultural mobility. So understood, the system of copyright requires the deliberate introduction and maintenance of legal and institutional discontinuities that shelter cultural play.

Copyright law purports to recognize a discontinuity principle, but increasingly pays only lip service to it. The contemporary approach to defining copyright rights assigns owners broad and often overlapping rights and then subjects those rights to narrow, situation-specific exceptions and limitations. The formulation of rights reflects what I have described as the logician's skepticism; it is deeply suspicious of approaches that might exclude new modes of expression or foreclose newly developing markets. In the realm of exceptions and limitations, however, law- and policy makers become mysteriously confident in their ability to define criteria for unremunerated uses in precise, granular terms, without regard to the inherent unpredictability of future events that might threaten such uses. Taking their guidance from these attitudes, courts interpret rights in an expansive fashion and construe exceptions narrowly. Both halves of this approach reflect a near allergy to logical gaps in copyright's coverage. Copyright rights have a protean quality, expanding into every avenue of potential profit. With one significant exception, copyright limitations generally have not demonstrated a parallel capacity to evolve as technologies change.

Copyright scholars and A2K advocates have advanced a variety of proposals for recalibrating the copyright balance. Those proposals generally fall into four categories. First, many argue that courts can and should interpret the fair use doctrine more expansively, developing a jurisprudence that would more predictably privilege a broader variety of uses. Second, advocates of fair use reform often argue that identifiable communities of practice—documentary filmmakers or fanvidders, for example—should develop statements of "best practices" that judges might consult for guidance. Third, copyright scholars have proposed statutory reforms to copyright formalities intended to speed the transfer of certain types of copyrighted content to the public domain. Fourth, the Creative Commons movement and similar open-access movements have sought to encourage more widespread use of open licensing regimes by which copyright holders can permit various uses of their works that satisfy particular criteria. All these proposals represent very good ideas. Without more, however, they are unlikely to yield the sort of meaningful recalibration that creative practice requires.

Within the U.S. legal system, the fair use doctrine has been the important exception to the general consensus that limitations on copyright must be narrow and precisely defined. Fair use shelters some uses in a way that purports to be open ended and sensitive to the ultimate value of the use in question. In practice, however, the shelter that fair use affords for everyday practice is not nearly as capacious as users tend to assume. Businesses and courts uncomfortable with open-ended exceptions have developed interpretive rules designed to make fair use more manageable. Those rules have operated to constrain user privilege within relatively narrow channels. They privilege uses that are clearly identifiable as criticism, parody, or biography, but do not reliably privilege many other forms of reworking that are central to contemporary creative practice, including allusion, homage, and pastiche, nor do they reliably privilege copying that situated users might undertake for other, less directly expressive reasons. In cases involving the literal copying of small excerpts—

for educational use, for inclusion in a documentary, or for any number of other purposes—a practice has emerged of licensing "clearances." Courts cite these emerging licensing markets as justifications for rejecting fair use arguments, producing a cycle of "doctrinal feedback" in which the zone of fair use continually shrinks.[20]

Although some aspects of fair use practice are probably amenable to reform, this history suggests that fair use likely cannot function as the general-purpose exception that some A2K advocates have envisioned. Even if courts took steps to end the problem of doctrinal feedback, the culture of licensing likely would persist because that culture is not only or even primarily a judicial creation. The culture of licensing is first and foremost a risk management culture; it is the by-product of culture facilitators' demand for clear rules with which to structure their dealings. Best-practice statements that are clear, concise, and aggressively promoted can counter that demand to some extent, but they confront a chicken-and-egg problem; to work most effectively, they must interrupt licensing norms at their inception. In addition, the best-practice model requires a community that is sufficiently well established to begin with. For the ordinary situated user of copyrighted content, who has only what Larry Lessig describes as "the right to hire a lawyer," best-practice statements offer little realistic possibility of shelter.[21]

Proposals for the "reformalization" of copyright and the adoption of open licensing norms, meanwhile, would simply reinforce the relative power of mass commercial culture. Consider, for example, the proposal that United States revert to a rule requiring renewal of copyright after an initial fixed term, or the proposal that it reinvigorate copyright registration and notice rules by making compliance with formalities a condition of claiming enhanced remedies.[22] To an overwhelming degree, copyright owners of mass commercial culture would take advantage of such rules, while many individual proprietors of copyright would not. Similarly, open-access initiatives such as Creative Commons have achieved very little penetration within the core domains of mass copyrighted culture, and those regimes often impose other transaction costs of their own.[23] Under either proposal, therefore, the common cultural baseline established by mass commercial culture most likely would remain off-limits to many forms of creative play. That result does not serve situated users' need to interact meaningfully with the constituent elements of the cultural landscape that surrounds them.

A different kind of strategy for privileging certain kinds of use would involve defining the copyright rights themselves in a more limited fashion. When confronted with this possibility, most copyright lawyers and scholars automatically resist it. If pressed, some will concede that copyright owners would not be materially worse off than they are now if they enjoyed only the right to control commercial exploitation of their works. Unremunerated but commercially harmful uses, such as P2P file sharing, could be addressed by defining the rights to include any exploitation that has significant commercial impact. Similarly, some U.S. copyright lawyers are willing to entertain the possibility of reformulating the derivative-work right as an adaptation right as long as it includes language that clearly signals the reservation of reasonably expected and commercially significant adaptations to the copyright owner. Commercial significance, though, is one of the most notoriously elastic concepts in copyright jurisprudence; it rapidly expands to cover everything in sight. Even in cases where evidence of commercial harm is deemed speculative, courts usually think it is important to leave the door open to a finding of harm later.[24] We might therefore be reasonably confident in predicting that rights defined by reference to commercial expectations, and unconstrained by any definite outer boundary, would be subject to continual judicial expansion.

In short, copyright lawyers and policy makers can talk the talk of limiting rights in the interest of "balance," but when it comes to actually ratcheting back the scope of copyright rights in any meaningful way, they become oddly reluctant to make changes that might affect the copyright owner's future bottom line—even though they can't predict whether there will actually be an effect or how much effect there might be. One reason for this reluctance, which is well understood by copyright scholars, is what we might call a naive restitutionary impulse—the idea that commercial gain to anyone else constitutes an injury that demands compensation so the copyright holder can be made whole.[25] If we need to adopt a broad reading of one or the other of the copyright exclusive rights to do this, then we should do it. However, the reluctance to limit rights does not depend entirely, or even principally, on the restitutionary impulse.

The more fundamental reason that copyright judges and policy makers resist setting meaningful limits has to do with the form of reasoning that our legal culture prizes most highly. It is best illustrated with an anecdote. Upon occasion, I have asked groups of upper-level law students to describe their exam-taking strategy. I ask them to imagine that they are taking an exam in some other, non-copyright-related subject— torts, or maybe constitutional law—and that they have been presented with a long, complicated fact pattern and been asked whether the plaintiff can succeed on any of a number of theories of relief. Then I ask whether they think they would get better grades by arguing that the plaintiff should succeed or fail. Except for the odd contrarian, who seeks to stand out by going against the trend, the students tend to believe that unless the professor has signaled a clear preference for a different strategy, they will get better grades by attempting to show how the plaintiff could succeed, even if it required an expansion of the grounds recognized by the law as basis for recovery.

That my students think the way they do about exam performance is no accident. We—I and my colleagues in law teaching—have taught them to think that way. To some extent, their response reflects successful internalization of the common-law method, in which the definition of legal rights proceeds by flexible incrementalism. But my students also understand arguments for extension as demonstrating both more technical creativity—more skill at lawyering—and more "true" understanding of the subject matter. You "really" understand torts or constitutional law or whatever when you can explain why a particular right "really" extends to cover situations in which it has never before been applied. Within the U.S. legal system, at least, the extension of rights and remedies into new territory is the essence of what lawyers do, and skill at it is a key indicator of professional and intellectual excellence.

That belief system, in turn, is both an intellectual legacy of Enlightenment rationalism and a more direct descendent of twentieth-century legal realism. The understanding of rights as narrow entities with fixed limits has become identified with the irrationality of nineteenth-century classical legal thought and the formalist categories on which it relied. At its inception, the realist project was both philosophical and political; it sought to show that limited understandings of legal rights and obligations served fundamentally antiprogressive ends. Over time, however, the reformist impetus waned and was replaced by a positivist anti-formalism.[26] Within the context of the original realist project, it made particular sense to interpret limits on rights and remedies as arbitrary fictions propped up by a discredited set of intellectual and political commitments. Positivist antiformalism affects a more neutral stance, resisting doctrinal distinctions that appear to have no foundation in logic. The 1976 Copyright Act and most other contemporary copyright laws and treaties are realist documents in this latter sense: they subordinate careful consideration of the balancing problems involved in copyright policy to the goal of drafting rights in a way that avoids artificial constraints. Within U.S. copyright circles, to suggest deviating from a baseline of broad entitlements subject to narrow limitations is to evoke the much-reviled categorical structure of the law that the 1976 Act replaced, the 1909 Copyright Act, which doled out narrower rights in an ad hoc, historically contingent fashion.

The limits of a legal methodology that treats limited rights as logically and intellectually disrespectable are particularly evident in contexts in which it is necessary to balance competing, equally important interests. If we think about the patchy, incomplete structure of the 1909 act from the perspective of the creative process, its logically discontinuous structure was a feature, not a bug. The 1909 act was a product of its time, a deeply formalist text whose authors understood, for example, "lectures" and "essays" as performing lexically different functions. That structure reflected a way of thinking about creative works that cannot, and likely should not, be recaptured. But principled insistence on real limitations is an intellectual stance that deserves better treatment. Creative practice flourishes most fully under conditions that permit unexpected encounters with new information and that provide room for reworking, tinkering, and other forms of creative play. As we saw in Chapter 6, the forms of creativity that we prize in artistic and intellectual endeavor, and that we cite when talking about what we expect the copyright system to protect, often turn out to depend centrally on imitation and reworking. From the perspective of creative practice, a legal regime characterized by formally incomplete rights—by logical gaps that permit at least some uncontrolled access and use—comes closer to solving the balancing problem that copyright confronts.

The 1909 act thus suggests a more general template for achieving semantic discontinuity in copyright law and practice: a copyright regime concerned with the balance between economic fixity and cultural mobility should replace broad, all-encompassing statutory provisions and generous, judicially created tests for infringement with narrower, clearly delimited formulations of copyright rights separated by deliberate gaps representing uses that are reserved in the service of cultural play, regardless of commercial consequence.

First, a regime of copyright recalibrated to prize and facilitate play should create broad zones of what Jessica Litman has called "lawful personal use"—uses of copyrighted works that are reserved to the situated user regardless of whether regimes of authorization might be developed to monetize them. Zones of lawful personal use should be defined using the sort of broad statutory language that until now has been reserved for the definition of copyright rights. A statutory provision for lawful personal use also should avoid subjecting such uses to a rigid form of the public-private distinction, such as the one that qualifies the current statutory definition of public performance. Many personal uses do occur in private spaces, but personal uses do not occur only at home or among a family and its circle of social acquaintances. They occur at work, at school, on trains and airplanes, and in many other places. Here copyright can usefully draw lessons from recent privacy scholarship's emphasis on the importance of context: like privacy, lawful personal use is subject to norms of contextual appropriateness and flow; copyright should recognize and respect those norms.[27]

Second, a regime of copyright recalibrated to facilitate play should sharply limit copyright owners' rights to control adaptations and remixes by third parties. It should do so by enumerating, in a fashion designed to emulate the 1909 act's discontinuous style, the list of adaptations to which copyright-holder control is permitted to extend. The list should not simply ignore fanworks and other examples of remix culture, as current copyright law now does, but should clearly reserve a broad range of remix privileges to users. Elsewhere I have written about how copyright law might apportion sequelization rights, reserving for authors the right to develop for commercial exploitation continuations of the original story while permitting users to experiment with fanworks and also to develop for commercial exploitation new stories set in other authors' fictional worlds.[28] In other cases—derivations of visual artworks or musical works, translations, and so on—the law should specify a similar apportionment and should instruct courts to safeguard the interests of users when deciding cases that fall near the boundary.

Third, in a regime of copyright recalibrated to facilitate play, rules about the privileges and obligations of information intermediaries should be designed with the balance between fixity and play in mind. They should facilitate, rather than impede, the efforts of intermediaries such as digital libraries and search engines to organize information and present search results in ways that are useful. The Google Book Search project is a paradigmatic example of the sort of use that should be permitted to both Google and would-be competitors because of the extraordinary social benefits it will produce. In addition, copyright law should set strict limits on indirect liability and technical-protection rules that cast a chill over the development of new technologies, including user-driven innovations. As we have seen, the problem is not simply that technology developers risk infringement liability for giving users too much flexibility, but also that the ongoing, legally mediated realignment of technology

247

markets encourages technology providers to overcompensate in the opposite direction, giving users too little flexibility. A properly constructed regime of indirect liability would seek to minimize both risks by explicitly inserting the legitimate interests of users into the liability calculus.

Reforms such as these, designed to restore interstitial complexity within the copyright system, would equip situated users of copyrighted content with the legal standing to direct flows of culture according to their own legitimate expectations and needs, and thereby to participate in the culture evolving around them. For exactly that reason, such reforms also would go a long way toward curing the legitimacy crisis that the copyright regime currently confronts. Although that crisis has resulted in part from market and enforcement behaviors that users perceive as abusive, it is also fueled by the copyright industries' habitual practice of normative overclaiming. Situated users are told that copyright is itself the font of all creativity, even as they daily experience that claim to be false. Clearer acknowledgment of limitations on what the copyright system can claim for itself would produce greater public respect for those claims.

Boundary Management within Social Landscapes

Chapter 6 developed a working definition of privacy as the process of differential boundary management by situated subjects and argued that privacy so defined is an indispensable enabler of the process of subject formation. In the case of privacy, the fixity that threatens emergent subjectivity is bound up with constitutive ideologies about the relationship between information processing and truth, and about the primacy of individualized treatment. While the ability to identify individuals persistently and accurately is important for some purposes, a just regime of information policy also must seek to provide the breathing room that critical subjectivity requires. Contextual integrity requires interstitial complexity; privacy law and policy should reinforce and widen gaps within the semantic web so that situated subjects can thrive.

Although privacy law purports to recognize a discontinuity principle, that principle operates primarily to protect small islands of concededly "intimate" or "sensitive" information and correspondingly small enclaves of acknowledged physical seclusion. In an age of distributed information processing, moreover, even those islands are fast eroding. As we saw in Chapter 3, discourse about surveillance practices and privacy laws operates primarily in the mode of technocratic confidence. Both private and public actors believe that if we can just collect enough information about people, the route to enlightened decision making in the realms of both profit and policy will be revealed. The information-processing imperative dictates that if more information can be collected and incorporated into predictive profiles and algorithms, it should be. We can be deeply troubled by particular uses of information but still believe, equally deeply, that the cure for misuses is even more and better information. Disrupting the information-processing imperative violates an implicit equation that is fundamental to the paradigm of liberal political economy: information equals truth.

Discourse about privacy protections, meanwhile, operates in the minor key of logical skepticism. The information-processing imperative has an important corollary, which I will call the "Luddism proviso": predetermined limits on information processing are a manifestation of irrationality, and those who endorse them are fundamentally antiprogress. Some kinds of information are more private than others, but to the extent that privacy protection for particular items of information can be made to appear arbitrary—because the information is relevant to a contracting party's decision to provide services, because its sharing might enable valuable efficiencies, or because it has already been disclosed to somebody else anyway—existing legal restrictions begin to fall away, and new, more effective privacy protections fail to materialize.

Consider, for example, the privacy provisions of the Gramm-Leach-Bliley Act, which governs the collection and exchange of information by U.S. financial institutions. Some legislators and privacy advocates favored restricting the extent to which such institutions could share customers' personal information with both affiliated and nonaffiliated companies. Lobbyists argued that such a rule would raise costs to firms seeking to market, and consumers seeking to comparison shop for, financial services. The bill reported from committee in the House of Representatives included an opt-out rule covering both affiliates and nonaffiliates. As finally enacted, the opt-out rule covers only information sharing with nonaffiliates. It permits information sharing with affiliates without limitation, on the implicit presumption that information given to one member of a corporate "family" isn't private as far as the other members are concerned.[29] Since both vertical and horizontal integration are widespread in the U.S. financial services industry, this rule facilitates an enormous amount of information sharing.

Next, consider the "deidentification" standard promulgated under the Health Insurance Portability and Accountability Act (HIPAA), which authorizes disclosure to third parties of data that includes birth year and partial zip code information. When combined with information from other readily available data sources, such entries can be reidentified with relative ease.[30] Interested parties have resisted additional restrictions on data disclosure, citing the need to conduct accurate population research. The specific nature of that need is left strategically vague, and the larger structure of privacy discourse allows it to remain that way. From a social welfare standpoint, not all needs are equal. We might think, for example, that medical researchers have greater need for population data than marketers of personal-care products do. To that extent, the drafters of the HIPAA rules agreed with the unequal-value proposition; medical researchers may acquire fully identified data if they observe other confidentiality requirements.[31] Yet they do not appear to have considered seriously whether some "population research"—for example, research designed to identify the population of potential customers for adult incontinence products, or research designed to develop more precise differential health-insurance pricing—has so little social value that we should not worry unduly about frustrating it.

Privacy scholars and advocates have advanced a variety of proposals for more effective protection, but proposals to impose substantive limits on information processing and sharing tend to make A2K advocates uncomfortable. Many U.S. legal scholars and technology commentators have tended to think that privacy problems can be addressed in a less heavy-handed fashion by giving people access to "privacy-enhancing technologies," such as services that enable anonymous Internet browsing, and by providing more comprehensive information about the privacy practices of public and privacy entities.[32] As the Gramm-Leach-Bliley and HIPAA examples illustrate, however, neither palliative affords meaningful shelter in the thousands of everyday contexts in which one must supply personal information in order to engage in ordinary transactions and receive important services.

But the liberal-rationalist tradition is not solely to blame for the dominance of the view that equates individualized information with truth and anti-individualization rules with antiprogressive animus. Liberal political theory's discourse of rights and human dignity also emphasizes individualized treatment at moments of decision. Privacy scholars sometimes draw explicit contrasts between aggregated treatment and individual dignity; thus described, the problem is not simply that invasions of privacy objectify individuals, but that they do so in a way that denies individuality itself, filtering out potentially individuating elements of context and subjecting individuals to categorical judgments. Yet that mode of reasoning about privacy contains the seeds of its own undoing. When the dignity interest is formulated in terms of a right to individualized treatment, it becomes difficult to argue that making health coverage or financial decisions based on highly granular profiles is fundamentally unjust.

The reluctance to make normative decisions about the limits of information processing is not well founded. First, a wealth of historical evidence undercuts the rationalist faith in the inevitable link between information processing and truth. Innovations in information processing are not invariably linked to just and wise social policy. Automated census technologies have been used to facilitate persecution and genocide, and automated surveillance technologies to support regimes of political repression.[33] Law- and policy makers tend to understand these examples as instances of conceptually unrelated (and morally repugnant) social ideology run amok. On that understanding, the problem is that bias occasionally diverts rationalism from its true course. But distinguishing rationalism from bias requires an omniscience that situated policy makers do not possess.

The insistence that dignitary concerns inevitably require individualization is equally curious. In the era of automated personalization, we have come to realize that individualization is not a sufficient condition of dignified treatment. The new personalized information services enabled by the semantic web are highly individualized, but still make judgments in formulaic and sometimes objectifying ways. Yet we have continued to act as though individualization is a necessary condition of dignified treatment. Scholars who study the moral dimensions of profiling argue that the notion of individualized treatment is inherently slippery because we cannot avoid inferring individual characteristics from group attributes.[34] On that account, the notion of perfectly individualized treatment is fictive, an unattainable ideal. It seems more sensible to inquire whether, both practically and theoretically, the ideal of individualized treatment simply cannot support the normative weight it has been asked to bear. Critics of the individualist tradition in liberal jurisprudence have long argued that it devalues other strands in our moral tradition that are predicated on equality and that are emphasized within the capabilities approach. In a world of increasingly ubiquitous information processing, perhaps the theory of privacy as room for boundary management can help point the way toward a different way of thinking about the requisites of human dignity.

If individualized treatment is not necessarily dignifying, perhaps the reverse is also true: perhaps dignifying treatment is not necessarily individualized. Put differently, if individualized treatment can be dignifying or objectifying, perhaps the same is true of aggregated treatment. Decisions affecting individuals and groups within society can be classified as individualized or aggregated, and as dignifying or objectifying, but the pairs of attributes need not always align in the same way. Legal and policy decisions affecting individuals and groups can be conceptualized using a matrix (below) that allows for the possibility of actions that are both aggregated and dignifying. Within privacy law and theory, as within liberal political theory more generally, the lower right quadrant of the matrix is undertheorized. It is occupied principally by the claims of various identity groups to equal protection of the law, but its potential extends far beyond such claims. An important purpose of privacy law and policy is to populate that quadrant of the policy matrix, advancing the concept of dignifying aggregation in a way furthers a more general, non-identity-based claim to the right to develop capabilities for human flourishing.

	Objectifying	Dignifying
Individualized	Profiling; Semantic Web	Due Process
Aggregated	Bureaucracy; "One-size-fits-all"	Equal Protection; Privacy

So conceptualized, a "just aggregation" principle underwrites an equality-based right to *avoid* individualized treatment, including both practices aimed at transparency and practices aimed at exposure. The situated subject requires protection against information-processing practices that impose a grid of highly articulated rationality on human activity, and against the reordering of spaces to institute norms of exposure and collective objectification. Against a background of increasing convergence, effective legal protection for privacy requires interventions aimed at preserving the commercial, technical, and spatial disconnects that separate contexts from one another. Policy interventions designed to promote semantic discontinuity should operate both informationally, by disrupting the grid, and spatially, by affording shelter. And on this understanding of privacy's purpose, privacy consists in the setting of limits precisely where logic would object to drawing lines.

A regime of discontinuity-based privacy protection informed by a just-aggregation principle would set stringent limits on the collection, use, retention, and transfer of personal information. Such restrictions in the United States too often reflect a purely proceduralist conception of consumer protection that revolves around notice and consent. Many other countries provide more meaningful protection, but have struggled to enforce privacy guarantees against data processors located outside their borders. For privacy protection to be effective in preserving room for emerging subjectivity, privacy guarantees must be substantive and global, aimed at introducing more than modest amounts of interstitial complexity into the semantic web.

For most cases involving use of personal information by commercial and nonprofit entities, a data fiduciary model based on fair information practices establishes a baseline standard for protection.[35] Some aspects of this protection might be waivable, but the conditions of waiver would need to be strictly defined and highly granular so that waiver could not become a tool for routine evasion of privacy obligations. In the Gramm-Leach-Bliley example discussed above, information sharing with both affiliates and nonaffiliates could proceed on an opt-in, unbundled (per-recipient) basis, subject to the operational-transparency requirements described earlier in this chapter. Where transfer is allowed, however, transferred information must be subject to strict purpose limitations, nonwaivable prohibitions on further transfer, and mandatory data-destruction rules. As Paul Ohm explains, some potential recipients of personal data are more trustworthy than others; to ensure compliance with privacy restrictions, privacy regulators should develop a system for certifying trustworthiness and prohibiting transfers to uncertified recipients.[36] The primary data fiduciary, meanwhile, would be subject to similar limits in its own uses of information. More particularly, either the law or implementing regulations would set restrictions on the types of personal information that the institution could use in making decisions about pricing and other terms of service.

Because privacy expectations and needs vary contextually, this basic structure would require modification for at least the following four special cases. First are contexts in which situated subjects' own well-being requires the collection, long-term retention, and more widespread sharing of individualized personal information. The most compelling example of such information is health-related information, which must be collected, kept, and often shared in order to enable successful treatment. In such circumstances, the governing law should waive data-destruction requirements and should permit data transfer as necessary for the effective provision of treatment, but should impose robust security requirements for information access and storage and should subject data custodians to periodic, publicly disclosed audits. Government entities that need to maintain and share certain permanent records, such as property records, benefits records, and judicial dockets, should be excused from data-destruction requirements, but should be required to redact designated categories of information before making the records available to the public.

The second special case involves databases used in research, including research on medical, public health, and social welfare issues. As noted above, the initial experience with data deidentification requirements has shown that data sets are much easier to reidentify than had been thought. In part, this results from the widespread public availability of partial data sets that can be cross-linked and correlated; many of the other proposals advanced here would reduce that availability simply because they would erect higher barriers to data exchange. In part, the ease of deidentification results from reliance on systematic and therefore predictable practices in the assignment of anonymous identifiers; in such cases, randomization of the assignment process would make reidentification more difficult.[37] The strength of the information-processing imperative, however, suggests that calls for the public release of deidentified data sets would remain strong and that incentives to develop new methods of reidentification would remain high. In some such cases, partial privacy protection can be achieved by introducing "noise" into data sets at a level that does not impair their utility. As long as that effect is reversible, however—a state of affairs that regulatory requirements requiring logical proof of concept tend to encourage—the likelihood of eventual reidentification is strong.[38] Ultimately, then, privacy policy makers must directly confront the extent of the stated need for accuracy. In contexts where accuracy is important—public health modeling for pandemic detection, for example—accuracy can be offset with confidentiality and security requirements. In other contexts, however, where there is no such compelling need, the balance should be struck differently. In particular, many for-profit acquisitions of population data for marketing and product research should not be permitted at all.

The third special case concerns disclosures of personal information via social-networking platforms. Regulation of the content of such disclosures would be difficult and ultimately counterproductive. Users derive important benefits from sharing the details of their lives with friends, family, and others. Yet users also derive important benefits from being able to establish and manage boundaries, and social-networking platforms have not met that demand with capabilities that remotely approach the context sensitivity that task requires. Part of the solution to that problem involves the tools used to designate disclosures for particular recipients, and will be discussed below. In addition, the privacy impact of social-networking disclosures can be minimized by implementing strict, nonwaivable rules governing commercial partnerships and the cross-linking of affiliated data services. Such rules should generally mirror the basic data-fiduciary model. Social-networking platforms should be able to share some information with trusted advertisers, but must do so without making users identifiable and without releasing the shared information for secondary uses or combination with data acquired elsewhere. Users who desire it should be offered the opportunity to contact advertisers without disclosing their profiles.

The fourth special case involves linkages between personal information and spatial management, including both generalized surveillance and processes for authentication of access. A regime of discontinuity-based privacy protection requires legal, policy, and technical interventions aimed at preserving adequate spatial privacy for situated subjects. Recall from Chapter 6 that the spatial-privacy interest operates in public spaces as well as private ones. In a networked information society, protection for spatial privacy requires strict limits on the retention of data establishing presence in most public spaces and in many technically private spaces that serve public functions (for example, a privately owned shopping center or the student commons at a private university). Transfers of such data during the term of its retention would be subject to the basic data-fiduciary model, and data-fiduciary rules also would operate to limit the real-time correlation of access records with stored profile data gathered from other sources. Both on- and off-line, surveillance should be visible; the persons or entities conducting it should be identified with particularity; and the rules governing the retention and processing of surveillance data should be publicly disclosed.

Finally, each of these proposed regimes also intersects with the problem of government data collection and use for law enforcement and national security purposes. As a practical matter, any privately held data set is potentially subject to compelled production, and we have seen that many government entities also participate actively in markets for personal information. A system of data-destruction mandates would not eliminate the latter activity, but instead would simply give the government incentive to acquire data before its destruction. Government practices with respect to personal information span a vast spectrum, and this chapter is already long. Many government uses of personal information are not different in kind from commercial uses and could be subjected to similar privacy rules. For present purposes, it is sufficient to note that the most pressing government needs for access to accurate personal information in real time, which relate to law enforcement and counterterrorism surveillance, are not inconsistent with the principled development and application of a just-aggregation principle. It is just such a principle that the U.S. system of constitutional and statutory protections has attempted to achieve by erecting procedural barriers that revolve around particularized showing of a need for access. In the post-9/11 world, many of those protections have eroded. Lawmakers, enforcement officials, judges, and public opinion have become increasingly willing to accept the argument that every piece of information, however seemingly innocuous, may reveal a threat to public safety when placed in context. Yet that proposition is too often asserted rather than argued for.

The push toward more complete profiling in the interest of security reflects a particular philosophy of risk management, which holds that risk is most usefully conceptualized as an inverse function of logical completeness in information systems. But the relationship between information processing and risk is much more complicated than that view acknowledges. Events in the post-9/11 world reveal a dialectical relationship between new technological methods of managing risks and risks that new technological methods create. Large-scale data mining and complex, automated systems for managing critical infrastructures rely heavily on algorithms that align and systematize the meanings of data about people and events. Formally, such systems approximate the requirement of logical completeness, an approximation that becomes stronger as more and more data are collected. Much evidence suggests, however, that relying on such techniques to the exclusion of human judgment does not eliminate the risk of system failure, but instead magnifies the probability that system failures will be large and catastrophic. The U.S. government's development of a profile-based system for screening airline passengers inspired the "Carnival Booth" study, in which a pair of MIT-based researchers demonstrated how a terrorist group might defeat the screening system by hiding its agents within designated low-risk groups.[39] In 2009, the Washington, D.C., Metro system's exclusive reliance on an automated network-management system produced the deadliest subway crash in U.S. history.[40] Security experts believe that many other critical infrastructure systems are vulnerable to similar disruptions.

Chapter 8 explored some of the ways in which discourses of secrecy and spectacle underwrite our information policy; automated information processes intersect with those discourses in ways that can increase the risks of harm. Regimes of secrecy premised on need-to-know access to critical information increase the likelihood of groupthink and reduce the likelihood that critical perspectives will be brought to bear on security practices. The Carnival Booth study demonstrates powerfully that insider bias may reinforce the shortcomings of automated systems rather than correct for them. Meanwhile, the events leading up to the attempted bombing of a Detroit-bound airliner in December 2009 demonstrate that the U.S. security apparatus retains an astonishing capacity to ignore the results of human intelligence gathering.[41] At the same time, the powerful conceptual link between comprehensive, rationalized information processing and security feeds the public demand for visible, information-intensive countermeasures without regard to whether they are also the most effective. As a result, security processes may tend to emphasize visibility over efficacy, or what Bruce Schneier has called "security theater."[42]

Security planning to minimize the likelihood of catastrophic harm requires due regard for the risks of too much information, too much automation, and too much secrecy. Many security experts argue that humans are the best threat detectors because the insistently analog human brain draws connections that automated algorithms may not. The surprising level of consensus on that view suggests that the right response to contemporary security threats may be counterintuitive: less reliance on predictive profiling and more emphasis on heterogeneous and often redundant layers of protection. For present purposes, it seems sound to conclude that the regime of privacy protection sketched in this chapter would not make us less secure, and might produce the opposite effect.

Legal and technical privacy rules animated by a just-aggregation principle would work to produce a networked information society characterized by respect for what Helen Nissenbaum calls context-relative informational norms.[43] Critically, this is so whether or not those rules are perfectly enforceable. Here, privacy theory and policy can draw useful lessons from the copyright experience. Legal prohibitions on infringement are relatively ineffective at preventing P2P file sharing of copyrighted sound recordings, but robust markets for digital music nonetheless have emerged, and the widespread availability of lawful, affordable access has supported the development of norms favoring payment. A system of privacy laws will always remain vulnerable to abuse. But the processes of norm formation do not run only one way; privacy expectations are shaped not only by what is possible, but also by discourses about the content of legal rights and the nature of good engineering practice. Meaningful privacy protection has been difficult to attain because we as a society have been unwilling to commit to it either formally or intellectually. If such a commitment could be made, there is every reason to think that, over time, a rigorous, principled commitment to just aggregation would generate its own supporting discourses and norms. Just as in the case of semantically discontinuous copyright, moreover, a privacy regime founded on principles of just aggregation likely would enhance the legitimacy of the surveillance practices that need to remain in place.

Material Practice within Technical Landscapes

Chapter 8 argued that the play of everyday practice has an important material dimension that requires room for experimentation and play by situated users of networked information technologies. Emergent regimes of authorization seek to stabilize commercial relationships and public functions in a way that systematically minimizes breathing room for everyday practice, and that threatens important social values. Rather than automatically reinforcing such regimes, laws governing copyright, trade secrecy, and privacy must work together to balance fixity and play. To promote semantic discontinuity, legal and technical rules governing interconnection should seek to foster a heterogeneous, imperfect technical landscape that allows scope for the play of everyday material practice while maintaining protection for the privacy of situated users.

In technical and policy discussions about the design of network architectures, the interplay between logical skepticism and technocratic confidence revolves around the tension between architectures that are "open," in the sense that no central decision maker controls their interoperability with networks, platforms, and tools, and architectures that are "closed." Technical communities and policy communities experience that tension differently. However, dynamics within each community contribute importantly to the emergence and gradual entrenchment of regimes of authorization.

Computer scientists and technology designers are inclined to view technical barriers to interoperability as artificial constraints to be overcome. That conviction derives partly from the information-processing imperative, already discussed. It also derives from a commitment to seamless, interoperable design that is both intellectual and aesthetic, and that is deeply internalized in the technoculture of computer science and engineering. Seamless interoperability and uninterrupted semantic flow are central goals in the theory and practice of network design. Belief in the fundamentally artificial nature of barriers to data interchange coexists, sometimes uneasily, with technocratic confidence in the possibility of defining increasingly granular, code-based rules for authorizing flows of information. As we have seen, that confidence manifests across each of the domains that this book has explored, in the development of rights-specification languages, surveillance systems, ubiquitous-computing systems, search algorithms, and so on. For technologists, the commitments to the foundational importance of openness and to the tantalizing possibility of control are reconcilable within a normative framework that expects, and indeed demands, continual challenge to reigning theoretical and technical frameworks. Most also recognize a role for legal and ethical rules that distinguish between productive inquiry and destructive vandalism.

For lawyers and policy makers, the considerations surrounding the interplay between openness and closure are more complex, reflecting the influence of additional, competing normative considerations that relate to social policy. Many (though not all) policy makers think that, other things being equal, open access to technical protocols promotes both innovation and competition. Other things often are not equal, however. As we saw in Chapter 8, the law protects technical secrets for a variety of reasons. In other cases, patent policy may support the development and licensing of technical protocols on a proprietary basis. In contemporary technology-policy debates, the intellectual property system's institutional support for closed systems based on proprietary technologies derives normative reinforcement from the seductive possibility of attaining more accurate regulation of behavior. Like Justice Holmes, we are skeptical of relying on the insubstantial reeds of virtue and internalized communal obligation to enforce rules of good conduct; unlike Justice Holmes, we are inclined to view the reed of law as equally insubstantial if there are technical measures that can accomplish the desired result. And once having committed to the importance of such systems, policy makers are inclined to think that they should not lightly be set aside. In particular, to the lawyers and businesspeople who play an instrumental role in defining and extending regimes of authorization, a professional culture that encourages the hacking of authorization systems seems exotic and alien.

Within the A2K paradigm, the ensuing controversies about access to and legal reinforcement of proprietary systems are most easily understood as debates about the relative merits of openness and closure. A2K advocates keenly appreciate the ways in which restrictions on technical accessibility have worked to tilt the playing field to the advantage of the economically and politically powerful. That history makes them enormously wary of legal involvement in standards setting, which they view as vulnerable to political capture, and of mandated restrictions on the technical accessibility of information systems, which they view as inevitably disadvantaging the powerless. Scholars like Jack Balkin, Yochai Benkler, and James Boyle have argued persuasively that in the realm of intellectual property, open access to networks, information, and technical protocols promotes not only innovation and competition, but also important equality-related goals, including freedom of expression and access to the fruits of technical innovation. Most A2K advocates acknowledge that unauthorized access to closed systems may legitimately be prohibited in some circumstances, but they would drastically narrow the law's protection of publicly available platforms for copyrightable content and other information services. They have advocated the adoption of national technology policies mandating technical openness in certain core capabilities, and they are inclined to view most legal restrictions on interconnection as normatively unjustifiable. When confronted with technical mash-ups that recast personal information about network users in new ways—for example, merging the "Twitter stream" with global positioning data to pinpoint users precisely in space and time—they have been inclined to praise the technical creativity involved and to overlook or excuse the privacy implications.

If we interrogate this binary framing of the relationship between openness and closure from the perspective of everyday practice, things become more complicated. The play of everyday practice thrives when openness and closure are in balance. Emerging regimes of authorization threaten the play of everyday practice not because they implement universal closure, but more precisely because of the ways that they change the patterns of openness and closure that everyday practice requires to thrive. Regimes of authorization establish closed circuits of information flow governed by their own internal logics. The patterns of information flow created by copyright management and security protocols produce important and highly artificial discontinuities for network users, subjecting them to technical and transactional barriers that interfere with creative and material practice. Yet regimes of authorization also benefit from openness with respect to the collection and flow of personal information about users and user communities. Openness and closure together supply the foundation for the dynamics of transparency and exposure discussed in Chapter 6, and eliminating only legal protection for closure would not rectify the problems that openness creates.

Consider Google's recent entry in the social-networking field, Google Buzz, which trumpeted its adoption of open-data standards. The most controversial aspect of Google Buzz was Google's decision to combine data streams from its Buzz and Gmail products and to display users' top Gmail correspondents as their publicly disclosed Buzz "friends." In response to public outrage over this unexpected blending of private and public, Google gave users a way to opt out of the default settings.[44] Substantive privacy protections such as those described in the previous section would limit Google's ability unilaterally to make such disclosures. But the open-data architecture of Google Buzz was no different from the proprietary architecture of market leader Facebook in one critical respect: it sharply limited users' power to create, maintain, and revise privacy-protective boundaries in context-specific ways. The Twitter stream example described above similarly exploits user powerlessness, a point powerfully demonstrated by the hack of Foursquare's constant stream of updates on users' whereabouts to generate Please Rob Me, a site that linked users' out-and-about updates with their home cities.[45]

When confronted with the privacy problems that unrestricted technical openness can create, A2K advocates tend to become sudden and unaccountable believers in the market's invisible hand. They argue that if platforms that allow social networking while protecting personal information are so desirable, users will create them, empowering new online communities to which other users will flock. As we saw in Part IV, that argument is structurally naive. The social and political effects of logical openness must be assessed in the context of a market structure that rewards transparency-promoting interconnection. Even new technical offerings touted as empowering users tend to harden their positions on transparency and exposure as they migrate out of the start-up phase. In addition, as James Grimmelmann explains, "The design of social network sites plays into plenty of well-understood social cognitive biases" by "activat[ing] the subconscious cues that make users think they are interacting within bounded, closed, *private* spaces."[46] Under current legal and market conditions, more effective tools for managing personal boundaries online are disfavored.

The A2K narrative about openness also tends to overlook the fact that even communities of practice organized around principles of technical openness and seamless interconnection sometimes pursue other values. A central tenet of open-source coding practice is that when serious disagreements about project direction arise, standards for the project can be "forked." Within the official discourse of open-source software-engineering practice, the possibility of forking serves as an important meritocratic corrective to the path-dependent engineering process. Yet forking also has other, geographic and political implications that are less well explored. The choice to fork an evolving protocol might be desirable precisely because it offers a choice to enable local platforms tailored to situated users' particular needs. Nor have open-source software designers fully rejected the closed systems characteristic of regimes of copyright authorization. In the DeCSS litigation, defendants argued that circumvention of the copy-protection system for DVDs was intended to create an open-source DVD player, and was necessary because no such player was available. Obtaining licensed access to the CSS technology would have required an agreement to embed robust, secret functionality at the core of an otherwise open product. While the two approaches are not incompatible from a technical perspective, some had raised questions about their philosophical compatibility. By the time the DeCSS case went to trial, however, the DVD Copy Control Association had granted two such licenses, evidence that at least two groups of developers had found the conflict to be reconcilable.[47]

These examples in turn suggest that the equation of logical openness with political freedom is too simple. Situated users value openness very highly, but many can neither fully embrace standardization nor abandon dialogue with closure. As we saw in Chapter 7, moreover, the alignment of unrestricted technical openness with political and expressive freedom simply restates the traditional liberal preoccupation with liberty and constraint. The play of everyday practice requires no such perfect alignment. Play is not, and could not be, wholly liberated from circumstantial constraint; it follows, then, that circumstantial constraints need not foreclose meaningful opportunities for play. The question is not whether constraints should exist at all, but how to locate them in a way that most effectively promotes all aspects of human flourishing. Wherever they are located, they will be challenged, but that does not necessarily make all constraints illegitimate. (Sometimes, transgression is just transgression.)

It is useful to disaggregate the problem of openness and closure into two narrower, functional categories subsumed within the paradigm of unauthorized access. One category of decisions concerns whether and when to penalize the act of unauthorized access to a closed system. The other concerns whether and when to enforce coordination around a closed standard. For regimes of authorization to succeed, the law must support both types of action. Many lawsuits that are framed as involving unauthorized access in fact involve the intersection of the "coordinated standardization" and "unauthorized access" categories, and those lawsuits suggest a template for resolution of the regulatory dilemma that the push for technical openness creates. The complex interrelationship between everyday practice and technical accessibility requires a regulatory landscape designed both to encourage certain kinds of interconnection and to promote certain kinds of closure.

Consider the recent litigation involving the RealNetworks Real-

DVD media player. RealNetworks designed a system that would enable users to play DRM-protected prerecorded DVDs, but it did not permit wholly unrestricted access to the content. Instead, it sought to provide access that, while it neither conformed in all respects to the applicable proprietary standard nor was authorized by the DVD Copy Control Association, nonetheless would provide meaningful copyright protection.[48] Plaintiffs objected not because the media player created an increased risk of infringement—by any objective standard, it did not—but rather because its development and distribution flouted the dominance of their regime of authorization. Although the suit was framed as one seeking to enjoin the provision of circumvention tools, the real dispute concerned the extent of legal support for privatized standardization—the extent to which law should delegate irrevocably to private actors the authority to specify how much content protection is enough. RealNetworks lost because the court read the statutory delegation as absolute, but the law could approach questions of privatized standardization differently.

The critical underpinning of regimes of authorization is legally sanctioned coordination around a closed standard. It is such coordination that most directly threatens human flourishing in the networked information society, and that a justice-promoting information policy should seek to neutralize. But the RealNetworks dispute suggests that the law could allow interconnection while imposing other conditions on it. Situated users should enjoy broad freedom to repurpose networked digital artifacts, but that freedom should end where legitimate interests—in copyright, in national security, or in meaningful privacy—begin. To provide meaningful shelter for the play of everyday practice, the law also should seek to counter the hardening of regimes of authorization more directly, by defining baseline implementation standards designed to preserve interstitial complexity in the technical environment.

In the case of technical protections for copyright, policy makers should seek to develop legal rules that differentiate more conscientiously between modes of unauthorized access that promote true piracy and modes that further the play of everyday practice. First, legal prohibitions on the act of unauthorized access should distinguish between circumvention for willful infringement and circumvention for the expanded set of lawful uses described earlier in this chapter. Second and correspondingly, legal prohibitions on the development and provision of circumvention tools should be narrowed to permit interconnection by new, unlicensed content services and media players that afford an adequate amount of protection against unrestricted reproduction and retransmission. Such prohibitions also should exempt the provision of circumvention tools designed simply to assist users in making lawful uses of technically protected content.

In addition, the law should decline to enforce copyright-protection regimes that unduly burden the play of everyday practice. Many current approaches to the design of copyright-protection systems attempt to satisfy users' desire for portability of media content without affording parallel flexibility to copy and remix. Emerging regimes of authorization encourage technology intermediaries to comply with technical and contractual restrictions to minimize their own exposure to liability. The law governing copyright protection systems should seek to reverse this polarity, giving both copyright owners and intermediaries incentives to design and implement systems that incorporate more tolerance for play. To claim the benefits of anticircumvention protection, copyright owners should be required to produce evidence of such design efforts. To claim the benefits of safe harbors from indirect-infringement liability, intermediaries should be required to show that their systems do not unduly restrict lawful uses. Such burdens are not unrealistic. Efforts by researchers and open-access advocates have shown that it is possible, for example, to define filtering protocols for user-generated content more or less restrictively.[49] The "least cost avoider" rationale for defining and enforcing intermediary obligations tends to magnify the importance of legal violations by end users; the more general point, which tends to get lost in enforcement-oriented discussions, is that cost considerations may make intermediaries an appropriate focus of regulatory leverage in either direction.

In the case of privacy, policy makers should develop regulatory interventions that differentiate between interconnection practices that magnify the transparency and exposure effects experienced by situated subjects, and other practices that offset or minimize such effects. First, the law should permit circumvention of technical-protection systems for proprietary social-networking and gaming platforms as necessary to enable users to make lawful use of their own information or transfer it to competing information platforms. Second, it should permit interconnection with proprietary platforms and services if and only if the new platforms and services enabled by the interconnection afford users adequate privacy protection. Such a rule would acknowledge the potential cultural and political value of technical mash-ups, but also require mash-up creators to introduce other protections to offset the new kinds of information that they make visible. For example, the creators of the Twitter stream/GPS mash-up described above might compensate for the increased geographic exposure that they create by limiting the accessibility of user-names so that only users specifically authorized to do so could connect a particular person to a particular location.

In addition, the law should discourage design decisions that unduly threaten the play of everyday practice by subjecting users to heightened transparency and exposure. Here, policy makers can draw concrete lessons from more theoretical scholarship about the historically and contextually contingent trajectories of human-designed artifacts. The flattened categorical structures and the lack of context sensitivity that so-called social software routinely exhibits are not inevitable, but rather reflect both the circumstances under which social-networking platforms arose and the values of their designers and operators. Two circumstantial factors in particular are worth considering more carefully. First, the vast majority of early adopters of social-networking technologies were quite young. Many (though not all) such individuals operate within flatter social schema than adults do, and consequently have less experience managing the boundaries that separate contexts from one another. This does not mean that the young do not value privacy; researchers who study online youth culture have shown that teens and twentysomethings often care deeply about preserving the contextual integrity of their online disclosures.[50] Nor does it mean that we should all simply learn to practice selective amnesia toward embarrassing antics and disclosures, as some commentators have argued. It means, instead, that the online behaviors of those who are still learning to construct and manage personal boundaries should not supply the normative baseline for policy making.

Second, as danah boyd has observed, certain design features of popular social-networking platforms—their relatively rigid, algorithmic categorization of people, and their inability to facilitate certain kinds of contextual separation—likely reflect the predilections and dysfunctions of geek culture rather than the preferences of social-networking participants more generally.[51] Whether to embrace those predilections is itself a choice, and one with large consequences. The failure to erect obstacles to the market-driven logics of transparency and exposure invites those logics to expand into the spaces where boundary management is impaired. The inability to reinforce contextual separation also intersects with and reinforces majority cultural norms; its "nothing to hide" ethos effectively privileges a way of being in the world that many people—immigrants bridging two cultures, gay and minority youth, people struggling to extricate themselves from difficult or abusive relationships—do not experience.

As in the case of copyright, regulators should seek to reverse the polarities in social-software markets that favor the provision of overly lax and contextually insensitive privacy-management features. In particular, regulators should pursue two kinds of intervention. First, they should require developers of social-networking services to implement strong pro-privacy default rules and to educate users on their importance. Second, they should promulgate standards regarding the substantive adequacy of privacy-management tools that create incentives to develop such tools and provide adequate instruction on their use. A conceptual template for this sort of regulation may be found in the movement for value-centered design, which stresses the iterative articulation of and engagement with normative values throughout the design process.[52] By analogy to the doctrines that establish secondary liability for copyright infringement, one might imagine a rule establishing liability for providing privacy-management tools that do not enable a reasonable degree of contextual variation and that do not afford a reasonable level of control. What is reasonable would depend on the state of the art, but would be the subject of an obligation to make continuing improvements.

A combination of conditional interconnection privileges and value-driven design obligations would work to sustain and reinforce interstitial complexity in the networked information environment. This in turn would help preserve semantic discontinuity within networked physical and digital spaces, safeguarding the processes and practices through which culture moves and changes and through which embodied, situated subjectivity is formed. Such a regime would entail a type of constraint on innovation; as we have seen, however, innovation in the service of openness is not an unmitigated good. We accept without question that new drugs should be evaluated for their effects on human health; so too, new technologies should be evaluated for their effects on human flourishing. Judged according to that standard, the regime I have sketched fares well. Most minimally, it is preferable to both of the currently existing alternatives—to the constraints on innovation imposed by regimes of authorization, on the one hand, and to the constraints on evolving subjectivity that result from transparency and exposure, on the other. More fundamentally, it would focus the attention of policy makers and technologists on the important and difficult challenge of facilitating the play of everyday practice so that the situated subjects and communities who engage in it can thrive.

CHAPTER 10

Conclusion: Putting Cultural Environmentalism into Practice

Thehe premise of this book has been that meaningful reform in information law and information policy requires a deep and fundamental rethinking of the most basic assumptions on which they are founded. Properly understood, "cultural environmentalism" requires engagement with culture in all its messy, materially embedded heterogeneity, and demands that we learn to value privacy as well as access and interstitial complexity as well as seamless rationalization. Put differently, it requires change in a culture that thinks culture and materiality unimportant and that treats gaps in market and informational frameworks as imperfections to be eliminated. That argument, though, suggests a chicken-and-egg problem: cultural change and legal change are both necessary, but each is dependent on the other. How are we to begin? A final lesson from everyday practice, however, is that practice does not need to wait for an official version of culture to lead the way. It seems appropriate, therefore, to close this extended meditation on the necessity of putting practice into cultural environmentalism with some thoughts on strategies for putting cultural environmentalism into practice.

Let us begin by returning to the point where we started: to the enclosure and environment analogies that proponents of free culture and A2K have invoked to support their arguments for reform. Reconsidered in historical and cultural perspective, those analogies usefully illuminate three important directions for the practice of cultural environmentalism.

One direction concerns the way that we talk about cultural environmentalism. Over the past decade, legal scholars have applied themselves with a will to the task of reimagining information-policy discourse in cultural environmentalism's image, producing new theoretical constructs

267

and elegant economic models. That work has produced much that is valuable, and has strengthened calls for a new way of thinking about information law and policy. What I have in mind here, however, are narratives that are relentlessly ethnographic and that force attention over and over again to the ways that culture moves, to the ways that subjectivity is made and remade, and to the ways that the play of everyday material practice leads to technical and social innovation. In a word, putting cultural environmentalism into practice requires good storytelling. We need stories that remind people how meaning emerges from the uncontrolled and unexpected—stories that highlight the importance of cultural play and of the spaces and contexts within which play occurs.

A second direction concerns the relationship between cultural environmentalism and the practice of regulation. Some scholars charge that if taken seriously as a prescription for law- and policy making, the theory of capabilities for human flourishing would undermine social welfare because its distributive-justice requirements would stifle technological and market innovation.[1] That argument presumes that innovative processes are not already constrained by the demands of existing interest groups; it presumes, in other words, that such processes now follow essentially neutral, merit-based trajectories, which the capabilities approach would derail. The presumption of a neutral baseline places the burden on reform proponents to prove that the changes they advocate will not make matters worse. And the argument about the vulnerability of innovative processes posits that the possibility of transformation in the technological and economic conditions of contemporary life is oddly fragile, simultaneously within our grasp and at constant risk of slipping away. But those conclusions are historically and theoretically unfounded.

In his history of the (first) enclosure movement and the industrial revolution in Britain, Karl Polanyi wrote about a "great transformation" of economic and social systems, driven by the need to subject labor, land, and money to the demands of a rapidly industrializing and increasingly nationwide market economy. As Polanyi explained, however, labor, land, and money are "fictitious commodities"; they are not produced for sale and exist independently of the market system that attempts to dispose of them. Although powerful social forces may press toward unrestricted commodification of these items, their regulation purely by market mechanisms

> would result in the demolition of society. For the alleged commodity "labor power" cannot be shoved about, used indiscriminately, or

even left unused, without affecting also the human individual who happens to be the bearer of this peculiar commodity. . . . Robbed of the protective covering of cultural institutions, human beings would perish from the effects of social exposure; they would die as the victims of acute social dislocation through vice, perversion, crime, and starvation. Nature would be reduced to its elements, neighborhoods and landscapes defiled, rivers polluted, military safety jeopardized, the power to produce food and raw materials destroyed. Finally, the market administration of purchasing power would periodically liquidate business enterprise, for shortages and surfeits of money would prove as disastrous to businesses as floods and droughts in primitive society.[2]

In fact, the dislocations and disasters described by Polanyi occurred, and caused immense suffering to the ordinary people who lived through them. The human suffering occasioned by enclosure and industrialization was alleviated not by the workings of the market, but by the development of "protective countermoves," such as regulation of wages and working hours, that were rudimentary precursors of the social safety net that modern industrial societies employ. Those reforms—all of which were experiments—did not stifle the burgeoning industrial economy, which proved more than robust enough to tolerate them. Instead, they prevented it from consuming itself.

This historical example holds three important lessons for policy makers in the emerging information society. The first lesson concerns the difference between historicism and determinism. Like the first "great transformation," the transformation now underway is probably inevitable. Fifty years from now, we will think of information networks and information markets differently than we do today. Many concepts that seemed unquestionable today will strike us as quaint and outmoded. That said, however, there is still enormous room for discussion about what the emerging information society will look like. Polanyi's analysis reminds us that the precise pathways of transformation are not predetermined. What is inevitable is change, not any particular set of economic, political, or social institutions.

The second lesson concerns the fiction of a self-regulating market economy. It is dangerous folly to think of markets as separate and independent from the societies in which they operate. In particular, the message that Polanyi sought to impart about the commodification of labor, land, and money applies to information as well. In the networked information society, human beings amass and trade or withhold information to promote self-interested economic goals. At the same time, information is stored in human minds and transmitted by human communication. It is the stuff of our collective culture, and a shift to the pure-commodity vision of information is neither feasible nor desirable. To avoid injustice, policy makers must consider the welfare of humans in addition to the welfare of markets.

The final lesson of the first enclosure movement is outside the frame of Polanyi's analysis. Those who opposed the first great transformation did not include only dispossessed tenant farmers, but also a group of agitators who have come to be called Luddites. Today, we think of a Luddite as someone who opposes technological advance, but historians have shown that this was not necessarily true. What the Luddites opposed, instead, was technology developed in a particular way and deployed in the service of an economic philosophy with which they deeply disagreed.[3] The Luddite challenge could not be met simply by enacting wage and working-hour regulation. It required recognition of the fact that the trajectories of technological development are not inevitable, and that some kinds of labor, though inefficient by commodity-market standards, may be worth privileging for their own sake. Such recognition was not forthcoming, and the Luddites became a vignette for the history books, a cautionary tale for technological naysayers.

So retold, the tale of the Luddites poses an important challenge for scholars and policy makers in the emerging networked information society. If technologies do not have natural trajectories, it is our obligation to seek pathways of development that promote the well-being of situated, embodied users and communities. When our preferred policy prescriptions persistently produce information architectures and institutions that undermine human flourishing in critical ways, it is time to question them and to experiment with ways of doing better. The tale of the development of regulatory countermoves to mitigate industrialization's costs, meanwhile, reminds us that attention to human values need not undermine the future of valuable innovation. Processes of technological and economic innovation are self-motivating; they are not so easily derailed. Both stories suggest that putting cultural environmentalism into regulatory practice entails looking backward and taking seriously history's lessons about the complex interrelationship of innovation, regulation, and social welfare. They suggest, as well, that those who oppose attention to human values should bear the burden of justifying their preference for existing patterns of influence over technological development.

A third direction for the practice of cultural environmentalism concerns the market valuation of information and information services. Technologies do not have fixed developmental trajectories, but they do have trajectories, which emerge gradually as the result of many decisions made by individual and institutional actors. Prevailing understandings of market value and market risk have large consequences for the design of information technology products and services and for the development and funding of new information technology ventures. Making different decisions requires different methods of assessing value and risk.

As we have seen throughout this book, the theme of risk management pervades debates about information law and policy. Firms that invest in copyrighted content argue that more complete copyright rights provide important security in an increasingly uncertain world. Firms and governments that make use of personal information advance a different version of the uncertain-world argument, asserting that derogating from their current freedoms will undermine profitability, sap innovation, and jeopardize security. These linked arguments for logical completeness in entitlements and regulatory restraint reflect an understanding of risk in which gaps in legal and informational frameworks produce vulnerability. That view in turn shapes the operation of capital markets, where a range of players from venture capitalists to private-equity analysts rely on financial projections to steer investment in information and technology firms.

The understanding of the relationship between information and risk management reflected in contemporary information-policy debates is a seductive one, but it is incomplete. Practices of risk identification and risk management are socially constructed in important ways. Although we are culturally predisposed to understand them that way, incomplete legal and informational frameworks do not themselves create risk. The possibility of harm from unpredictable future events is an unavoidable fact; to undertake any prospective enterprise is to confront risks of all sorts. Strategies focused on the elimination of gaps in informational frameworks can magnify risk, either by exacerbating preexisting dangers or by creating new ones. One seeking evidence for that proposition need look no farther than the recent and still-ongoing meltdown of the global financial system, an event precipitated by the toxic combination of reliance on automated, logically complete financial models and regulatory deference to those models.[4] In a similar way, reliance on the logics of commodification, transparency, and exposure simultaneously creates large risks to the processes of human flourishing and disables policy makers from recognizing those risks.

Meanwhile, there is ample evidence that capital markets do not understand how to value either the positive externalities that result from imperfect ownership rights in intellectual goods or those that result from incomplete access to consumers' personal information. Consider You-Tube, which has struggled to turn a profit despite its high market valuation. YouTube's owner, Google, faces ongoing pressure from investors who fail to see the profit potential in users' home-created videos of themselves, their children, and their pets, and who would prefer to see Google devote more efforts to attracting mainstream, predictably monetizable content. Social-networking giant Facebook has pursued a variety of schemes for monetizing users' personal information, repeatedly angering its subscribers, because extant metrics for market success demand and reward such monetization.

Putting cultural environmentalism into practice requires sweeping changes in the theory and practice of valuing information so that market logics will not push quite as inexorably toward commodification, transparency, and exposure. Corporations and financial institutions have struggled with the balance sheet and stock market implications of sustainable-development policies. Efforts to generate an "economics of sustainability" and associated metrics for corporate social responsibility have borne some fruit, but work in that direction is still preliminary. In a similar way, the institutional actors that play central roles in the cultural ecology will need to struggle with the financial implications of sustainable-development policies designed to nurture the cultural environment. Financial accounting and projection are decidedly unromantic topics, but the central importance of financial markets in the organization of cultural and technological production suggests that practitioners of cultural environmentalism should give those topics their sustained attention.[5]

Strategies for implementing cultural environmentalism will not emerge full-blown. As we have seen, that is not the way either culture or innovation works. They will emerge gradually as the result of situated actions taken in the belief that a just information society should prize both openness and privacy (even though that requires difficult distinctions to be made and maintained), that innovation can serve human values (even if the endpoints are not clearly in view), and that human flourishing requires the relaxation of technocratic logics (even in the face of our own discomfort). This great transformation too seems unthinkable, but it is within our reach.

Notes

Chapter 1: Introduction: Imagining the Networked Information Society

1. See, for example, Benkler, "Free as the Air to Common Use," 354–59; Boyle, "The Second Enclosure Movement," 33–40.

2. Boyle, "A Politics of Intellectual Property."

3. See, for example, Balkin, *Cultural Software*; Crawford, "The Biology of the Broadcast Flag," 621–29.

4. See, for example, Landes & Posner, *The Economic Structure of Intellectual Property Law*, 71–84; Yoo, "Copyright and Product Differentiation."

5. See, for example, Cohen, "Examined Lives"; Schwartz, "Privacy and Democracy in Cyberspace"; Solove, "The Virtues of Knowing Less."

6. See, for example, Posner, "Privacy, Surveillance, and Law"; Strahilevitz, "Privacy versus Antidiscrimination"; Stigler, "An Introduction to Privacy in Economics and Politics."

7. See Polly Sprenger, "Sun on Privacy: 'Get Over It,'" *Wired*, Jan. 26, 1999, http://www.wired.com/politics/law/news/1999/01/17538.

8. This observation is not new. See Kennedy, "The Stages of the Decline of the Public/Private Distinction," 1354–56.

9. See John Perry Barlow, A Declaration of the Independence of Cyberspace, Feb. 8, 1996, at http://homes.eff.org/~barlow/Declaration-Final.html; Johnson & Post, "Law and Borders."

10. See, for example, Easterbrook, "Cyberspace and the Law of the Horse"; Volokh, "Cheap Speech," 1833–47.

11. Lessig, *Code and Other Laws of Cyberspace*, 24–29. See also Reidenberg, "Lex Informatica."

12. See, for example, Mann & Belzley, "The Promise of Internet Intermediary Liability"; Picker, "From Edison to the Broadcast Flag"; Picker, "Rewinding *Sony*."

13. See, for example, Benkler, *The Wealth of Networks*; Lessig, *The Future of Ideas*, 120–40; Hunter & Lastowka, "Amateur-to-Amateur."

14. Hayles, *How We Became Posthuman*, 4.

15. See, for example, Lemley, "Property, Intellectual Property, and Free Riding,"1031–32; McGowan, "Copyright Nonconsequentialism," 1–5.

16. See Benkler, *The Wealth of Networks*, 278–85. Unlike many others, Benkler does not duck the problem of culture, but instead tries to work around it by specifying a set of minimal conditions vis-à-vis culture that cohere most closely with the aims of liberal political theory.

17. Solove, *Understanding Privacy*, 14–38.

18. For the classic form of the argument that privacy rights are subsumed within rights to liberty and property, see Thomson, "The Right to Privacy." A provocative recasting of privacy interests vis-à-vis liberty and property interests is Matheson, "A Distributive Reductionism about the Right to Privacy."

19. Sociological theories of privacy include Post, "The Social Foundations of Privacy"; Schoeman, *Privacy and Social Freedom*. For an illuminating analysis of the differences between liberal and dignitary conceptions of privacy, see Whitman, "The Two Cultures of Privacy"; see also Bloustein, "Privacy as an Aspect of Human Dignity"; Reiman, "Privacy, Intimacy, and Personhood."

20. On constitutive privacy, see Allen, "Coercing Privacy," 738–40; Cohen, "Examined Lives," 1424–25; Schwartz, "Privacy and Democracy in Cyberspace," 856–57. Solove's pragmatist theory of privacy is developed most fully in *Understanding Privacy*; for Nissenbaum's theory of privacy as contextual integrity, see Nissenbaum, *Privacy in Context*.

21. The characterization of Sen's capabilities approach as consequentialist will, I hope, be relatively uncontroversial. The description of Nussbaum's capabilities approach as a consequentialist one is somewhat more unusual, but I think it is justified. Nussbaum roots her understanding of capabilities for flourishing in a theory of the good life that is predominantly Aristotelian. Within that theory, the ultimate good is a life that is lived in a particular way. Nussbaum's approach differs from Aristotle's in its egalitarianism, which translates into a concern for distributive effects.

22. See, for example, Sen, *Development as Freedom*, 247; Nussbaum, "Public Philosophy and International Feminism," 770–73; see also Benkler, *The Wealth of Networks*, 279–85 (advancing an account of culture developed from within liberal political theory). As to Chon and Sunder, the pun is very much intended; their greater skepticism toward the liberal tradition is no accident.

23. See, for example, Sugden, "Welfare, Resources, and Capabilities." Other scholars argue that the theory's egalitarian prescriptions would operate to society's ultimate detriment by draining away social resources and impeding innovation. See, for example, Epstein, "Decentralized Responses to Good Fortune and Bad Luck"; Stein, "Nussbaum." This, of course, depends rather substantially on how social utility is measured.

24. For illuminating perspectives on liberalism as culture, see Paul Kahn, *Putting Liberalism in Its Place*; Taylor, *Modern Social Imaginaries*.

25. See Latour, *We Have Never Been Modern*, 1–12, 39–47.

26. See, for example, Bourdieu, *Distinction*; DiMaggio, "Culture and Cognition"; Foucault, *The Archaeology of Knowledge*; Giddens, *The Constitution of Society*.

27. Eagleton, *The Idea of Culture*, 96.

28. See, for example, Bowker & Star, *Sorting Things Out*; Gandy, *The Panoptic Sort*; Lyon, *Surveillance Society*.

29. Lessig, *Code*, 86–95.

30. Marvin, *When Old Technologies Were New*, 4–8.

31. Winner, "Do Artifacts Have Politics?," in *The Whale and the Reactor*, 19–39.

32. Different perspectives on that process include Dourish, *Where the Action Is*; Haraway, *Simians, Cyborgs, and Women*; Ihde, *Bodies in Technology*; Verbeek, *What Things Do*; Woolgar, "Configuring the User."

33. On culture and the production of space, see, for example, Harvey, *The Condition of Postmodernity*; Lefebvre, *The Production of Space*; and Soja, *Postmodern Geographies*. On surveillance and spatial production, see, for example, Foucault, *Discipline and Punish*; Lyon, *Surveillance Society*; Ball, "Exposure"; and Koskela, "The Gaze Without Eyes."

34. See Foucault, "Of Other Spaces"; Hetherington, *The Badlands of Modernity*, 20–40.

35. For a useful perspective on interdisciplinarity, see Garber, *Academic Instincts*, 72–79.

Chapter 2: From the Virtual to the Ordinary

1. The term "digital sublime" is Vincent Mosco's. See generally Mosco, *The Digital Sublime*; Nye, *American Technological Sublime*. On the nineteenth-century response to electric communication technologies, see Marvin, *When Old Technologies Were New*.

2. On the commodification of land, labor, and money during the industrial revolution, see Polanyi, *The Great Transformation*, 72–75.

3. For Hayles's recounting of the intellectual history of cybernetics, see Hayles, *How We Became Posthuman*. On the self as flows of information, see, for example, Floridi, "The Ontological Interpretation of Information Privacy," 189–90.

4. On mobile personal communication, see Fortunati, "The Mobile Phone"; Gergen, "The Challenge of Absent Presence." For accounts of virtuality as an escape from the particularities of embodiment, see Kang, "Cyber-Race"; Stone, *The War of Desire and Technology*. For challenges to that understanding of virtuality, see Nakamura, *Cybertypes*; White, *The Body and the Screen*.

5. Garfinkel, *Studies in Ethnomethodology*, 10–34, 68–73. See Bourdieu, *Distinction*; Geertz, *The Interpretation of Cultures*; Goffman, *The Presentation of Self in Everyday Life*.

6. See, for example, Butler, *Bodies That Matter*; Bordo, "Bringing the Body to Theory"; Yoshino, "Covering"; Young, "Throwing like a Girl."

7. Contemporary interest in phenomenology generally traces its roots to Heidegger's early elaboration of "being in the world" as the basis for knowledge, but the most systematic effort to develop a phenomenological theory of knowledge is Merleau-Ponty's *Phenomenology of Perception*.

8. See Crossley, *The Social Body*; Grosz, *Volatile Bodies*; Shilling, *The Body in Social Theory.*

9. Lakoff and Johnson, *Philosophy in the Flesh*, 97.

10. Wang & Spelke, "Human Spatial Representation," 376; see also Spelke, "Origins of Visual Knowledge." On the Western philosophical tradition's understanding and misunderstanding of space, see Curry, "Discursive Displacement."

11. See, for example, Foucault, "Of Other Spaces"; Lefebvre, *The Production of Space*; Soja, *Postmodern Geographies.*

12. Lakoff & Johnson, *Metaphors We Live By*, 139–46.

13. Lefebvre, *The Production of Space*, 86.

14. See generally Jeremy Black, *Maps and Politics*; Harley, *The New Nature of Maps*; Pickles, *A History of Spaces.*

15. For a comprehensive study of approaches to mapping the Internet, see Dodge & Kitchin, *Mapping Cyberspace.*

16. Castells, *The Rise of the Network Society*, 378–428. On the linkages between information technologies and material infrastructures, see Sassen, ed., *Global Networks, Linked Cities.*

17. Barabási, *Linked*, 69–72.

18. Sassen, "Locating Cities on Global Networks," 2–4.

19. A provocative effort to theorize this process within legal theory is Radin, "Online Standardization and the Integration of Text and Machine."

20. Mirchandani, "Practices of Global Capital," 370. On globalization and flows of culture, see generally Appadurai, *Modernity at Large.*

21. Haraway, *Simians, Cyborgs, and Women*, 149–81.

22. See, for example, Sheets-Johnstone, "Corporeal Archetypes and Power," 152–53.

23. Verbeek, *What Things Do*, 123–38, 195–99. See also Ihde, *Bodies in Technology*; Ihde, *Postphenomenology.*

24. Hansen, *Bodies in Code*, 20–22.

25. See http://geekfeminism.wikia.com/wiki/Category:Incidents.

26. Hayles, *How We Became Posthuman*, 192–207.

27. Haraway, *Simians, Cyborgs, and Women*, 161–72. For William Mitchell's more optimistic vision, see *Me++.*

28. See Certeau, *The Practice of Everyday Life*; Geertz, *The Interpretation of Cultures.*

29. See "NYC Surveillance Camera Project," http://www.mediaeater.com/cameras/; HollabackNYC, http://hollabacknyc.blogspot.com/.

30. See Dourish, "What We Talk About When We Talk About Context"; Suchman, *Plans and Situated Actions.*

31. Hickman, *Philosophical Tools for Technological Culture*; McCarthy & Wright, *Technology as Experience.*

32. Benkler, *The Wealth of Networks*, 60–63.

33. Bruns, *Blogs, Wikipedia, Second Life, and Beyond*, 9–30.

34. See generally Stuart Brown, *Play*; Gardner, *Developmental Psychology*, 228–47; Pellegrini, *The Oxford Handbook of the Development of Play*; Wenner, "The Serious Need for Play."

35. Sutton-Smith, *The Ambiguity of Play*, 221–31.

36. Lyotard explicates his theory of games in *The Postmodern Condition*. For some useful discussions of transgressive play in a variety of contexts, see Butler, *Gender Trouble*; Coombe, *The Cultural Life of Intellectual Properties*; McGrath, *Loving Big Brother*. A thought-provoking exploration of boundary play divorced from explicitly political ideas of transgression is Nippert-Eng, "Boundary Play."

37. Pickering, *The Mangle of Practice*, 21–24.

38. On liberal commitments in open-source communities, see Coleman & Golub, "Hacker Practice," 259–63; Kelty, *Two Bits*, 36–94. On media fandoms, see Rebecca Tushnet, "Payment in Credit." On communities of practice generally, see Wenger, *Communities of Practice*.

39. Gadamer, *Truth and Method*, 102–10.

Chapter 3: Copyright, Creativity, and Cultural Progress

1. Peters, "Copyright Enters the Public Domain," 708. On the public effects of private uses, see also Goldstein, *Copyright's Highway*, 23–24, 144–46, 199–208.

2. Feist Publications, Inc. v. Rural Telephone Service Co., 499 U.S. 340 (1991).

3. Hughes, "The Personality Interests of Authors and Inventors," 119–24; Bracha, "The Ideology of Authorship Revisited," 112–29, 133–35, 153–56.

4. Craig, "Reconstructing the Author-Self," 228–33.

5. See, for example, Gordon, "A Property Right in Self-Expression," 1555–60; Netanel, *Copyright's Paradox*, 38–41; Rubenfeld, "The Freedom of Imagination," 32–43.

6. Kwall, "Inspiration and Innovation," 1951–70.

7. Hughes, "The Personality Interests of Authors and Inventors," 116.

8. See, for example, Goldstein, *Copyright's Highway*, 200–201; Landes & Posner, *The Economic Structure of Intellectual Property Law*, 37–84; Yoo, "Copyright and Product Differentiation," 214–19.

9. Boyle, "Second Enclosure Movement," 44–49; see also Benkler, *Wealth of Networks*, 91–127.

10. See Amabile, *Creativity in Context*; Csikszentmihalyi, *Creativity*; Gardner, *Creating Minds*.

11. See, for example, Lemley & Reese, "Reducing Digital Copyright Infringement," 1373–78, 1391–94. An important departure from the narrative of the economic user is Liu, "Copyright Law's Theory of the Consumer."

12. For an overview of the dominant "tragedy" framework, see Ostrom, *Governing the Commons*, 2–13.

13. Finding representative discussions of the transformative user is surprisingly difficult. Users are largely absent from discussions about transformative uses. My claim

here is that the latter discussions implicitly presume a user with fully formed intent. See, for example, Campbell v. Acuff-Rose Music, Inc., 510 U.S. 569, 579–83 (1994); Leval, "Toward a Fair Use Standard," 1111–16.

14. Judge Posner's complements-substitutes distinction probably comes closest to being workable. See Ty, Inc. v. Publications International Ltd., 292 F.3d 512 (7th Cir. 2002), *cert. denied*, 537 U.S. 1110 (2003). That distinction, though, does not tell us what to do about literary borrowings such as sequels and fanworks, which have both complementary and substitutive effects. For an elegant meditation on the limits of the romantic view of copying implicit in the fair use doctrine, see Rebecca Tushnet, "Copy This Essay."

15. Bleistein v. Donaldson Lithographing Co., 188 U.S. 239 251–52 (1903).

16. Boyle, *Shamans, Software, and Spleens*; Chon, "Postmodern 'Progress'"; Coombe, *The Cultural Life of Intellectual Properties*; Elkin-Koren, "Cyberlaw and Social Change"; Jaszi, "On the Author Effect"; Lange, "At Play in the Fields of the Word"; Woodmansee, "On the Author Effect." On the non-neutrality of copyright's categories, see, for example, Arewa, "From J. C. Bach to Hip Hop"; Barron, "Copyright Law's Musical Work"; Barron, "The Legal Properties of Film"; Chon, "New Wine Bursting from Old Bottles."

17. See, for example, Ginsburg, "Authors and Users in Copyright," 7–8.

18. Lange, "Recognizing the Public Domain"; Litman, "The Public Domain"; Madison, "A Pattern-Oriented Approach to Fair Use."

19. See, for example, Lemley, "Romantic Authorship and the Rhetoric of Property," 878 n35.

20. Hayles, *How We Became Post-Human*, 12–13.

21. This formulation originated in Nichols v. Universal Pictures Corp., 45 F.2d 119, 121 (2d Cir. 1930), *cert. denied*, 282 U.S. 902 (1931).

22. For examples, see Yankee Candle Co. v. Bridgewater Candle Co., 259 F.3d 25, 35–37 (1st Cir. 2001) (applying the merger doctrine); Williams v. Crichton, 84 F.3d 581, 589 (2d Cir. 1996) (applying the *scènes à faire* doctrine).

23. For examples, see Boisson v. Banian, Ltd., 273 F.3d 262, 271–76 (2d Cir. 2001) (finding infringing similarity between two alphabet quilts because of similarity in "total concept and feel"); Satava v. Lowry, 323 F.3d 805, 810–12 (9th Cir. 2003) (declining to find infringing similarity between two glass jellyfish sculptures because only ideas and standard features were copied), *cert. denied*, 540 U.S. 983 (2003); Herbert Rosenthal Jewelry Corp. v. Kalpakian, 446 F.2d 738, 742 (9th Cir. 1971) (declining to find infringing similarity between two jeweled bee pins because the idea of a jeweled bee pin merged with its expression).

24. For examples, see Computer Associates International, Inc. v. Altai, Inc., 982 F.2d 693, 708 (2d Cir. 1992) ("[T]he more efficient a set of modules are, the more closely they approximate the idea or process embodied in that particular aspect of the program's structure."); Lotus Development Corp. v. Borland International, Inc., 799 F. Supp. 203, 217–19 (D. Mass. 1992) (holding that the particular arrangement of commands in spreadsheet menu was an expression of the idea of a spreadsheet menu), *reversed*, 49 F.3d 807, 816–17 (1st Cir. 1995) (holding that the arrangement of commands in the spreadsheet menu was analogous to a "method for operating a VCR" and that "'methods

of operation' are not limited to mere abstractions"); Mitel, Inc. v. Iqtel, Inc., 124 F.3d 1366, 1373 (10th Cir. 1997) (criticizing *Lotus* on the ground that copyright "does not extinguish the protection accorded a particular expression of an idea merely because that expression is embodied in a method of operation at a higher level of abstraction"), American Dental Association v. Delta Dental Plans Association, 126 F.3d 977, 979 (7th Cir. 1997) (holding that the arrangement of items in taxonomy of dental procedures was copyrightable expression because it expressed particular judgments about classification).

25. On the Lockean approach, see Gordon, "A Property Right in Self-Expression," 1581–81, 1568–72. On freedom of expression and ideas, see Netanel, "Copyright and a Democratic Civil Society," 347–64. For a representative discussion of the economic approach, see Landes & Posner, *The Economic Structure of Intellectual Property Law*, 90–97.

26. See, for example, Burkholder, "The Uses of Existing Music"; Clayton & Rothstein, eds., *Influence and Intertextuality in Literary History*; Hermeren, *Influence in Art and Literature*; Orr, *Intertextuality*; Pasco, *Allusion*.

27. For examples, see Castle Rock Entertainment v. Carol Publishing Group, Inc., 150 F.3d 132 (2d Cir.1998) (holding that a trivia guide to the *Seinfeld* television show infringed the show's copyright); Metro-Goldwyn-Mayer, Inc. v. American Honda Motor Co., 900 F. Supp. 1287, 1293 (C.D. Cal. 1995) (holding that a daredevil character in a Honda commercial infringed the copyright in "the James Bond character as expressed and delineated in Plaintiff's sixteen films").

28. See Thomson v. Larsen, 147 F.3d 195 (2d Cir. 1998).

29. See Newton v. Diamond, 204 F. Supp. 2d 1244 (C.D. Cal. 2002), *affirmed on other grounds*, 388 F.3d 1189 (9th Cir. 2004), *cert. denied*, 545 U.S.1114 (2005).

30. See Benkler, "Through the Looking Glass"; Benkler, "Free as the Air to Common Use"; Boyle, "Second Enclosure Movement"; Lange, "Recognizing the Public Domain"; Litman, "The Public Domain"; Lessig, *The Future of Ideas*; Samuelson, "Mapping the Digital Public Domain."

31. See, for example, Landes & Posner, *The Economic Structure of Intellectual Property Law*; Landes & Posner, "Indefinitely Renewable Copyright."

32. See Liu, "Copyright and Breathing Space"; Pessach, "[Networked] Memory Institutions," 90. For court decisions characterizing copyright as requiring "breathing space" or "breathing room" for subsequent creators, fair users, and innovators, see Metro-Goldwyn-Mayer Studios, Inc. v. Grokster, 545 U.S. 913, 933 (2005); Campbell v. Acuff-Rose, 510 U.S. 569, 579 (1994); Blanch v. Koons, 467 F.3d 244, 251 (2d Cir. 2006); Universal City Studios, Inc. v. Corley, 273 F.3d 429, 443 (2d Cir. 2001); Field v. Google, Inc., 412 F. Supp. 2d 1106, 1119 (D. Nev. 2006); Leibovitz v. Paramount Pictures Corp., 948 F. Supp. 1214, 1226 (S.D.N.Y. 1996), *affirmed*, 137 F.3d 109 (2d Cir. 1998).

Chapter 4: Decentering Creativity

1. Craig, "Reconstructing the Author-Self," 265.

2. See, for example, de la Peña, *The Body Electric*; Marvin, *When Old Technologies Were New*, 109–51; Hayles, *How We Became Posthuman*, 25–49, 192–221; Coppa, "Writing Bodies in Space."

3. For an exploration of textuality's roots in oral tradition, see Clanchy, *From Memory to Written Record*, 266–93.

4. Coppa, "Writing Bodies in Space," 243.

5. For an introduction to the "Mary Sue" genre, see Chander & Sunder, "Everyone's a Superhero."

6. See Katyal, "Semiotic Disobedience"; see also Peñalver & Katyal, *Property Outlaws*, 169–82.

7. Schur, *Parodies of Ownership*, 65–66.

8. For discussion of the role of the copy over time, see Homburg, *The Copy Turns Original*.

9. See J. Peter Burkholder, ed., "Musical Borrowing: An Annotated Bibliography," http://www.music.indiana.edu/borrowing/.

10. A useful introduction to SCOT is Brey, "Social Constructivism for Philosophers of Technology." On deconstruction, see Derrida, *Of Grammatology*; Balkin, "Deconstruction's Legal Career."

11. For examples of this approach, see Bijker, *Of Bicycles, Bakelites, and Bulbs*; Latour, *The Pasteurization of France*; Law, "Technology and Heterogeneous Engineering."

12. See Bourdieu, *The Field of Cultural Production*, 29–73; Csikszentmihalyi, *Creativity*, 36–45; Gardner, *Creating Minds*, 34–40.

13. See generally Becker, *Art Worlds*.

14. See Farley, "The Lingering Effects of Copyright's Response to the Invention of Photography"; Schur, *Parodies of Ownership*, 166–87.

15. See Sunder, "Intellectual Property and Identity Politics," 71–73, 91–94; Arewa, "From J. C. Bach to Hip Hop," 79–86; Schur, *Parodies of Ownership*, 24–41.

16. See, for example, Lange, "Reimagining the Public Domain," 482–83; Lange, "At Play in the Fields of the Word," 148–51; Moglen, "Anarchism Triumphant," 126–29.

17. On the relationship between art and play, see Sutton-Smith, *The Ambiguity of Play*, 133–50; see also Eisner, *The Arts and the Creation of Mind*. On the relationship between creativity and open-endedness, see Amabile, *Creativity in Context*, 115–20, 231–32: Csikszentmihalyi, *Creativity*, 120–21.

18. Discussions of the origins of paradigm-shifting theories in science include Simonton, *Origins of Genius*, 123–25; Galison, *Einstein's Clocks, Poincaré's Maps*, 221–63. Discussions of the origins of artistic inspiration include Boorstin, *The Creators*, 384–94; Geller, "*Hiroshige v. Van Gogh*," 39–42; Randall, *Pragmatic Plagiarism*, 238–40.

19. See, for example, Pessach, "Copyright Law as a Silencing Restriction."

20. Mezey & Niles, "Screening the Law," 100. On the creative fruitfulness of culture markets generally, see Cowen, *In Praise of Commercial Culture*.

21. See, for example, Aufderheide & Jaszi, *Untold Stories*; Heins & Beckles, *Will Fair Use Survive?*; Lessig, *Free Culture*.

22. See Amabile, *Creativity in Context*, 115–20, 231–32; Csikszentmihalyi, *Creativity*, 120–21.

23. See, for example, Michael Brown, *Who Owns Native Culture?*, 209–27; Riles, "Anthropology, Human Rights, and Legal Knowledge," 52–65.

24. Mezey, "Law as Culture," 35.

25. Burrell & Coleman, *Copyright Exceptions*, 188–91.

26. See, for example, Ku, "The Creative Destruction of Copyright," 294–311. The theory of creative destruction originates in Schumpeter, *Capitalism, Socialism, and Democracy*, 81–86.

27. Benkler, *The Wealth of Networks*, 19.

Chapter 5: Privacy, Autonomy, and Information

1. For a useful overview of the survey evidence and of behavioral and cognitive factors affecting consumer behavior, see Nehf, "Shopping for Privacy Online," 6–32.

2. Galison & Minow, "Our Privacy, Ourselves."

3. Richards, "Intellectual Privacy."

4. DeCew, *In Pursuit of Privacy*, 77–78. See, for example, Roe v. Wade, 410 U.S. 113 (1973); Eisenstadt v. Baird, 405 U.S. 438 (1972); Griswold v. Connecticut, 381 U.S. 479 (1965).

5. See, for example, Watchtower v. Village of Stratton, 535 U.S. 150 (2002); McIntyre v. Ohio Elections Comm'n, 514 U.S. 334 (1995).

6. For good discussions of the history and purposes of constitutional protection against unreasonable searches and seizures, see Harris v. United States, 331 U.S. 145, 155–74 (1947) (Frankfurter, J., dissenting); Boyd v. United States, 116 U.S. 616, 625–32 (1886).

7. For an example, see the Gramm-Leach-Bliley Act, Pub. L. No. 106–102, 113 Stat. 1437 (codified at 15 U.S.C. §6802(b)). Exceptions involve information-gathering activities that relate to intellectual privacy and therefore implicate the romantic dissenter. See, for example, the Video Privacy Protection Act, Pub. L. No. 100–618, 102 Stat. 3195 (codified at 18 U.S.C. §2710); Richards, "Intellectual Privacy," 387 (summarizing state laws mandating privacy protections for library records).

8. See Schwartz, "Privacy and Democracy in Cyberspace," 1660–62.

9. For classic expositions of the negative liberty thesis and the positive liberty thesis, see Berlin, *Two Concepts of Liberty*, and Raz, *The Morality of Freedom*.

10. See Allen, "Coercing Privacy"; Cohen, "Examined Lives"; Schwartz, "Privacy and Democracy in Cyberspace."

11. For a perceptive analysis of privacy and contextual variation, see Nissenbaum, *Privacy in Context*.

12. Rosen, *The Unwanted Gaze*, 166.

13. See, for example, Rosen, *The Unwanted Gaze*.

14. For the communitarian argument, see Etzioni, *The Limits of Privacy*. For the argument from security, see Posner, "Privacy, Surveillance, and Law," 245.

15. See Bennett & Raab, *The Governance of Privacy*; Post, "The Social Foundations of Privacy"; Rao, "A Veil of Genetic Ignorance?"; Regan, *Legislating Privacy*; Schoeman, *Privacy and Social Freedom*; Solove, *Understanding Privacy*.

16. For a perceptive discussion of the process by which privacy concerns give way to countervailing interests, see Regan, *Legislating Privacy*.

17. Schauer, *Profiles, Probabilities, and Stereotypes.*

18. Strahilevitz, "Privacy versus Antidiscrimination," 376–81.

19. See Rosen, *The Unwanted Gaze*, 8, 55–56, 198–06. In a similar vein, some economically inclined privacy scholars argue that the phenomenon of bounded rationality may mean that privacy has a valuable role to play in saving us from ourselves. See Strandburg, "Privacy, Rationality, and Temptation."

20. On the constitutive importance of risk and risk management in contemporary economic and social organization, see Beck, *Risk Society.*

21. On privacy protection for residential tenants, see Hamberger v. Eastman, 206 A.2d 239, 242 (N.H. 1964). On airplane overflight, see Florida v. Riley, 488 U.S. 445, 451 (1989); California v. Ciraolo, 476 U.S. 207, 214–15 (1986). On privacy interests in garbage, see California v. Greenwood, 486 U.S. 35, 40 (1988).

22. See O'Connor v. Ortega, 480 U.S. 709, 713–14 (1987); Mancusi v. DeForte, 392 U.S. 364, 369 (1968).

23. Kyllo v. United States, 533 U.S. 27, 34 (2001).

24. See, for example, Lisa Austin, "Privacy and the Question of Technology," 126; Gavison, "Privacy and the Limits of Law," 432.

25. United States v. Orito, 413 U.S. 139, 142–43 (1973).

26. Weinreb, "The Right to Privacy," 26–27.

27. In constitutional privacy case law, the "zone" metaphor originates in Griswold v. Connecticut, 381 U.S. 479, 484–85 (1965). For examples of subsequent federal cases invoking the "zone" and "sphere" metaphors, see Ohio v. Akron Center for Reproductive Health, 497 U.S. 502, 529–32 (1990) (Blackmun, J., dissenting); New Jersey v. T.L.O., 469 U.S. 325, 361 (Brennan, J., dissenting); Rakas v. Illinois, 439 U.S. 128, 159–60, 164 (1978) (White, J., dissenting); Zablocki v. Redhail, 434 U.S. 374, 397 (1978) (Powell, J., concurring); Dietemann v. Time, Inc., 449 F.2d 245, 248–49 (9th Cir. 1971). For examples of state privacy tort cases employing the "zone" and "sphere" metaphors, see Shulman v. Group W Productions, Inc., 955 P.2d 469, 498 (Cal. 1998); Stall v. Long, 570 So. 2d 257, 269 (Fla. 1990); Young v. Jackson, 572 So. 2d 378, 381 (Miss. 1990); Luedtke v. Nabors Alaska Drilling, Inc., 768 P.2d 1123, 1135–36 (Alaska 1989); Rhinehart v. Seattle Times Co., 654 P.2d 673, 679–82 (Wash. 1982); Multimedia WMAZ, Inc. v. Kubach, 443 S.E.2d 491, 499 (Ga. Ct. App. 1994); Urbaniak v. Newton, 277 Cal. Rptr. 354, 357–61 (Cal. Ct. App. 1991).

28. See, for example, Schartum, "Designing and Formulating Data Protection Laws," 2 ("I understand 'privacy' to be a concept that first and foremost expresses the state in which a person is inaccessible to others, for instance within a private sphere"); Schwartz, "Preemption and Privacy," 907 ("Tort privacy . . . creates a legal process for negotiation of limits . . . on the individual's desire for zones of privacy without community scrutiny"); Strahilevitz, "Reputation Nation," 1736 ("True enough, the private sphere of the home will remain a respite . . . and there will be market demand for zones of privacy"); West, "The Story of Us," 594 ("[W]hile it is troubling to give Henry the ability to silence Emily, it is a matter of no small concern that Emily is in a position to destroy Henry's personal zone of privacy").

29. For an overview of the common-law privacy torts, see Keeton, *Prosser and Keeton on the Law of Torts*, §117, 851–56.

30. See, for example, Dwyer v. American Express Co, 652 N.E.2d 1351, 1355–56 (Ill. App. Ct. 1995); Castro v. NYT Television, 851 A.2d 88, 98 (N.J. Super. Ct. 2004).

31. See, for example, Singleton, "Privacy versus the First Amendment," 121–33.

32. For a good overview of this literature and for the "project" nomenclature, see Richards, "The Information Privacy Law Project." On the particular problem of privacy in public, see Nissenbaum, *Privacy in Context*, 113–26; Nissenbaum, "Protecting Privacy in an Information Age."

33. Solove, *Digital Person*, 44–47.

34. See, for example, Lyon, *The Electronic Eye*; Rosen, *Unwanted Gaze*; Reiman, "Driving to the Panopticon." For the classic analysis of the Panopticon, see Foucault, *Discipline and Punish*, 200–09.

35. Solove, *Digital Person*, 36–41.

36. Descartes, *Rules for the Direction of Mind*. On the iconography of the linkage between vision, knowledge, and power, see Schmidt-Burkhardt, "The All-Seer," 18–26.

37. Solove, *Digital Person*, 33–35.

Chapter 6: Reimagining Privacy

1. See Nissenbaum, *Privacy in Context*; Nissenbaum, "Privacy as Contextual Integrity"; Solove, *Understanding Privacy*.

2. See, for example, Parker & Sedgwick, *Performativity and Performance*.

3. See Warner, *Publics and Counterpublics*.

4. See, for example, Spelke, "Origins of Visual Knowledge"; Wang & Spelke, "Human Spatial Representation." For a representative and eloquently argued example of the feminist critique, see Nedelsky, "Law, Boundaries, and the Bounded Self."

5. Westin, *Privacy and Freedom*, 32–42.

6. Altman, *The Environment and Social Behavior*, 3.

7. See Altman, "Privacy Regulation."

8. For useful discussions of collective subjectivity, see DiMaggio, "Culture and Cognition"; Holland et al., *Identity and Agency in Cultural Worlds*; Zerubavel, *Social Mindscapes*.

9. On liberal individualism as culture, see Paul Kahn, *Putting Liberalism in Its Place*; Taylor, *Modern Social Imaginaries*.

10. See, for example, Foucault, "Technologies of the Self"; Giddens, *Modernity and Self-Identity*.

11. See, for example, Cohen, "A Right to Read Anonymously," 1006–07; Cohen, "Examined Lives," 1406–08; Richards, "Intellectual Privacy," 416–21.

12. Foucault, *Discipline and Punish*, 223.

13. For useful overviews, see Lyon, *Surveillance Society*; Wood, *A Report on the Surveillance Society*; Ball, "Elements of Surveillance."

14. The sources cited in note 13 elaborate in detail the relationship between

surveillance and discrimination. In addition, see Gandy, *The Panoptic Sort*; Gandy, "Data Mining, Surveillance, and Discrimination."

15. Haggerty & Ericson, "The Surveillant Assemblage," 614–15.

16. See, for example, McGrath, *Loving Big Brother*, 12–16; Koskela, "Webcams, TV Shows, and Mobile Phones," 206–07; Phillips, "From Privacy to Visibility," 101.

17. Koskela, "The Gaze Without Eyes," 250.

18. Ibid., 257.

19. See, for example, Merriman, "Driving Places."

20. Altman, *The Environment and Social Behavior*, 6, 53–62.

21. For a utilitarian argument in favor of social discipline through structured shaming, see Strahilevitz, "'How's My Driving?'"

22. Mann, Nolan, and Wellman, "Sousveillance," 348.

23. See, for example, Wayne Harrison, "CU Posts Pictures of Pot-smoking Event: Reward Offered for Information about People in Photos," *ABC 7 News Online* (Apr. 28, 2006), http://www.thedenverchannel.com/news/9063737/detail.html.

24. See, for example, Bailey & Kerr, "Seizing Control?," 132, 137; Alan Finder, "When a Risque Online Persona Undermines a Chance for a Job," *New York Times*, June 11, 2006, 1.

25. Ball, "Exposure," 641, 643–45.

26. For representative examples, see Fried, "Privacy," 484; Inness, *Privacy, Intimacy, and Isolation*, 74–94.

27. Altman, *The Environment and Social Behavior*, 6, 156–61.

28. See Dean, *Publicity's Secret*, 3–13.

29. On tribal or essentialized identity, see Barber, *Jihad vs. McWorld*; Castells, *The Power of Identity*. On hivelike identity, see Alexander Galloway, *Protocol*; see also Baudrillard, *Simulacra and Simulation*.

30. For a useful historical overview of Westin's privacy surveys and methodology, see Kumaraguru & Cranor, "Privacy Indexes."

31. See Foucault, "The Subject and Power," 222–26; see also Reiman, "Privacy, Intimacy, and Personhood," 310–13.

32. See Jonathan Kahn, "Controlling Identity"; Matheson, "A Distributive Reductionism about the Right to Privacy." Studies of the use of surveillance techniques in social welfare systems include Gilliom, *Overseers of the Poor*; Monahan, *Surveillance and Security*. Notably, Gilliom criticizes the "privacy rights paradigm" for its insensitivity to the power dynamics of surveillance (121–34).

33. See Amabile, *Creativity in Context*, 115–20, 231–32; Csikszentmihalyi, *Creativity*, 120–21.

Chapter 7: "Piracy," "Security," and Architectures of Control

1. Lessig, *Code and Other Laws of Cyberspace*, 88.

2. This terminology, which originates in the political science literature, helpfully reminds us that regulatory modalities are means by which self-interested actors

pursue institutional change. See, for example, Raab & De Hert, "Tools for Technology Regulation." See generally Giddens, *The Constitution of Society*.

3. On the organizational changes enabled by the advent of information processing technologies, see Beniger, *The Control Revolution*.

4. Computer Fraud and Abuse Act of 1984, Pub. L. No. 98–473, 98 Stat. 2190 (codified as amended at 18 U.S.C. §1030). For the 1986 amendments extending the statute's coverage to nongovernment computers, see Pub. L. No. 99–474, 100 Stat. 1213. For the 1994 amendments, see Pub. L. No. 103–322, 108 Stat. 2097.

5. For good summaries of these changes and their effects on prosecutorial behavior, see Ohm, "The Myth of the Superuser," 1349–51; Skibell, "Cybercrimes and Misdemeanors," 927–33.

6. The "surface level" terminology is my own. See Cohen, "Pervasively Distributed Copyright Enforcement," 4–7.

7. For good descriptions of the music industry's failure to implement a coordinated strategy for surface-level protection and of the motion picture industry's relatively successful implementation, see Gillespie, *Wired Shut*, 137–91.

8. Pub. L. No. 105–304, 112 Stat. 2863–77 (codified at 17 U.S.C. §§1201–1204).

9. For a fuller description, see Cohen, "Pervasively Distributed Copyright Enforcement," 9–11.

10. See Electronic Frontier Foundation, "Unintended Consequences: Twelve Years under the DMCA" (2010), http://www.eff.org/files/eff-unintended-consequences-12-years.pdf, 2–6.

11. Failed legislative efforts include the Consumer Broadband and Digital Television Promotion Act of 2002, Proposed Bill No. S. 2048, 107th Congress, 2nd Session; the Digital Transition Content Security Act of 2005, Proposed Bill No. H.R. 4569, 109th Congress, 2nd Session; and the Audio Broadcast Flag Licensing Act of 2006, Proposed Bill No. H.R. 4861, 109th Congress, 2nd Session. In 2003, the entertainment industries successfully prevailed on the Federal Communications Commission to issue a broadcast-content protection rule, but the rule was invalidated on jurisdictional grounds. See American Library Association v. Federal Communications Commission, 406 F.3d 689 (D.C. Cir. 2005). For the FCC's cable plug-and-play rule, see Federal Communications Commission, "Commercial Availability of Navigation Devices and Compatibility between Cable Systems and Consumer Electronics Equipment," 68 Fed. Reg. 66,728 (Nov. 28, 2003).

12. See High Level Group on Digital Rights Management, Final Report (2004), http://ec.europa.eu/information_society/eeurope/2005/all_about/digital_rights_man/doc/040709_hlg_drm_2nd_meeting_final_report.pdf.

13. Intel, "Technology Overview: Intel Trusted Execution Technology," http://www.intel.com/technology/security/downloads/TrustedExec_Overview.pdf.

14. Pub. L. No. 105–304, 112 Stat. 2877–86 (codified at 17 U.S.C. §512).

15. Quilter & Urban, "Efficient Process or 'Chilling Effects'?"

16. The statutory provision authorizing injunctive relief against backbone providers is 17 U.S.C. §512(j)(1)(b)(ii). For a discussion of the Listen4Ever case, see

Daniel W. Kopko, "Looking for a Crack to Break the Internet's Back: The Listen4ever Case and Backbone Provider Liability Under the Copyright Act and the DMCA," *Computer Law Review and Technology Journal* 8 (2003): 83.

17. Higher Education Opportunity Act, Pub. L. No. 110–315, 122 Stat. 3078 (codified at 20 U.S.C. §1094(a)(29)). For the background notice-of-repeat-infringement rule, see 17 U.S.C. §512(e).

18. See Rick Mitchell, "French Constitutional Panel OKs Piracy Law, Cutting Internet Access After 'Three-Strikes,'" BNA *Patent, Trademark & Copyright Journal*, Oct. 30, 2009, 804.

19. See Sarah McBride & Ethan Smith, "Music Industry to Abandon Mass Suits," *Wall Street Journal*, Dec. 19, 2008.

20. See ibid.

21. See Eriq Gardner, "EXCLUSIVE: 'Expendables' Producer Next to Sue Thousands of Online Pirates," *Hollywood Reporter*, Jan. 4, 2011, http://www.hollywood reporter.com/blogs/thr-esq/expendables-producer-sue-thousands-online-68257.

22. For a good summary of the rhetoric deployed by representatives of the motion picture industry, see Gillespie, *Wired Shut*, 118–25.

23. See Gillespie, "Characterizing Copyright in the Classroom."

24. See U.S. Department of Homeland Security, "US-VISIT Biometric Identification Services," http://www.dhs.gov/files/programs/gc_1208531081211.shtm; Peter Alford, "Japan Immigration to Scan Foreign Faces," *Australian*, Oct. 25, 2007, 11; Wilmer Heck & Annemarie Kas, "Fingerprints in Passports Can't Be Used by the Police—Yet," *NRC Handelsblad*, Sept. 18, 2009, 1.

25. The most recent report, *Privacy and Human Rights 2006*, can be found online at http://www.privacyinternational.org/article.shtml?cmd[347]=x-347-559458.

26. See U.S. Department of Homeland Security, "DHS Announces $12 Million for Operation Stonegarden to Support Local Border Security Efforts," Dec. 15, 2006, http://www.dhs.gov/xnews/releases/pr_1166216119621.shtm; U.S. Department of Homeland Security, "Secretary Napolitano Announces $60 Million in Operation Stonegarden Grants for Border States," June 4, 2009, http://www.dhs.gov/ynews/releases/pr_1244070019405.shtm.

27. On the privatization of public space, see generally Kohn, *Brave New Neighborhoods*, and Low & Smith, *The Politics of Public Space*.

28. See Communications Assistance for Law Enforcement Act, Pub. L. No. 103–414, 108 Stat. 4279 (codified at 47 U.S.C. §§1001–10); U.S. Federal Communications Commission, "Communications Assistance for Law Enforcement and Broadband Access and Services," 20 *F.C.C. Record* 14989 (2005), *affirmed*, American Council on Education v. F.C.C., 451 F.3d 226 (D.C. Cir. 2006).

29. See Foreign Intelligence Surveillance Act, Pub. L. No. 95–511, 92 Stat. 1783 (codified at 50 U.S.C. §1801); Schwartz, "Warrantless Wiretapping, FISA Reform, and The Lessons of Public Liberty," 411–17.

30. See Eric Lichtblau & James Risen, "Spy Agency Mined Vast Data Trove, Officials Report," *New York Times*, Dec. 24, 2005; Leslie Cauley, "NSA Has Massive Data-

base of Americans' Phone Calls," *USA Today*, May 11, 2006; Alexander Dryer, "How the NSA Does 'Social Network Analysis,'" *Slate*, May 15, 2006, http://www.slate.com/id/2141801; Siobhan Gorman, "NSA's Domestic Spying Grows as Agency Sweeps Up Data," *Wall Street Journal*, Mar. 10, 2008.

31. See Ohm, "The Rise and Fall of Invasive ISP Surveillance," 1432–37.

32. See Comcast Corp. v. Federal Communications Commission, 600 F.3d 642 (D.C. Cir. 2010); Paul Barbaglio, "House Commerce Adopts Resolution to Overturn FCC's Net Neutrality Rules," *BNA Electronic Commerce & Law Report*, Mar. 16, 2011, 420; John Letzing, "As Debate Intensifies, Net Neutrality Rivals Invest in D.C. Influence," *Wall Street Journal*, Apr. 7, 2010, https://secure.marketwatch.com/story/net-neutrality-rivals-invest-in-dc-influence-2010-04-06; Kevin Bogardus & Kim Hart, "Companies Lobby Newest FCC Members on Net Neutrality Rule," *Hill*, Nov. 11, 2009, 16.

33. For a summary of official policy on fusion centers and links to reports and guidelines, see U.S. Department of Justice, "Fusion Centers and Intelligence Sharing," http://www.it.ojp.gov/default.aspx?area=nationalInitiatives&page=1181. A wider variety of information can be found at Electronic Privacy Information Center, "Information Fusion Centers and Privacy," available at http://epic.org/privacy/fusion/.

34. Hoofnagle, "Big Brother's Little Helpers," 598–618.

35. See Electronic Communications Privacy Act, Pub. L. 99–508, 100 Stat. 1848 (codified as amended at 18 U.S.C. §2703(f)); Directive 2006/24/EC of the European Parliament and of the Council of 15 March 2006 on the retention of data generated or processed in connection with the provision of publicly available electronic communications services or of public communications networks, 2006 O.J. (L 105) 54.

36. Spencer S. Hsu, "States Get More Time to Comply with Real ID," *Washington Post*, Dec. 19, 2009.

37. DeNardis, *Protocol Politics*, 79.

38. See Ashlee Vance, "Microsoft Office 2010 Starts Ascension to the Cloud," Bits Blog, *New York Times*, July 13, 2009, http://bits.blogs.nytimes.com/2009/07/13/microsoft-office-2010-starts-ascension-to-the-cloud/.

39. See, for example, Nik Bonopartis, "Net Vigilantes Go Where Police Can't: Groups Help Identify Pedophiles," *Poughkeepsie Journal*, Oct. 4, 2004. Texas Border Watch, http://www.texasborderwatch.com/. For a good general discussion of the dynamic by which ordinary people are recruited as participants in surveillance activities, see Andrejevic, *iSpy*, 175–82. To be fair, vigilance by ordinary citizens has achieved some spectacular successes. See, for example, Corey Kilgannon & Michael S. Schmidt, "Street Vendors' Keen Eyes Alerted Police to Threat," *New York Times*, May 3, 2010 (attempted bombing of Times Square in New York City); Anahad O'Connor & Eric Schmitt, "Terror Attempt Seen as Man Tries to Ignite Device on Jet," *New York Times*, Dec. 26, 2009 (attempted bombing of Detroit-bound airliner on Christmas Day).

40. For examples, see "Address by the Right Honorable Tony Blair, Prime Minister of the United Kingdom of Great Britain and Northern Ireland," *Congressional Record* 149: H7060 ("The virus is terrorism"); "Authorizing Use of United States Armed Forces against Those Responsible for Recent Attacks against the United States," *Congres-*

sional Record 147: H5638 (statement of Rep. Hoyer) ("[W]e must cut out and destroy this cancer which plagues civilized society"); "National Security in the Wake of Events of September 11," *Congressional Record* 147: H6121 (statement of Rep. McInnis) ("My analogy . . . is a battle . . . against a cancer").

41. See U.S. Department of Homeland Security, "About the Homeland Security Advisory System," http://www.dhs.gov/files/programs/Copy_of_press_release_0046 .shtm#2.

42. Lessig, *Code and Other Laws of Cyberspace*, 88.

43. See, for example, Dam, "Self-Help in the Digital Jungle," 394–97, 407–09; Smith, "Self-Help and the Nature of Property," 101–06.

44. Bracha, "Standing Copyright Law on Its Head?," 1806.

45. See, for example, Balkin, "Digital Speech and Democratic Culture"; Benkler, "Free as the Air to Common Use."

46. See, for example, von Lohmann, "Measuring the Digital Millennium Copyright Act against the Darknet," 640–43.

47. Biddle et al., "The Darknet and the Future of Copyright Protection."

48. For a well-supported argument that not all copy protection will be broken, see Ohm, "The Myth of the Superuser," 1359–62.

49. See http://www.freedom-to-tinker.com/.

50. See, for example, Dam, "Self-Help in the Digital Jungle," 407–12; Picker, "From Edison to the Broadcast Flag," 293–96.

51. See, for example, Cybersecurity Enhancement Act of 2010, Bill Number H.R. 4061.EH, §105(a), 111th Congress, 1st Session (version enacted in House).

52. See Birnhack & Elkin-Koren, "The Invisible Handshake."

53. See In re Charter Communications, Inc. Subpoena Enforcement Matter, 393 F.3d 771 (8th Cir. 2005); Recording Industry of America v. Verizon Internet Services, Inc., 351 F.3d 1229 (D.C. Cir. 2003), *cert. denied*, 543 U.S. 924 (2004).

54. Zittrain, *The Future of the Internet*, 57–59.

55. See Grimmelmann, "Regulation by Software"; Wagner, "On Software Regulation."

56. Zittrain, *The Future of the Internet*, 70–73.

57. Foucault, *Discipline and Punish*, 200–09.

58. Katyal, "The New Surveillance," 309–20; Katyal, "Privacy vs. Piracy," 244–51.

59. Foucault, *Discipline and Punish*, 135–69, 210–28.

60. Boyle, "Foucault in Cyberspace."

Chapter 8: Rethinking "Unauthorized Access"

1. Sassen, *Territory, Authority, Rights*, 379–86.

2. For a description of this process, see Barabási, *Linked*, 41–92.

3. Swyngedouw, "Neither Global Nor Local," 140–42.

4. On global standardization of copyright rules, see Birnhack, "Global Copyright, Local Speech." On convergence in social networking, see Ching-man Au Yeung,

Ilaria Liccardi, Kanghao Lu, Oshani Senaviratne, & Tim Berners-Lee, "Decentralization: The Future of Online Social Networking," W3C *Workshop on the Future of Social Networking*, Jan. 2009, http://www.w3.org/2008/09/msnws/papers/decentralization.pdf; Keven Moffitt, "Facebook's Open Graph: Could It Be the End of the Walled Garden?" *E-Commerce Developer*, May 13, 2010, http://www.ecommercedeveloper.com/articles/1903-Facebook-s-Open-Graph-Could-It-Be-the-End-of-the-Walled-Garden-; Juan Carlos Perez, "Data Portability: Reasonable Goal or Impossible Dream?," *PCWorld*, Jan. 21, 2008, http://www.pcworld.com/businesscenter/article/141541/data_portability_reasonable_goal_or_impossible_dream.html.

5. For a comprehensive discussion of the challenges of cultural preservation in the networked information environment, see Pessach, "[Networked] Memory Institutions."

6. For a helpful summary of Google's policies regarding the display of books still under copyright, see Jonathan Band, "A Guide for the Perplexed: Libraries and the Google Library Project Settlement," American Library Association and the Association of Research Libraries, Nov. 13, 2008, 4–5, http://www.arl.org/bm~doc/google-settlement-13nov08.pdf.

7. See Eric Bangeman, "Internet Archive Settles Suit over Wayback Machine," *Ars Technica*, Aug. 31, 2006, http://arstechnica.com/old/content/2006/08/7634.ars; Steve Lohr, "It's History, So Be Careful Using Twitter," *New York Times*, Apr. 15, 2010.

8. See Curry & Lievrouw, "Places to Read Anonymously." On the geographies of digital memory and forgetting, see also Blanchette & Johnson, "Data Retention and the Panoptic Society"; Mayer-Schönberger, *Delete*.

9. See U.S. Federal Communications Commission, "In the Matter of Preserving the Open Internet: Broadband Industry Practices," No. 10-201, Dec. 21, 2010, Appendix A, http://www.fcc.gov/Daily_Releases/Daily_Business/2010/db1223/FCC-10-201A1.pdf; U.S. Federal Communications Commission, "In the Matter of Preserving the Open Internet: Broadband Industry Practices," No. 09-93, Oct. 22, 2009, ¶¶ 118–132, http://hraunfoss.fcc.gov/edocs_public/attachmatch/FCC-09-93A1.pdf. As of this writing, Congress may block the 2010 regulation from taking effect. See Paul Barbaglio, "House Commerce Adopts Resolution to Overturn FCC's Net Neutrality Rules," *BNA Electronic Commerce & Law Report*, Mar. 16, 2011, 420.

10. On affordances, see Norman, *The Design of Everyday Things*, 9–11, 87–104; Pfaffenberger, "Social Anthropology of Technology," 503–07.

11. See, for example, U.S. Federal Communications Commission, "Digital Broadcast Content Protection: Notice of Proposed Rulemaking," 68 Fed. Reg. 67,624, 67,625 (Dec. 3, 2003); U.S. Federal Communications Commission, "Report and Order and Further Notice of Proposed Rulemaking: In the Matter of Digital Broadcast Content Protection," No. 03-273, Nov. 4, 2003, ¶ 63. For an early model of digital rights management contemplating atomized authorization, see Stefik, "Letting Loose the Light," 226–34.

12. See Gillespie, *Wired Shut*, 236–40.

13. Weiser, "Creating the Invisible Interface." A fuller exposition of Weiser's vision of computing appears in Weiser, "The Computer for the 21st Century."

14. In a provocative article, Jerry Kang and Dana Cuff suggest that users might employ pervasive computing capabilities to bring the public sphere into the shopping mall, tagging places and products with persistent, user-generated commentary and critique; see Kang & Cuff, "Pervasive Computing." In a similar vein, see Anne Galloway, "Intimations of Everyday Life."

15. See Saul Hansell, "AOL Removes Search Data on Vast Group of Web Users," *New York Times*, Aug. 8, 2006; Michael Barbaro & Tom Zeller, Jr., "A Face Is Exposed for AOL Searcher No. 4417749," *New York Times*, Aug. 9, 2006.

16. See Louise Story and Brad Stone, "Facebook Retreats on Online Tracking," *New York Times*, Nov. 30, 2007; Caroline McCarthy, "Facebook Beacon Has Poked Its Last," *CNet News*, Sept. 18, 2009, http://news.cnet.com/8301-13577_3-10357107-36.html; Tomio Geron, "Judge Approves Facebook's Privacy Settlement," *Wall Street Journal*, Mar. 19, 2010, Tech, http://online.wsj.com/article/SB1000142405274870358090457 5131742105971382.html.

17. See Mike Musgrove, "Google E-Mail Ad Plans Raise Fears About Privacy," *Washington Post*, Apr. 2, 2004; John Markoff, "Google Sends a Message to Competitors," *New York Times*, Apr. 1, 2004.

18. See Google Privacy Policy ("Information We Collect and How We Use It"), revised Oct. 3, 1010, http://www.google.com/privacypolicy.html; Louise Story and Miguel Helft, "Google Buys Online Ad Firm for $3.1 Billion," *New York Times*, Apr. 14, 2007; Miguel Helft, "Google to Offer Ads Based on Interests," *New York Times*, Mar. 11, 2009.

19. Pasquale, "Beyond Competition and Innovation"; see also Introna & Nissenbaum, "Shaping the Web."

20. Google Corporate Information, "Company Overview," http//www.google .com/corporate/index.html.

21. Carroll, "Creative Commons and the New Intermediaries," 59. The "semantic web" nomenclature originates with Tim Berners-Lee. See Berners-Lee, Hendler, and Lassila, "The Semantic Web."

22. See Goldman, "A Coasean Analysis of Marketing."

23. The classic statement of this argument is Winner, *Autonomous Technology*.

24. See Kephart & Chess, "The Vision of Autonomic Computing"; IBM, "Autonomic Computing: IBM's Perspective on the State of Information Technology," http://www.research.ibm.com/autonomic/manifesto/autonomic_computing.pdf. For a set of thought-provoking meditations on the philosophical and legal implications of IBM's project, see Hildebrandt & Rouvroy, *Law, Human Agency, and Autonomic Computing*.

25. Zittrain, *The Future of the Internet*, 67–74.

26. See ibid., 104–26.

27. Ohm, "The Myth of the Superuser." For a representative analysis of the different subvarieties of hacking, see Skibell, "Cybercrimes and Misdemeanors."

28. For perceptive accounts of this evolution, see Kerr, "Cybercrime's Scope"; Winn, "The Guilty Eye." The relevant provisions of the CFAA are 18 U.S.C. §1030(2) and (4).

29. The access-control protections are codified at 17 U.S.C. §1201(a)(1)–(2);

the prohibition on trafficking in devices for circumventing rights controls is codified at 17 U.S.C. §1201(b). For the legislative history, see House of Representatives Report No. 105–551, part 1, 17–19 (1998), reprinted in Melville B. Nimmer & David Nimmer (2000), *Nimmer on Copyright: Congressional Committee Reports on the Digital Millennium Copyright Act and Concurrent Amendments,* 5-1, 5-24 to 5-26; Senate Report No. 105-190, at 28–30 (1998), reprinted in Nimmer & Nimmer, ibid., 4-1, 4-33 to 4-35.

30. See Universal City Studios, Inc., v. Reimerdes, 111 F. Supp. 2d 294, 317–19 (S.D.N.Y. 2000), *affirmed,* Universal City Studios, Inc. v. Corley, 273 F.3d 429 (2d Cir. 2001).

31. Digital Millennium Copyright Act, Pub. L. No. 105–304, 112 Stat. 2866 (codified at 17 U.S.C. §1201(f)). For examples of cases rejecting the interoperability defense for unauthorized media and game players, see *Reimerdes,* 111 F. Supp. 2d at 320; Davidson & Associates v. Jung, 422 F.3d 630, 641–42 (8th Cir. 2005).

32. See U.S. Copyright Office, "Exemption to Prohibition on Circumvention of Copyright Protection Systems for Access Control Technologies: Final Rule," 71 Fed. Reg. 68,472, 68, 476 (Nov. 27, 2006) (codified at 37 C.F.R. §201.40(b)(5)).

33. See Katie Hafner, "Altered iPhones Freeze Up," *New York Times,* Sept. 29, 2007.

34. See, for example, U.S. Federal Trade Commission, staff report, "Monitoring Software on Your PC: Spyware, Adware, and Other Software," Mar. 2005, 2–4, http://www.ftc.gov/os/2005/03/050307spywarerept.pdf; Dave Morgan, Interactive Advertising Bureau, Testimony Before the Subcommittee on Commerce, Trade, and Consumer Protection on H.R. 964, "Securely Protect Yourself Against Cyber Trespass Act," U.S. House of Representatives, Committee on Energy & Commerce, Mar. 17, 2007, available at http://www.iab.net/media/file/Morgan-Testimony_SPYACT.pdf.

35. Dean, *Publicity's Secret.*

36. See, for example, New York Times Co. v. U.S. Department of Defense, 499 F. Supp. 2d 501 (S.D.N.Y. 2007); American Civil Liberties Union v. F.B.I., 429 F. Supp. 2d 179 (D.D.C. 2006); American Civil Liberties Union v. U.S. Department of Justice, 265 F. Supp. 2d 20 (D.D.C. 2003).

37. Freedom of Information Act, Pub. L. No. 89–554 , 80, Stat. 383 (codified as amended at 5 U.S.C §552(b)(1)-(7)).

38. The statute authorizing the court is the Foreign Intelligence Surveillance Act, Pub. L. No. 95–511, 92 Stat. 1783 (codified at 50 U.S.C. §1801 *et seq.*). For the secrecy provisions, see 50 U.S.C. §1803(b). For examples of post-9/11 press coverage relatively critical of the secrecy surrounding the FISA court, see John Lancaster & Walter Pincus, "Proposed Anti-Terrorism Laws Draw Tough Questions," *Washington Post,* Sept. 25, 2001; Philip Shenon, "Secret Court Says F.B.I. Aides Misled Judges in 75 Cases," *New York Times,* Aug. 23, 2002. For examples of coverage more favorable to FISA following discovery of the Bush Administration's warrantless wiretapping program, see James Risen & Eric Lichtblau, "Bush Lets U.S. Spy on Callers without Courts," *New York Times,* Dec. 16, 2005; Neil King, Jr., "Senators Focus on Wiretapping Program," *Wall Street Journal,* Jan. 18, 2006.

39. For decisions according trade-secret protection to search algorithms, see

Viacom Intern. Inc. v. YouTube Inc., 253 F.R.D. 256, 259–60 (S.D.N.Y. 2008); Gonzales v. Google, Inc. 234 F.R.D. 674, 684–86 (N.D. Cal. 2006). On trade-secret protection for DRM protocols, see DVD Copy Control Association, Inc. v. Bunner, 31 Cal. 4th 864 (2003); and DVD Copy Control Association, Inc. v. Bunner, 116 Cal. App. 4th 241 (2004). The California Supreme Court ruled that enjoining defendant from distributing DeCSS over the Internet did not violate the First Amendment; on remand, however, the Court of Appeal vacated the injunction because the evidence showed that DeCSS already had been widely distributed to the public at the time the defendant posted it.

40. The leading text on accountability for data-processing practices, the *OECD Guidelines on the Protection of Privacy and Transborder Flows of Personal Data* (1980), requires that individuals be given the right to inspect and correct data maintained about them, and requires disclosure of the purpose for which data processing is being conducted. See ibid., ¶¶9, 13, http://www.oecd.org/document/18/0,3343,en_2649_34255_1815186_1_1_1_1,00.html.

41. Universal City Studios, Inc., v. Reimerdes, 111 F. Supp. 2d 294, 331–32 (S.D.N.Y. 2000), *affirmed*, Universal City Studios, Inc. v. Corley, 273 F.3d 429 (2d Cir. 2001).

42. See note 40 to Chapter 7, above.

43. See Buzan, Waever, and de Wilde, *Security*, 21–42; Der Derian, "The Value of Security."

44. Foucault, *Discipline and Punish*, 195–98.

45. For a perceptive analysis, see Nissenbaum, "Where Computer Security Meets National Security."

46. See, for example, Ellen Nakashima & Alec Klein, "U.S. Agency Tries to Fix No-Fly List Mistakes," *Washington Post*, Jan. 20, 2007; John Schwartz, "She Says She's No Music Pirate. No Snoop Fan, Either." *New York Times*, Sept. 25, 2003; John Schwartz, "High-Tech Voting System Is Banned in California," *New York Times*, May 1, 2004; Clint Ecker, "Massive Spyware-Based Identity Theft Ring Uncovered," *Ars Technica*, Aug. 6, 2005, http://arstechnica.com/old/content/2005/08/5175.ars.

47. For a comprehensive discussion of the politics of network standards, see DeNardis, *Protocol Politics*.

48. See 17 U.S.C. §1201(f), (g), (j). For an analysis of the ways that the DMCA works to prevent "disruptive innovation," see Seltzer, "The Imperfect Is the Enemy of the Good."

49. See Castells, *The Power of Identity*; Castells, *The Rise of the Network Society*; Deleuze, *Negotiations*; Baudrillard, *Simulacra and Simulation*; see also Galloway & Thacker, *The Exploit*.

50. Madison, "Complexity and Copyright in Contradiction"; see also Kang & Cuff, "Pervasive Computing," 122-28. On the tension between order and vibrancy in urban planning, see generally, Jacobs, *The Death and Life of Great American Cities*; Lang, *Creating Architectural Theory*.

51. See Andrejevic, *iSpy*; Haggerty & Ericson, "The Surveillant Assemblage."

52. Coombe, *The Cultural Life of Intellectual Properties*; McGrath, *Loving Big Brother*.

Chapter 9: The Structural Conditions of Human Flourishing

1. See Nussbaum, *Frontiers of Justice*, 76–78.

2. Ibid.

3. Shaver, "Defining and Measuring A2K," 239.

4. See Rebecca Tushnet, "I Put You There," 921–24; 17 U.S.C. §1201(a)(1)(C).

5. For examples illustrating the range of producer responses to user innovation, see Fisher, "The Implications for Law of User Innovation," 1435–41. On play rhetoric and user labor, see, for example, Banks & Humphreys, "The Labour of User Co-Creators"; Zwick, Bonsu, and Darmody, "Putting Users to Work." For a similarly skeptical perspective on the culture of digital gaming, see Grimes & Feenberg, "Rationalizing Play."

6. The automatic license for the preparation of sound recordings is set forth in 17 U.S.C. §115. For the automatic-licensing provisions that apply to digital public performances, see 17 U.S.C. §114(d)(2) & (f). Section 114(f)(e)(2) prohibits collective rate negotiation for performances that do not qualify for the statutory license.

7. See Chon, "Intellectual Property 'From Below'"; Okediji, "Sustainable Access to Copyrighted Digital Information Works."

8. Chon, "Intellectual Property and the Development Divide," 2893.

9. Okediji, "Sustainable Access to Copyrighted Digital Information Works," 180.

10. Berkman Center for Internet and Society, *Next Generation Connectivity*, 3.

11. See Lee, "Warming Up to User Generated Content"; Wu, "Tolerated Use."

12. See, for example, Benkler, "Free as the Air to Common Use," 361–63; Boyle, "The Second Enclosure Movement," 58–69.

13. See Organization for Economic Cooperation and Development, "OECD Guidelines on the Protection of Privacy and Transborder Flows of Personal Data," http://www.oecd.org/document/18/0,3343,en_2649_34255_1815186_1_1_1,00.html; Directive 95/46/EC of the European Parliament and of the Council of 24 October 1995 on the protection of individuals with regard to the processing of personal data and on the free movement of such data, 1995 O.J. (L 281) 31.

14. See Organization for Economic Cooperation and Development, "The 30th Anniversary of the OECD Privacy Guidelines," http://www.oecd.org/document/35/0,3343,en_2649_34255_44488739_1_1_1_1,00.html; see also Organisation for Economic Co-operation and Development, "The Seoul Declaration for the Future of the Internet Economy," 9–10, http://www.oecd.org/dataoecd/49/28/40839436.pdf.

15. See Citron, "Technological Due Process"; Citron, "Open Code Governance."

16. See Pasquale, "Beyond Competition and Innovation"; see also Introna & Nissenbaum, "Shaping the Web."

17. DeNardis, *Protocol Politics*, 219.

18. Ibid., 225.

19. Holmes, "The Path of the Law," 459–61.

20. See Gibson, "Risk Aversion and Rights Accretion," 887–906.

21. Lessig, *Free Culture*, 187.

22. See Landes & Posner, "Indefinitely Renewable Copyright"; Sprigman, "Reform(aliz)ing Copyright," 553–56.

23. See Elkin-Koren, "What Contracts Cannot Do," 397–419.

24. See, for example, Campbell v. Acuff-Rose Music, Inc., 510 U.S. 569, 590–94 (1994) ("Although 2 Live Crew submitted uncontroverted affidavits on the question of market harm to the original, neither they, nor Acuff-Rose, introduced evidence or affidavits addressing the likely effect of 2 Live Crew's parodic rap song on the market for a nonparody, rap version of 'Oh, Pretty Woman.'"); Perfect 10, Inc. v. Amazon.com, Inc., 508 F.3d 1146, 1168 (9th Cir. 2007) ("[T]he district court did not make a finding that Google users have downloaded thumbnail images for cell phone use. This potential harm to Perfect 10's market remains hypothetical.").

25. See Cohen, "*Lochner* in Cyberspace," 504–14; Gordon, "On Owning Information," 166–80.

26. See Horwitz, *The Transformation of American Law*, 208–12.

27. Nissenbaum, *Privacy in Context*, 127–57. For Litman's argument about shelter for personal use of copyrighted works, see Litman, "Lawful Personal Use." For the statutory definition of the public performance right, see 17 U.S.C. §101 ("To perform or display a work 'publicly' means–(1) to perform or display it at a place open to the public or at any place where a substantial number of persons outside of a normal circle of a family and its social acquaintances are gathered.").

28. See Cohen, "Creativity and Culture," 1198–1205; Cohen, "Copyright, Commodification, and Culture," 160–64.

29. Compare Gramm-Leach-Bliley Act, Pub. L. No. 106–102, 113 Stat. 1437 (codified at 15 U.S.C. §6802), with Financial Services Act of 1999, H.R. No. 10.RH, §501 (version reported in the House).

30. See Ohm, "Broken Promises of Privacy," 1719–20, 1723–27; Latanya Sweeney, "Computational Disclosure Control: A Primer on Data Privacy Protection," Jan. 8, 2001, http://groups.csail.mit.edu/mac/classes/6.805/articles/privacy/sweeney-thesis-draft.pdf. For the HIPAA deidentification regulations, see 45 C.F.R. §164.514.

31. See 45 C.F.R. §164.512(i); Institute of Medicine, *Beyond the HIPAA Privacy Rule: Enhancing Privacy, Improving Health Research*, 162–87, Washington, D.C.: National Academics Press, 2009.

32. An early and well-known statement of this view is Lessig, *Code*, 156–63. For a devastating rejoinder, see Rotenberg, "Fair Information Practices and the Architecture of Privacy." See also Schwartz, "Beyond Lessig's *Code* for Internet Privacy."

33. The classic study is Edwin Black, *IBM and the Holocaust*.

34. See, for example, Schauer, *Profiles, Probabilities, and Stereotypes*, 199–223.

35. One recent thought experiment that moves in this direction is Hoofnagle & Solove, "A Model Regime of Privacy Protection."

36. Ohm, "Broken Promises of Privacy," 1765–71.

37. See Acquisti & Gross, "Predicting Social Security Numbers from Public Data."

38. I thank Allan Friedman for enlightening me on this point.

39. See Robert O'Harrow, Jr., "Intricate Screening of Fliers in Works: Database Raises Privacy Concerns." *Washington Post*, Feb. 1, 2002; Chakrabarti & Strauss, "Carnival Booth."

40. See Lena H. Sun & Lyndsey Layton, "At Least 6 Killed in Red Line Crash," *Washington Post*, June 23, 2009.

41. See Mark Mazzetti & Eric Lipton, "U.S. Spy Agencies Failed to Collate Clues on Terror," *New York Times*, Dec. 31, 2009; Scott Shane, "Wide U.S. Failures Helped Airliner Plot," *New York Times*, May 19, 2010.

42. Schneier, *Beyond Fear*, 38–40.

43. See Nissenbaum, *Privacy in Context*, 140–48.

44. See Miguel Helft, "Anger Leads to Apology from Google about Buzz," *New York Times*, Feb. 15, 2010.

45. See Ryan Kim, "'Rob Me' Site Points Out Security Concerns," *San Francisco Chronicle*, Feb. 18, 2010.

46. Grimmelmann, "Privacy as Product Safety," 803.

47. See Universal City Studios, Inc., v. Reimerdes, 111 F. Supp. 2d 294, 311, 319–20 (S.D.N.Y. 2000), *affirmed*, Universal City Studios, Inc. v. Corley, 273 F.3d 429 (2d Cir. 2001).

48. See RealNetworks, Inc. v. DVD Copy Control Association, 641 F. Supp. 2d 913, 924–27 (N.D. Cal. 2009).

49. See, for example, Electronic Frontier Foundation et al., "Fair Use Principles for User Generated Content," http://www.eff.org/files/UGC_Fair_Use_Best_Practices_0.pdf. For a comprehensive discussion and evaluation of a variety of less restrictive designs for technical-protection systems, see Armstrong, "Digital Rights Management and the Process of Fair Use." See also Burk & Cohen, "Fair Use Infrastructure for Rights Management Systems."

50. See Jones et al., "Everyday Life Online"; Livingstone, "Taking Risky Opportunities," 404–07; Moscardelli & Divine, "Adolescents' Concern for Privacy"; "Steeves & Webster, Closing the Barn Door," 14–15.

51. See boyd, "Autistic Social Software."

52. See, for example, the essays and case studies collected in Friedman, *Human Values and the Design of Computer Technology*.

Chapter 10: Conclusion: Putting Cultural Environmentalism into Practice

1. See, for example, Epstein, "Decentralized Responses to Good Fortune and Bad Luck."

2. Polanyi, *The Great Transformation*, 73.

3. See Jones, *Against Technology*, 9, 47–49.

4. For discussion of the role that technologically driven risk management

played in the collapse of the global financial system, see Bamberger, "Technologies of Compliance." On the cultural construction of risk more generally, see Beck, *Risk Society*; Douglas, *Risk and Blame*; Ericson & Doyle, *Risk and Morality*.

     5. See, for example, Heal, *Valuing the Future*; Rogers, Jalal, and Boyd, *An Introduction to Sustainable Development*, 260–312. One noteworthy early effort to develop practices for valuing the cultural environment is Pasquale, "Toward an Ecology of Intellectual Property."

Bibliography

Acquisti, Alessandro & Ralph Gross. "Predicting Social Security Numbers from Public Data." *Proceedings of the National Academy of Sciences* 106.27 (July 27, 2009): 10975–80.

Adorno, Theodor & Max Horkheimer. "The Culture Industry: Enlightenment as Mass Deception." In Simon During, ed., *The Cultural Studies Reader,* 2nd ed., 31–43. New York: Routledge, 1999.

Allen, Anita L. "Coercing Privacy." *William and Mary Law Review* 40.3 (1999): 723–57.

Altman, Irving. *The Environment and Social Behavior: Privacy, Personal Space, Territory, Crowding.* Monterey, Calif.: Brooks/Cole Publishing, 1975.

——. "Privacy Regulation: Culturally Universal or Culturally Specific?" *Journal of Social Issues* 33.3 (1977): 66–84.

Amabile, Teresa M. *Creativity in Context.* Boulder, Colo.: Westview Press, 1996.

Anderson, Benedict. *Imagined Communities,* rev. ed. New York: Verso, 1991.

Andrejevic, Mark. *iSpy: Surveillance and Power in the Interactive Era.* Lawrence: University Press of Kansas, 2007.

Appadurai, Arjun. *Modernity at Large: Cultural Dimensions of Globalization.* Minneapolis: University of Minnesota Press, 1996.

Arewa, Olufunmilayo B. "From J. C. Bach to Hip Hop: Musical Borrowing, Copyright, and Cultural Context." *North Carolina Law Review* 84.2 (2006): 547–645.

Armstrong, Timothy K. "Digital Rights Management and the Process of Fair Use." *Harvard Journal of Law and Technology* 20.1 (2006): 49–121.

Aufderheide, Patricia & Peter Jaszi. *Untold Stories: Creative Consequences*

Bibliography

of the Rights Clearance Culture for Documentary Filmmakers. Washington, D.C.: Center for Social Media, 2004.

Augé, Marc. *Non-Places: Introduction to an Anthology of Supermodernity*. Translated by John Howe. New York: Verso, 1995.

Austin, J. L. *How to Do Things with Words*. Cambridge, Mass.: Harvard University Press, 1962.

Austin, Lisa. "Privacy and the Question of Technology." *Law and Philosophy* 22.2 (2003): 119–66.

Bailey, Jane & Ian Kerr. "Seizing Control? The Experience Capture Experiments of Ringley and Mann." *Ethics and Information Technology* 9.2 (2007): 129–39.

Balkin, Jack M. *Cultural Software: A Theory of Ideology*. New Haven, Conn.: Yale University Press, 1998.

——. "Deconstruction's Legal Career." *Cardozo Law Review* 27.2 (2005): 719–40.

——. "Digital Speech and Democratic Culture: A Theory of Freedom of Expression for the Information Society." *New York University Law Review* 79.1 (2005): 1–58.

Ball, Kirstie S. "Elements of Surveillance: A New Framework and Future Directions." *Information, Communication, and Society* 5.4 (2002): 573–90.

——. "Exposure: Exploring the Subject of Surveillance." *Information, Communication, and Society* 12.5 (March 2009): 639–57.

Bamberger, Kenneth A. "Technologies of Compliance: Risk and Regulation in a Digital Age." *Texas Law Review* 88.4 (March 2010): 669–739.

Banks, John & Sal Humphreys. "The Labour of User Co-Creators: Emergent Social Network Markets?" *Convergence* 14 (2008): 401–18.

Barabási, Albert-László. *Linked: The New Science of Networks*. Cambridge, Mass.: Perseus Publishing, 2002.

Barber, Benjamin R. *Jihad vs. McWorld: How Globalism and Tribalism Are Reshaping the World*. New York: Ballantine Books, 1995.

Barron, Anne. "Copyright Law's Musical Work." *Social and Legal Studies* 15.1 (March 2006): 101–27.

——. "The Legal Properties of Film." *Modern Law Review* 67.2 (2004): 177–208.

Baudrillard, Jean. *Simulacra and Simulation*. Translated by Sheila Glaser. Ann Arbor: University of Michigan Press, 1996.

Beck, Ulrich. *Risk Society: Towards a New Modernity*. Translated by Mark Ritter. London: Sage, 1992.

Becker, Howard. *Art Worlds*. Berkeley and Los Angeles: University of California Press, 1982.

Bibliography

Beniger, James R. *The Control Revolution: Technological and Economic Origins of the Information Society.* Cambridge, Mass.: Harvard University Press, 1986.

Benjamin, Walter. "The Work of Art in the Age of Mechanical Reproduction." In *Illuminations*, trans. Harry Zohn, 217–51. New York: Schocken Books, 1969.

Benkler, Yochai. "Free as the Air to Common Use: First Amendment Constraints on the Enclosure of the Public Domain." *New York University Law Review* 74.2 (1999): 354–445.

———. "Through the Looking Glass: Alice and the Constitutional Foundations of the Public Domain." *Law and Contemporary Problems* 66.1–2 (Winter/Spring 2003): 173–224.

———. *The Wealth of Networks: How Social Production Transforms Markets and Freedom.* New Haven, Conn.: Yale University Press, 2006.

Bennett, Colin & Charles Raab. *The Governance of Privacy: Policy Instruments in Global Perspective.* Cambridge, Mass.: MIT Press, 2006.

Berkman Center for Internet and Society. *Next Generation Connectivity: A Review of Broadband Internet Transitions and Policy from around the World.* Cambridge, Mass.: Berkman Center for Internet and Society, 2010.

Berlin, Isaiah. *Two Concepts of Liberty.* London: Oxford University Press, 1959.

Berners-Lee, Tim, James Hendler, and Ora Lassila. "The Semantic Web." *Scientific American* 284.4 (April 2001): 34–43.

Biddle, Peter, Paul England, Marcus Peinado, and Bryan Willman. "The Darknet and the Future of Content Protection." In *Lecture Notes in Computer Science: Digital Rights Management*, 155–176. Berlin: Springer, 2003.

Bijker, Wiebe. *Of Bicycles, Bakelites, and Bulbs: Toward a Theory of Sociotechnical Change.* Cambridge, Mass.: MIT Press, 1995.

Birnhack, Michael D. "Global Copyright, Local Speech." *Cardozo Arts and Entertainment Law Journal* 24.2 (2006): 491–547.

Birnhack, Michael D. & Niva Elkin-Koren. " The Invisible Handshake: The Reemergence of the State in the Digital Environment." *Virginia Journal of Law and Technology* 8.6 (2006): 1–57.

Black, Edwin. *IBM and the Holocaust: The Strategic Alliance between Nazi Germany and America's Most Powerful Corporation.* New York: Crown Books, 2001.

Black, Jeremy. *Maps and Politics.* Chicago: University of Chicago Press, 1997.

Bibliography

Blanchette, Jean-François & Deborah Johnson. "Data Retention and the Panoptic Society: The Social Benefits of Forgetfulness." *Information Society* 18.1 (2002): 33–45.

Bloustein, Edward J. "Privacy as an Aspect of Human Dignity." In Ferdinand Schoeman, ed., *Philosophical Dimensions of Privacy*, 156–202. New York: Cambridge University Press, 1984.

Blumenthal, Marjory & David Clark. "Rethinking the Design of the Internet: The End to End Arguments vs. the Brave New World." *ACM Transactions on Internet Technology* 1.1 (August 2001): 70–109.

Bonsu, Samuel K. & Aron Darmody. "Co-creating Second Life: Market Consumer Cooperation in Contemporary Economy." *Journal of Macromarketing* 28.4 (2008): 355–68.

Boorstin, Daniel. *The Creators: A History of Heroes of the Imagination*. New York: Random House, 1993.

Bordo, Susan. "Bringing the Body to Theory." In Welton, *Body and Flesh*, 84–97.

Borgmann, Albert. *Crossing the Postmodern Divide*. Chicago: University of Chicago Press, 1992.

Bourdieu, Pierre. *Distinction: A Social Critique of the Judgement of Taste*. Translated by Richard Nice. Cambridge, Mass.: Harvard University Press, 1984.

———. *The Field of Cultural Production*. New York: Columbia University Press, 1993.

Bowker, Geoffrey C. & Susan Leigh Star. *Sorting Things Out: Classification and Its Consequences*. Cambridge, Mass.: MIT Press, 1999.

boyd, danah. 2005. "Autistic Social Software." In Joel Spolsky, ed., *The Best Software Writing*, 35–45. New York: Apress.

———. "Facebook's Privacy Trainwreck." *Convergence: The International Journal of Research into New Media Technologies* 14.1 (February 2008): 13–20.

———. "Why Youth (Heart) Social Network Sites: The Role of Networked Publics in Teenage Social Life." In David Buckingham, ed., *Youth, Identity, and Digital Media*, 119–142. Cambridge, MA: MIT Press, 2007.

Boyle, James. "Foucault in Cyberspace: Surveillance, Sovereignty, and Hard-Wired Censors." *University of Cincinnati Law Review* 66.1 (Fall 1997): 177–205.

———. "A Politics of Intellectual Property: Environmentalism for the Net?" *Duke Law Journal* 47.1 (October 1997): 87–116.

———. *The Public Domain*. New Haven, Conn.: Yale University Press, 2009.

———. "The Second Enclosure Movement and the Construction of the

Public Domain." *Law and Contemporary Problems* 66.1–2 (Winter/ Spring 2003): 33–74.

――. *Shamans, Software, and Spleens: Law and the Construction of the Information Society.* Cambridge, Mass.: Harvard University Press, 1998.

Bracha, Oren. "The Ideology of Authorship Revisited." *Yale Law Journal* 118.1 (October 2009): 186–271.

――. "Standing Copyright Law on Its Head? The Googlization of Everything and the Many Faces of Property." *Texas Law Review* 85.7 (June 2007): 1799–1869.

Brey, Philip. "Social Constructionism for Philosophers of Technology: A Shopper's Guide" *Techne: Journal of the Society for Philosophy and Technology* 2.3–4 (Spring/Summer 1997): 56–78.

Brown, Michael F. *Who Owns Native Culture?* Cambridge, Mass.: Harvard University Press, 2003.

Brown, Stuart. *Play: How It Shapes the Brain, Opens the Imagination, and Invigorates the Soul.* New York: Penguin Group, 2009.

Bruns, Axel. *Blogs, Wikipedia, Second Life, and Beyond: From Production to Produsage.* New York: Peter Lang, 2008.

Burk, Dan L. "Legal Consequences of the Cyberspatial Metaphor." In Mia Consalvo et al., eds., *Internet Research Annual: Selected Papers from the Association of Internet Researchers Conferences 2000–2002,* 17–24. New York: Peter Lang, 2003.

Burk, Dan L. & Julie E. Cohen. "Fair Use Infrastructure for Rights Management Systems." *Harvard Journal of Law and Technology* 15.1 (2001): 42–83.

Burkholder, J. Peter. "The Uses of Existing Music: Musical Borrowing as a Field." *Notes* 50.3 (March 1994): 851–70.

Burrell, Robert & Alison Coleman. *Copyright Exceptions: The Digital Impact.* New York: Cambridge University Press, 2005.

Butler, Judith. *Bodies That Matter: On the Discursive Limits of "Sex."* New York: Routledge, 1993.

――. *Gender Trouble: Feminism and the Subversion of Identity.* New York: Routledge, 1990.

Buzan, Barry, Ole Waever, and Jaap de Wilde. *Security: A New Framework for Analysis.* Boulder, Colo.: Rienner, 1998.

Carroll, Michael W. "Creative Commons and the New Intermediaries." *Michigan State Law Review* 2006.1 (Spring 2006): 45–65.

Carson, Rachel. *Silent Spring.* New York: Houghton Mifflin, 1962.

Castells, Manuel. *The Power of Identity.* Cambridge, Mass.: Blackwell, 1997.

――. *The Rise of the Network Society.* Cambridge, Mass.: Blackwell, 1996.

Bibliography

Certeau, Michel de. *The Practice of Everyday Life.* Translated by Steven
Rendall. Berkeley and Los Angeles: University of California Press, 1984.

Chakrabarti, Samidh & Aaron Strauss. "Carnival Booth: An Algorithm for
Defeating the Computer-Assisted Passenger Screening System." *First
Monday* 7.10 (October 2002). http://firstmonday.org/htbin/cgiwrap/bin/
ojs/index.php/fm/article/view/992/913.

Chander, Anupam & Madhavi Sunder. "Everyone's a Superhero: A Cultural Theory of 'Mary Sue' Fan Fiction as Fair Use." *California Law Review* 95.2 (April 2007): 597–626.

Chon, Margaret. "Intellectual Property and the Development Divide." *Cardozo Law Review* 27.6 (April 2006): 2821–912.

———. "Intellectual Property 'From Below': Copyright and Capability for Education." *University of California Davis Law Review* 40.3 (2007): 803–54.

———. "New Wine Bursting from Old Bottles: Collaborative Internet Art,
Joint Works, and Entrepreneurship." *Oregon Law Review* 75.1 (Spring
1996): 257–76.

———. "Postmodern 'Progress': Reconsidering the Copyright and Patent
Power." *DePaul Law Review* 43.1 (Fall 1993): 97–146.

Citron, Danielle Keats. "Open Code Governance." *University of Chicago
Legal Forum* 2008 (2008): 355–87.

———. "Technological Due Process." *Washington University Law Review*
85.6 (2008): 1249–313.

Clanchy, M. T. *From Memory to Written Record: England, 1066–1307*, 2d
ed. Malden, Mass.: Blackwell, 1993.

Clayton, Jay & Eric Rothstein, eds. *Influence and Intertextuality in Literary
History.* Madison: University of Wisconsin Press, 1991.

Cohen, Julie E. "Copyright and the Perfect Curve." *Vanderbilt Law Review*
53.6 (November 2000): 1799–819.

———. "Copyright, Commodification, and Culture: Locating the Public
Domain." In Lucie Guibault & P. Bernt Hugenholtz, eds., *The Future
of the Public Domain: Identifying the Commons in Information Law,*
121–166. The Hague: Kluwer Law International, 2006.

———. "Creativity and Culture in Copyright Theory." *University of California Davis Law Review* 40.3 (2007): 1151–1205.

———. "Cyberspace as/and Space." *Columbia Law Review* 107.1 (January
2007): 210–255.

———. "DRM and Privacy." *Berkeley Technology Law Journal* 18.2 (Spring
2003): 575–617.

———. "Examined Lives: Informational Privacy and the Subject as Object."
Stanford Law Review 52.5 (May 2000): 1373–438.

Bibliography

———. "*Lochner* in Cyberspace: The New Economic Orthodoxy of 'Rights Management.'" *Michigan Law Review,* 97.2 (November 1998): 462–563.

———. "Network Stories." *Law and Contemporary Problems* 70.2 (Spring 2007): 91–95.

———. "Pervasively Distributed Copyright Enforcement." *Georgetown Law Journal* 95.1 (November 2006): 1–48.

———. "The Place of the User in Copyright Law." *Fordham Law Review* 74.2 (November 2005): 347–374.

———. "Privacy, Ideology, and Technology: A Response to Jeffrey Rosen." *Georgetown Law Journal* 89.6 (June 2001): 2029–45.

———. "Privacy, Visibility, Transparency, and Exposure." *University of Chicago Law Review* 75.1 (Winter 2008): 181–201.

———. "A Right to Read Anonymously: A Closer Look at 'Copyright Management' in Cyberspace." *Connecticut Law Review* 28.4 (Summer 1996): 981–1039.

Coleman, E. Gabriella & Alex Golub. "Hacker Practice: Moral Genres and the Cultural Articulation of Liberalism." *Anthropological Theory* 8.3 (September 2008): 255–77.

Coombe, Rosemary. *The Cultural Life of Intellectual Properties: Authorship, Appropriation, and Law.* Durham, N.C.: Duke University Press, 1998.

Coppa, Francesca. "Writing Bodies in Space: Media Fan Fiction as Theatrical Performance." In Karen Hellekson & Kristina Busse, eds., *Fan Fiction and Fan Communities in the Age of the Internet: New Essays,* 225–44. Jefferson, N.C.: McFarland, 2006.

Cowen, Tyler. *Creative Destruction: How Globalization Is Changing World Culture.* Princeton: Princeton University Press, 2004.

———. *In Praise of Commercial Culture.* Cambridge, Mass.: Harvard University Press, 1998.

Craig, Carys J. "Reconstructing the Author-Self: Some Feminist Lessons for Copyright Law." *American University Journal of Gender, Social Policy, and the Law* 15.2 (2007): 207–68.

Crawford, Susan P. "The Biology of the Broadcast Flag." *Hastings Communications and Entertainment Law Journal* 25.3–4 (2003): 603–52.

Crossley, Nick. *The Social Body: Habit, Identity and Desire.* London: Sage, 2001.

Csikszentmihalyi, Mihalyi. *Creativity: Flow and the Psychology of Discovery and Invention.* New York: HarperCollins, 1996.

Curry, Michael R. "Discursive Displacement and the Seminal Ambiguity of Space and Place." In Leah A. Lievrouw & Sonia M. Livingstone, eds.,

Handbook of New Media: Social Shaping and Consequences of ICTs, 2d ed., 502–17. London: Sage, 2002.

Curry, Michael R. & Leah A. Lievrouw. "Places to Read Anonymously: New Media Technologies, Intellectual Freedom, and Ecologies of Attention and Forgetting." *Proceedings of the American Society for Information Science and Technology* 43.1 (2007): 1–4.

Dam, Kenneth W. "Self-Help in the Digital Jungle." *Journal of Legal Studies* 28.2 (June 1999): 393–412.

Dean, Jodi. *Publicity's Secret: How Technoculture Capitalizes on Democracy.* Ithaca, N.Y.: Cornell University Press, 2002.

DeCew, Judith Wagner. *In Pursuit of Privacy: Law, Ethics, and the Rise of Technology.* Ithaca, N.Y.: Cornell University Press, 1997.

de la Peña, Carolyn Thomas. *The Body Electric: How Strange Machines Built the Modern American.* New York: New York University Press, 2004.

Deleuze, Gilles. *Negotiations, 1972–1990.* Translated by Martin Joughin. New York: Columbia University Press, 1995.

Deleuze, Gilles & Felix Guattari. *A Thousand Plateaus: Capitalism and Schizophrenia.* Translated by Brian Massumi. Minneapolis: University of Minnesota Press, 1987.

DeNardis, Laura. *Protocol Politics: The Globalization of Internet Governance.* Cambridge, Mass.: MIT Press, 2009.

Der Derian, James. "The Value of Security: Hobbes, Marx, Nietzsche, and Baudrillard." In D. Campbell & M. Dillon, eds., *The Political Subject of Violence,* 94–113. Manchester, UK: Manchester University Press, 1993.

Derrida, Jacques. *Margins of Philosophy.* Translated by Alan Bass. Chicago: University of Chicago Press, 1982.

———. *Of Grammatology.* Translated by Gayatri Chakravorty Spivak. Baltimore, Md.: Johns Hopkins University Press, 1976.

Descartes, Rene. *Rules for the Direction of Mind.* Translated by Elizabeth S. Haldane & G.R.T. Ross. Chicago: Encyclopaedia Britannica, 1952.

Dewey, John. *Art as Experience.* New York: Perigee, 1934.

DiMaggio, Paul. "Culture and Cognition." *Annual Review of Sociology* 23 (1997): 263–87.

Dodge, Martin & Rob Kitchin. *Mapping Cyberspace.* New York: Routledge, 2001.

Douglas, Mary. *Risk and Blame: Essays in Cultural Theory.* New York: Routledge, 1992.

Dourish, Paul. "What We Talk About When We Talk About Context." *Personal and Ubiquitous Computing* 8.1 (February 2004): 19–30.

Bibliography

——. *Where the Action Is: The Foundations of Embodied Interaction.* Cambridge, Mass.: MIT Press, 2001.

Dreyfuss, Hubert L. & Paul Rabinow. *Michel Foucault: Beyond Structuralism and Hermeneutics,* 2d ed. Chicago: University of Chicago Press, 1983.

Eagleton, Terry. *The Idea of Culture.* Malden, Mass.: Blackwell, 2000.

Easterbrook, Frank. H. "Cyberspace and the Law of the Horse." *University of Chicago Legal Forum* 1996: 207–16.

Eisner, Elliott W. *The Arts and the Creation of Mind.* New Haven, Conn.: Yale University Press, 2002.

Elkin-Koren, Niva. "Cyberlaw and Social Change: A Democratic Approach to Copyright Law in Cyberspace." *Cardozo Arts and Entertainment Law Journal* 14.2 (1996): 215–295.

——. "What Contracts Cannot Do: The Limits of Private Ordering in Facilitating a Creative Commons." *Fordham Law Review* 74.2 (November 2005): 375–422.

Epstein, Richard A. "Cybertrespass." *University of Chicago Law Review* 70.1 (Winter 2003): 73–88.

——. "Decentralized Responses to Good Fortune and Bad Luck." *Theoretical Inquiries in Law* 9.1 (January 2008): 309–41.

Ericson, Richard V. & Aaron Doyle, eds. *Risk and Morality.* Toronto: University of Toronto Press, 2003.

Etzioni, Amitai. *The Limits of Privacy.* New York: Basic Books, 1999.

Farley, Christine Haight. "The Lingering Effects of Copyright's Response to the Invention of Photography." *University of Pittsburgh Law Review* 65.3 (Spring 2004): 385–456.

Fisher, William W. "The Implications for Law of User Innovation." *Minnesota Law Review* 94.5 (May 2010): 1417–77.

Flanagan, Mary. *Critical Play: Radical Game Design.* Cambridge, Mass.: MIT Press, 2009.

Floridi, Luciano. "Four Challenges for a Theory of Informational Privacy." *Ethics and Information Technology* 8.3 (July 2006): 109–19.

——. "The Ontological Interpretation of Information Privacy." *Ethics and Information Technology* 7.4 (December 2005): 185–200.

Fortunati, Leopoldina. "The Mobile Phone: Towards New Categories and Social Relations." *Information, Communication and Society* 5.4 (2002): 513–28.

Foucault, Michel. *An Archaeology of Knowledge.* Translated by Alan Sheridan. New York: Routledge, 1989.

——. *Discipline and Punish: The Birth of the Prison*. Translated by Alan Sheridan. New York: Vintage Books, 1978.

——. "Of Other Spaces." Translated by Jay Miskowiec. *Diacritics* 16.1 (Spring 1986): 22–27.

——. "The Subject and Power." Afterword to Hubert Dreyfus & Paul Rabinow, *Michel Foucault: Beyond Strucuturalism and Hermeneutics*, 208–26. Chicago: University of Chicago Press, 1982.

——. "Technologies of the Self." In Luther H. Martin, Huck Gutman, and Patrick H. Hutton, eds., *Technologies of the Self: A Seminar with Michel Foucault*, 16–49. Amherst: University of Massachusetts Press, 1988.

Fried, Charles. "Privacy." *Yale Law Journal* 77.3 (January 1968): 475–93.

Friedman, Batya, ed. *Human Values and the Design of Computer Technology*. New York: Cambridge University Press, 1997.

Frischmann, Brett M. "Cultural Environmentalism and the Wealth of Networks." *University of Chicago Law Review* 74.3 (Summer 2007): 1083–138.

——. "An Economic Theory of Infrastructure and Commons Management." *Minnesota Law Review* 89.4 (April 2005): 917–1030.

Gadamer, Hans-Georg. *Truth and Method*. 2nd rev. ed. Translated by Joel Weinsheimer & Donald G. Marshall. New York: Continuum, 2004.

Galison, Peter. *Einstein's Clocks, Poincaré's Maps: Empires of Time*. New York: Norton, 2003.

Galison, Peter & Martha Minow. "Our Privacy, Ourselves in an Age of Technological Intrusions." In *Human Rights and the "War on Terror,"* ed. Richard Ashby Wilson, 258–94. New York: Cambridge University Press, 2005.

Galloway, Alexander R. *Protocol: How Control Exists After Decentralization*. Cambridge, Mass.: MIT Press, 2004.

Galloway, Alexander R. & Eugene Thacker. *The Exploit: A Theory of Networks*. Minneapolis: University of Minnesota Press, 2007.

Galloway, Anne. "Intimations of Everyday Life: Ubiquitous Computing and the City." *Cultural Studies* 18.2/3 (March/May 2004): 384–408.

Gandy, Oscar H., Jr. "Data Mining, Surveillance, and Discrimination in the Post-9/11 Environment." In Kevin D. Haggerty and Richard V. Ericson, eds., *The New Politics of Surveillance and Visibility*, 363–84. Toronto: University of Toronto Press, 2006.

——. *The Panoptic Sort: A Political Economy of Personal Information*. Boulder, Colo.: Westview, 1993.

Garber, Marjorie. *Academic Instincts*. Princeton, N.J.: Princeton University Press, 2001.

Bibliography

Gardner, Howard. *Creating Minds: An Anatomy of Creativity as Seen through the Lives of Freud, Einstein, Picasso, Stravinsky, Eliot, Graham, and Gandhi.* New York: Basic Books, 1993.

——. *Developmental Psychology: An Introduction.* Boston, Mass.: Little, Brown, 1978.

Garfinkel, Harold. *Studies in Ethnomethodology: Some Essential Features of Common Understandings.* Englewood Cliffs, N.J.: Prentice-Hall, 1967.

Gavison, Ruth. "Privacy and the Limits of Law." *Yale Law Journal* 89.3 (January 1980): 421–71.

Geertz, Clifford. *The Interpretation of Cultures: Selected Essays.* New York: Basic Books, 1973.

Geller, Paul J. "*Hiroshige v. Van Gogh*: Resolving the Dilemma of Copyright Scope in Remedying Infringement." *Journal of the Copyright Society of the U.S.A.* 46 (1998): 39–70.

Gergen, Kenneth J. "The Challenge of Absent Presence." In James E. Katz & Mark A. Aakhus, eds., *Perpetual Contact: Mobile Communication, Private Talk, Public Performance,* 227–41. New York: Cambridge University Press, 2002.

Gibson, James. "Risk Aversion and Rights Accretion in Intellectual Property Law." *Yale Law Journal* 116.5 (March 2007): 882–951.

Giddens, Anthony. *The Constitution of Society: Outline of the Theory of Structuration.* Berkeley and Los Angeles: University of California Press, 1986.

——. *Modernity and Self-Identity: Self and Society in the Late Modern Age.* Stanford, Calif.: Stanford University Press, 1991.

Gillespie, Tarleton. "Characterizing Copyright in the Classroom: The Cultural Work of Anti-Piracy Campaigns." *Communication, Culture, and Critique* 2.3 (September 2009): 274–318.

——. *Wired Shut: Copyright and the Shape of Digital Culture.* Cambridge, Mass.: MIT Press, 2007.

Gilliom, John. *Overseers of the Poor: Surveillance, Resistance, and the Limits of Privacy.* Chicago: University of Chicago Press, 2001.

Ginsburg, Jane C. "Authors and Users in Copyright." *Journal of the Copyright Society of the U.S.A.* 45 (1997): 1–20.

Goffman, Erving. *The Presentation of Self in Everyday Life.* New York: Anchor Books, 1959.

——. *Relations in Public: Microstudies of the Public Order.* New York: Basic Books, 1971.

Goldman, Eric. "A Coasean Analysis of Marketing." *Wisconsin Law Review* 2006.4 (2006): 1151–221.

Bibliography

Goldstein, Paul. *Copyright's Highway: From Gutenberg to the Celestial Jukebox*. Palo Alto, Calif.: Stanford University Press, 2003.

Gordon, Wendy J. 1992. "Intellectual Property as Price Discrimination: Implications for Contract." *Chicago-Kent Law Review* 73.4 (1998): 1367–90.

———. "On Owning Information: Intellectual Property and the Restitutionary Impulse." *Virginia Law Review* 78.1 (February 1992): 149–281.

———. "A Property Right in Self-Expression: Equality and Individualism in the Natural Law of Intellectual Property." *Yale Law Journal* 102.7 (1993): 1533–609.

Graham, Stephen. "The End of Geography or the Explosion of Place? Conceptualizing Space, Place and Information Technology." *Progress in Human Geography* 22.2 (June 1998): 165–85.

Grimes, Sara M. & Andrew Feenberg. "Rationalizing Play: A Critical Theory of Digital Gaming." *The Information Society* 25.2 (March 2009): 105–18.

Grimmelmann, James. "Privacy as Product Safety." *Widener Law Review* 19.3 (2010): 793–827.

———. "Regulation by Software." *Yale Law Journal* 114.7 (May 2005): 1719–58.

———. "Saving Facebook." *Iowa Law Review* 94.4 (May 2009): 1137–1206.

Grosz, Elizabeth. *Volatile Bodies: Toward a Corporeal Feminism*. Bloomington: Indiana University Press, 1994.

Haggerty, Kevin D. & Richard V. Ericson. "The Surveillant Assemblage." *British Journal of Sociology* 51.4 (2000): 605–22.

Hansen, Mark B.N. *Bodies in Code: Interfaces with Digital Media*. New York: Routledge, 2006.

Haraway, Donna J. *Simians, Cyborgs, and Women: The Reinvention of Nature*. New York: Routledge, 1991.

Harley, J. B. *The New Nature of Maps: Essays in the History of Cartography*. Baltimore: Johns Hopkins University Press, 2002.

Harvey, David. *The Condition of Postmodernity*. Cambridge, Mass.: Blackwell, 1989.

Hayles, N. Katherine. *How We Became Posthuman: Virtual Bodies in Cybernetics, Literature, and Informatics*. Chicago: University of Chicago Press, 1999.

Heal, Geoffrey. *Valuing the Future: Economic Theory and Sustainability*. New York: Columbia University Press, 1998.

Heidegger, Martin. *Being and Time*. Translated by John Macquarrie and Edward Robinson. New York: Harper Perennial, 1962.

Heins, Marjorie & Tricia Beckles. *Will Fair Use Survive? Free Expression in the Age of Copyright Control.* New York: Brennan Center for Justice at NYU School of Law, 2005.

Hermeren, Goran. *Influence in Art and Literature.* Princeton, N.J.: Princeton University Press, 1975.

Hetherington, Kevin. *The Badlands of Modernity: Heterotopia and Social Ordering.* New York: Routledge, 1997.

Hickman, Larry A. *Philosophical Tools for Technological Culture: Putting Pragmatism to Work.* Bloomington: Indiana University Press, 2001.

Hildebrandt, Mireille & Rouvroy, Antoinette, eds. *Law, Human Agency, and Autonomic Computing: The Philosophy of Law Meets the Philosophy of Technology.* New York: Routledge, 2011.

Holland, Dorothy, William Lachicotte, Jr., Debra Skinner, and Carole Cain. *Identity and Agency in Cultural Worlds.* Cambridge, Mass.: Harvard University Press, 1998.

Holmes, Oliver Wendell, Jr. "The Path of the Law." *Harvard Law Review* 10.8 (1897): 457–78.

Homburg, Cornelia J. *The Copy Turns Original.* Amsterdam: Benjamins, 1996.

Hoofnagle, Chris Jay. "Big Brother's Little Helpers: How ChoicePoint and Other Commercial Data Brokers Collect and Package Your Data for Law Enforcement." *North Carolina Journal of International Law and Commercial Regulation* 29.4 (Summer 2004): 595–637.

Hoofnagle, Chris Jay & Daniel J. Solove. "A Model Regime of Privacy Protection." *University of Illinois Law Review* 2006.2 (2006): 357–403.

Horwitz, Morton J. *The Transformation of American Law, 1870–1960: The Crisis of Legal Orthodoxy.* New York: Oxford University Press, 1992.

Hughes, Justin. "The Internet and the Persistence of Law." *Boston College Law Review* 44.2 (March 2003): 359–96.

———. "The Personality Interests of Authors and Inventors in Intellectual Property." *Cardozo Arts and Entertainment Law Journal* 16.1 (1998): 81–181.

Huizinga, Johan. *Homo Ludens: A Study of the Play-Element in Culture.* Boston: Beacon Press, 1995.

Hunter, Dan. "Cyberspace as Place and the Tragedy of the Digital Anti-commons." *California Law Review* 91.2 (March 2003): 439–519.

Hunter, Dan & F. Gregory Lastowka. "Amateur-to-Amateur." *William and Mary Law Review* 46.3 (December 2004): 951–1030.

Ihde, Don. *Bodies in Technology.* Minneapolis: University of Minnesota Press, 2002.

———. *Postphenomenology: Essays in the Postmodern Context.* Chicago: Northwestern University Press, 1993.

Inness, Julie C. *Privacy, Intimacy, and Isolation*. New York: Oxford University Press, 1992.

Introna, Lucas D. & Helen Nissenbaum. "Shaping the Web: Why the Politics of Search Engines Matters." *Information Society* 16.3 (July-September 2000): 169–85.

Jacobs, Jane. *The Death and Life of Great American Cities*. New York: Vintage Books, 1961.

Jaszi, Peter. "On the Author Effect: Contemporary Copyright and Collective Creativity." In Martha Woodmansee & Peter Jaszi, eds., *The Construction of Authorship: Textual Approaches in Law and Literature*, 29–56. Durham, N.C.: Duke University Press, 1994.

Johnson, David R. & David Post. "Law and Borders—The Rise of Law in Cyberspace." *Stanford Law Review* 48.5 (May 1996): 1367–1402.

Jones, Steve, Camille Johnson-Yale, Sarah Millermaier, and Francisco Seoane Perez. "Everyday Life, Online: U.S. College Students' Use of the Internet." *First Monday* 14.10 (October 5, 2009). http://firstmonday.org/htbin/cgiwrap/bin/ojs/index.php/fm/article/viewArticle/2649/2301.

Jones, Steven E. *Against Technology: From the Luddites to Neo-Luddism*. New York: Routledge Taylor & Francis Group, 2006.

Kahn, Jonathan. "Controlling Identity: *Plessy*, Privacy, and Racial Defamation." *DePaul Law Review* 54.3 (Spring 2005): 755–81.

Kahn, Paul. *Putting Liberalism in Its Place*. Princeton, N.J.: Princeton University Press, 2005.

Kang, Jerry. "Cyber-Race." *Harvard Law Review* 113.5 (March 2000): 1130–208.

Kang, Jerry & Cuff, Dana. "Pervasive Computing: Embedding the Public Sphere." *Washington and Lee Law Review* 62.1 (Winter 2005): 93–146.

Kapczynski, Amy. "Access to Knowledge Mobilization and the New Politics of Intellectual Property." *Yale Law Journal* 117.5 (March 2008): 804–85.

Katyal, Sonia K. "The New Surveillance." *Case Western Reserve Law Review* 54.2 (Winter 2003): 297–385.

———. "Privacy vs. Piracy." *Yale Journal of Law and Technology* 7 (2006): 222–320.

———. "Semiotic Disobedience." *Washington University Law Review* 84.3 (2006): 489–571.

Keeton, W. Page, ed. *Prosser and Keeton on the Law of Torts*, 5th ed. St. Paul, Minn.: West, 1984.

Kelty, Christopher M. "Punt to Culture." In Christopher M. Kelty, ed., "Culture's Open Sources: Software, Copyright, and Cultural Critique." Special issue, *Anthropological Quarterly* 77.3 (Summer 2004): 547–58.

Bibliography

——. *Two Bits: The Cultural Significance of Free Software.* Durham, N.C.: Duke University Press, 2008.

Kennedy, Duncan. "The Stages of the Decline of the Public/Private Distinction." *University of Pennsylvania Law Review* 130.6 (June 1982): 1349–57.

Kephart, Jeffrey O. & David M. Chess. "The Vision of Autonomic Computing," *Computer* 36.1 (January 2003): 41–50.

Kerr, Orin S. "Cybercrime's Scope: Interpreting 'Access' and 'Authorization' in Computer Misuse Statutes." *New York University Law Review* 78.5 (November 2003): 1596–668.

Kohn, Margaret. *Brave New Neighborhoods: The Privatization of Public Space.* New York: Routledge, 2004.

Koskela, Hille. "The Gaze Without Eyes: Video Surveillance and the Changing Nature of Urban Space." *Progress in Human Geography* 24.2 (June 2000): 243–65.

——. "Webcams, TV Shows, and Mobile Phones: Empowering Exhibitionism." *Surveillance and Society* 2.2/3 (2004): 199–215.

Ku, Raymond Shih Ray. "The Creative Destruction of Copyright: Napster and the New Economics of Digital Technology." *University of Chicago Law Review* 69.1 (Winter 2002): 263–324.

Kuhn, Thomas S. *The Structure of Scientific Revolutions*, 2nd ed. Chicago: University of Chicago Press, 1970.

Kumaraguru, Ponnurangam & Lorrie Faith Cranor. "Privacy Indexes: A Survey of Westin's Studies." Unpublished manuscript (2005). *Institute for Software Research International*, CMU-ISRI-5–138, http://reports-archive.adm.cs.cmu.edu/anon/isri2005/CMU-ISRI-05-138.pdf.

Kwall, Roberta Rosenthal. "Inspiration and Innovation: The Intrinsic Dimension of the Artistic Soul." *Notre Dame Law Review* 81.5 (June 2006): 1945–2012.

Lakoff, George & Mark Johnson. *Metaphors We Live By.* Chicago: University of Chicago Press, 1980.

——. *Philosophy in the Flesh: The Embodied Mind and Its Challenge to Western Thought.* New York: Basic Books, 1999.

Landes, William M. & Richard A. Posner. *The Economic Structure of Intellectual Property Law.* Cambridge, Mass.: Harvard University Press, 2003.

——. "Indefinitely Renewable Copyright." *University of Chicago Law Review* 70.2 (Spring 2003): 471–518.

Lang, Jon. *Creating Architectural Theory: The Role of the Behavioral Sciences in Environmental Design.* New York: Van Nostrand Reinhold, 1987.

Bibliography

Lange, David. "At Play in the Fields of the Word: Copyright and the Construction of Authorship in the Post-Literate Millennium." *Law and Contemporary Problems* 55.2 (Spring 1992): 139–51.

———. "Recognizing the Public Domain." *Law and Contemporary Problems* 44.4 (Autumn 1981): 147–78.

Latham, Robert & Saskia Sassen. "Digital Formations: Constructing an Object of Study." In Robert Latham & Saskia Sassen, eds., *Digital Formations: IT and New Architectures in the Global Realm*, 1–33. Princeton, N.J.: Princeton University Press, 2005.

Latour, Bruno. *The Pasteurization of France.* Translated by Alan Sheridan & John Law. Cambridge, Mass.: Harvard University Press, 1988.

———. *We Have Never Been Modern.* Translated by Catherine Porter. New York: Harvester Wheatsheaf, 1993.

Law, John, ed. *A Sociology of Monsters: Essays on Power, Technology, and Domination.* New York: Routledge, 1991.

———. "Technology and Heterogeneous Engineering: The Case of Portuguese Expansion." In Wiebe Bijker et al., eds., *The Social Construction of Technological Systems: New Directions in the Sociology and History of Technology,* 111–134. Cambridge, Mass.: MIT Press, 1987.

Lee, Edward S. "The Public's Domain: The Evolution of Legal Constraints on the Government's Power to Control Public Access through Secrecy or Intellectual Property." *Hastings Law Journal* 55.1 (November 2003): 91–209.

———. "Warming Up to User-Generated Content." *University of Illinois Law Review* 2008.5 (2008): 1459–548.

Lefebvre, Henri. *The Production of Space.* Translated by Donald Nicholson-Smith. Cambridge, Mass.: Blackwell, 1974.

Lemley, Mark A. "Property, Intellectual Property, and Free Riding." *Texas Law Review* 83.4 (March 2005): 1031–75.

———. "Romantic Authorship and the Rhetoric of Property." *Texas Law Review* 75.4 (March 1997): 873–906.

Lemley, Mark A. & R. Anthony Reese. "Reducing Digital Copyright Infringement Without Reducing Innovation." *Stanford Law Review* 56.6 (May 2004): 1345–1434.

Lessig, Lawrence. *Code and Other Laws of Cyberspace.* New York: Basic Books, 1999.

———. *Free Culture: How Big Media Uses Technology and the Law to Lock Down Culture and Control Creativity.* New York: Penguin Press, 2004.

———. *The Future of Ideas: The Fate of the Commons in a Connected World.* New York: Random House, 2001.

———. "The New Chicago School." *Journal of Legal Studies* 27.2, pt. 2 (June 1998): 661–91.

———. *Remix: Making Art and Commerce Thrive in the Hybrid Economy.* New York: Penguin Press, 2008.

Leval, Pierre N. "Toward a Fair Use Standard." *Harvard Law Review* 103.5 (March 1990): 1105–36.

Levin, Thomas Y., Ursula Frohne, and Peter Weibel, eds. *CTRL[SPACE]: Rhetorics of Surveillance from Bentham to Big Brother.* Cambridge, Mass.: MIT Press, 2002.

Litman, Jessica. "Lawful Personal Use." *Texas Law Review* 85.7 (June 2007): 1871–920.

———. "The Public Domain." *Emory Law Journal* 39.4 (Fall 1990): 965–1023.

Liu, Joseph P. "Copyright and Breathing Space." *Columbia Journal of Law and the Arts* 30.3–4 (2007): 429–51.

———. "Copyright Law's Theory of the Consumer." *Boston College Law Review* 44.2 (March 2003): 397–431.

Livingstone, Sonia. "Taking Risky Opportunities in Youthful Content Creation: Teenagers' Use of Social Networking Sites for Intimacy, Privacy and Self-Expression." *New Media and Society* 10.3 (June 2008): 393–411.

Low, Setha & Neil Smith, eds. *The Politics of Public Space.* New York: Routledge, 2006.

Lyon, David. *The Electronic Eye: The Rise of Surveillance Society.* Minneapolis: University of Minnesota Press, 1994.

———. *Surveillance Society: Monitoring Everyday Life.* Philadelphia: Open University Press, 2001.

Lyotard, Jean-François. *The Postmodern Condition: A Report on Knowledge.* Translated by Geoff Bennington & Brian Massumi. Minneapolis: University of Minnesota Press, 1984.

Macklem, Timothy. *Independence of Mind.* New York: Oxford University Press, 2006.

Madison, Michael J. "Complexity and Copyright in Contradiction." *Cardozo Arts and Entertainment Law Journal* 18.1 (2000): 125–74.

———. "A Pattern-Oriented Approach to Fair Use." *William and Mary Law Review* 45.4 (March 2004): 1525–690.

Mann, Ronald J. & Seth R. Belzley. "The Promise of Internet Intermediary Liability." *William and Mary Law Review* 47.1 (October 2005): 239–307.

Mann, Steve, Jason Nolan, and Barry Wellman. "Sousveillance: Inventing and Using Wearable Computing Devices for Data Collection in Surveillance Environments." *Surveillance and Society* 1.3 (2003): 331–55.

Marvin, Carolyn. *When Old Technologies Were New: Thinking about Com-*

munication in the Late Nineteenth Century. New York: Oxford University Press, 1998.

Matheson, David. "A Distributive Reductionism about the Right to Privacy." *Monist* 91.1 (2008): 108–29.

Mayer-Schönberger, Viktor. *Delete: The Virtue of Forgetting in the Digital Age.* Princeton, N.J.: Princeton University Press, 2009.

McCarthy, John & Peter Wright. *Technology as Experience.* Cambridge, Mass.: MIT Press, 2004.

McGowan, David. "Copyright Nonconsequentialism." *Missouri Law Review* 69.1 (Winter 2004): 1–72.

McGrath, John E. *Loving Big Brother: Performance, Privacy, and Surveillance Space.* New York: Routledge, 2004.

Merleau-Ponty, Maurice. *Phenomenology of Perception.* Translated by Colin Smith. London: Routledge, 1962.

Merriman, Peter. "Driving Places: Marc Augé, Non-places and the Geography of England's M1 Motorway." *Theory, Culture, and Society,* 21.4–5 (October 1, 2004): 145–67.

Mezey, Naomi. "Law as Culture." *Yale Journal of Law and the Humanities* 13.1 (2001): 35–67.

Mezey, Naomi & Mark Niles. "Screening the Law: Ideology and Law in American Popular Culture." *Columbia Journal of Law and the Arts* 28.2 (2005): 91–185.

Mirchandani, Kirin. "Practices of Global Capital: Gaps, Cracks and Ironies in Transnational Call Centres in India." *Global Networks* 4.4 (October 2004): 355–73.

Mitchell, Don. *The Right to the City: Social Justice and the Fight for Public Space.* New York: Guilford, 2003.

Mitchell, William J. *City of Bits: Space, Place, and the Infobahn.* Cambridge, Mass.: MIT Press, 1995.

———. *Me++.* Cambridge, Mass.: MIT Press, 2004.

Moglen, Eben. "Anarchism Triumphant: Free Software and the Death of Copyright." In Niva Elkin-Koren & Neil Weinstock Netanel, eds., *The Commodification of Information,* 107–31. The Hague: Kluwer Law International, 2002.

Monahan, Torin, ed. *Surveillance and Security: Technological Politics and Power in Everyday Life.* New York: Routledge, 2006.

Moscardelli, Deborah M. & Richard Divine. "Adolescents' Concern for Privacy When Using the Internet: An Empirical Analysis of Predictors and Relationships with Privacy-Protecting Behaviors." *Family and Consumer Sciences Research Journal* 35.3 (March 2007): 232–52.

Mosco, Vincent. *The Digital Sublime.* Cambridge, Mass: MIT Press, 2004.

Nakamura, Lisa. *Cybertypes: Race, Ethnicity, and Identity on the Internet.* New York: Routledge, 2002.

Nedelsky, Jennifer. "Law, Boundaries, and the Bounded Self." In Robert Post, ed., *Law and the Order of Culture,* 162–89. Berkeley and Los Angeles: University of California Press, 1991.

Nehf, James P. "Shopping for Privacy Online: Consumer Decision-Making Strategies and the Emerging Market for Information Privacy." *University of Illinois Journal of Law, Technology, and Policy* 2005.1 (2005): 1–54.

Netanel, Neil Weinstock. "Copyright and a Democratic Civil Society." *Yale Law Journal* 106.2 (November 1996): 283–387.

———. *Copyright's Paradox.* New York: Oxford University Press, 2008.

Nippert-Eng, Christena. "Boundary Play." *Space and Culture* 8.3 (2005): 302–34.

Nissenbaum, Helen. "Privacy as Contextual Integrity." *Washington Law Review* 79.1 (February 2004): 119–57.

———. *Privacy in Context: Technology, Policy, and the Integrity of Social Life.* Stanford, Calif.: Stanford University Press, 2009.

———. "Protecting Privacy in an Information Age: The Problem of Privacy in Public." *Law and Philosophy* 17.5–6 (November 1998): 559–96.

———. "Where Computer Security Meets National Security." *Ethics and Information Technology* 7.2 (June 2005): 61–73.

Norman, Donald. *The Design of Everyday Things.* New York: Doubleday, 1988.

Nussbaum, Martha C. "Aristotelian Social Democracy." In R. Bruce Douglass et al., eds., *Liberalism and the Good,* 203–52. New York: Routledge, 1990.

———. *Frontiers of Justice: Disability, Nationality, Species Membership.* Cambridge, Mass.: Harvard University Press, 2006.

———. "Public Philosophy and International Feminism." *Ethics* 108.4 (July 1998): 762–96.

Nye, David E. *American Technological Sublime.* Cambridge, Mass.: MIT Press, 1994.

Ohm, Paul. "Broken Promises of Privacy: Responding to the Surprising Failure of Anonymization." *UCLA Law Review* 57.6 (August 2010): 1701–77.

———. "The Myth of the Superuser: Fear, Risk, and Harm Online." *University of California Davis Law Review* 41.4 (April 2008): 1327–402.

———. "The Rise and Fall of Invasive ISP Surveillance." *University of Illinois Law Review* 2009.5 (2009): 1417–96.

Okediji, Ruth L. "Sustainable Access to Copyrighted Digital Information Works in Developing Countries." In Keith E. Maskus & Jerome H. Reichman, eds., *International Public Goods and Transfer of Technology under a Globalized Intellectual Property Regime*, 142–87. New York: Cambridge University Press, 2005.

Orr, Mary. *Intertextuality: Debates and Contexts.* Malden, Mass.: Polity, 2003.

Ostrom, Elinor. *Governing the Commons: The Evolution of Institutions for Collective Action.* New York: Cambridge University Press, 1990.

Palen, Leysia & Paul Dourish. "Unpacking 'Privacy' for a Networked World." In *Proceedings of the SIGCHI Conference on Human Factors in Computing Systems*, 129–36. New York: ACM, 2003. http://doi.acm.org.ezp-prod1 .hul.harvard.edu/10.1145/642611.642635.

Parker, Andrew & Eve Kosofsky Sedgwick. *Performativity and Performance.* New York: Routledge, 1995.

Pasco, Allan H. *Allusion: A Literary Graft.* Toronto: University of Toronto Press, 1994.

Pasquale, Frank. "Beyond Competition and Innovation: The Need for Qualified Transparency in Internet Intermediaries." *Northwestern University Law Review* 104.1 (2010): 105–73.

———. "Toward an Ecology of Intellectual Property: Lessons from Environmental Economics for Valuing Copyright's Commons." *Yale Journal of Law and Technology* 8 (Spring 2006): 78–135.

Pellegrini, Anthony D., ed. *The Oxford Handbook of the Development of Play.* New York: Oxford University Press, 2010.

Peñalver, Eduardo Moises & Sonia K. Katyal. *Property Outlaws: How Squatters, Pirates, and Protesters Improve the Law of Ownership.* New Haven, Conn.: Yale University Press, 2010.

Pennock, J. Roland & John W. Chapman, eds. *Nomos XIII: Privacy.* New York: Atherton Press, 1971.

Pessach, Guy. "Copyright Law as a Silencing Restriction on Noninfringing Materials: Unveiling the Scope of Copyright's Diversity Externalities." *Southern California Law Review* 76.5 (July 2003): 1067–104.

———. "[Networked] Memory Institutions: Social Remembering, Privatization and Its Discontents." *Cardozo Arts & Entertainment Law Journal* 26.1 (2008): 71–149.

Peters, Marybeth. "Copyright Enters the Public Domain." *Journal of the Copyright Society of the U.S.A.* 51.4 (Summer 2004): 701–28.

Petersen, Søren Mørk. "Mundane Cyborg Practice: Material Aspects of Broadband Internet Use." *Convergence: The International Journal of Research into New Media Technologies* 13.1 (2007): 79–91.

Bibliography

Pfaffenberger, Brian. "Social Anthropology of Technology." *Annual Review of Anthropology* 21.1 (1992): 491–516.

Phillips, David J. "From Privacy to Visibility: Context, Identity, and Power in Ubiquitous Computing Environments." *Social Text* 23.2 (Summer 2005): 95–108.

Picker, Randal C. "From Edison to the Broadcast Flag: Mechanisms of Consent and Refusal and the Propertization of Copyright." *University of Chicago Law Review* 70.1 (Winter 2003): 281–97.

———. "Rewinding *Sony*: The Evolving Product, Phoning Home and the Duty of Ongoing Design." *Case Western Reserve Law Review* 55.4 (Summer 2005): 749–75.

Pickering, Andrew. *The Mangle of Practice: Time, Agency, and Science.* Chicago: University of Chicago Press, 1995.

Pickles, John. *A History of Spaces: Cartographic Reason, Mapping, and the Geo-Coded World.* New York: Routledge, 2004.

Polanyi, Karl. *The Great Transformation: The Political and Economic Origins of Our Time.* Boston: Beacon Press, 1957.

Posner, Richard. "Privacy, Surveillance, and Law." *University of Chicago Law Review* 75.1 (Winter 2008): 245–60.

Post, Robert. "The Social Foundations of Privacy: Community and Self in the Common Law Tort." *California Law Review* 77.5 (October 1989): 957–1010.

Pozen, David. E. "The Mosaic Theory, National Security, and the Freedom of Information Act." *Yale Law Journal* 115.3 (2005): 628–79.

Quilter, Laura & Jennifer Urban. "Efficient Process or 'Chilling Effects'? Takedown Notices under Section 512 of the Digital Millennium Copyright Act." *Santa Clara Computer and High Technology Law Journal* 22.4 (2005): 621–93.

Raab, Charles D. & Paul De Hert. "Tools for Technology Regulation: Seeking Analytical Approaches beyond Lessig and Hood." In *Regulating Technologies: Legal Futures, Regulatory Frames, and Technological Fixes,* 263–86. Portland, Ore.: Hart Publishing, 2008.

Radin, Margaret Jane. 2002. "Online Standardization and the Integration of Text and Machine." *Fordham Law Review* 70.4 (March 2002): 1125–46.

Randall, Marilyn. *Pragmatic Plagiarism: Authorship, Profit, and Power.* Toronto: University of Toronto Press, 2001.

Rao, Radhika. "A Veil of Genetic Ignorance? Protecting Genetic Privacy to Ensure Equality." *Villanova Law Review* 51.4 (2006): 827–40.

Raz, Joseph. *The Morality of Freedom.* Oxford: Clarendon Press, 1986.

Regan, Priscilla. *Legislating Privacy: Technology, Social Values, and Public Policy.* Chapel Hill: University of North Carolina Press, 1995.

Bibliography

Reidenberg, Joel R. "Lex Informatica: The Formulation of Information Policy Rules Through Technology." *Texas Law Review* 76.3 (February 1998): 553–93.

Reiman, Jeffrey H. "Driving to the Panopticon: A Philosophical Exploration of the Risks to Privacy Posed by the Highway Technology of the Future." *Santa Clara Computer and High Technology Law Journal* 11.1 (1995): 27–44.

———. "Privacy, Intimacy, and Personhood." In Ferdinand Schoeman, ed., *Philosophical Dimensions of Privacy*, 300–16. New York: Cambridge University Press, 1984.

Richards, Neil. "The Information Privacy Law Project." *Georgetown Law Journal* 94.4 (April 2006): 1087–140.

———. "Intellectual Privacy." *Texas Law Review* 87.2 (December 2008): 387–445.

Riles, Annelise. "Anthropology, Human Rights, and Legal Knowledge: Culture in the Iron Cage." *American Anthropologist* 108.1 (March 2006): 52–65.

Rogers, Peter P., Kazi F. Jalal, and John A. Boyd. *An Introduction to Sustainable Development*. London: Earthscan, 2008.

Rose, Carol M. "The Comedy of the Commons: Custom, Commerce, and Inherently Public Property." *University of Chicago Law Review* 53.3 (Summer 1986): 711–81.

———. "Romans, Roads, and Romantic Creators: Traditions of Public Property in the Information Age." *Law and Contemporary Problems* 66.1–2 (Winter/Spring 2003): 89–110.

Rosen, Jeffrey. *The Naked Crowd*. New York: Random House, 2004.

———. *The Unwanted Gaze: The Destruction of Privacy in America*. New York: Random House, 2000.

Rotenberg, Marc. "Fair Information Practices and the Architecture of Privacy (What Larry Doesn't Get)." *Stanford Technology Law Review* 2001 (February 2001): 1. http://stlr.stanford.edu/pdf/rotenberg-fair-info-practices.pdf.

Rubenfeld, Jed. "The Freedom of Imagination: Copyright's Constitutionality." *Yale Law Journal* 112.1 (October 2002): 1–60.

———. "The Right of Privacy." *Harvard Law Review* 102.4 (February 1989): 737–807.

Samuelson, Pamela. "Mapping the Digital Public Domain: Threats and Opportunities." *Law and Contemporary Problems* 66.1–2 (Winter/Spring 2003): 147–71.

Sassen, Saskia. "Locating Cities on Global Circuits." Introduction to Saskia

Sassen, ed., *Global Networks, Linked Cities*, 1–36. New York: Routledge, 2002.

———. *Territory, Authority, Rights: From Medieval to Global Assemblages.* Princeton, N.J.: Princeton University Press, 2006.

Schartum, Dag Wiese. "Designing and Formulating Data Protection Laws." *International Journal of Law and Information Technology* 18.1 (Spring 2010): 1–27.

Schauer, Frederick. *Profiles, Probabilities, and Stereotypes.* Cambridge, Mass.: Harvard University Press, 2003.

Schmidt-Burkhardt, Astrit. "The All-Seer: God's Eye as Proto-surveillance." In Thomas Y. Levin, Ursula Frohne, and Peter Weibel, eds., *CTRL [SPACE]: Rhetorics of Surveillance from Bentham to Big Brother*, 16–31. Cambridge, Mass.: MIT Press, 2002.

Schneier, Bruce. *Beyond Fear: Thinking Sensibly about Security in an Uncertain World.* New York: Copernicus, 2003.

Schoeman, Ferdinand. *Privacy and Social Freedom.* New York: Cambridge University Press, 1992.

Schumpeter, Joseph. *Capitalism, Socialism, and Democracy.* New York: Harper & Row, 1950.

Schur, Richard L. *Parodies of Ownership: Hip Hop Aesthetics and Intellectual Property Law.* Ann Arbor: University of Michigan Press, 2009.

Schwartz, Paul M. "Beyond Lessig's *Code* for Internet Privacy: Cyberspace Filters, Privacy-Control, and Fair Information Practices." *Wisconsin Law Review* 2000.4 (2000): 743–88.

———. "Preemption and Privacy." *Yale Law Journal* 118.5 (March 2009): 902–47.

———. "Privacy and Democracy in Cyberspace." *Vanderbilt Law Review* 52.6 (November 1999): 1609–702.

———. "Warrantless Wiretapping, FISA Reform, and the Lessons of Public Liberty: A Comment on Jorde's Holmes Lecture." *California Law Review* 97.2 (April 2009): 407–32.

Seltzer, Wendy. "The Imperfect Is the Enemy of the Good: Anticircumvention versus Open Development." *Berkeley Technology Law Journal* 25.2 (2010): 910–73.

Sen, Amartya. *Development as Freedom.* New York: Anchor, 1999.

———. "Elements of a Theory of Human Rights." *Philosophy and Public Affairs*, 32.4 (October 2004): 315–56.

———. *Inequality Reexamined.* Cambridge, Mass.: Harvard University Press, 1992.

Shaver, Lea Bishop. "Defining and Measuring A2K: A Blueprint for an

Index of Access to Knowledge." *I/S: A Journal of Law and Policy for the Information Society* 4.2 (Summer 2008): 235–69.

Sheets-Johnstone, Maxine. "Corporeal Archetypes and Power: Preliminary Clarifications and Considerations of Sex." In Welton, *Body and Flesh*, 149–79.

Shilling, Chris. *The Body in Social Theory.* London: Sage, 2003.

Simonton, Dean Keith. *Origins of Genius: Darwinian Perspectives on Creativity.* New York: Oxford University Press, 1999.

Singleton, Solveig. "Privacy versus the First Amendment: A Skeptical Approach." *Fordham Intellectual Property, Media, and Entertainment Law Journal* 11.1 (Autumn 2000): 97–153.

Skibell, Reid. "Cybercrimes and Misdemeanors: A Reevaluation of the Computer Fraud and Abuse Act." *Berkeley Technology Law Journal* 18.3 (Summer 2003): 909–44.

Smith, Henry E. "Self-Help and the Nature of Property." *Journal of Law, Economics, and Policy* 1 (Winter 2005): 69–107.

Soja, Edward. *Postmodern Geographies: The Reassertion of Space in Critical Social Theory.* New York: Verso, 1989.

Solove, Daniel J. *The Digital Person.* New York: New York University Press, 2004.

———. *Understanding Privacy.* Cambridge, Mass.: Harvard University Press, 2008.

———. "The Virtues of Knowing Less: Justifying Privacy Protections against Disclosure." *Duke Law Journal* 53.3 (December 2003): 967–1065.

Spelke, Elizabeth S. "Origins of Visual Knowledge." In Daniel N. Osherson & Howard Lasnik, eds., *An Invitation to Cognitive Science: Visual Cognition in Action* 2:99–127. Cambridge, Mass.: MIT Press, 1990.

Sprigman, Christopher. "Reform(aliz)ing Copyright." *Stanford Law Review* 57.2 (November 2004): 485–568.

Steeves, Valerie & Cheryl Webster. "Closing the Barn Door: The Effect of Parental Supervision on Canadian Children's Online Privacy." *Bulletin of Science, Technology, and Society* 28.1 (February 2008): 4–19.

Stefik, Mark. "Letting Loose the Light: Igniting Commerce in Electronic Publication." In Mark Stefik, ed., *Internet Dreams: Archetypes, Myths, and Metaphors*, 219–53. Cambridge, Mass.: MIT Press, 1996.

Stein, Mark S. "Nussbaum: A Utilitarian Critique." *Boston College Law Review* 50.2 (March 2009): 489–532.

Stigler, George. "An Introduction to Privacy in Economics and Politics." *Journal of Legal Studies* 9.4 (December 1980): 623–44.

Stone, Allucquere Roseanne. *The War of Desire and Technology at the End of the Mechanical Age.* Cambridge, Mass.: MIT Press, 1995.

Bibliography

Strahilevitz, Lior Jacob. "'How's My Driving?' For Everyone (and Everything?)." *New York University Law Review* 81.5 (November 2006): 1699–765.

———. "Privacy Versus Antidiscrimination." *University of Chicago Law Review* 75.1 (Winter 2008): 363–81.

———. "Reputation Nation: Law in an Era of Ubiquitous Personal Information." *Northwestern University Law Review* 102.4 (2008): 1667–738.

Strandburg, Katherine. "Privacy, Rationality, and Temptation: A Theory of Willpower Norms." *Rutgers Law Review* 57.4 (Summer 2005): 1235–306.

Suchman, Lucy A. *Plans and Situated Actions: The Problem of Human-Machine Communication.* New York: Cambridge University Press, 1987.

Sugden, Robert. "Welfare, Resources, and Capabilities." *Journal of Economic Literature* 31.4 (December 1993): 1947–62.

Sunder, Madhavi. "Intellectual Property and Identity Politics: Playing with Fire." *Journal of Gender, Race, and Justice* 4.1 (Fall 2000): 69–98.

———. "IP³." *Stanford Law Review* 59.2 (November 2006): 257–332.

Sunstein, Cass. *Republic.com.* Princeton, N.J.: Princeton University Press, 2001.

Sutton-Smith, Brian. *The Ambiguity of Play.* Cambridge, Mass.: Harvard University Press, 1997.

Swyngedouw, Eric. "Neither Global nor Local: 'Glocalization' and the Politics of Scale." In *Spaces of Globalization: Reasserting the Power of the Local,* ed. Kevin R. Cox, 137–66. New York: Guilford Press, 1997.

Taylor, Charles. *Modern Social Imaginaries.* Durham, N.C.: Duke University Press, 2004.

Thomson, Judith Jarvis. "The Right to Privacy." In Ferdinand Schoeman, ed., *Philosophical Dimensions of Privacy: An Anthology,* 272–89. New York: Cambridge University Press, 1984.

Tushnet, Mark V. "'Everything Old Is New Again': Early Reflections on the 'New Chicago School.'" *Wisconsin Law Review* 1998.2 (1998): 579–90.

Tushnet, Rebecca. "Copy This Essay: How Fair Use Doctrine Harms Free Speech and How Copying Serves It." *Yale Law Journal* 114.3 (December 2004): 535–90.

———. "Economies of Desire: Fair Use and Marketplace Assumptions." *William and Mary Law Review* 51.2 (November 2009): 513–46.

———. "I Put You There: User-Generated Content and Anti-Circumvention." *Vanderbilt Journal of Entertainment and Technology Law* 12.4 (2010): 889–945.

———. "My Library: Copyright and the Role of Institutions in a Peer-to-Peer World." *UCLA Law Review* 53.4 (April 2006): 977–1029.

———. "Payment in Credit: Copyright Law and Subcultural Creativity." *Law and Contemporary Problems* 70.2 (Spring 2007): 135–74.

Bibliography

Vaidhyanathan, Siva. *The Anarchist in the Library: How the Clash between Freedom and Control Is Hacking the Real World and Crashing the System.* New York: Basic Books, 2004.

Verbeek, Peter-Paul. *What Things Do: Philosophical Reflections on Technology, Agency, and Design.* University Park: Pennsylvania State University Press, 2005.

Vinge, Vernor. *Rainbow's End: A Novel with One Foot in the Future.* New York: Tor Books, 2006.

Volokh, Eugene. "Cheap Speech and What It Will Do." *Yale Law Journal* 104.7 (May 1995): 1805–50.

Von Hippel, Eric. *Democratizing Innovation.* Cambridge, Mass.: MIT Press, 2005.

von Lohmann, Fred. "Measuring the Digital Millennium Copyright Act Against the Darknet: Implications for the Regulation of Technological Protection Measures." *Loyola of Los Angeles Entertainment Law Review* 24.4 (2004): 635–48.

Wagner, R. Polk. "On Software Regulation." *Southern California Law Review* 78.2 (January 2005): 457–519.

Wang, Ranxiao Frances & Elizabeth S. Spelke. "Human Spatial Representation: Insights from Animals." *Trends in Cognitive Science* 6.9 (September 2002): 376–82.

Warner, Michael. *Publics and Counterpublics.* New York: Zone Books, 2002.

———. *The Trouble with Normal: Sex Politics and the Ethics of Queer Life.* New York: Free Press, 2000.

Weinberg, Jonathan. "RFID and Privacy." In M. J. Radin, A. Chander, and L. Gelman, eds., *Securing Privacy in the Internet Age: Cultural Memory in the Present,* 245–70. Stanford, Calif.: Stanford University Press, 2008.

Weinreb, Lloyd. "The Right to Privacy." *Social Philosophy and Policy* 17.2 (June 2000): 25–44.

Weiser, Mark. "The Computer for the 21st Century." *Scientific American* 265.3 (March 1995): 94–104.

———. "Creating the Invisible Interface." In *Proceedings of the ACM Symposium on User Interface Software and Technology.* Marina del Rey, Calif.: ACM, 1994.

Welton, Donn, ed. *Body and Flesh: A Philosophical Reader.* Oxford: Blackwell, 1998.

Wenger, Etienne. *Communities of Practice: Learning, Meaning, and Identity.* New York: Cambridge University Press, 1998.

Wenner, Melinda. "The Serious Need for Play." *Scientific American Mind* 20.1 (Feb.–Mar. 2009): 22–29.

Bibliography

West, Sonja R. "The Story of Us: Resolving the Face-Off between Autobiographical Speech and Information Privacy." *Washington and Lee Law Review* 67.2 (Spring 2010): 589–650.

Westin, Alan F. *Privacy and Freedom.* New York: Atheneum, 1967.

White, Michele. *The Body and the Screen: Theories of Internet Spectatorship.* Cambridge, Mass.: MIT Press, 2006.

Whitman, James Q. "The Two Western Cultures of Privacy: Dignity versus Liberty." *Yale Law Journal* 113.6 (April 2004): 1151–222.

Winn, Peter A. "The Guilty Eye: Unauthorized Access, Trespass, and Privacy." *Business Lawyer* 62.4 (August 2007): 1395–437.

Winner, Langdon. *Autonomous Technology: Technics Out-of-Control as a Theme in Political Thought.* Cambridge, Mass.: MIT Press, 1978.

——. *The Whale and the Reactor: A Search for Limits in an Age of High Technology.* Chicago: University of Chicago Press, 1986.

Wood, David Murakami, ed. *A Report on the Surveillance Society for the Information Commissioner by the Surveillance Studies Network.* London: Mark Siddoway/Knowledge House, 2006.

Woodmansee, Martha. "On the Author Effect: Recovering Collectivity." In Martha Woodmansee & Peter Jaszi, eds., *The Construction of Authorship: Textual Approaches in Law and Literature,* 14–28. Durham, N.C.: Duke University Press, 1994.

Woolgar, Steve. "Configuring the User: The Case of Usability Trials." In John Law, ed., *A Sociology of Monsters: Essays on Power, Technology, and Domination,* 57–99. London: Routledge, 1991.

Wu, Tim. "Tolerated Use." *Columbia Journal of Law and the Arts* 31.3–4 (2008): 617–35.

Yoo, Christopher S. "Copyright and Product Differentiation." *New York University Law Review* 79.1_(April 2004): 212–280.

Yoshino, Kenji. "Covering." *Yale Law Journal* 111.4 (January 2002): 769–939.

Young, Iris Marion. "Throwing like a Girl." In Welton, *Bodies and Flesh,* 259–73.

Zerubavel, Eviatar. *Social Mindscapes: An Invitation to Cognitive Sociology.* Cambridge, Mass.: Harvard University Press, 1997.

Zittrain, Jonathan. *The Future of the Internet—And How to Stop It.* New Haven, Conn.: Yale University Press, 2008.

——. "The Generative Internet." *Harvard Law Review* 119.7 (May 2006): 1974–2040.

Zwick, Detlev, Samuel K. Bonsu, and Aron Darmody. "Putting Consumers to Work: 'Co-Creation' and New Marketing Govern-Mentality." *Journal of Consumer Culture* 8.2 (July 2008): 163–96.

Index

accessibility, 187–220, 223–224, 249–250, 271–272; limitations to, 206–213, 256, 263; operational transparency and, 236–237. *See also* authentication; unauthorized access

access-to-knowledge (A2K), 6, 223, 225–226, 229–234, 242, 243; free culture movement and, 4, 8, 267; intellectual property and, 259–260; limits to, 261–262; privacy protection and, 250, 261, 267

airline security, 167, 212, 256, 257

Altman, Irwin, 131, 143, 146

amateurism, 95, 97

Anderson, Benedict, 28

AOL, 197, 198, 199

Apple Computer, 206

appropriation art, 31, 72, 87

architectures, network. *See* architectures of control; *Code*

architectures of control, 155–186, 187; authorization and, 188–189, 202–220; emergence of, 156–171, 202–203; legal disputes about, 176; legislation and, 157–158, 160, 161, 162, 163; property rights and, 172–173; security and, 155, 164–171, 261; surface level protection and, 159–160; trusted systems and, 160–161. See also *Code*; freedom/control binary

association, freedom of, 20, 110–111

A2K. *See* access-to-knowledge

Augé, Mark, 141

authentication, 107, 109, 155, 165, 168–169, 170, 178, 255

authoritarianism, 124, 184, 189, 214

authorization. *See* regimes of authorization; unauthorized access

authorship, 17, 61–64, 66, 78, 80, 85–87, 91, 93, 151, 248; contributions of others to, 77, 96; copyright incentive and, 230; deliberate purpose and, 94; fan fiction and, 55–56, 69–70, 87, 97; ideas and, 74–75; motivation and, 64; originality test of, 63; reconceptualization of, 84; sequelization rights and, 247; user relationship with, 69–70, 83

Index

autonomic technologies, 200–202
autonomy, 10, 51, 53, 104, 132, 216;
  positive liberty and, 173; privacy
  and, 109–115, 128, 132, 138, 149;
  technology and, 200–202. *See also*
  selfhood
Axciom, 167

Balkin, Jack, 99, 259–260
Ball, Kirstie, 145
Baudrillard, Jean, 215
belief, freedom of, 110–111, 115
Benkler, Yochai, 7, 23, 53, 65, 96, 99,
  103–104, 259–260
Bennett, Colin, 116, 117
Bentham, Jeremy, 124, 136
Berkman Center for Internet and Society
  (Harvard), 233
"best-practices" statements, 242, 243
Big Brother, 124
biometric screening, 165, 168, 207
Birnhack, Michael, 179
black spaces, 175, 176
Blair, Tony, 210–211
body, 35, 36, 38, 40–41, 86–87, 124, 125;
  critical theory of, 49–50; spaces and,
  46–47. *See also* embodied perception;
  embodied self
borders, national, 162, 165, 167, 168, 169,
  190
borders, networked space, 190, 219, 224–
  225, 258; crossings between overlapping,
  93, 95; operational transparency in, 235
Bordo, Susan, 37
borrowing/reworking, 72, 93, 97–99, 246;
  creative centrality of, 87–88
Bourdieu, Pierre, 37
boyd, danah, 265
Boyle, James, 7, 8, 65, 71, 184, 259–260
Bracha, Oren, 63
Brand, Stewart, 12
Bruns, Axel, 53

Burrell, Robert, 102
Butler, Judith, 37

cameras. *See* photography; surveillance;
  videos
capabilities theory, 6, 16, 21–24, 225–239,
  268; components of, 229–239. *See also*
  human flourishing
capital markets, 44, 271–272
Carnival Booth study (MIT), 256–257
Carson, Rachel, *Silent Spring*, 8
Cartesian philosophy, 125
Castells, Manuel, 43, 215
categorical imperative, 16–17
censorship, 64
Central Intelligence Agency, 166
Certeau, Michel de, 51
ChoicePoint, 167
Chon, Margaret, 23, 71, 232
Citron, Danielle, 237
civil society, 116, 149
cloud storage, 234, 237, 238
Coasean filter, 199
Code, 13–14, 20, 26, 27, 171–188, 220;
  assessments of, 182–184; four-part
  framework of, 155–156, 186; liberal
  arguments against, 171–175, 181–185
cognitive science, 38–40
Coleman, Allison, 102
collectivity, 132–134, 147, 150
commodification of cultural goods, 7–8, 9,
  95; copyright and, 55, 64–65
commodification of information, 8, 13,
  34, 269–272; authorization and, 258;
  privacy and, 112, 113, 114, 237
common law: flexible incrementalism,
  245; privacy doctrines, 112, 123, 157
commons, metaphor of, 7, 8
Communications Assistance to Law
  Enforcement Act (1994), 166
communitarian theory, 116
communities, 28, 55–56, 149, 204, 224

Index

Computer Fraud and Abuse Act (1984), 157–158, 203, 206

conformity, 37, 54

consequentialism, 21–22

constitutional privacy doctrine, 108, 110–111; reasonable expectations test, 121–122

consumers, 53, 68, 82, 83, 129, 179, 197–198, 249–250, 252

Content Scramble System. *See* CSS

control. *See* architectures of control; freedom/control binary

cookies, 207

Coombe, Rosemary, 71, 216–217

Coppa, Francesca, 86

copying, 66, 67, 68–69, 75–77, 95, 264; consumptive vs. transformative, 69; darknet hypothesis and, 174, 175–176; disease metaphor for, 210; limits on, 242–243; permitted situations for, 75. *See also* borrowing/reworking

Copy Protection Technical Working Group, 161–162

copyright, 3–4, 5, 6, 17–18, 23, 25, 61–66, 70–79, 85, 230, 240, 241–248, 260; abuse potential of, 257; accessibility and, 192, 205; arguments for, 100, 177–178, 185, 271; attribution rules of, 56; authorization and, 262, 263–264; authorship concept and, 63–64; balance and, 100, 102–103, 241–244, 246, 258; boundaries and, 224; circumvention rules of, 263–264; content's nature and, 74–79; coverage extent of, 57; "creative destruction" and, 103; cultural mobility and, 31, 99–104; defects of, 78–79; digital enforcement and, 155–164; expansion harms of, 77–78, 81, 101; expansion of, 7–8, 9, 57, 61, 81, 242; fandom and, 55–56, 69, 97, 228, 242, 247; foundational abstractions and, 74–78; free/lower-cost access and, 230–231; ideas

excluded from, 62, 74, 75; incentive function of, 62, 65, 66, 67, 100, 101, 230; indirect infringement liability and, 179, 247–248, 266; infringement of, 158–164, 210, 263; infringement test for, 75; lawful personal use and, 247–248; music sampling disputes and, 92–93; open-source programmers and, 55; play of everyday practice and, 57, 246–247, 263–264; progress and, 70–74, 81; property-rights framework for, 172–173, 185; protection systems market and, 179–180; public domain models of, 77–78; public-private distinction of, 61, 247; purpose of, 63; reform proposals for, 242–248; secondary liability and, 160, 266; situated user and, 82–83, 87, 242–244, 246–247, 248; social value vs. cost of, 70–74; standardization in, 191; "tinkering" and, 176, 219; unauthorized access and, 204, 205–206; value-neutral markets and, 72; values and, 94–95, 151. *See also* intellectual property

Copyright Act (1909), 246, 247

Copyright Act (1976), 245, 246

Copyright Office, 206, 228

Copyrights Register, U.S., 61

coveillance, 144–148

Craig, Carys, 63–64, 84

Craigslist.org, 44

Creative Commons movement, 242, 243

creativity, 17, 30–31, 32, 57, 63–104, 152, 220, 267; accessibility and, 192, 198; basis of, 63–65; borrowing and (*see* borrowing/reworking); commonly held assumptions about, 63, 81; constituent elements of, 90; constraints on, 64, 82–83; copyright and, 4, 5, 8, 61–62, 65, 66, 67, 74–79, 81, 100, 101, 230; copyright conflict with, 103, 240; decentered model of, 81–95, 100, 101; democratization of, 99; end product vs.

Index

DVD Copy Control Association (DVD-CCA), 159, 262, 263

Eagleton, Terry, 25
eBay, 43, 44
economic theory, 7, 9, 16–18, 19, 21; authorization and, 214; *Code* and, 156, 171; copyright functions and, 100, 103, 241; creativity and, 64–68, 82, 100, 103; freedom to copy and, 75, 76; openness and, 147, 208; privacy and, 19, 20, 152. *See also* markets
Electronic Privacy Information Center, 165
electronic voting, 212
Elkin-Koren, Niva, 71, 99, 179
e-mail, 142, 166, 168, 197
embodied perception, 30, 33, 48–50, 56, 57, 85–87, 92; primacy of, 36–41
embodied self, 34–35, 37–38, 129, 135, 195–197; information flows and, 46–49; invisible bubble surrounding, 143. *See also* disembodiment; selfhood
enclosure movement, 7, 8, 11, 267; lessons of, 268–270
Enlightenment, 16–17, 118, 239, 245
environmentalism. *See* cultural environmentalism
equality, 22, 116, 252, 260
Ericson, Richard, 137
European Union, 163, 235–236
everyday practice, 17, 30, 32, 33, 50–57, 128–132, 169–170; authorization access and, 206–207, 217–220; autonomic technologies and, 200–202; copyright law and, 57, 246–247, 263–264; definition of, 201; fair use limits and, 242; material dimension of, 258–266, 268; network use and, 187, 225–229; privacy and, 125, 128–129, 135, 264–265. *See also* play
Experian, 167
exposure, 143–147, 148, 152, 234, 260, 261, 265, 271, 272; limitation rules, 266

expression, freedom of, 20, 32, 44, 50, 76, 172, 176; A2K argument and, 260; copyright challenge to, 173, 174; ideas vs., 62, 74–76, 78, 79; openness and, 262; privacy protection for, 11, 112, 118

Facebook, 45, 197, 198, 199, 261, 272
facts, as ideas, 75
fair information practices, 235–236
fair use practice, 66–68, 69, 71, 78; reform proposals, 242–243
fandom, 55–56, 228, 247
fanvids, 69, 97, 228, 242
Federal Communications Commission, 161, 166, 194, 233
Federal Trade Commission, 235
feminism, 130, 140, 145
file sharing, 164, 169, 180, 183, 195, 244, 257
film, 87, 88, 97, 98, 99, 242. *See also* videos
Foreign Intelligence Surveillance Act (1978), 166, 209
Foucault, Michel, 28, 37, 132, 136–137, 138, 140, 143, 149, 150, 183, 184, 215
Foursquare, 261
Frankfurt School, 91
free culture movement, 4, 8, 11–12, 96, 267
freedom/control binary, 4, 6–7, 10–15, 224; authorization and, 202, 214, 216; cyberspace and, 12–15; information and, 6, 10–14, 110, 117–120, 146–148, 178, 249; openness and, 259–262; privacy and, 11–12, 134. *See also Code*
Freedom of Information Act, 209
freedoms, 23; capabilities theory and, 16, 21, 225; *Code* relationship with, 171–172; definition of, 22; protected, 172. *See also* rights; *specific freedoms*
Frischmann, Brett, 7

Gadamer, Hans-Georg, 56, 134–135
Galison, Peter, 109–110

Index

geek culture, 265
Geek Feminism Wiki, 49–50
Geertz, Clifford, 37, 51
gender theory, 37, 55
General Agreement on Tariffs and Trade, 232
Gibson, William, 35
globalization, 44, 95–96, 191–192; cultural access disparities and, 232–233; privacy guarantees and, 253
global positioning systems. *See* GPS
glocal space, 191
Gmail, 197, 199, 260
Goffman, Erving, 37, 130
Google, 48, 197–198, 272; Google Book Search, 192, 198, 231, 247; Google Buzz, 260–261
government: data mining and, 167–168, 209, 255; monitoring and, 107, 108, 166; networked information independence from, 214; openness vs. secrecy and, 207–213; permanent record databases and, 253–254; privacy and, 150–151, 157–158; surveillance and, 139, 142, 165, 166, 178, 209, 255–256
GPS, 45, 48–49, 168, 260, 264–265
Gramm-Leach-Bliley Act (1999), 249, 250, 253
Grimmelmann, James, 182, 183, 184, 261
Grosz, Elizabeth, 38
Guattari, Felix, 137

Habermas, Jürgen, 16
hacking, 203, 204, 206, 210, 259, 261; legal theory and, 218, 219
Haggerty, Kevin, 137
Hansen, Mark, 49, 50
Haraway, Donna, 47–48, 51
Hayles, Katherine, 16, 35, 50, 74
health data. *See* medical data
Health Insurance Portability and Accountability Act (1996), 249–250
Hegel, G. W. F., 16

hip-hop, 87, 92
Hollabacknyc (Web forum), 52, 55
Holmes, Oliver Wendell, 70–71, 240, 259
home, protected privacy of, 111, 112, 113, 121, 122, 142–143
Homeland Security (Department of), 165, 170
Hughes, Justin, 63, 64
Huizinga, Johan, 54
human flourishing, 104, 152, 175, 189, 219, 220, 223–272; capabilities theory of, 6, 16, 21–24, 225–229, 268; collective interest in, 150; operational transparency and, 234–239; societal definition of, 116
human rights. *See* rights
hybridity, cultural, 28–30, 97–99

IBM, "Autonomic Computing Manifesto," 200
idea-expression distinction, 62, 74–76, 78, 79
identification systems, 45, 47, 165, 168–169
identity theft, 155, 168, 170, 212
Ihde, Don, 48
indigenous cultures, 92, 98
individualism. *See* autonomy; selfhood
individualized treatment, 251–252
individuation, 128–129, 130, 132
industrial revolution, 268–269
information: capability dimensions of, 229–230; cultural meanings of, 26, 28; freedom/control binary and, 6, 10–14, 110, 146–148, 178; human flourishing and, 3, 6, 21–24, 189, 225–229; as ultimate good, 20; valuation of, 117–120, 147, 249, 271
information collection and processing, 10, 48, 107–126, 155–186, 190, 201, 212, 240; accessibility and, 4, 6, 187–202, 223, 225–226, 229–234; authentication and, 168–169; authorized flow and,

Index

Index

Index

Index

Index